RECKONING
WITH SLAVERY

RECKONING WITH SLAVERY

Gender, Kinship, and Capitalism
in the Early Black Atlantic

JENNIFER L. MORGAN

Duke University Press   Durham and London   2021

Printed and bound by CPI Group (UK) Ltd, Croydon, CR0 4YY
Project editor: Lisa Lawley
Designed by Courtney Leigh Richardson
Typeset in Arno Pro by Westchester Publishing Services

Library of Congress Cataloging-in-Publication Data
Names: Morgan, Jennifer L. (Jennifer Lyle), author.
Title: Reckoning with slavery : gender, kinship, and capitalism
    in the early Black Atlantic / Jennifer L. Morgan.
Description: Durham : Duke University Press, 2021. |
    Includes bibliographical references and index.
Identifiers: LCCN 2020038911 (print)
LCCN 2020038912 (ebook)
ISBN 9781478013235 (hardcover)
ISBN 9781478014140 (paperback)
ISBN 9781478021452 (ebook)
Subjects: LCSH: Slavery—Political aspects—America. |
    Slavery—Economic aspects—America. | Women slaves—America. |
    Women slaves—Atlantic Ocean Region. | Slave trade—
    America—History. | Slave trade—Atlantic Ocean Region—History.
Classification: LCC HT871 .M67 2021 (print) | LCC HT871 (ebook) |
    DDC 306.3/62—dc23
LC record available at https://lccn.loc.gov/2020038911
LC ebook record available at https://lccn.loc.gov/2020038912

Cover art: Annibale Carracci (attributed), *Portrait of an African Woman Holding a Clock*, detail of a larger painting, ca. 1580s. Oil on canvas, 23¾ × 15½ inches. Courtesy Louvre Abu Dhabi.

Dedicated to the memory of
John P. Morgan and Claudia B. Morgan
and to Adrienne Lash Jones.
Teachers.

I was desperate to reclaim the dead, to reckon with the lives undone and obliterated in the making of human commodities.

—SAIDIYA HARTMAN, *Lose Your Mother:*
A Journey along the Atlantic Slave Route, 2008

CONTENTS

Sometime in the years before 1585 in the town of Bologna, Italy, the woman on the cover of this book sat for a portrait, painted by a man who would become famous. I won't give you his name because it's not important to the story that I am trying to tell. I can't tell you hers, although her anonymity is at the very heart of the story that I am trying to tell. As you can see in the portrait on the cover of this book, she is dressed well, and she holds an ornate clock that may indicate the kind of wealthy household she was a part of. The painting was damaged, so we do not know who else was in the portrait, only that—at one point—she was not alone. If you look closely at the bodice of her gown, you will see straight pins. She may or may not have sewed the dress and the decorative collar she wears. She may or may not have been a seamstress. She may or may not have been paid for her labor. She may or may not have been free. Hundreds of Africans, both enslaved and free, were in Italy at the end of the sixteenth century.[1]

At the time when the woman was painted, the legality of African enslavability had circulated around the Mediterranean for almost 150 years—but art historians don't know who this woman is. They can't. Black woman

---

1 On the long history of black women and men in Italy and in Italian art, see Kaplan, "Italy, 1490–1700."

with a Clock. Slave woman with a Clock. African Woman with a Clock.[2] She marks time with the object that she holds but marks so much more time with the gaze that holds us. Her visage conveys nothing if not knowing. She knows who she is in relation to the painter; she knows what she sees. She locks eyes with her viewers and comes close to dismissing us with the turn of her lip—dismissing, perhaps, our questions about who she is. When I look at her, I see someone who understands her own value—both the value that can't be quantified and that which can. I see a woman who reaches out across the centuries to say, "Look at me, and see what brought me here."

What follows is my effort to do so.

2 The portrait has been variously titled, most recently as *Portrait of an African Woman Holding a Clock*, Annibale Carracci, 1583/5. Tomasso Brothers, London. https://www .tomassobrothers.co.uk/artworkdetail/781241/18036/portrait-of-an-african-woman -holding.

This project has been many years in the making. When it began, I felt as though I were working relatively alone, on questions that emerged on the edges of a range of fields—the history of political economy, of early modern slavery, of racial formations prior to the nineteenth century. But as I draw near completion, I see that I have many fellow travelers. The fact that this field has grown exponentially since I began is one of the unexpected pleasures of the long gestation of this book. I am now part of a community whose scholarship on the history of race and gender in the Black Atlantic world is fueled by our collective commitments to political intentionality. My work has benefitted tremendously from being part of the collective endeavors of my collaborators and interlocutors who work on the histories of gender and slavery. They include Daina Ramey Berry, Deirdre Cooper Owens, Erica Dunbar, Marisa Fuentes, Thavolia Glymph, Kim Hall, Tera Hunter, Jessica Johnson, Celia Naylor, and Sasha Turner. As this project came to a close, I have keenly felt the absence of Stephanie Camp, a feeling I know I share with so many. And, as always, I am deeply grateful for the trailblazing work and critical support of Deborah Gray White, whose scholarship continues to set the stage for those of us who follow in her wake.

I began working on this book as I joined the faculty at New York University. In addition to institutional support through the auspices of Deans Thomas Carew, Antonio Merlo, Joy Connolly, and Gigi Dopico, I owe much to the conversations and exchange of ideas that I have been a part of in both the Department of Social and Cultural Analysis and the Department of History. I am particularly grateful to colleagues Carolyn Dinshaw, Lisa Duggan, Nicole Eustace, Ada Ferrar, Rebecca Goetz, Gayatri Gopinath, Phil Harper, Martha Hodes, Andrew Ross, and Deb Willis. When Covid made us feel like we were at the End of Days, the Future of America Working Group—Julie Livingston, Nikhil Singh, Thuy Tu, and honorary SCA-ers Herman Bennett and Behrooz Tabrizi-Ghamari—offered, as they always have, a rare overlapping space of love and scholarship. Deb Willis and Ellyn Toscano's Women and Migrations project provided a long set of critical engagements with colleagues at NYU and beyond. I am grateful to Uli Baer, who helped me reckon through a moment of serious trouble. Conversations with students have been both sustaining and generative, and I appreciate my work with Thulani Davis, Miles Grier, Laura Helton, Ebony Jones, Justin Leroy, Max Mischler, Samantha Seeley, Shauna Sweeney, Chinua Thelwell, and, currently, with Lila Chambers, Erica Duncan, Justin Linds, Alejandro McGee, Elise Mitchell, Joan Morgan, Shavagne Scott, and Amrit Trewn. I owe a particularly sweet debt to my colleagues (and former students) Ebony Jones and Shauna Sweeney, whose enthusiastic loyalty and support has lifted me (much more than they know) at crucial moments.

There are many colleagues who have read multiple drafts of this manuscript and whose suggestions and support have been essential to what you now hold in your hands. Being available to read again and again is an extraordinary mark of friendship and collegiality. Antoinette Burton has had faith in me for a Very Long Time. I cannot tally the debt I owe her. She has read every sheepishly sent draft and has offered enduring support. Her help in conceptualizing and finishing this project has been tremendous. Herman Bennett has always dropped everything at a moment's notice to read and engage with my work. Daina Ramey Berry has travelled miles to write and read together. Marisa Fuentes has become a crucial interlocutor, whose insight and probing engagement has helped me to clarify the stakes of my work. And Julie Livingston has read with care and offered generative support over innumerable anxious conversations. They all have read at least one full copy of this manuscript, if not more. I appreciate their time and attention tremendously.

Along the way, I have drawn strength from the engagement of friends and colleagues who have posed questions and offered support in ways that have incalculably contributed to this project and to my work more broadly.

For this I am deeply grateful to Sharon Block, Jennifer Brier, Christopher L. Brown, Catherine Hall, Kim Hall, Saidiya Hartman, Walter Johnson, Robert Reid-Pharr, David Scott, Stephanie Smallwood, Alys Weinbaum, and Karin Wulf.

I have benefitted from a long friendship with Joyce Seltzer, whose advice has been an important source of guidance as I navigated through the terrain of publication. I am lucky that this manuscript has found a home with Duke University Press and the enthusiastic support of Ken Wissoker. Anonymous readers at the press have strengthened this manuscript with their critical engagement. Thank you to Josh Gutterman Tranen, Lisa Lawley, and Kim Miller for bringing it across the finish line.

I've been in a conversation with Professor Julius S. Scott since I began graduate school more than three decades ago. Sometimes he is actually present, sometimes I am just imagining his response to my ideas, but always he makes me a more careful and grounded scholar. Similarly, and as I think we all do, I have a community of intellectuals and friends who comprise my ideal readers and with whom I have crafted so many of the arguments of this text in both actual conversation and in the kinds of exchanges that occur over the work that I strive to emulate. For this I am particularly grateful for the work of Vincent Brown, Marisa Fuentes, Saidiya Hartman, Walter Johnson, Fred Moten, Katherine McKittrick, Christina Sharpe, and Stephanie Smallwood.

Framing the work of the archive is, of course, a task of translation. Since 2010, I have appreciated Lynn Paltrow's insistence that I reckon with the contemporary consequences of the histories that I have traced both here and elsewhere. My time spent with her and my colleagues at the National Advocates for Pregnant Women saturates the work that I have done in this volume. Working with Stanley Nelson, Marcia Smith, and Naz Habtezghi and the scholars they have assembled for conversations about the slave trade has had a major impact on my efforts to clarify my thinking about the experience of enslavement. Zillah Watson and Andy Neather have constantly opened their home and their family to me and mine, providing a comfortable landing spot for those research trips to London. Conversations with Emma Morgan-Bennett concerning her work as a doula and an activist have brought crucial perspectives on the afterlife of slavery and reproductive justice to my scholarship.

I have presented versions of this work in so many venues that I am afraid to try to list them all! Suffice it to say that the reception of and engagement with my ideas has been hugely important as I attempted to reconcile my efforts with my abilities. Generous invitations to share my work have placed me in conversation with colleagues and students at many institutions; this has made the book significantly better than it would have been had I worked in isolation. Thank you to Hazel Carby and African American Studies at Yale University; Chris Brown and the Society of Fellows at Columbia University; the Newberry Library; the Feminism and Critical Race Theory group at UNC-Charlotte; the Institute for Historical Studies at University of Texas, Austin; Rosemary Brana-Shute and the Carolina Lowcountry and the Atlantic World seminar at the College of Charleston; Alys Weinbaum, Stephanie Smallwood, and Moon-Ho Jung and the Empires of Capital symposium at the University of Washington, Seattle; Sharon Block and the Department of History at the University of California, Irvine; Alexandra Juhasz and the Monroe Center for Social Inquiry at Pitzer College; Jim Downs and his students at Connecticut College; Cynthia Young and the Department of African American Studies at Penn State; Tony Bogues and the Center for the Study of Slavery and Justice at Brown University; Justin Leroy and the Racial Capitalism Sawyer Seminar at the University of California, Davis; Kirsten Fischer and the Early American Atlantic Workshop at the University of Minnesota; Diana Paton and the Edinburgh Center for Global History at the University of Edinburgh; April Haynes, Pablo Gomez, the Program in Gender and Women's History, and the Plantationocene Seminar at the University of Wisconsin, Madison; Stephanie Shaw and the 1619 and Beyond seminar at the Ohio State University; the Center for the Humanities at the University of Miami; and Ayanna Thompson and the Arizona Center for Medieval and Renaissance Studies. More than a decade's worth of conversations with my colleagues at the Berkshire Conference of Women Historians—the Big and Little Berks—have shaped this project from its inception. I am deeply grateful to Barbara Balliet, Jennifer Brier, DeeDee Cooper Owens, Claire Potter, Susan Yohn, and so many others who have done the hard work to sustain the organization as a place for crucial conversation.

Many of the ideas that frame this project were developed in conversation with the Slavery and Freedom Working Group, which I convened at the Humanities Institute at New York University with support from Jane Tylus. A first draft finally came to completion while I was a member of the School of Social Sciences at the Institute for Advanced Studies in Princeton under the direction of Didier Fassin, Danielle Allen, and Joan Scott. The opportunity to exchange ideas there with Brady Bower, Brian Connolly, Michael Hanchard, Julilly Kohler-Hausmann, Jill Locke, Maurizio Meloni,

Charles Payne, Sophia Rosenfeld, and Mara Viveros Vigoya was such a gift. Final thoughts came together while convening a year-long seminar on Gender, Race, and Finance at the Folger Shakespeare Library, through the support of Michael Whitmore and Owen Williams. There, bracing conversations with Vanessa Braganza, Holly Brewer, Urvashi Chakravarty, Sherri Cummings, Emilee Durand, Valerie Forman, Marisa Fuentes, Atsede Makonnen, J. E. Morgan, Kyle Repella, Ricardo Salazar-Rey, David Sartorius, Gregory Smaldone, Shauna Sweeney, and Andrew Young shaped the final version of the manuscript. I am grateful to the latter two institutions for their longstanding formal support, which allows scholars to share ideas in beautiful places while shielded, at least temporarily, from the distractions and enervations of daily life.

As it turns out, those who have nothing to do with the book actually are at its heart. Chris Veljovic and Ana Baptista have given me a place to regain strength and to laugh and remind me every week of the connection between mind and body; in particular, Chris has shown me that if you find the work, you end with exaltation. My Danby Harbor peeps personify my history, and for that I am always grateful to Peter Bergman, Benedicte de Montlaur, Lisa Waller, Sidney Whelan, and Keith Yazmir. Genevieve and Gabrielle Waller-Whelan, Chloe and Luca Goldmansour, and Susanna and Daniel De Martino have always honed my attention onto what is most important. Tim Tyson is never surprised. Marlene Brito and Marty Correia are daily reminders of all that is right with the world. Steven Amsterdam once said that I could do anything. I do not think that he was right, but his faith in me has been a touchstone. He and Corry DeNeef also offered me the time, space, and comfort I needed in the final stage of writing and revising amidst the kangaroos and wombats of Venus Bay. Abigail Asher is vital to whatever capacity I have to restore myself to balance in proximity to open waters. Lisa Waller and Kristen Goldman are my sisters in the truest possible meaning of the word and show me every day that there is actually nothing imaginary at all about fictive kin.

My children, Carl Fraley-Bennett and Emma Morgan-Bennett, have grown into astonishing adults as I have labored over this book. I love them beyond words. My brother and sister-in-law, Zachary Morgan and Cynthia Young, have always offered me unquestioning love and necessary laughter. Lee and Helga Bennett have been a beacon in a time of loss, and my beloved grandmother, Maymette Carter, is a source of enduring stability. Jaiden, Julian, and Oliver care not at all about this book, and for that I am forever in their debt! Losing both my parents during the time that I have been working on this book was both devastating and disorienting. They were always my most constant supporters and I feel their absence almost every day. The dedication of this book would make perfect sense to them, and they would have also understood why I want them to share it. Professor Adrienne Lash Jones set me on a path in 1984 that I have continued to follow and provided me with a constant model of what it means to be, in the words of my father, a scholar and a gentlewoman.

Finally, everyone who knows us can see that Herman L. Bennett and I are indivisible. What they cannot always see is how much I have learned both from him and with him about the politics and pleasures of lingering. It would all mean nothing without him. Herman, "part of you flows out of me, in these lines from time to time." You know the rest.

INTRODUCTION. Refusing Demography

In the 1640s, as a child, Elizabeth Keye found herself misidentified on an estate in Virginia. A white boy named John Keye called her "Black Besse." Overhearing it, the overseer's wife "checked him and said[,] Sirra you must call her Sister for shee is your Sister," whereupon "the said John Keye did call her Sister."[1] Keye, the daughter of a free white Englishman and an enslaved African woman, occupied a space in seventeenth-century Virginia in which she could simultaneously be "Black Besse" and the sister of a white boy. In this space a Black woman could claim ties of kinship that would be recognized and legislated, but this was both anomalous and temporary. In the coming years, the logic of the paternal link formally unraveled as hereditary racial slavery congealed. Kinship could be claimed only in freedom, and by the middle of the seventeenth century in the English colonies, Blackness generally signified freedom's opposite.

At some point in the late 1620s, the free white Englishman Thomas Keye, a member of the Virginia House of Burgesses, had impregnated Elizabeth's enslaved Africa-born mother. What this woman (who is never actually named, appearing only as "woman slave" in the documentary record) hoped or believed about her daughter's future is utterly lost. What is clear is that Thomas Keye's death threw that future into some confusion.

1 "The Case of Elizabeth Key, 1655/6," in Billings, Old Dominion, 195–99; Billings, "Cases of Fernando and Elizabeth Key."

Although Elizabeth had been placed in indenture as a child, after her father's death she (or her indenture) was sold to another Virginia landowner. Selling the remaining term of an indenture was not uncommon, but because she was the daughter of an African woman, her race made her vulnerable to abuses from which an Englishwoman would have been protected. Although the English had embraced the system of African slavery elsewhere in the Atlantic, in Virginia they relied on indentured servants, the vast majority of whom were themselves English. In the 1650s, there were fewer than three hundred Africans in the colony, or about 1 percent of the population of English settlers. There were many people like Elizabeth Keye, women and men of African origin or descent whose lives detoured from the trajectory of brutal racial slavery associated with Black people in the Americas.

For the historian Ira Berlin, Keye would count as an Atlantic Creole, a person who traversed the Atlantic in relative or absolute freedom in a milieu that was soon to generate hardened categories of racial subjugation.[2] In the late sixteenth and early seventeenth centuries, in Europe and in European colonies in the Americas, such individuals could acquire land, other forms of wealth, and the mobility conferred by these. The experiences of these women and men demonstrate the uneven development of racial hierarchy in the Atlantic world, a reminder that racial categories could be less fixed than they appeared.[3] Keye understood that she was in danger, that her color could indeed dictate her status.

Keye spent her life assessing the terrain of race, inheritance, value, slavery, and freedom in the seventeenth-century world, which was at once a localized space configured around the English Atlantic and also part and parcel of a multicultural, multi-imperial universe. She lived in a community that accepted her paternal lineage, but kinship faltered when its members were asked to testify about her status. Some said she was a slave, some that

2 While Berlin didn't discuss Keye in the landmark article where he introduced the notion of the Atlantic Creole, she would fit squarely in his exploration of seventeenth-century colonial Virginia and the Tidewater free Blacks he does name. Berlin, "From Creole to African," 276–78. The case plays an important role in Heywood and Thornton, *Central Africans*.

3 Along with the work of Berlin, historical biographies written by scholars like James Sweet, Linda Heywood, and Vincent Carretta similarly seek to wrench Black lives from the chokehold of the history of slavery. Similarly, Rebecca Goetz and others have carefully interrogated the history of race in the early Atlantic world in pursuit of the nuances that historicizing race reveals. See Carretta, *Equiano the African*; Goetz, *Baptism of Early Virginia*; Heywood, *Njinga of Angola*; Sweet, *Domingos Álvares*.

she was free, and some that she was indentured.[4] She had a child, fathered by a free white Englishman, but this brought no clarity. When she petitioned the court to affirm her freedom in 1655, she clearly had a precise understanding of how her statuses as a woman, as a mother, and as a descendant of an enslaved African intersected. Her suit was granted, then overturned, and finally won when the Englishman who was the father of her child brought her case to the General Assembly. After she was deemed free, the two wed, their marriage a buttress to the freedom of her descendants, as well as to her own.

For historians, the fact that she prevailed shows that in seventeenth-century Virginia, racialized categories of enslavement were neither inevitable nor hardened.[5] In the history that follows, within which Keye was situated, the life circumstances and experiences of those defined as Black were already brutally marked; the transatlantic slave trade had already indelibly shaped notions of race, the market, and the family. By the mid-seventeenth century, the underlying forces structuring the slave trade were steadfastly shaping ideas of difference, commerce, and kinship. This is not an argument opposed to historicizing the concept of race; rather, it brings kinship and commodification to bear on seventeenth-century ideologies to ask both how the obscene logics of racial slavery came to make sense to Europeans and also what Africans and their descendants in the early modern Atlantic could and did know about the terms of their captivity. It is also an effort to dislodge the English Atlantic from its anglophone perch by placing it firmly in the longer history of the Atlantic. To understand Keye and the forces she navigated, we must conceive of a history in which the notions of heredity, motherhood, commodity, and race all cohered in and on the body of the daughter of an enslaved African woman and a free Englishman.

For Keye, the case rested on the assumption that affective relationships—those between father and daughter, husband and wife, mother and children—would prove a bulwark against the intrusions of the commercial market into her and her children's lives and labors. Historians are accustomed to thinking of Keye as a woman enmeshed in these relationships, not as an economic thinker (a person versed in political arithmetic, speculative thought, and social calculation). Yet economic concerns were the source of danger for Keye, and economic concerns drove the legislators to revisit this case less than a decade later. In 1662 the colonial legislators reconvened to decree that in all future cases, the condition of a child born to

4 "Case of Elizabeth Key."
5 "Case of Elizabeth Key."

an African woman and a free man would follow that of the mother.[6] As English colonial settlers legislated new economic formulations that extended masters' property rights to other humans, they brought matters of intimacy and affect out of the household and into the marketplace. Using arguments based in law, religion, and race, they located Africans and their descendants in ledgers and bills of sale, not as members of households or families. This social transformation was saturated with both spectacular violence and the brutality of everyday cruelties.

The insinuation of economic rationality into colonial intimacies is the crux of the matter. The mechanisms and ideas that emerged in the early modern Atlantic world situated economy and kinship as not just distinct but antithetical. As anthropologist Claude Meillassoux noted more than three decades ago, slavery produced social relations that are the antithesis of kinship relations.[7] On the other side of the Atlantic, Hortense Spillers suggested that if scholars were to "overlap kinlessness on the requirements of property," it could enlarge our understanding of what enslavement entailed.[8] Examining the Keye case from these perspectives, we see that it refracted the gradual recognition among colonial legislators that intimacy needed to be carefully navigated because kinship posed dangers for an economic system in which race demarcated human beings as property.

The intimacy that concerned slave-owning legislators was sexual. But as the cultural theorist Lisa Lowe has argued, intimacy is a framework that reveals the relatedness of phenomena that have been constructed as distinct and unrelated. For Lowe, those categories are liberalism, the slave trade, settler colonialism in the Americas, and the China and East Indies trade.[9] She mobilizes intimacy as a category that exceeds the spheres of sexuality and household relations, writing that she uses "the concept of intimacy as a heuristic, and a means to observe the historical division of world processes into those that develop modern liberal subjects and modern spheres of social life, and those processes that are forgotten, cast as failed or irrelevant because they do not produce 'value' legible within modern classifications."[10] *Reckoning*

---

6 "Negroe Women's Children to Serve according to the Condition of the Mother," Act XII, in Hening, *Statutes at Large*, 170. The law was soon adopted by all English colonies as they defined the status of the enslaved. It stood as law until the abolition of slavery in 1863. For a fuller discussion of this case, see J. L. Morgan, "*Partus Sequitur Ventrem*."

7 Meillassoux, *Anthropology of Slavery*, 85–98.

8 Spillers, "Mama's Baby, Papa's Maybe," 73.

9 Lowe, *Intimacies of Four Continents*, 1–42.

10 Lowe, *Intimacies of Four Continents*, 17–18.

with Slavery is similarly concerned with the processes that divide people and economies along distinct axes of value and commodity. I draw on Lowe's methodological intervention to consider the relationship between early modern concepts of numeracy, slavery, and kinship in constructing the rationale for hereditary racial slavery and in positioning African women as particularly illegible—both historically and archivally.

Doing so highlights the range of meanings attached to Keye, her children, and her legal case. Virginia lawmakers faced the quotidian consequences of sex between free subjects and those who were or could be enslaved. Keye assumed she had a kinship relationship to her father. Her freedom suit was rooted in the notion that his paternal line was hers to claim. However, in the context of a labor system wherein white men routinely, and possibly systematically, raped the women they claimed as property, their own paternity could not devolve to their children. Indeed, in this system, only women who were the daughters of free white men and white women could convey kinship, and thus freedom, to their children. The legislative intervention associated with Keye's case did more than just clarify the heritability of slavery; it also assigned legitimacy to white women's kinship ties and white men's property claims. The inability to convey *kinship*—to have family represent something other than the expansion of someone else's estate—is at issue here. If the children of white men and African women could assert their freedom, the primacy of property claims would be dislodged. But Englishmen did not want their property rights unsettled by sexual congress. Reproduction (and thus enslavability) was tethered to enslavement in a way that foreclosed the possibility that kinship might destabilize capital. To be enslaved meant to be locked into a productive relationship whereby all that your body could do was harnessed to accumulate capital for another. In this case, sex, inheritance, property, race, and commodification were both displayed and delineated as the House of Burgesses amplified its core assumptions about the nature of racial inheritance in the New World.

Scholars who analyze the 1662 code reanimate the word *condition* as we discuss the implications of the rule that the condition of the child would follow that of the mother. But I am compelled to push back against that word and the stasis it invokes. In the historian Vincent Brown's engagement with Orlando Patterson's concept of social death, he concludes that instead of understanding slavery as a condition, we should see it as a "predicament, in which enslaved Africans and their descendants never ceased to pursue a politics of belonging, mourning, accounting, and regeneration."[11] For Brown, the notion of social death as the condition of slavery fixes the enslaved person too statically in the category. I too want to problematize social death as a static condition that evokes but doesn't actually engage with the maternal figure who is incapable of counteracting natal alienation. I suggest here that enslaved parents understood the potential birth of children as a predicament that clarified the foundations on which their enslavement was erected. The violence that suffused that predicament was regularized and indeed world defining. In her critical formulation of social death, which she renders as *zombie biopolitics*, Elizabeth Dillon has argued that such violence produced the "resourced, white, genealogically reproductive, legally substantiated, Enlightenment man."[12] The archival silences around the lived experiences of enslaved women at the birth of racial capitalism are themselves the technologies that rendered those women as outside history, feeling, and intellect.

How were race, inheritance, trade, freedom, value, and slavery condensed in the competing desires of white men and of Black women and men as the former sought to retain property in persons by destroying kinship and the latter sought to produce families opposed to that destruction? Both white elites and the women whose corporeal integrity was so profoundly violated by the rule of property understood, experienced, and responded to these new ideas in ways that we still do not fully understand. Women who lived through the early decades of enslavement saw the identity of their children and the assumptions that governed their futures change drastically. That shift was rooted in a relatively new set of ideas concerning trade, value, population, and commodification, all of which might qualify as forms of numeracy. Spillers wrote in 1987 that the captive body becomes the site of a "metaphor for *value*" that renders useless any distinction between the literal and figurative violences that enslaved persons were subjected to.[13] Further, as I argue in this book, the metaphors of value and valuelessness owe at least part of their power to the knowledge regimes set in motion by the transatlantic slave trade. Rational equivalence was increasingly understood as the antithesis of social, emotional, or familial categories, which were simultaneously delimited as the sole purview of Europeans. As a result, African women and their descendants—all members of families—were locked together into the very space that built a market based on the denial

11 V. Brown, "Social Death and Political Life," 1248.
12 Dillon, "Zombie Biopolitics," 626.
13 Spillers, "Mama's Baby, Papa's Maybe," 68.

that they were there. This book argues that perhaps it is possible to discern the developments that brought these categories into being in the modern world when we examine them from the point of view of these women.

How does the concept of value, or currency, or marketing, connect with the experience of being enslaved? How did enslaved people interpret the illusory claims of rationality when such claims laid a price on both their heads and those of their unborn children? As early as 1971, the scholar and activist Angela Davis asked historians to consider the trauma that enslaved women experienced when they "had to surrender child-bearing to alien and predatory economic interests."[14] Answering such questions calls for a reading and a research strategy that takes as its starting point the assumption that both enslaved Africans and their captors simultaneously enacted meanings as they navigated the very new terrain of hereditary racial slavery and its consequences. By examining the moments when ideas about rationality and race appear to cohere, we can unearth the lived experiences and analytic responses to enslavement of those whose lives have most regularly and consistently fallen outside the purview of the archive. The question, as posed by the anthropologist Stephan Palmié, is, How did enslaved women and men "not just experience but actively analyze and render comprehensible" the violent transformations wrought upon them?[15] Being locked into a juridical category of perpetual servitude based on an inherited status had particular meaning for those who produced that inheritance inside their own bodies. To return to Davis's important work, enslaved women were positioned to "attain a practical awareness" of both the slave owner's power and the slave owner's dependence on her productive and reproductive body.[16] Thus, these women embodied both the apex of slavery's oppressive extractions and its potential undoing.

If we assume that Elizabeth Keye entered the House of Burgesses with little ability to comprehend the calculus working on and through her, we overlook her relationship to and understanding of all that was unfolding around her. She was embedded in a foundational epoch from which race, forced labor, capitalism, and modern economies emerged. While the actions she undertook to protect her children show that she did not see herself as commodified, they offer tacit proof that she saw that some around her were. What can we learn from the moments when those being commodified catch the process

14 Davis, "Reflections on the Black Woman's Role."
15 Palmié, *Wizards and Scientists*, 3.
16 Davis, "Reflections on the Black Woman's Role."

in action? From actions that reveal layers of meaning and complexities? It is obvious that Keye experienced this transformation, but might she have formulated thoughts about what she glimpsed? The seventeenth-century English Atlantic world was a tangle of overlapping hierarchies, ideas of difference, and newly sharpened ideas about rationality and value. Concepts about race entwined with those about value, and ideas about inheritance with those about social reproduction and childbirth in ways that we still do not adequately understand.

Thus, we need to reexamine the new ideas about commerce, finance, value, and money that came to be understood as the heart of what was rational, knowable, and scientific. In the early modern period, the number of people in England with numerical literacy increased significantly across the population, including among the writers and critical thinkers of the time. Keith Thomas argues that the field of seventeenth-century political arithmetic emerged from a "faith in the power of statistics to resolve the problem of government and administration."[17] But it was also the product of a faith in the work that rationality could do. Faced with the notion that an investment in forced labor could become a valuable asset for individuals and for the nation, Europeans ascribed stable value to Black bodies as commodities and claimed that the province of assessing value belonged only to whites (that is, to those who came to see themselves primarily as white). However, if we read race back onto political arithmetic, its faulty calculus and claims to logical certitude become increasingly apparent, as do the roots of racial thinking at its core. There was nothing purely rational about the turn to racial slavery, regardless of the wealth it produced. Yet the self-evidence of that statement still requires a caveat concerning the role of racism in rendering slavery irrational. In the arena of culture, racial slavery made no sense. In the realm of the economy, however, it did.

Locating the connections between the history of difference and the history of value demands a recognition that ideas about value developed alongside other concepts that were meant to position economics as the site of rationality and knowability. The same process that led the accounts of courts, trade, commerce, and governments to be archived ended with no accounting at all of the lived experiences of Africans as commodities, of the lives of seventeenth-century African women and their descendants.[18]

17 K. Thomas, "Numeracy in Early Modern England," 104.
18 Gregory, "Cowries and Conquest," 207. In *A History of the Modern Fact*, Mary Poovey asks us to "map the complex history of the relationship between numerical representation

It is impossible to approach the histories of slavery and gender without confronting the problem of the archive. As Marisa Fuentes has generatively shown, doing so requires us to understand that "enslaved women appear as historical subjects through the form and content of archival documents in the manner in which they lived: spectacularly violated, objectified, disposable, hypersexualized, and silenced. The violence is transferred from the enslaved bodies to the documents that count, condemn, assess, and evoke them, and we receive them in this condition."[19]

Fuentes's observations are crucial. The processes she describes apply to the production of these women and to the production of the ideas that situated them as counted and condemned. Before we received these women, they were captured by the Atlantic market through a set of ideas and practices that enabled the damage white people did to them and ensured that such damage could only result in archival obscurity. Making visible the process by which this happened is as important as recognizing the problem of its outcome. If the archives make it impossible to receive African women as other than historically obscure, damaged, and violated, then redressing that damage requires a clear understanding of what situated them as such. And while the manifestations of racial hierarchy are inescapably violent, they gestate in the claims of neutrality, calculability, and rationality. The practices that locate trade as rational and Black women as entries in ledgers transformed these women from subjects to objects of trade through the concepts of population, value, market, currency, and worth. So much has been lost to the pages of legislative debates, merchant ledgers, and calculations of risk, finance, fluctuating value, tariffs, products, and trade. The archives of gender and slavery emerged in a maddening synchronicity of erasure and enumeration.[20]

---

and figurative language" (26). (In this foundational text, Poovey completely omits any discussion of race and its connection to the accumulation of wealth in early modern Europe.) And in *Wizards and Scientists*, Palmié worries that the "truly stunning wealth of aggregate data" on slavery and the slave trade may form a "mounting heap of abstract knowledge that . . . may well contribute to blocking from view" the ghosts of the men and women who are our concern (8).

19 Fuentes, *Dispossessed Lives*, 5.

20 More than thirty years ago, Sidney Mintz and Richard Price argued that the core contradiction of American slave societies was the assertion that the enslaved were not fully human even as slave owners lived intimately with those they enslaved and thus were fully cognizant of their humanity. The records perform a similar act of recognition and disregard. Understanding the role of numerical abstraction in the reduction of persons

In recent years, scholars of slavery have attended carefully and productively to the archive, insisting on recognizing the particular problems that archival research poses for the study of gender, power, and enslavement. Social historians who focus on the issue of resistance are also intent on unearthing the lives of the enslaved by reconsidering the nature of archival evidence. While both of these historiographical trends are critical to the state of the fields in which this study is situated, here I want to emphasize something that has all too often been lost. Elizabeth Keye and the other women with whom I am concerned were sentient beings who themselves generated an intellectual and political response to the profoundly new circumstances that were unfolding around them. To center the cognizant work of enslaved women, this study seeks to denaturalize the systems of thought that were only just emerging in the early modern Black Atlantic. It considers economy, ideology, and kinship as mutually constituted and explores *how* they are mutually constituted. Insisting that the logic that defined slaves and a range of seventeenth-century commodities and values was shaped by the concept of race and racial hierarchy enacts a methodology of relatedness. In what follows, I use the sources and techniques of social history and of Black feminist theory together in an effort to excavate hauntings. I am interested in articulating a set of relationships and ideologies that emerged in the sixteenth and seventeenth centuries (the period that is my primary focus) but that congealed in the eighteenth and nineteenth centuries into commonsense understandings whose ghosts, implications, and undercurrents are with us still.

Reckoning with Slavery is concerned with the triangle of economic logic, the Black radical tradition, and kinship as the basis of both racial formation and Blackness as enslavability. It is the symbolic underpinnings of race and capitalism that I am after, and in the archival places where the details of those underpinnings are legible, I will follow them with fidelity. But I also write in the tradition of Hortense Spillers and Cedric Robinson—indeed, I am trying to understand some of the viscera of what Spillers laid out so brilliantly when she mobilized the notion that enslaved women were forced to "reproduce kinlessness."[21] This project reads across academic disciplines and geographies and takes on the archival data produced in this

to commodities is another way to unpack the contradictory source of the violence inflicted on both the Africans caught in the slave trade and their descendants. Mintz and Price, *Birth of African-American Culture*, 25.

21 Spillers, "Mama's Baby, Papa's Maybe," 74.

historical moment as a space of collusion with the politics of erasure that has for so long produced segregated inquiries into the Atlantic past. My work here is that of a historian who is deeply committed to interdisciplinarity and is in dialogue with diasporic theorists of race and slavery. As I hope to illustrate through this study, the work of excavating the history of the Black Atlantic—the categories it produced, the violent destructions it wrought—requires a broad set of approaches united by a political and ethical stance toward academic practices that is capacious and omnivorous.[22] Racial identity, economy, value, and sociality emerged—and thus must be examined—in proximity to one another.

The explicit link between human commodification and the rise of market economies expands the impact of slavery beyond the cultural and ideological problem it has posed for social and intellectual historians in the past. The imperative to clarify the provenance of race and racial ideology produced a scholarly focus on the history of ideology, exemplified by the crucial work of scholars like Winthrop Jordan. This work sets aside the economic impact of racial slavery in a quest to understand the problem of race as a matter of culture. Jordan and Alden Vaughan mounted arguments that England's alleged insularity from contact with Africans rendered the experience of racial difference a shock.[23] New scholarship on slavery and capitalism reframes the economic by insisting on its social and ideological valence and takes Eric Williams's *Capitalism and Slavery* as its starting point.[24]

This book contributes to that reframing and insists that we still need to attend to beginnings, to how "a seventeenth-century faith in a well-regulated marketplace as a mechanism . . . of social and economic inclusion" produced instead an increasingly fixed and identifiable social category of exclusion.[25] Kim Hall observed in 1995 that "the many ways in which African trade

<hr />

22 The work that follows has been shaped by and through the scholarship of Herman Bennett, Christopher Brown, Vincent Brown, Ada Ferrer, Marisa Fuentes, Kim Hall, Saidiya Hartman, Jessica Johnson, David Kazanjian, Lisa Lowe, Katherine McKittrick, Fred Moten, M. NourbeSe Philip, Neil Roberts, David Scott, Christina Sharpe, Stephanie Smallwood, Michel-Rolph Trouillot, Sasha Turner, Alexander Weheliye, Alys Weinbaum, Sylvia Wynter, and others who work across disciplines and across time periods.
23 Jordan, "Modern Tensions"; Vaughan, "Origins Debate."
24 Smallwood's *Saltwater Slavery* exemplifies (and indeed in many ways inaugurates) this effort to think through the cultural weight of economy.
25 Briggs, "John Graunt, Sir William Petty," 20.

provided the practice, theory, and impetus for English trade [in the Elizabethan and Jacobean ages] remain unremarked."[26] The twinned concepts of social and economic inclusion produced categories of humans and markets that were excluded. There is no need to revisit the extensive scholarship here on medieval and early modern notions of difference. We understand the multiple taxonomies of savagery and monstrosity that came to undergird the emerging categories of race. The work of Renaissance scholars Kim Hall, Imtiaz Habib, Elizabeth Spiller, and others on the circulation of free and enslaved Black people in late Renaissance and early modern England has clarified that English merchants and elites were far less vulnerable to the shock of encounter with racialized difference than was earlier presumed.[27] Yet the connection between, on the one hand, new notions of population and ascriptions of racial difference to categories of people and, on the other, the new frameworks that valued and commodified human beings remains undertheorized. The history of slavery has been routed down one path or the other—economy or ideology. The division between these two paths owes its distinction, in part, to the work that the transition to racialized slavery performed in the formation of the Atlantic world.

In the sixteenth century, the space of the Atlantic was becoming manifest for traders, rulers, colonists, and courtiers in both Europe and Africa. As vistas expanded, a range of material and ideological technologies came into play for rulers, merchants, ideologues, and travelers in both Europe and West Africa. Numeracy—fluency in the concepts of trade and exchange, as well as attention to demographics—was just one of many new modes of thinking that accompanied the origins of the modern Atlantic world. There were always arguments about whether slavery was right or not, which suggests that from the onset European slave owners had to create some rationalizing meaning out of what would otherwise be clearly understood as irreligious abuse. In England and on the West African coast, traders and scholars were reconsidering their understanding of economy alongside its components: wealth, trade, and the notion of population. For English theorists, *political arithmetic* came to mean the ways that states benefited from a clear understanding of their demographic strengths and vulnerabilities; this theorization developed concurrently with the slave trade, yet

---

26 K. Hall, *Things of Darkness*, 16.
27 K. Hall, *Things of Darkness*; Habib, *Black Lives*; Spiller, *Reading and the History*.

has been sublimated by both contemporaries and their historians.[28] As some persons were transformed into mercantilist units of production, others became subject to the demographic manipulations of the state.

As we untangle the connections between early modern English ideas about the body, the emergence of a capitalist trade in human beings, the emergence of "population," and the discursive construction of race as logic, we need to pay particular attention to the process by which the strange became the fungible. At the end of the Middle Ages, Europeans understood Africans as oddities—as spectacles, objects that indicated strangeness (such as monstrous, quasi-human beings with eyes in their chest or breasts on their backs) to be displayed on the stage and at the fair. Their strangeness was defined through their exhibition. But "the circular procession of the 'show' [was replaced] with the arrangement of things in a 'table.'"[29] Over the course of the sixteenth century, white elites moved Africans from the stage to the double-entry record books of slave traders and buyers. Africans were no longer primarily spectacular; they had become speculative items of calculus. But turning African human beings into commodified objects was neither a simple nor an untempered process. The language of commodity, of sale and value, of populational assessments and equivalent currencies, all of these instruments of numerical rationalism sat quite uncomfortably upon human beings. As much as mobilizing these instruments was an act of distinguishing Europeans from Africans, the proximity between them continued to upset the claim that people could ever be fully reduced to things.

The enslavement of Africans raised moral and ethical questions in Europe to be answered or evaded as the slave trade became increasingly central to the growth of European economies. The possibility of European commodification and the intense need to interrupt it laid the foundation for racialist philosophies, articulations of the interconnected logic of

28 An attentive reader will recognize *political arithmetic* as a potent turn of phrase in Saidiya Hartman's introduction to *Lose Your Mother*. Here, as she defines the afterlife of slavery, she writes that "black lives are still imperiled and devalued by a racial calculus and a political arithmetic that were entrenched centuries ago" (6). It is instructive to me that her recourse to calculus in 2007 was rooted in a seventeenth-century phrase designed to capture the ideological reverberations of demographic data.

29 Foucault, *Order of Things*, 131. Absent from this, and most work on the early emergence of modernity, is a discussion of how this move into tables and record books was experienced by Africans.

natural philosophy, political arithmetic, and the theories of value exemplified by the trade in human bodies across the Atlantic. On the African coast, traders began to see populations as marketable in new and more fungible ways as slavery came to mean something entirely different than it had before—premised on an unspoken assumption that the enslavable population was clearly definable, permanent, and infinite. Simultaneously, the languages of race and racial hierarchy changed long-standing conceptions of who was different, who was foreign, who was an ally, and who was an enemy. These changed ideas shaped the trade in slavery, the goods produced by slave labor, and the settler colonialism that would become the core means by which wealth was transferred across and around the Atlantic. Both the application of numerical abstraction to goods and people and the race thinking that it compelled were shaped by the social and cultural processes that attended their use. Neither was a fixed or static tool, but together they forged meaning through the interplay between the supposed logic of calculus and the alchemy of race making.

Despite their historical proximity, numeracy and race have rarely been examined under the same lens. New ways of thinking were the norm in the seventeenth-century Atlantic world. Contemporary observers understood that significant shifts in the roles merchants and traders played in producing the wealth of monarchies and states were underway and took pains to explore and understand them. Seventeenth-century English policies related to trade and commerce reflected a crucial moment in the development of Atlantic markets. This was the moment when the English state made foundational commitments to an empire that was rooted in colonial commodities markets and was dependent on slave labor. The transformations that led up to these commitments were the products of many political, material, and ideological convergences: a monarchy open to new kinds of growth, the shifting parameters of commerce and credit, the fact that a portion of the population was willing to resettle, shipbuilding technology that brought both the western African and eastern American coasts within reach, and an ideological shift in how people and things acquired factuality in the service of secular governance—to name just a few. The growth of England's involvement in the transatlantic slave trade coincided with currency crises rooted in (though not limited by) the false hope of New World gold, the escalation of intra-European military conflicts fueled by claims on emerging markets, and the ascendency of a pseudoscientific moralistic ideology of race, money, and civility that justified the relentless violation of human community.

The slave trade—the reliance on slave labor to extract commodities and to function as currency—was not simply one trade system among many. Rather, slavery exemplified the brutal logics of a new order, one based on a form of wealth that was produced not by exalted bloodlines but by commodity exchanges that were increasingly dependent on the invention of race to justify the inheritances of slavery—both those that adhered to the slave owner and those that adhered to the enslaved. The role of hereditary racial slavery in consolidating modern economic systems has been either overlooked or misplaced as marginal to the core text of early modern economic formations. Historians understand the relationship among early modern Atlantic settler colonialism, commodity extraction, and the transatlantic slave trade, but scholarship on the relationship between money (or, more broadly, the systems of abstraction that I link in this study as numeracy) and the transatlantic slave trade as simultaneously an economic and a cultural phenomenon is rare.[30]

Arguments about the origins of racial thinking turn on economics to explain the why of slavery but don't consider that economics and race might be mutually constitutive. To approach them, then, as two distinct arenas of thought misses the ways in which, for example, ideas about the English population are linked to ideas about Africans. The constellation of early modern ideas related to trade, currency, population, and civility that formed the ideological foundation for the logics of race produced categories of thinking that depended on the ejection of reproduction from kinship and women from the category of the enslaved. Sexual violence, reproduction, and the conceptual importance of infants and children undergirded the work that race would do in justifying Atlantic slavery and had brutal consequences for women and men exploited by regimes of terror and control in slave societies across the Americas.

Much of the historical attention to the relationship between slavery and capitalism is framed by ideas of cause and effect—does slavery undergird capitalism, or does capitalism produce the conditions that allow slavery to develop? The way I navigate this question is substantially influenced by the foundational work of the political scientist Cedric Robinson, whose 1983 text *Black Marxism* has enjoyed a well-deserved resurgence in the fields of African American history and philosophy since its republication in 2000. Robinson rereads the history of feudal Europe's turn to capitalism and critiques Karl Marx for situating capitalism as the revolutionary rejection of

30 For a crucial provocation along this line, see Smallwood, "Commodified Freedom."

feudal economic relations. Instead, Robinson argues that both capitalism and racism emerged, simultaneously, from the European feudal order, that the earliest proletariats in Europe were racialized, and that this gave rise to a modern system rooted in both slavery and violence. Here I join scholars of slavery and its afterlives (like Walter Johnson, Robin Kelley, Stephanie Smallwood, Alys Weinbaum, and others) to build on Robinson's work by exploring the fixed categories of labor, hierarchy, and race.

In particular, I engage Robinson in tandem with the concept of reproduction—both as used by Marx and as used by scholars of gender and slavery. Slavery is not a residual form in emergent capitalism, nor are reproductive capacities and the gendered meanings attached to them residual to the emergence of early modern racial formations.[31] How, then, does the notion of reproduction undergird the emergence of the category and the practice of slavery and slave labor? How might the experience of enslaved women have given rise to a Black radical tradition (another of Robinson's core interventions) that was rooted in the intersections between birth and commodification? These questions emerge by centering enslaved women—and suggest that racial capitalism offers us a way not just to understand the simultaneity of these large historical forces but also to see how the logics of reproduction undergird both. It is only recently that historians of capitalism have considered slavery as central to the emergence of capitalism in the early modern Atlantic world.[32]

But questions remain as to how slavery might be understood not just as bound up with the emergence of capitalist economies but as constitutive of commerce, value, money, and the new cultural logics embedded therein. The questions I engage in this study are clearly related to and in dialogue with the newly invigorated scholarship that has revisited Eric Williams's foundational *Capitalism and Slavery*.[33] Building on these ideas, I exam-

---

31 The relationship between the appropriation of women's reproductive lives and the emergence of capitalism has long been at the core of feminist Marxist scholarship. My interest here is in elaborating the relationship between the history of racial capitalism and the production of enslaved women as vectors of kinlessness.

32 For an overview of this turn, see Beckert and Rothman, introduction, 1–28.

33 In "Reckoning with Williams," Russell Menard offers a good overview of why Williams's work is crucial to the history of slavery in the colonial Americas. For a clear and generative articulation of why capitalism and slavery should no longer be thought of as two distinct things, see W. Johnson, "To Remake the World." For more on the resurgent engagement with Williams's *Capitalism and Slavery*, see Beckles, *Britain's Black Debt*, 100–108; Draper, *Price of Emancipation*, 1–16.

ine the emergence of a cultural logic that regarded a specific category of human beings as commodities and, based on that belief, created the slave-based economies of the early modern period. These economies, rooted in the sixteenth-century Spanish colonies in the Caribbean and Latin America and expanded by the Dutch, English, and French in the seventeenth century, are crucial to understanding the historical connections among slavery and capitalism as well as the cultural and ideological formations that undergirded those connections.

While we are quite certain about the role the American colonies and the trade associated with them played in transforming European states into empires, questions remain around the cultural and economic connections between the rationalizing of the transatlantic slave trade, the political economy of settler colonialism, and the efforts on the part of the enslaved to refuse their commodification. These three areas of historiography—racial ideology, economics, and the political life of enslaved peoples—are most often addressed as distinct by scholars trained in subdisciplines of history that continue to be seen as merely adjacent rather than co-constitutive. As Kris Manjapra has argued, contemporary racial capitalism "depends on the financial apparatus to conceal"—and such dependence has deep roots.[34] There are obscene abstractions at the heart of the slave trade that reverberated across the social and economic categories that racial slavery would call into being—race thinking, speculative economic thinking, political economies of both enslaved people and slave owners, arguments about ethics and finance, and the relative autonomy and safety of family life among people of European and African descent. They set in motion a series of relationships and inequities that are at the heart of modern capitalism and whose half-lives we can only fully comprehend through an accounting practice rooted in the traditions and interpretive strategies of Black radicalism. These connections are at the heart of the intervention I seek to make with Reckoning with Slavery.

In 1776 Adam Smith argued in An Inquiry into the Nature and Causes of the Wealth of Nations that the crucial mark of the civilizing process was the accumulation of "objects of comfort." Such commodities were the things that distinguished the "savage" from the "civilized and thriving nation."[35] By the latter part of the eighteenth century, it was clear that such a division existed, even as political economists like Smith struggled to articulate the

34 Manjapra, "Necrospeculation," 34.
35 A. Smith, Wealth of Nations, 2.

logical connections between wealth and national sovereignty. That connection was often made manifest through metaphors of the body. This was a body, according to philosopher Susan Buck-Morss, "composed of things, a web of commodities circulating in an exchange that connects people who do not see or know each other. These things make it a civilized body."[36] But by the time Smith wrote *The Wealth of Nations*, it was taken for granted that the commodities that distinguished one "great body of the people" from others could in fact *be* bodies. The false universalism embedded in the corporeal metaphor is thus already a violation, an act of erasure that ensures the exclusion of Africans from the categories of civility, citizenship, and nationhood, all of which rest on the accumulation of capital.

While invulnerability and bodily integrity were by no means assured in an era of plagues and famines, Barbary captivity and indentured servitude, the ability to accumulate things ultimately defined some bodies as decidedly not things. They were instead subjects whose identities were coterminous with the political and economic project of the nation, rather than objects whose value fueled it. These bodies were demarcated as white, civilized, and sovereign; they were defined in contradistinction to the enslavable, the commodifiable, the countable, and thus the unfree. That the Enlightenment notion of the universal subject rested on the erasure of another's corporeal integrity warrants careful consideration. Indeed, it may well have been the most foundational concept in the making of the modern world.[37]

Writing about the concept of "wealth in people" as a metaphor for understanding the ways human beings could be valued in Africa, anthropologist Jane Guyer insisted that "the history of exchange and the history of relationships must permeate one another."[38] While narratives about trade, commerce, and the exchanges that led to the transatlantic slave trade frequently situate African women at the margins of the relationships deemed critical, they were crucial indicators of the boundaries of sovereignty, of the customs that ultimately marked Africans as different, and of the potentialities of hereditary enslavement. The cultural shifts that marked the

36 Buck-Morss, "Envisioning Capital," 450. Identifying the circulatory paths of wealth—like blood—through the body politic was a crucial task for Enlightenment thinkers, who were often driven to metaphors of the body.

37 Michel-Rolph Trouillot's elaboration of the unthinkable brings the diaspora and its consequences to bear on Michel Foucault's anemic and deracinated notion of what it is impossible to think. See Foucault, *Order of Things*, xv–xxiv; Trouillot, *Silencing the Past*.

38 Guyer, "Wealth in People, Wealth in Things," 87.

emergence of modernity for late sixteenth- and early seventeenth-century England, including the decoupling of wealth from nobility and the capacity to relocate and remain English, depended on the possible commodification of all bodies. And it was in the bodies of the enslaved that this fundamental transformation found its rawest and most devastating articulation.

Descriptions of women as part of diplomatic or trade negotiations, as an index of the strangeness of African customs or as evidence that reproduction took place in the absence of kinship, all became part of the arsenal of difference and enslavability deployed by European writers in defining their relationship to the African continent and its people. Elsewhere, Guyer asks why so little sustained social history or social theory exists that explores African concepts of self-valuation.[39] She poses this question while considering a very different time and place than the sixteenth- and seventeenth-century origins of the transatlantic slave trade, but that question of the history of self-valuation persists. As women and men were forcibly removed from their homes and communities, they carried a deep and multivalent sense of value across the Atlantic. They knew their own value as kin, as producers, as reproducers, as marketers, as objects of trade, as currency. It must be considered, then, that during the Middle Passage they might have begun to discern the larger meaning of their capture.

In the seventeenth century, Elizabeth Keye inhabited a world in which the languages of trade, equivalency, and commodification had seeped into the worldviews of Europeans and West Africans alike. European expansion and its cultural logics significantly altered the geographies of trade and affect in which Keye lived, but because those transformations involved her parents and her children, indeed because it depended on them and all they represented, the ability to read the parameters of that expansion became part of her commonsense understanding of the world and of her place in it. The calculation of value, worth, and commodity and the extent to which they impinged on human life was not just the jurisdiction of slave owners and merchants calculating worth, of indentured servants calculating time, or of white women and free Black men calculating risk. It featured in the thinking of the Keye family as they calculated freedom through a newborn who evidenced the interdependency between the receding possibilities of her future and her newly calculated value.

As we will see, traders and shell divers, philosophers and griots, outlaws and Irishmen, were all embedded in patterns of thought about rationality,

39 Guyer, "Wealth in People and Self-Realization," 243–65.

numeracy, and calculability that were being newly honed and becoming rationalized. In the process, they produced knowledge systems that were isolated from one another in the binaries of the sacred and the profane, the sentimental and the analytic, and the economic and the poetic. All of this removed the stench of bruised and putrefying flesh from the bookkeeper's ledger. The end result was so exquisitely rendered that Keye's comprehension of her embeddedness in Atlantic modernity fades from view. It is left out of the archives we have inherited and created because motherhood came to occupy a different location than economy. But of course that was not the case for Keye.

Kinship, motherhood, population, currency, migration, commodification, and race were conceptually intertwined, both for those who were slave owners and for those who were enslaved. However, the latter population tends to fall out of our studies of early modern Atlantic slave societies because of the limits of both our archives and our analysis. How can we comprehend the alchemy of commerce, race, and slavery in women's lives when those who chose which documents to archive so consistently erased its traces? Perhaps we must insist that in the fields of meaning that were coming into practice in the English Atlantic in the late sixteenth and early seventeenth centuries, racialized maternity was entirely synchronous with commodity.

Susan Sontag has argued that "the sufferings most often deemed worthy of representation are those understood to be the product of wrath, divine or human."[40] Those of us who study the impact of the transatlantic slave trade often find that the victims of wrath have disappeared into merchant ledgers, planter inventories, and modern databases. This renders the processes that put them there indiscernible. Despite what we know to be the case, the range of emotions associated with human wrath—acquisitiveness, selfishness, greed, and rage—don't figure in these accounts; they are neutralized as they are transformed into commerce.

And, indeed, it is hard not to believe that recourse to the logics of trade and commerce was the first effort to cover up the bodies. The bodies we can no longer see or even conjure up enter the historical record, then, only as numbers—or sometimes as the familiar cross section of the slave ship *Brookes*, in which the very quantity of bodies is the evidence of their disembodiment. As far as slave owners and settlers were concerned, there was

40 Sontag, *Regarding the Pain of Others*, 7, 40.

no divine or human anger here, no spectacle, nothing to see. But one of the less common meanings of the word *wrath* is "to afflict harm or injure; to bring to grief or disaster."[41] And even without the help of etymological investigation, it isn't too difficult to locate wrath in the transactions of the transatlantic slave trade. Wrath is intimately connected to the violation that transforms a human being into a commodity, but because that transformation takes place through the calculus of trade, the violation that we identify most immediately is how racism interrupts and perverts humanity. We overlook the process that fixes human beings in the ledger books and accounting practices of merchants on both sides of the Atlantic.

This, then, is a question of knowledge production. It speaks to the project of knowing Man—the rational, spiritual, economic, and political universal male who was forged in the ideological spaces of the early modern. How does the history of slavery comport with the ideological processes that positioned public and private life as oppositional, defined the citizen, and delimited reason and intellect as the province of only the European man? As enslaved people were produced as outside the category of humanity, the notion that enslaved women or men could generate coherent assessments of the terms of their enslavement fell increasingly outside the realm of the possible. Slave owners, ministers, chroniclers, European travelers, and economic thinkers all managed to both record and erase the presence of Africans in connection to structures of community that they claimed were the sole province of Europeans, such as family, church, trade, and markets. European writers produced copious records in the wake of contact with Africans that reflected both mutual confusion and disdain but also a burgeoning interest in quantification and in understanding populations as distinct, quantifiable, and transferable.

Historians have used these data to reveal the violence of the transatlantic slave trade and the suffering it caused. But rarely do we see these data as part of the prisons of meaning enslaved people struggled against. Too often the quantitative evidence of Black suffering and commodification is treated as if it is irrefutably transparent. The data are situated, albeit with regret, as all that historians have. This kind of evidence is both efficacious and dulling—it makes a certain kind of scholarship possible while rendering another quite impossible. By carefully tracing the ideological

---

41 *Oxford English Dictionary*, online ed., s.v. "wrath, v.," accessed April 16, 2019, http://www.oed.com/view/Entry/230557?rskey=l8z9WI&result=3&isAdvanced=false.

work attached to the reputed logic of trade, taxation, and migration in concert with that of inheritance and race, we can more fully understand the emergent overlapping logics of race, gender, and numeracy in the early modern period.[42]

A political economy of women in early modern slavery is called for, and with it a new methodology. Our ability to excavate men and women embedded in social, ethical, and political lives from the sedimentation that is commerce, colonialism, abolition, and moral suasion is profoundly compromised not just by the archives we inherit but by the siloed categories of knowledge that accompany the production of those archives. The economic goals of the transatlantic slave trade—the transformation of humans into cargo—mobilized discursive strategies that became embedded in the logics of market capitalism and the efforts to oppose them. To argue that the Middle Passage was embedded in a particular script is not to suggest that the corporeal agony of the journey is not real. Rather, it is to take seriously the work of generations of cultural critics who have argued that the discursive fields in which social-historical experiences occur not only matter but are analytic categories that fully shape both our rendering of those experiences and the experiences themselves.

Writing the history of Black people, particularly in the early modern period, continues to be a struggle against the disciplining forces of knowledge production and the claim that Africa is a place without history. The longstanding accusation that Africans have no legible past is older than Georg Wilhelm Friedrich Hegel and as contemporary as the hundreds of lives lost to the Mediterranean Sea as North African refugees desperately tried to enter Italy in recent years.[43] Efforts to rewrite the history of slavery and the Middle Passage, to restore African captives to the narrative of events that so profoundly shaped them, sometimes reproduce the very narrative structures that positioned Africans as outside historical change. The Middle Passage becomes the raw material through which the violences of early modern capital are rendered legible, a script whose "stains won't wash out."[44] But we still need to ask what it means to write histories that acknowledge

---

42 Stephanie Smallwood and Daina Ramey Berry both refuse the kind of static relationship with numerical data with which I am also concerned. Berry, *Price for Their Pound of Flesh*; Smallwood, *Saltwater Slavery*.

43 For a foundational discussion of the role of discursive erasures in European thought, see Gates, *Figures in Black*, 14–24.

44 Kearney, "Swimchant," 62–63.

that the silences in the records are evidence of "an irrecoverable w/hole."[45] These histories are often a search for surrogates, an effort to find stand-ins for "the missing voices of those enslaved, dead and forgotten."[46] The Middle Passage and the logbooks that record it mark an archive of beginning: "This is where historic blackness comes from: the list, the breathless numbers, the absolutely economic, the mathematics of the unliving."[47]

My work here is an attempt to write a counterhistory of the origins of racial slavery, one that is not an effort to restore an irrecoverable whole but rather a response to Katherine McKittrick's exhortation that we can "write blackness" by "reading the mathematics of [anti-black] violences as possibilities that are iterations of black life that cannot be contained by black death."[48] Doing so requires us to inhabit multiple spaces: the deadening enumeration of the slave trader's account book and the slave owner's plantation inventory, the absence of women in discursive records except as wenches or madwomen, and the refusal to imagine that a rebel might also be a woman.

What follows is not a formal history, for gathering a series of archive-based linear narratives is not possible here. Indeed, the very idea of a formal history is predicated on rules of evidence, sources, and strategies of interpreting that depend on the very denial that Black people are the agents and subjects of such formal histories. *Reckoning with Slavery* is an interdisciplinary examination of ideas newly circulating in the early modern Atlantic world, their consequences, and their reverberations. It considers the writings and experiences of Africans, Iberians, and English by drawing on records produced in the context of contact and trade with the aim of understanding something about the current of ideas that would shape the experience of enslavement in English colonies in the seventeenth century. I use sixteenth-century sources and evidence concerning English, Iberian, and West African notions of trade, wealth, and encounter to provide a context for ideas that would cohere later on. I also lean heavily on the work of historians, geographers, anthropologists, legal scholars, cultural critics, and literary scholars whose close reading practices offer grounded theoretical insight.

45 Shockley, "Going Overboard," 806.
46 Tillet, *Sites of Slavery*, 108. For a discussion of contemporary efforts to reconcile the absences produced by the Middle Passage, see Tillet, *Sites of Slavery*, 95–131.
47 McKittrick, "Mathematics Black Life," 17.
48 McKittrick, "Mathematics Black Life," 17.

While my commitments to archival research drive this project, part of my intention is to interrogate the impasse that the social historian of Black women's early modern history faces, to engage the extant source materials with care, and to bring as broad a methodological arsenal as I am capable of to bear upon these sources. The women who are my primary concern occupied a crucial conceptual position in the unfolding of racial slavery in the Americas. Their presence as laborers was dependent on their absence as historical subjects. But that absence fluctuates. Women appear in some archives and disappear elsewhere. Instead of lamenting the woefully un-even record, the chapters that follow weave extant evidence about enslaved women with the ideological developments that produced their absence. The book argues that embracing and legitimizing the appropriation of en-slaved women's and men's bodies depended on fields of meaning that were coming into being at the time. These are not reducible to racism or colo-nialism, even though the admixture of new ideas produced those concepts.

At the core of that process of appropriation are, of course, the men, women, and children who were taken captive and sold as forced laborers in the Americas. Thus, chapter 1 begins with a review of what evidence we have concerning the numbers of women on board Atlantic slave ships and how we come to know them. We need to ask both how the presence of those women affected the construction of the racialized category of the slave in the eyes of European traders and settlers and what the consequences of such enslavement were for how early enslaved Africans understood the vi-olent transformations that they endured. Such transformations, I suggest, need to be considered a kind of alchemy: slave traders had the notion that they could transform human beings into wealth, assigning them a value that rendered them exchangeable and distributable through transport and markets. The foundations for this alchemy are laid in both the materiality of the slave trade and the records produced to render it legible—records that situate kinship as commodity. Here I introduce a key question that runs throughout this project: In the face of the commodification of human beings, what did New World kinship come to mean?

This question hovers in the background of chapter 2, which considers the problem of evidence regarding the scope and scale of the slave trade from the perspective of the history of mathematical thinking and record keeping. I argue that Europeans' growing conviction that they could trade in human cargo and still retain their moral core was more closely entwined with numeracy than we have presumed. Neutral categories of thought such as "population" and "currency" came into circulation in England at the same time that commitments to the slave trade were becoming more robust. As English writers mulled over the new landscape of currency and wealth, they did so in relationship to the idea of Africa and the wealth of the Americas. The categories of thought that distinguished spaces of scholarly inquiry—economy, culture, literature, and politics—were emerging at this juncture in ways that were deeply influenced by concepts of difference and human hierarchies.

Chapter 3 extends this discussion of numeracy to the West African coast. Here I discuss how African women and men on or near the coast would have encountered commodification both before and after European contact. I also consider how Europeans wielded numeracy in their arsenal of meaning making in a way that denied African people sovereignty and autonomy. Such denials were at the core of how the subject with universal rights came to be so narrowly defined. Thus, they need to be understood not just as impacting the Africans whose numerical literacy and economies were mobilized against them but also as shaping the archive that erased Africans.

The second part of *Reckoning with Slavery* follows enslaved Africans across the Atlantic and into the colonies. Chapter 4 considers women's experience of capture and the Middle Passage. Exposed to the sexual predation of crew members and tasked with the care of infants and children on board, women experienced a multifaceted and profoundly inhumane passage. Centering these women undoes the refusal of ship captains to acknowledge their presence in their formal records and casts a critical eye on the production of silence in archival remnants of the slave trade. Further, it suggests that erasure was important for the ideological production of race as a vector of human hierarchy. Finally, I argue in this chapter that African women who endured the Middle Passage were uniquely positioned to understand the role of kinship at the heart of early modern slavery and thus to understand racial capitalism.

This capacity to know is also at the core of chapter 5, which explores the phenomena of sales and the experience of being sold. The sale of human beings was a clear and intimate lesson in how racial capitalism was unfolding, both for those being sold and for those doing the buying and selling. Here I explore the concepts of value and alienation that were unearthed at the moment of the sale, using advertisements posted in colonial newspapers as an entry point into this conversation. The proximity of advertisements of slaves for sale and advertisements for runaways generates a discussion on

the idea of "stealing oneself" and a consideration of the potentially liberatory counternarratives of commodification.

Finally, chapter 6 considers a range of efforts by enslaved women to disrupt their commodification on both small and large scales. Here I revisit
the question of archival tracings, centering the ways that the ideological
edifice of slavery meant that English slave owners were disinclined to report or acknowledge women's participation in marronage or slave revolts.
By situating a discussion of women's rejection of the terms of enslavement
at the close of this study, I intend to highlight the productive consequences
of early modern racial capitalism. Here we understand that the assumptions that drive histories of slavery wherein women's lives and experiences
are cordoned off as falling within the realm of family are entangled with the
structures of knowledge production that produced these women's enslavement in the first place.

My overarching concern is how the use and abuse of enslaved women
reverberated in the development of the slave-owning Atlantic world. I situate these women through a discussion of the role of kinship in authorizing
hereditary racial slavery and in shaping the development of slavery as a financial and commercial instrument. Understanding the role of numeracy
and accounting practices that both recognize and sublimate gender is critical to my intervention—these practices and processes have made finding
these women difficult in both our archives and in our conceptions of the
past.

In producing a study of women's lives that is also concerned with mapping ideologies and knowledge production, I attempt to integrate social,
economic, and cultural histories while being attentive to the impact of such
histories on our ability to think through or past these categories. The notion of palimpsest is helpful here because it marks a transformation that
builds on earlier forms of knowing even as it produces new ones. Those old
forms of knowing are not confined to a single African or European time
or place even though they called very specific times and places into being.
Thus, while this study is rooted in the English Atlantic world of the seventeenth century, it detours into fifteenth- and sixteenth-century West Africa
and Iberia and calls for a methodology that centers enslaved women over
geographies. Loosely, this book follows an Atlantic arc that begins in Iberia
and England, moves to the West African coast, crosses the Atlantic in the
Middle Passage, lands in the Caribbean, and works its way up to the North
American colonies. Throughout, I ask where and how enslaved women
were situated by the European men who claimed them as objects of com-

merce and what effect that had on the women so positioned and the ideological formations that swirled around them. I am interested in both the social history of enslaved women—their material experiences—and the ideological consequences of that materiality on them and on those who appropriated their labors.

ONE. Producing Numbers: *Reckoning with the Sex Ratio in the Transatlantic Slave Trade, 1500–1700*

Any social history begins with an accounting of subjects. Who was there? What was the impact of their presence? On the surface, these appear to be routine social-historical questions. But in the history of the Atlantic world we have only just begun to ask these questions regarding African women. It is not only that histories of slavery and the slave trade have rarely centered women's lives; it is also that in the effort to write those histories, we are always faced with distorted evidence. Women's lives during capture, transport, and enslavement are obscured; as a consequence, they can drop out of our understanding of how slavery as an Atlantic system unfolded. Scholars of slavery and its afterlives need to consider how difficult it is to answer a relatively simple question: How many African women were enslaved in Europe and the Americas? Also, how can we determine the answer? Everything that follows hinges on these questions, including the claim that women were crucial to both the economy of slavery and the development of racial ideologies in the early modern Atlantic world.

Women were captured, transported, and sold in Europe and the Americas from the onset of the Atlantic slave trade in 1444. That is irrefutable even as their exact numbers are difficult to extrapolate from the pastiche of records left behind by crowns and courts, customs and treasury officials, slave traders and sellers, trading companies and abolitionists, diplomats and patrollers. Apprehending those numbers is important for many reasons, not least because demographic clarity (a social fact, or numbers) transforms the transatlantic slave trade's profound violence and destruction from rhetoric and representation into tangible reality. The slave trade, slavery, and the slave all functioned as financial and commercial instruments as well as being collectively configured as an economic institution. The epistemological problem of representation that haunts our efforts to tell and retell this story is, in part, rooted in the alchemy of counting and accounting, of reckoning with the scope of this traffic in all its meanings. David Eltis framed the terrain appropriately: among voluntary and involuntary migrants who crossed the Atlantic before 1800, African women outnumbered European women by four to one. The question that must follow is therefore not, Were African women there?[1] It is, rather, Who were they?

Questions about the scope and scale of the slave trade have long been at the forefront of histories of Africa and the Americas. Phillip Curtin opened his foundational 1972 study with a chapter titled "The Slave Trade and the Numbers Game," in which he named the rise and fall of the Atlantic slave trade an "important quantitative problem."[2] Because what follows situates the problem of demography as a "game," the answer to this quantitative problem served as evidence mobilized to support an argument—a supposition neither flippant nor, ultimately, incorrect—even as the terms of the argument have shifted. No longer are historians driven by a desire to cast the slave trade as solvable riddle, but the unintended consequences of approaching the slave trade as a problem of quantification remain.[3]

An international multidisciplinary team of researchers with the Trans-Atlantic Slave Trade Database project (on the Slave Voyages website) have collected and organized the most comprehensive data on the slave trade to date. Some 36,110 voyages are currently accounted for in this database, including information about ships, captains and crew, points of origin and disembarkation, numbers of captives, and, most important for my purposes, ages and sex ratios.[4] The database is a model of collaborative empirical scholarship. But in deriving its organizing principles from the beneficiaries

1 Eltis, *Rise of African Slavery*, 97.
2 Curtin, *Atlantic Slave Trade*, 3.
3 In her introduction to a special issue of the *William and Mary Quarterly* on the Slave Voyages database project, Barbara Solow writes, "We can learn a good deal from the undeniable success Europeans had in assimilating eleven million human beings to an item in the balance of international payments." Solow, "Transatlantic Slave Trade," 11.
4 The project is ongoing, and new data are continually added. The figures cited here and elsewhere in this volume date from October 2020.

of a trade in humans—the evidence is gleaned from merchants, traders, and ship captains—it produces problems for scholars even as it answers queries. Determining the sex ratio in the slave trade from the available data is difficult, despite the confidence with which researchers use the data. Out of 36,110 voyages recorded between 1514 and 1866 (carrying 10,665,103 enslaved men, women, and children), a mere 3,426 record sex ratios, disaggregating the total number of captives into men and women, or males and females. Of the 4,358 voyages recorded for the period between 1514 and 1700, 336 disaggregate captives by sex.[5]

The researchers associated with the database project are well aware of its limits, and historical records outside of those directly related to the voyages have been crucial to the myriad scholars who have worked assiduously to clarify the rhythms of sex and age ratios in the transatlantic slave trade.[6] The point here is not that historians have been unable to ascertain the sex and age ratios. Rather, it is that turning to the database to answer questions about sex ratios means extrapolating from severely incomplete data. We know that among this small percentage of voyages, ship captains reported that males averaged 63 percent of the captives. But why do almost nine-tenths of voyages not contain information on the sex of the captives? And what further evidence do we need regarding the 37 percent of females on the voyages where they were counted? Is such a small piece of data even useful for constructing a history of women and slavery, or does it say more about the history of gender, trade, and racial ideology?

Historians have worked diligently to disaggregate these numbers. In early arguments that drew on this evidence, David Eltis and Stanley Engerman concluded that adult men "made up less than half" of all Africans forced to endure the Middle Passage. They also show that the proportion of women

5 In the introduction to the database, written in 2018, Eltis notes that there are a total of 3,731 voyages in which the age *and* sex of captives was recorded at the place of landing, and only 1,970 voyages where it was recorded at the place of embarkation. There are data on both age and gender (men, women, boys, girls) for a total of 3,404 voyages. David Eltis, "Age and Gender Ratios," in *Slave Voyages—Methodology* (2018), https://www.slavevoyages.org/voyage/about#methodology/age-and-gender-ratios/16/en/. The figure of 36,110 is taken from the total number of entries in the database as of November 2020. The figure of 3,426 is derived from a search of the database for all voyages that record at least 1 percent women on board.
6 For example, Paul Lovejoy has articulated some of the concerns about using the database to construct African histories. See Lovejoy, "Upper Guinea Coast," esp. 12.

was at its highest before 1700.[7] If we consider the wider range of source material available to scholars, then, it is clear that while women were out-numbered in the transatlantic slave trade by men and children, in the first century and a half of the trade numbers of women and men were relatively balanced, with women sometimes constituting the majorities.[8] Much of the scholarly analysis of the data on sex and age ratios on the Slave Voyages website is primarily concerned with explanations for differences across re-gion and time that rest on questions of labor demands, European gender norms, and the sociopolitical and demographic factors in the regions from which captives were taken. But these are not the primary questions of this study. In this chapter I am concerned with clarifying the significant pres-ence of women in the slave trade before 1700 and with attending to how evi-dence of their presence is both visible and elusive in the archives of slavery. This means translating the demographic data into social-historical evidence or, in this case, thinking about the ways in which the market for slavery and the suppression of kinship ultimately are consolidated as capitalism. For the anthropologists Sidney Mintz and Richard Price, the emergence of African American cultures and societies in the early years of colonial settlement re-flects a profound dynamism and creativity in the face of the violence of cap-ture and transport.[9] Here I want to suggest that that dynamism was rooted in the gendered realities of the captives who arrived in these early years and to explore further the social and economic realities accompanying their captivity.

New evidence of the first wave of slave trading to Spanish America is particularly important for the study of gender and slavery.[10] In sixteenth-

7 Eltis and Engerman, "Was the Slave Trade Dominated?," 237, 241. Eltis and Engerman were core contributors to the Trans-Atlantic Slave Trade Database, and this article drew on early findings.
8 See also J. L. Morgan, *Laboring Women*, 50–51.
9 Mintz and Price, *Birth of African-American Culture*, 49.
10 For an overview of new work on the Slave Voyages database, see Borucki, Eltis, and Wheat, "Atlantic History and the Slave Trade." The attention of historians of Africa to the structures that funneled captives into the hands of traders has increased clarity about the early decades of the slave trade by leaps and bounds and has added tens of thousands of captives to the database, increasing our understanding of the reach of the transatlantic slave trade before 1650. David Wheat has brought to the data set new evidence of close to eighty thousand African captives who disembarked in Cartagena from 1570 to 1640. See Wheat, "First Great Waves"; Wheat, *Atlantic Africa*. See also

century Ecuador, for example, records of slave sales indicate that nearly equal numbers of men and women were purchased to labor in the city of Quito; broader population figures for that country suggest at least 40 percent of enslaved Africans were female.[11] In Lima, censuses and tax records put women at just over 50 percent of the Black and mulatto population by 1600.[12] Indeed, in Peru enslaved women were so common that policing their movement and their garb became a crucial aspect of seventeenth-century Spanish colonial law, as historian Tamara Walker has shown.[13] Tatiana Seijas and Pablo Miguel Sierra Silva have shown that the persistence of the slave market in central Mexico in the seventeenth century was fueled by the lure of natural reproduction among Africans; this led to the enduring presence of enslaved women as valuably marketable.[14] Alex Borucki, David Eltis, and David Wheat suggest that the new evidence on the scope of the slave trade to Spanish America, particularly to Mexico, Columbia, Ecuador, and Peru, offers further clarity on the natural growth of African populations.[15] These figures have long been known to the handful of scholars working on slavery and the slave trade in the Iberian world of the fifteenth and sixteenth centuries, although they continue to surprise the larger field of colonial Latin Americanists.[16]

As research on the transatlantic slave trade has grown, more data and different questions allow us to engage further with the numbers as a problem of both ideology and evidence. The reach of numbers into social life is enormous. They impute neutrality to deeply contested and constructed ideas about worth and value. As historian Michelle Murphy has argued, reworking Marx's notion of the phantasmagorical powers of the commodity, ideas regarding population might usefully be considered *phantasmagrams*—"quantitative practices that are enriched with affect . . . and hence have supernatural effects in surplus of their rational precepts."[17]

Eltis, *Rise of African Slavery*, 85–113; Green, *Rise of the Trans-Atlantic* , 179, 238; Nwokeji, *Slave Trade and Culture*, 144–77.

11 Lane, "Captivity and Redemption," 228.
12 Bowser, *African Slave in Colonial Peru*, 337–41.
13 Walker, *Exquisite Slaves*, 33–34.
14 Seijas and Sierra Silva, "Persistence of the Slave Market," 316.
15 Borucki, Eltis, and Wheat, "Atlantic History," 458.
16 On the persistent need to emphasize the presence of enslaved Africans in early Latin American colonies see, for example, Herman L. Bennett's *Africans in Colonial Mexico* and *Colonial Blackness*.
17 Murphy, *Economization of Life*, 24.

In regard to slavery and the slave trade, transforming human beings into commodities produced abstract ideas about African populations that are obviously racist fantasies but are also, less clearly, linked to more dispersed modern phantasmagrams of value, disposability, and reproduction.

"Not a Sixth Part Are Women"

If we are clear that captive women, particularly before 1700, formed a significant proportion of enslaved laborers throughout Europe and the Atlantic world, we are perhaps less clear as to how their presence shaped the unfolding of the institution of racial slavery and its connection to emergent early modern capitalism. Richard Ligon, a royalist who was exiled from England after parliamentary forces defeated Charles I in the English Civil War, spent three years traveling to the Cape Verde Islands and then on to Barbados before returning to England. After his return, he published a history of Barbados that functioned as both a memoir and a guide; historian Karen Kupperman has called his text "an excellent example of something that was new in his period: an Atlantic life."[18] Ligon's movements sketch out the contours of the seventeenth-century Atlantic world, thus providing plans for other Englishmen hoping to profit from enslaving African laborers on stolen land in the Americas. Ligon ended his *True and Exact History of the Island of Barbados* (1657) with a long, detailed account of how a planter might establish a sugar plantation.[19] He wrote that planters purchased men and women in equal numbers; in his description of an imagined plantation, the "negroes . . . will account to be a hundred of both sexes . . . divide[d] equally."[20] Ligon was writing here in the mode of the promotional, describing an ideal.

The statement that a seventeenth-century plantation should contain equal numbers of men and women has been treated as anomalous or reinterpreted as a recommendation that planters change their policy of buying men in much larger numbers than women—in other words, it has not challenged the assumption that seventeenth-century planters with the power to shape their labor force eschewed sex balance in favor of robust male majorities in the sugar fields.[21] The notion that English planters in the

---

18 Kupperman, introduction, 1.
19 Ligon, *True and Exact History*, 110–18.
20 Ligon, *True and Exact History*, 115.
21 Eltis and Engerman, "Was the Slave Trade Dominated?," 237.

seventeenth century were able to enact a desire for an all-male workforce comes through an amalgam of beliefs on the part of both early modern slave owners and twentieth-century historians that needs to be carefully unpacked. The association of the slave or "negro" with maleness was laid down at precisely this juncture, and not until the 1980s would historians of women and slavery begin to marshal arguments and evidence about the lives of African women in the transatlantic slave trade. The words *negro* and *slave* were gendered male in the earliest records of European contact with Africans, as were all references to population, government officials, merchants, slave traders, and white laborers. On the island of Barbados, however, where female majorities predominated among the enslaved population from the mid-seventeenth century on, there is no discernible trace of those women in the language used by slave owners or legislators to describe the enslaved laborers.[22]

Unearthing the impact of women's presence requires, then, an attentive archival practice and a recognition that the effort to normalize the appropriation of other people for hard labor in Europe and the Americas was rooted in an ideological maneuver that erased captives' gender and kinship and family ties, which makes women that much more difficult to trace. It also requires a skepticism regarding the gendered assumptions that inform the foundational work on enslavement, the slave trade, and the history of slavery. Ligon wrote that "though we breed both Negroes, horses, and Cattle; yet that increase will not supply the moderate decays which we find in all those; *especially in our Horses and Cattle*."[23] If we approach Ligon free from the assumption that all slaves were male, we see that, for him, the presence of enslaved women on Barbadian plantations was as unremarkable as that of cows. For Ligon, not only were women a key aspect of plantation management, but their reproductive capacity apparently exceeded that of horses and cattle. The only women who are outnumbered by men in Ligon's account are "Christian [white] women," who were outnumbered by their male counterparts by two to one. Elsewhere in Ligon's account, it seems quite clear that African women were a common sight in the fields. He wrote, "We buy them so as the sexes may be equal" and described the work women performed in the fields.[24]

---

22 On the presence of female majorities on the island of Barbados, see Beckles, *Natural Rebels*, 7–23; J. L. Morgan, *Laboring Women*, 69–87.

23 Ligon, *True and Exact History*, 114 (italics added).

24 Ligon, *True and Exact History*, 44; see also 48–49 for his discussion of women's labor.

Ligon does not, of course, explicitly discuss the sex ratios on slave ships docking in Barbados or the relationship between the ideal number of women on a plantation and the reality. Instead, he offers glimpses that raise more questions than they answer. As Eltis and Engerman point out, the published and unpublished accounts of most other seventeenth-century writers constitute evidence of the "unquestioned 'given' that male majorities predominated in the trade."[25] Such misreadings have persisted in the historical literature despite the weight of numerical evidence. Indeed, the archival record, embedded as it is in the effort to justify and rationalize the slave trade and slavery, is replete with moments when numeracy and racialist prejudice coincide or buttress one another. More than a hundred years later, the propagandist and apologist for slavery Edward Long claimed in *The History of Jamaica* (1774) that "not a sixth part [of the enslaved population] are women."[26] For Long, the observation about the lack of women in Jamaica was keyed to an interpretation of the relationship among sexuality, population, and culture that exonerated the English from wrongdoing on the African continent. The slave trade, he argued, benefited Africa: by removing so many men, Europeans had helped forestall what would have been a "superabundance of inhabitants, if the slave trade did not take so many off."[27] His comments read in full:

> Of the slaves shipped from the coast, not a sixth part are women; and this happens from there being fewer female criminals to be transported, and no female warriors to be taken prisoners. The number of females born exceeds the males, and though some Blacks in the inland countries have ten, others an hundred wives, yet by the strictest enquiries from the inland merchants, it appears that no man goes without a wife from a scarcity of women; and that although the richest have many wives, the poorest are not thereby precluded from having one or two; in short, that an unpaired man or woman is seldom or never seen. Thus of many hindrances to population in Europe, not one takes place in Afric; and such is the rapidity of propagation here, that it should seem there would be a superabundance of inhabitants, if the slave trade did not take so many off. . . . It seems from hence

25 Eltis and Engerman, "Was the Slave Trade Dominated?," 237.
26 Long, *History of Jamaica*, 386–87.
27 Long, *History of Jamaica*, 386–87.

very probable, that Afric not only can continue supplying the West Indies with the same quantities as hitherto; but, if necessity required it, could spare thousands, nay millions more, and continue doing the same to the end of time, without any visible depopulation.[28]

Long, a Jamaican slave owner from 1757 to 1769 and an influential proslavery advocate in England once he returned there, did much, in the words of historian Catherine Hall, to inscribe the figure of the degraded African into British consciousness.[29] He does so here by drawing liberally from the well of populational abstraction, embedding prurient claims about the sexual proclivities of African men into an apologia for his compatriots' capturing and enslaving of tens of thousands of Africans in the West Indies.

Long's claim that so few women were enslaved on Jamaica is an example of late eighteenth-century proslavery agitation in the face of a growing abolitionist movement in Britain; the two-hundred-year-old trade was rationalized by embedding it in a narrative structure from which no recognizable women or children could emerge. Even though European slave traders and slave owners had little compunction about enslaving women, the archival silence around their presence remains challenging. The challenge is not insurmountable, as I hope this book will testify. The women are there. Their hazy presence marked the claims of early modern capitalists, despite—indeed, because of—the ways that the edifice of racial hierarchy and political arithmetic obscured them. Inattention to the particulars of their presence cannot be dismissed as simple omission; rather, it reflects an alchemy of race and commerce in the service of rendering African captives unrecognizable, as humans whose precarity was articulated through claims that they lived outside of kinship or civilization.[30]

Enslaved women provided crucial labor in American colonies but were also key in the emergent rationale for hereditary racial slavery, a rationale attached to the idea of kinless populations. Claims about the sex ratio of enslaved laborers, such as those iterated by Long, often hinge on the suggestion that plantation owners were loath to put women to work in plantation production or mining; this supposition itself hinges partially on the

28 Long, *History of Jamaica*, 386–87.
29 C. Hall, "Whose Memories?," 133.
30 I am using the Hegelian notion of recognition as modified by Judith Butler in her discussion of precarity and grievability. Butler, *Frames of War*, 4–5.

presumption that slave owners recognized African women as gendered in familiar ways that would make slave owners loath to submit them to capture and enslavement. And yet even in the eighteenth century, when women were certainly outnumbered in the slave trade, they often constituted the majority of laborers in sugar, rice, and tobacco fields.[31] The question remains, What were the consequences for slave owners, for the enslaved, and for the development of the Atlantic economy when women's labor was even more ubiquitous than it was in later decades? Asking this is a crucial response to the call to center the culture and the politics of enslaved people in histories of the slave trade.[32]

Kinship occupies a complicated space in the narrative evidence of the transatlantic slave trade. Although kinship was fundamentally erased by the violations of capture and transport, chroniclers and travelers to the African coast throughout the early modern period provide glimpses of both kinship structures in African communities and their own contradictory recognition of ties of affinity among captives. The alleged failure of Africans to form families or mother-child bonds of connection was a key aspect of early musings about savagery and enslavability. The inability to form families, or thwarted kinship, became a key manifestation of hereditary racial slavery as men, women, and children who survived the transatlantic slave trade were actively mourning the loss of family, even as they were thrust into a market in which their ability to convey enslavability to their descendants was part of what marked them as enslaved. The processes of family formation that shaped life for those who migrated both voluntarily and involuntarily to the Americas unfolded in profoundly precarious ways. At the same time, among all those who crossed the Atlantic to the Americas, it was only among Africans that anything approaching natural age and sex ratios occurred. As we know from records of sales and plantation inventories, in the middle of the seventeenth century, for example, the sex ratio among enslaved captives in the English colonies was almost at parity, while free migrants to the Caribbean and Virginia or Maryland ranged from 75 to 88 percent

---

31 For a discussion of women's role in cultivation, see Beckles, *Natural Rebels*, 24–55; Bush, *Slave Women in Caribbean Society*, 33–45; Carney, *Black Rice*, 107–41; Moitt, *Women and Slavery*, 34–56; J. L. Morgan, *Laboring Women*, 144–61; Steckel, "Women, Work, and Health".

32 V. Brown, "Social Death and Political Life."

male.[33] These uneven sex ratios among English settlers have garnered significant attention from scholars of colonial settlements across the Americas and have been mobilized to explain the incidence of sex "across the color line" between European men and indigenous or African women.[34] And yet in the foundational decades of Iberian, Dutch, and English settlement in the Americas, enslaved women constituted majorities in most cities and reached parity in the countryside.[35] Thus, it was only among enslaved Africans that the possibility of regular family formation existed—a possibility routinely destroyed by the violations that accompanied enslavement.

The labor of enslaved women had been an aspect of the landscape for European elites across the continent well before the onset of the transatlantic slave trade. Slavery in Europe—the enslavement of Europeans by Europeans—was a predominantly female institution. From Italy to Iberia to England, women who were defined as different worked in European households and fields. This situation laid the groundwork for the assumption that gendered notions of protection extended only to women who were attached to property-owning men, a mindset that would have epic ramifications for African women in the Americas.[36] Once the fixity of racial inheritance adhered to the concept of the slave, something changed about how women either came into or were erased from view. Although the trade in slaves was a trade in women and children and men, as slavery began to be associated with a notion of bodily and heritable difference, the presence of women signaled new meanings linked to Europeans' concepts of the fungible, the irrational, and the quantifiable in ways that exceed the disciplinary boundaries placed around the history of racial slavery. These concepts laid crucial groundwork in the alchemy of gender, race, labor, and value in the early modern Atlantic world—the

---

33 Eltis and Engerman, "Fluctuations in Sex and Age," 309; Eltis, *Rise of African Slavery*, 85–103, esp. 98, table 4.3.

34 See, for example, Bardaglio, "'Shamefull Matches'"; Spear, *Race, Sex, and Social Order*, 17–51.

35 For colonial New York, see L. Harris, *In the Shadow of Slavery*, 14–29; for colonial Mexico, see Bennett, *Africans in Colonial Mexico*, 1–32, esp. 23; for seventeenth-century Guadaloupe, Martinique, and St. Christopher, see Moitt, *Women and Slavery*, 1–18; for the metaquestions raised by the database regarding sex ratio, see Geggus, "Sex Ratio and Ethnicity"; Geggus, "Sex Ratio, Age and Ethnicity."

36 Robinson, *Black Marxism*, 10–18, esp. 16. This evidence for Iberia has been elaborated in Blumenthal, *Enemies and Familiars*, 18; and Phillips, *Slavery in Medieval*, 84–85.

conversion of people into a legitimized form of wealth. For historians of the slave trade, the demographic profile of the population of captives has been a concern insofar as the scope of the trade and its rhythms over time and space speak to its large-scale impact.[37] But demographic analyses have not substantively contributed to a deeper understanding of how gendered patterns of knowledge and experience on the West African coast and during the Middle Passage might have contributed to particular ways of experiencing the transition into slavery. They also have not clarified how those patterns in Europe and among European traders and travelers positioned the transatlantic slave trade as a rational component in the extraction of wealth from the Americas.

Demographic Archives

While estimating the volume of the transatlantic slave trade is essential to comprehending its human toll, doing so comes with some costs that are hard to disentangle from the evidence, precisely because of how such evidence comes to be housed in slavery's archive. The effort to understand the scale of the transatlantic slave trade has launched a wide-ranging historiography that is rooted in the work of W. E. B. Du Bois and continues to drive new scholarship.[38] At the heart of the effort to clarify and refine the demographic impacts of the slave trade is a set of arguments concerning the place of slavery in the development of the modern world. Those include situating Africans as victims or agents in the trade, unpacking the economic impact of the trade on the African continent, considering the

---

37 The large-scale impact of the trade has driven the study of its mechanisms, including discussions of warfare and the role of European weaponry in intensifying military conflicts on or near the African coasts. These discussions have led, for example, to clarity about the importance of prisoners of war in the slave trade and later in large-scale uprisings on the other side of the Atlantic, where the background of male warriors supported efforts to overturn slave societies in South Carolina, the West Indies, and Brazil. For studies on the role of the military experience of African men in rebellions in the Americas, see Landers, "Transforming Bondsmen into Vassals"; Price, *Maroon Societies*; Rucker, *Gold Coast Diasporas*, 162–93; Thornton, "African Dimensions."

38 For foundational studies on the scope of the slave trade and its consequences for the history of Africa and the Americas, see Curtin, *Atlantic Slave Trade*; Du Bois, *Suppression*; Inikori, *Forced Migration*; M. Klein and Inikori, *Atlantic Slave Trade*; and Solow, "Slavery and the Rise."

different roles of slave labor in the economic development of various colonies in the Americas, and assessing the development of race and racism as ideological formations.[39] This scholarship is grounded in a set of questions about how many people were caught up in the trade, and it propagates inquiries about the impact of the trade on African, European, and American economies. It relies on demographic and econometric analytics and is fundamentally important for questions related to cultural transmission, social history, and political economy on both sides of the Atlantic.

The demographics of the slave trade drive the scholarship on the cultural and social history of slavery: investigations of ethnogenesis and resistance, cultivation and culture, and religion and creolization. Demographic data have become a requisite, though incomplete, tool for scholars invested in what might be termed a project of rehumanizing the enslaved. The data are used to make arguments about resiliency in the face of devastating loss and to analyze the systemic and structural politics of abjection at the core of burgeoning Western democratic notions of freedom. We can see how these inquiries are also at the heart of a guiding moral economy in slavery studies that fuels debate about how devastating its impact was on African development or how deep its roots traveled in the development of Euro-American wealth and depravity.

But scholarship regarding the place of slavery has only recently begun to grapple with the possibility that slavery and racial capitalism do not occupy a discrete and bounded place in the history of the West but instead are at its very heart.[40] As a consequence, I argue here that a methodological

39 The bulk of this work has been coterminous with post–World War II transformations in academia and is therefore implicitly or explicitly embedded in contemporary arguments about the role of racism in local and international political, social, economic, and intellectual life. In other words, it sets out to respond to a series of debates about the place of Black people in the history of the Americas and, as such, offers a crucial and productive intervention in scholarship that had for generations proceeded from the assumption that all important historical actors were white. For an early and explicit discussion of the impact of race on the historical profession, see Meier, *Black History and the Historical Profession*. For an intervention that focuses on the role of Black women scholars in shaping the discipline of history, see White, *Telling Histories*.

40 This work might be said to originate in the rich interventions of Gilroy, *Black Atlantic*; Robinson, *Black Marxism*; Spillers, "Mama's Baby, Papa's Maybe"; Trouillot, *Silencing the Past*; and Wynter, "Unsettling the Coloniality of Being." These have been generatively elaborated by Moten, *Universal Machine*; Sharpe, *In the Wake*; and Weheliye, *Habeas Viscus*. These authors are diasporic scholars of culture and history whose interventions in the history of race, slavery, and power have often been siloed. This productive

approach steeped in the ideological currents that produced demographic data is required. Demographic data do particular ideological work in histories of slavery: they convey a troubling moral compass. It is hard to avoid the conclusion that quantification introduces Western rationalism and that the arguments over the demographic impact of the slave trade are rooted in a perverse arithmetic whereby evidence of fewer numbers of captives is couched as scholarly and rational and evidence of greater numbers is linked to a dogmatic Afrocentrism. In the face of a contentious history whose violence continues to animate the present, demography offers a soothing chimera, suggesting that quantifying the totality of the transatlantic slave trade will refute passionate accusations of *maafa*—African devastation caused by the slave trade, underdevelopment, and persistent European and Euro-American extractive violence. Meanwhile, some of the most prescient theories of violence and the state—including Hannah Arendt's totalitarianism, Walter Benjamin's concept of history, Michel Foucault's biopolitics, and Giorgio Agamben's bare life—demonstrate an utter disregard for the four-hundred-year-long iniquity meted out on the bodies of 9 million or 13 million or 15 million African men, women, and children.[41] In these theorists we see enacted the disturbing propensity for scholars of the West to treat slavery and the slave trade as an aberration—a discrete and distinct phenomenon that might be of interest to the scholar of Black life or culture but that has no impact on larger ideologies or structures. The number of bodies conveyed across the Atlantic is, ultimately, incidental to the West. As the sociologist Paul Gilroy wrote, "It is hardly surprising that if it is perceived to be relevant at all, the history of slavery is somehow assigned to blacks. It becomes our special property rather than a part of the ethical and intellectual heritage of the West as a whole."[42] And yet any understanding of the modern West that fails to account for those lives and for the wealth that slave owners accrued as a result of this human traffic sits at the nexus of racism and numeracy— at the juncture where the refusal to see the history of slavery and the slave trade as part and parcel of the history of Europe meets the rationalizing patina of political arithmetic, namely, the way that sixteenth- and

---

and visionary work has not yet been fully taken up by scholars of Atlantic economies and slavery.

41 Arendt, *Origins of Totalitarianism*; Benjamin, "Philosophy of History"; Foucault, *Birth of Biopolitics*; Agamben, *Homo Sacer*.

42 Gilroy, *Black Atlantic*, 49.

seventeenth-century European writers and traders mobilized accounting practices, and the ideologies that accompanied them, to discount massive numbers of people.[43] Demography performs subtle and normalizing work. It hides prejudice under the disinterest of numbers. Its origins in the seventeenth century set in motion an economization of life that merged human potential and racial hierarchies.[44] The ideological work that situates human beings in abstract groups is embedded in the same processes that Karl Marx identified as the ones that turn an idea into a commodity. Michelle Murphy reminds us that "quantitative modeling is more than the mere tabulating of numbers." It produces categories of aggregate forms of life that can be mobilized in the service of economies of extraction, gains, and losses. Further, aggregate numbers—"the population" instead of communities—tend to "erase their own conditions of creation."[45] In other words, we use numbers without awareness of how they come to be. In the case of the demographic data regarding the slave trade, the erased conditions include the systems of logic that situate enslaved people in ledger and account books and those that regard sex differences among captives as not worthy of note. Indeed, one might well argue that the subtle and normalizing work that demography does in the context of academic study may itself be rooted in the historical juncture it emerged from: the period associated with both the birth of the modern world and the rise of the transatlantic slave trade. The very data through which specificity can be achieved are part of the technology that renders Africans and their descendants outside the scope of modernity, but a recognition of this is fundamentally absent from the scholarship on the demographics of the slave trade. As historian Stephanie Smallwood has argued, the slave trader's ledger book transformed individual captives into "the aggregate that formed the 'complete' human cargo."[46] This sleight of hand reverberates in the work of scholars who disconnect the data from the context that produced them.[47] If, as Mary Poovey argues, English efforts to render theories of wealth and society legible have been "pervaded

43 This is, of course, the core intervention of Sylvia Wynter's work. See, for example, Wynter, "Unsettling the Coloniality of Being."
44 Murphy, *Economization of Life*, 24.
45 Murphy, *Economization of Life*, 53.
46 Smallwood, *Saltwater Slavery*, 68.
47 For an example of this gesture as well as the pushback it received from other historians, see Eltis, Morgan, and Richardson, "Agency and Diaspora"; and responses from a wide range of scholars in "*AHR* Exchange," 123–71.

by the metaphor of bookkeeping" since the seventeenth century, then we need to think more carefully about the bookkeepers of the slave trade, who generated a logical system in which African laborers were routinely brutalized in the service of national accumulations of wealth and at the same time omitted from the categories of subject and citizen.[48]

Counting Women

Underpinning our efforts is the recognition that the data were never meant to serve the historian of the African or Afro-diasporic past. While this is the case for most contributions to our archive, it is particularly true with regard to data on slave voyages. The effort to quantify and clarify the scope of the trade continues to drive the Slave Voyages database project, which exemplifies both the promise and the limitations of aggregate data. This data set has been extremely productive for scholarship on the transatlantic slave trade and has led to new understandings of the dimensions of the slave trade, its economic impacts, its regulations and rhythms, and the experience of the Middle Passage. I leave the experiential for last because the nature of these data poses particular challenges to the social historian of the slave trade. The protocols of aggregation and extrapolation at the heart of an economic history data set prove to be particularly vexing for the scholar of gender and enslavement. Broad trends marginalize women's presence in the Middle Passage and thus in the foundational generations of New World slave societies. The effort to disaggregate the sexes reveals the extent to which the records of the Slave Voyages project illustrate both the roots of the traffic in human commodities and the unwillingness to recognize its history and its afterlife.[49]

The problems and potentials of using the extant data to clarify the presence of women on slave ships are clear.[50] The Slave Voyages database

---

48 Poovey, *History of the Modern Fact*, 29.

49 In *Lose Your Mother*, Saidiya Hartman writes, "If slavery persists as an issue in the political life of black America . . . it is because black lives are still imperiled and devalued by a racial calculus and a political arithmetic that were entrenched centuries ago. This is the afterlife of slavery—skewed life chances, limited access to health and education, premature death, incarceration, and impoverishment" (6).

50 The Slave Voyages project's most enduring impact may well be found in the work it has set in motion to engage its logics and omissions. See, most recently, Gregory E. O'Malley's work on the secondary shipments endured by those who survived the Middle Passage and his contribution of those voyages to the Slave Voyages data set

documents 4,358 slave-trading voyages (out of the total 36,110) that departed from Africa in the first period of the slave trade, from 1514 to 1700.[51] Understanding both the demographic profiles of the captives on those ships and the processes by which ship captains assigned such profiles is crucial to understanding how racial slavery evolved in the sixteenth and seventeenth centuries. Yet fewer than 8 percent of those records, or 336, contain information about the percentage of men and women on board the ships (figures 1.1 and 1.2).[52] In these early voyages, adult men were not in the majority, and thus, for captains recording their cargo, *slave* was not actually synonymous with *male*. Figures throughout eighteenth-century North America derive from a minuscule sample of voyages. For example, for the Carolinas, only 14 of 538 voyages contain data on sex ratios, or 3 percent of the available voyages. Out of 1,551 voyages destined for mainland Latin America, we have data on the sex ratio for only 7. Only on voyages to the Caribbean does the percentage of captains who recorded the sex ratio rise into the double digits—of 1,600 voyages to the Caribbean, 300 contain such data. What we can know from using these data is that of the ships whose captains recorded the sex ratio, more than 32 percent carried more adult women than men and 53 percent carried more women and girls than men and boys. The difference in these figures leads immediately to the question of children. On the ship *Mary and Margaret Galley*, for example, which landed in Jamaica in 1699 from Whydah, 45 percent of the captives were male, while 33 percent were men.[53] As was often the case with ships whose captains recorded the sex ratio, the *Mary and Margaret* also contained children. Indeed, of the 336 voyages for which the sex ratio is reported, 310 reported the presence of children.

One can read these data in a number of ways. They seem to indicate that in the sixteenth and seventeenth centuries, most ships carried both women and children, but given the small proportion of voyages that include data on the sex ratio, that conclusion feels tenuous until bolstered

---

in https://www.slavevoyages.org/american/database. See O'Malley, *Final Passages*. Other scholars of the South Atlantic slave trade, including Wheat (*Atlantic Africa*) and the scholars collected in Richardson and Ribeiro da Silva (*Networks and Trans-cultural Exchange*), are also doing crucial work in this field. See also Lovejoy, "Upper Guinea Coast."

51 Figures compiled in November 2019.

52 Figure 1.2, then, is derived from a mere 10 percent of all known voyages.

53 Voyage 9718, *Mary and Margaret Galley* (1699), http://slavevoyages.org/voyages /database.

with other evidence.[54] We need to consider the implications, for both slave traders and the enslaved, that although the slave trade would rest on the claim that Africans produced no kin, some of the earliest captives were tasked with protecting children—children whose very presence proved Africans' kinlessness a lie. This is not merely a historiographical or method-ological issue; it is epistemic. It suggests a crucial originary moment when the erasure of gendered categories of meaning became constitutive of the most profoundly inscribed racial subordination. The proportions of men, women, and children who were captured, transported, and forced to labor in the Americas were of crucial significance to the captives, to the lives they constructed and those they mourned, to the possible futures embodied in one another's differences and similarities. But to the captain, the imper-ative was only the total number of bodies on board that he successfully delivered to port cities along the Atlantic littoral, minus those lost to the Atlantic graveyard.

The gaps in the data can be filled in from other sources. But the gaps also speak to the incompleteness of statistical reckoning, something that is usu-ally not associated with economic history, numeracy, or statistics. Some patterns suggest that English slave captains provided the most data related to the age or sex of the captives they transported and sold into slavery.[55] While only 30 percent of all slaving ships before 1700 sailed under an En-glish flag, 85 percent of the voyages that specify the number of women on board were English. The captains of 288 voyages that originated in England in this period provided data related to the sex ratio of the captives (out of a total of 1,128). The degree to which the practice of recording the gender

54 There are, of course, related questions to be asked. Eight of the ships for which the sex ratio is known reported some type of revolt or attempted revolt: on four of these, men accounted for less than 50 percent, and on the other four, men accounted for more than 50 percent. The accounting of mortality is slightly more complete. Of the ships for which the sex ratio is recorded, 131, or slightly more than a third, provide mortality rates (not disaggregated by sex) for the voyage. The aggregate figures are useful, but they generate as many questions as answers for those who want to understand both women's experi-ences during the Middle Passage and women's impact on the outcome of the voyages.

55 Before 1700 it appears that England retains the most data related to characteristics; 288 voyages out of 1,123 total voyages for the period of 1514–1700 that include data related to the percentage of women, still only a small percentage. For 1701–1800: total voyages are 9,830, with 809 voyages recording the percentage of women. I am grateful to Marcia Tucker, librarian at the Institute for Advanced Study, for this insight and for her help with the data set.

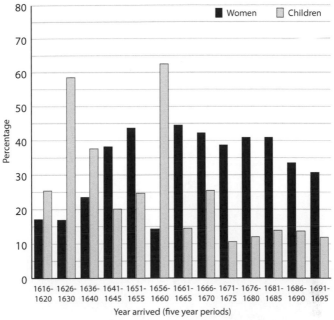

FIGURE 1.1 Women and children as a percentage of captives, 1585–1695, derived from 10 percent of extant voyages. http://slavevoyages.org/voyage/data.

of those on board accords with national origin of the voyages raises some interesting questions about the correlation between certain notational and national assumptions of accountability.

But mostly these data tell us that for the vast majority of voyages, the priorities of ship captains did not include recording sex ratios. This suggests a particular way that the trade in human beings was enmeshed in the fields of race and gender. As I discuss more fully in chapter 4, the captains' silence about the numbers of women on their ships stands in sharp contrast to the persistent ways that captains and their crew used those women during the journey as well as the degree to which the women were presumed to be connected to birth and children even as their exposure in the Atlantic markets that awaited them destroyed the affective nature of those connections. Women and girls were consistently subjected to rape. Sometimes they were pregnant when they boarded or became pregnant during their capture and transport. A captain would not be unaware of their presence.

Instead, the silence regarding the sex ratio of captives should lead us to ask what productive work such omission did for ship captains involved

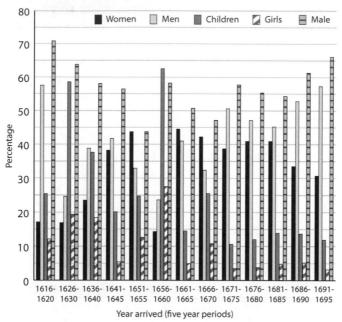

FIGURE 1.2 Sex and age ratios among captives, 1585–1695, derived from 10 percent of extant voyages. http://slavevoyages.org/voyage/data.

in a profoundly violent process of rendering human beings into cargo.[56] To recognize women in the transatlantic slave trade ran the risk of situating them in relationship to men and children, to kin from whom they had just been violently sundered. It ran the risk of ascribing the same human capacity for familial connection to captives that the captain and crew members ascribed to themselves. It ran the risk of inserting grief into the business of capture, transport, and sale—an insertion that would be wildly disruptive. As social theorist Judith Butler writes, lives framed as grievable are lives recognized as those that count. To be ungrievable is to be "already lost or forfeited." In the case of the victims of the trade, those lives are outside community, lost to the marketplace.[57] By bringing this type of silence into proximity with the qualitative discussions of women on transatlantic slave ships, we can reckon with what it meant for female African captives to be so unrecognizable. Their presence as commodities

56 Smallwood, *Saltwater Slavery*, 65–100.
57 Butler, *Frames of War*, 30–31.

cannot be unlinked from their vulnerability to rape, their centrality to uprisings, their role as mothers, and the space their pregnant bodies demanded.[58]

The lacuna between what the records of the slave trade say and what they refuse to say echoes the simultaneity involved in knowing and not knowing that African captives were embedded in family and community. Slave owners routinely described African peoples in terms that recognized them as members of families and communities while in the next breath denying them any human connections. The records of slave traders and plantation managers indicate that bookkeeping was often the technology they used to do so.[59] Plantation records are often a clearer window onto the presence of women, as inventories and bills of sale routinely differentiate men from women, adults from children, and boys from girls—although they do so without validating kinship ties. For slave traders, refusing to record the sex ratios on board their ships was perhaps part of their ideological strategy for rationalizing the trade. I am not alone in arguing that the process of distancing themselves from their part in transforming members of families into cargos on board ships demanded willful blindness, but recognizing the particular erasure of women's presence in that process requires more attention. By failing to record the sex and age of captives, merchants construed the social spaces marked by sex and age (family, household, kin networks) as outside the space of the market. In turn, this becomes part of the racialized logic of modernity—as the notion of public and private life emerged as both crucial to the concept of citizenship and fully embedded in an ideological structure that indelibly marked those categories as white. Thus, when gender, parenthood, or other familial relations make their way into the records, they need to be understood as a particular type of irruption.

In some instances, that irruption may have been shaped by surprise about the number of women aboard. In 1642 the Dutch ship *Prinses* made the trip from Luanda to Pernambuco in about a month loaded with 152 captives,

---

58 On women's role in shipboard revolts, see Richardson, "Shipboard Revolts," 76.
59 While Poovey does not include a discussion of slavery or the slave trade in her exploration of the emergence of factual knowledge in early modern European thought, she does situate double-entry bookkeeping as a crucial development in naturalizing facticity during this moment. Poovey, *History of the Modern Fact*, 29–91.

98 percent of whom were women.[60] Evidence of this ship full of women may survive in the archives owing to its rarity because even as early as the seventeenth century, Angola was known as a port of embarkation primarily for male prisoners of war.[61] The dread that gripped these captives in the face of all that was unknown about their destination may have been augmented by their collective vulnerability to the sexual depravity of the crew and by the fact that in the region they came from, women were normally the ones the white men's slave ships left behind. It is difficult to comprehend how saturated that ship must have been with rape and sexualized violence. The women must have concluded that they were to be delivered as sexual objects to be consumed at their ultimate destination, wherever that was, and perhaps they were correct. The captain's impulse to record the presence of those women may well have been shaped by a similar moment of recognition that he tacitly acknowledged with the census of his captives. However, there is an analytic danger that may well attend situating records of sex ratios as evidence of anomaly. Ship captains conducted sex and age censuses on ships where the percentage of men ran from 1 percent to 100 percent. In other words, demographic reports were not triggered by unusually high or low numbers of female captives. Among the vessels for which such data are available, there is no discernible pattern in the recording of sex ratios. We have no way to ascertain why we know about the women aboard the *Prinses*, but situating the accounting practices in the fields of meaning associated with culture and family may help us get closer to an answer.

Rather than bemoan the accounting protocols that leave so many questions unanswered, we might consider how those practices bolstered the ideological formations that in the broadest terms made the slave trade possible. What work did it do for captains and merchants, who were fully versed in the mercantilist practices of the day, to refuse to record the most basic information concerning their human cargo? Writing about the 1783 *Zong* massacre, in which a slave ship captain threw 133 living men and women overboard in order to make an insurance claim on their lives, the literary theorist Ian Baucom writes:

> What haunts the accounting procedures and the econometric logic . . .
> is not only the specter of a modern principle of bookkeeping and a

60 Voyage 11330, *Prinses* (1642), http://slavevoyages.org/voyages/database.
61 Miller, *Way of Death*, 160–67.

modern system of finance capital capable of converting anything it touches into a monetary equivalent, but the specter of something else such financial protocols made possible . . . the specter of slavery, the slave auction block, the slave trader's ledger book; the specter, quite precisely, of another wounded, suffering human body incessantly attended by an equal sign and a monetary equivalent.[62]

In the seventeenth century, as the accounting protocols that concern Baucom were coming into being, a similar haunting was underway. Clearly, data regarding sex were inconsequential to the monetary returns on a voyage's investments: had it been financially significant to have more men than women, those data would have been more scrupulously recorded. Indeed, in the next hundred-year period, between 1700 and 1800, only 2,396 of 21,001 ships provided information on the number of women on board, suggesting that such information remained of negligible importance to those responsible for monitoring the financial losses and gains of human cargos. Of the captains who piloted the 12,065 ships bound for the Caribbean during that hundred years, 2,108 disaggregated their cargo based on sex.[63] This does not mean that sex ratios were unimportant to slave owners or the sellers of human property once the ships reached the colonies. We have obtained crucial data on sex and age ratios among the enslaved from plantation inventories and the account books that recorded slave sales. Still, I would like to linger here on the records of ship captains and slave-trading companies.[64]

At a very prosaic level, the absences in the shipping records are simply a call for good historical research. Evidence that colonial Barbados and New York were home to female majorities, for example, comes from

62 Baucom, *Specters of the Atlantic*, 7.
63 The figure for sex disaggregation was arrived at by searching the database for voyages that include at least 1 percent males. This captures records that note either women or girls among the captives.
64 For the eighteenth century, the summary statistics indicate that 70 percent of all the captives who survived the Middle Passage to disembark in North America were male, but that figure is based on an aggregate of only fifty voyages. Records indicate that males accounted for 68.4 percent of all captives unloaded in the Carolinas and 72.3 percent of those in the Mississippi Delta. Based on such evidence, it might be tempting to discount the influence of African women in these colonies. The figures for Maryland seem to indicate something a bit different: for the same period only 58.9 percent of captives were male, but that number derives from only two out of the hundred voyages included in the database.

careful examination of tax, probate, and census records. Yet of the 449 voyages under the English flag that ended in Barbados before 1700, only 128 recorded the proportion of women on board, and more than 80 percent of those had male majorities.[65] The records are much thinner for New York; only seventy-six vessels arrived there under any flag before 1800. Only one, a Dutch ship called *Gideon* that reached its destination in 1664, recorded the sex ratio; 47 percent of its captives were female.[66] The story these bookkeepers of human traffic told is not just crucial to understanding the trade itself; it is also at the heart of how such compounded violence directed at generations of Africans and their descendants became so thoroughly absorbed into the record of human progress as to be rendered invisible by crucial theorists of modernity and violence, from Hegel to Marx to Foucault to Agamben.

The absence of this basic index of human identity compels a range of questions both methodological and ideological. The journey of the Middle Passage is unearthed only through a methodological approach that enables us to see its violences as both inscribed in and willfully set outside the frame of the early modern nation-state. Together, the slave trade and the colonial occupation of the Americas set in motion the political, economic, and social forces that built the modern nation-state. But simply reinscribing that violence through a new narrative cannot be the goal. As Smallwood writes, "It takes no great insight to point to the role of violence in the Atlantic slave trade. But to understand what happened to Africans in this system of human trafficking requires us to ask precisely what kind of violence it required to achieve its end, the transformation of African captives into Atlantic commodities."[67]

Erasing Women

What kind of violence was involved in erasing women from the records of more than 95 percent of all slave-trading voyages to North America or 85 percent of all slave-trading voyages to the Caribbean? What kind of violence was involved in doing so while casually leaving evidence that their presence was in fact crucial to the captains' ability to offset the discomfort of the voyage for himself and his crew by brutally using those same

65 That is, 103 voyages had at most 50 percent women.
66 Voyage 11414, *Gideon* (1664), http://slavevoyages.org./voyage/database.
67 Smallwood, *Saltwater Slavery*, 36.

women as a form of sexual release and a reward to white men for enduring the transatlantic passage? What kind of violence led them to be grossly examined for reproductive potential at points of sale even as their capacity to parent was denigrated and denied? The transformation of these women into Atlantic commodities was systematic, not singular: it occurred tens of thousands of times on ships and millions of times at points of sale up and down the Atlantic littoral. It required enormous collective effort on the part of slaveholding individuals and polities to maintain a fictive reality in which torture became commerce, and family—the most fundamental of human social forms—disintegrated in the face of financial calculations. And yet in part because of an inability to understand Africa as a place of sovereignty, political economy, and complex social and cultural forms, we have failed to grapple with the histories that preceded and constituted the "catastrophic rupture" of the Middle Passage, which set the modern world in motion. Instead, we focus on the suturing that followed that rupture.[68] Moreover, the nature of the archival traces of the Middle Passage produces a lasting bifurcation in which mathematically fixed data are in the hands of economists, while malleable claims rooted in culture are in the hands of humanists and artists. Culture becomes the category open to the poetics of African American history, while economy remains the province of neutrality and rigor.

The call to fully engage with the role of slavery and enslavement in the Atlantic world has been at the forefront of scholarship on the Black Atlantic for decades. Still, the categories scholars have taken up either position the involvement of Africans in the slave trade as a matter of political economy or register its impact on the African diaspora in the realms of language, religion, and family.[69] Such divisions are long-standing and exceed the confines of the archive, but our relationship to archival evidence undergirds such hierarchies of meaning and saturates the conclusions we are able to draw. The records of the slave trader are a crucial piece of archival evidence, but they impose their own suprarational strictures on conceptual possibilities. What remains unclear is the role that gender played in the process of commodifying African people. As slave traders caught women and children in the grasp of the trade, how did these captives perceive their enslavability? How did women exposed to the trade come to understand

---

68 Gilroy, *Black Atlantic*, 197. On Gilroy's notion of time and rupture in the Black Atlantic, see Piot, "Atlantic Aporias."

69 For this observation see Lindsay, "Extraversion, Creolisation, and Dependency," 136.

both their commodification and the degree to which their sexual and gendered identities were embedded in that process? Ultimately, we must refuse the analytic divide imposed by the construction of rational economies in the service of willful blindness. Thus, as Saidiya Hartman argues, the archive must be deranged—unsettled, reconfigured, and entered with a clear understanding of the political intentions that bolstered its construction.[70] The arrangement of archival evidence testifies to the violence the archive claims to depict and thus poses challenges to the historian, who can no longer imagine that there is nothing to be said. Faced with the accounting practices that grew from the trade in slaves, the geographer Katherine McKittrick writes that "this is where we begin, this is where historic blackness comes from: the list, the breathless numbers, the absolutely economic, the mathematics of the unliving."[71]

70 Hartman, "Venus in Two Acts," 13.
71 McKittrick, "Mathematics Black Life," 17.

TWO. "Unfit Subjects of Trade":
Demographic Logics and Colonial Encounters

That who in numbring has no skill, is numbred for a beast.
THOMAS HYLLE, *Arte of Vulgar Arithmaticke,* 1600

Numbers have mattered. . . . We would do well to remember it.
FERNAND BRAUDEL, *The Structures of Everyday Life,* 1979

Normative processes of violence are embedded in numerical evidence, in the development of demography and other quantitative approaches to population, and in the ways men and women were reduced to monetary or commercial value. Scholars of economic history, of political economy, and of the postcolonial have long been attuned to the disciplinary power of quantification.[1] But for the early modern period, a clear boundary has been drawn between the political implications of mathematics and the transatlantic slave trade. Today the two areas are largely framed as distinct and discrete domains, even though they actually emerged as closely interwoven arenas of thought. Linking the processes by which writers and political theorists mobilized categories of socioreligious difference in the first decades of the seventeenth century and firmly attached them to native and African peoples through new ideas about trade, value, and relationality will

1 See, for example, Cohn, *Colonialism,* 8, 16–20, 80–88.

magnify the cruelty of racialist logics. In search of stable and legible markers of value, European slave traders and colonial settlers applied such racialist logics to African men, women, and children, mobilizing ideas of race and racial hierarchy to buttress the profoundly unstable claim that Africans were, like silver or gold, symbols of and for exchange.

Yet the connections between the history of slavery and the history of European capitalism have been largely deferred. In *The Wheels of Commerce*, when Fernand Braudel examined the labor market in the early history of capitalism, he prefaced this with a note that he would leave slavery "aside."[2] With this decision, Braudel exemplified much of the foundational work on the history of European capitalisms. The institution of slavery has long been situated as something that happened offstage in the development of the capitalist world economy. Even when slavery is acknowledged to be a key part of capitalist development, its role is defined by its location in peripheral zones.[3] Eric Williams's foundational *Capitalism and Slavery*, which argued forcefully for considering the relationship between the two, has until recently been widely dismissed as a polemic—further marginalizing the study of slavery in the emergence of capitalism.

At the same time, historians have long agreed that the economic transformations of the late sixteenth and early seventeenth centuries were accompanied by new symbolic meanings that went far beyond the realm of the economy. As the historian Hilary Beckles has noted, "Capitalist political economy found expression during the 16th and 17th centuries in a proliferation of mercantilist tracts . . . preaching the values of large scale production, surplus generation and the accumulation of wealth through foreign trade."[4] In the

2 Braudel, *Wheels of Commerce*, 51. Karl Marx himself, while firmly situating slavery in the preliminary stage of capitalism, was well aware of the simultaneity of nineteenth-century capitalism and racial slavery. Writing to Abraham Lincoln on the ending of the Civil War, Marx certainly drew on his long engagement with the contest over slavery in North America when he congratulated Lincoln on the nation's entry into modernity. More than simply a pithy asterisk to the historiography that shapes this work, the inability to connect the conflict in North America with the economic theory regarding slavery in world history is possibly emblematic of the ideological work that race came to perform in the nineteenth century and beyond—work that is rooted in the terms of its emergence in the sixteenth century. I am grateful to Andrew Young and the Folger Shakespeare Library seminar Finance, Race, and Gender in the Early Modern World for helping me to formulate this intervention. See also Blackburn, "Lincoln and Marx."

3 Wallerstein, *Modern World System I*, 86–90.

4 Beckles, "Capitalism, Slavery and Caribbean Modernity," 778.

process, the world of commerce became increasingly cordoned off from the aspects of life ascribed to culture; merchants and their work were set outside of the proper space of sociability and gentility. Commerce transformed the way Englishmen thought about space, effectively separating the economic from the social and producing new ways of navigating societal spheres.[5] But the role of the simultaneous emergence of the slave trade as both the authorizer of colonial extraction and the financial instrument through which significant aspects of foreign trade were negotiated still remains peripheral to histories of early modern European culture and trade.

This chapter asks whether the economy that emerged as a mode of thought in seventeenth-century England might be more enmeshed in ideas of racial slavery than economic historians' peripheral treatment of slavery might suggest. Slavery and the processes that came to define it—commodification, the regulation of people, the emergence of new forms of being and kinlessness—were intrinsic to emerging Atlantic economies.[6] Scholars such as Kim Hall and Michael Guasco have made it abundantly clear that sixteenth- and seventeenth-century English men and women were familiar with both the idea and the material possibilities of slavery and that that familiarity was made manifest in their material culture, their religious ideology, and their concepts of politics, economics, and punishment.[7] Here I build on this important work, examining the extent to which seventeenth-century notions of markets, values, numeracy, and race intertwined in early modern English thought and laid the groundwork for the moral and economic confidence that came to be attached to the practice of purchasing and appropriating the labor of slaves. Confidence in the use of

---

5 Appleby, *Economic Thought and Ideology*, 26.
6 Slavery introduced a range of new ideas about freedom, race, and autonomy to the Atlantic world. It also was deeply enmeshed in ideas about consumption. In their foundational work on consumption, Mary Douglas and Baron Isherwood argue that "the very idea of consumption . . . has to be set back into the social process." In many conversations about economy and race, the idea of consumption—what can be consumed and how one obtains the resources required to deliver goods to be consumed—was implicitly shaped by the conceptual frameworks that emerged in the seventeenth century that linked color, enslavability, and the capacity to be a consumer. These connections continue to echo in the twenty-first century, both in the connection between race and dispossession and in that between consumer behavior and the prerogatives of citizenship. Douglas and Isherwood, *World of Goods*, 4; and Streeck, "Citizens as Customers."
7 K. Hall, *Things of Darkness*; and Guasco, "Settling with Slavery."

slave labor was also the preamble to the bleak and horrifying claim to certitude and facticity that was at the heart of nineteenth-century racial science.

The logics of mercantilism were organized around notions of exchange rooted in fungibility. The products entering the mercantilist market in this era were more often than not extracted through another node of equivalency: human fungibility, or the idea that a human being had a monetary value and could thus be exchanged for money or goods. This commodity market in human beings functioned with much the same rationality and systemic structure as other markets but required some ideological leaps and claims to logic that bridged the disturbing messiness of prejudiced racialist thought and the crisp clarity that underpinned economies of exchange.

Racing Economies

Seventeenth-century English writers who wrote about trade, wealth, and the state built a comprehensive literature on early modern economic thinking. Recognizing the connection between that literature and England's embrace of the transatlantic slave trade requires an engagement with the intersections between economic and racial thinking. The abstractive processes that ensnared so many Africans and their descendants were rooted in markets. Moral clarity about the trade in slaves came to many English investors through obfuscating rhetoric about finance, valuation, and risk that linked New World gold to foreign trade while sidestepping the very real moral challenges of an economy based on African slave labor.

But even here there were important wrinkles. As new investment mechanisms opened in the form of joint-stock companies (an Elizabethan innovation) and merchants and gentlemen forged new alliances, much ink was devoted to comprehending the changing terrain of wealth and the processes that undergirded its accumulation. Political thinkers debated the implicit value of gold and silver coins and considered the idea that relocating English or Irish subjects could solve both social and economic problems for the kingdom. These numerically situated discussions were always closely related to questions about the African and American continents and to the efforts of European travelers, merchants, and statesmen to locate African and American peoples along a continuum from sovereign to commodified savage.[8] That proximity has not, however, driven economic

---

8 These efforts are deeply familiar to scholars of the Black Atlantic, but they have primarily been located in the realm of religious, corporeal, and aesthetic philosophies rather

histories of early modern Europe. Nor have contemporary writers taken up this convergence.

If we presume that Europeans simply felt that Africans *should* be enslaved and attribute that feeling to animus, fear, or the illogic of religious prejudice, we fail to understand how and where racial slavery was justified and rationalized. The idea of race emerged out of older notions of "the other" rooted in religion, language, wealth, and sovereignty historically grounded in medieval Europe. Rationalizing the practices of selling and distributing human beings demanded that the concept of kinship be subordinated to the mathematical logics of the marketplace. However, recognizing those deep roots does not suggest a natural precondition for race thinking but rather historicizes it. As a system of thought, race emerged at a specific point in time to do particular work.[9] The turn to hereditary racial slavery happened in tandem with the emergent economics that marked European exploration and colonial expansion in the fifteenth and sixteenth centuries.[10]

Although rooted in early notions of antagonistic difference, what becomes race emerged in the context of new ideas about finance, commerce, economy, and empire. For some who watched, the evolution was at times quite jarring. Despite being well versed in the business of slavery, as any Iberian associated with the royal court would have been in the fifteenth century, Portuguese chronicler Gomes Eannes de Zurara lingered rather intently on the inherent violence done to families by merchants' value systems when he wrote of the arrival in Portugal of the first slave ship from Africa in 1444. He wrote of the grief of the 250 African captives who were unloaded on the docks of Lagos:

> Though we could not understand the words of their language, the sound of it right well accorded with the measure of their sadness. But to increase their sufferings still more, there now arrived those who had charge of the division of the captives, and who began to separate one

---

than in that of mercantile economies, population theories, and the bimetallic currency crisis. It is a mistake to leave the question of racial thinking to an ideological realm understood as distinct from the economic: as I argue in the following, the two were mutually constitutive in a number of suggestive ways.

9 For key interventions in the history of race as ideology, see Vaughan, "Origins Debate"; Jordan, "Modern Tensions"; Patterson, *Slavery and Social Death*; K. Brown, *Good Wives, Nasty Wenches*; and Goetz, *Baptism of Early Virginia*.

10 See Robinson, *Black Marxism*, 10–18.

from another, in order to make an equal partition. . . . And then was it needful to part fathers from sons, husbands from wives, brothers from brothers. . . . The mothers clasped their other children in their arms, and threw themselves flat on the ground with them, receiving blows with little pity for their own flesh, if only they might not be torn from them.[11]

Zurara's language—of division, equal partitions, fathers, mothers, sons, and wives—conveys hereditary enslavement's essential conflict between market and kin.

This passage is so important for thinking about the conflict between kinship and the market that I will return to it throughout the chapters that follow. Here I want to emphasize what his language marks. In the starkest possible terms, we see the challenge human cargo posed for Europeans: how to bring the logics of commerce to bear on the affective space of kinship. This is, of course, a recurring aspect of slavery in the Atlantic world, one that we see reverberating in plantations, urban work sites, and households wherever the demands of labor clashed with the ties of kinship. For Zurara, the pathos of enslavement was best evoked by the contrast between the rationality of dividing up merchandise for distribution and a mother's willingness to sacrifice herself in an effort to protect her child. The ties of family that connected these men, women, and children were explicit and specific. They had been captured in groups by an early Portuguese slave raider and thus shared connections obvious even to those observing from a cultural and linguistic distance. The efforts of the enslaved to interrupt their commodification by refusing to remain categorized in "equal partition" instead of as fathers and sons or wives and husbands were clear to Zurara. They also suggest a foundational refusal or counternarrative of commodification among the enslaved.

Here is a conceptual space where we might imagine the roots of dissent, the nascent articulation of what would become a diasporic theory of resistance, a recognition on the part of the enslaved that the marketing of their bodies was nothing less than a systematic denial of their kinship ties that had to be refused. The captives' refusal to comply with the logics of the marketplace emerged as a fundamental problem; in the context of an enslavement that came to rest on a hereditary mark, the market depended on kinship even as it refused it. The logic that produced women and men as

11 Zurara, *Discovery and Conquest of Guinea*, 81–82.

commodities to be traded, based on a spurious claim to hereditary enslavability, rendered kin ties as obstacles to fungibility. Yet the enslaved mother was simultaneously made impossible (as the child was wrenched from her grasp) and crucial (as her womb marked the child as a product legitimately offered on the Atlantic market). The recurring rupture of the parental bond by the commercial link would define the circuit of human production in the marketplace of hereditary racial slavery.

As we seek to understand how race emerged in and shaped the space of commerce, it is useful to consider how the language of commerce cohered within the worldview from which racial slavery emerged. As Europeans encountered Africans and Native Americans, they developed new ways of thinking to situate themselves in relation to peoples whom they needed to characterize as different. But they did so slowly over time. As historian Herman Bennett has argued, when Iberians encountered West Africa in the fifteenth century, they did not mobilize the notion of difference as the core of their thinking about Africans. Initially, Iberians wrote of Africans in terms that recognized their status as *extra ecclesium*—those who did not accept the Christian faith but who remained sovereign and had obligations and rights that were discernible to European Catholics.[12] But as the century unfolded, the ascendency of commerce and new fields of value created the need for Iberians (and later other Europeans) to frame Africans through increasingly rigid notions of difference that codified race and capital as mutually produced sites of meaning in the Atlantic world, mobilizing savagery and skin color to do so.

Iberian Foundations

While my concern here is primarily with English ideas about Africa, the broader history of European concepts of race in the Atlantic world begins with Iberians, whose encounters with and writings about Africa would frame England's entry into the Atlantic world.[13] This literature forms the corpus that historians and literary scholars have used to frame the encounter between Europe

12 Bennett, *African Kings and Black Slaves*, 69–74.
13 It is beyond the scope of this project to engage with all the writings and negotiations crisscrossing Europe in regard to Africa and the Americas in this period. I see the Spanish writings as pivotal for England—both because of their circulation in England and because of England's particular relationship with Spain in the sixteenth and early seventeenth centuries—and hope to illustrate this in the following.

and sub-Saharan Africa. English reading of Spanish literature and travel or navigation accounts (both in Spanish and in translation) can be traced back to Catherine of Aragon, who sparked an interest in reading Spanish literature both at the English court and at universities.[14] Beginning in the Elizabethan era, English readers could obtain translated travel accounts from Iberia and elsewhere. Their access to descriptions of faraway lands produced an increasingly robust sense of England's boundaries in relationship to Europe, Asia, and Africa in the sixteenth century.[15] Elizabeth Spiller has argued that with the introduction of printing, the English acquired a sense of their own racial identity through the circulation of early modern English works of ethnography, geography, and history.[16] Thus, even in a study that largely concerns the beliefs and behaviors of Englishmen in the Atlantic, we must begin with Christopher Columbus's voyages to the Indies and with what they both consolidated and inaugurated.

In the journal entry on his first encounter with Native Americans, Columbus described offering the inhabitants glass beads and other items "of little value." He alleged that the people were so taken by them that they "ended up being ours to an amazing extent," and that he offered the beads knowing "they were a people who could be more easily freed and converted to our holy faith by love than by force."[17] The romance of capturing hearts and minds through trinkets—a low-cost exchange for Europeans—is articulated with a breathlessness that exudes Columbus's, and indeed Spain's, hopes for gold and converts in equal measure. This is precisely the sort of exchange that Europeans longed for, and it fueled Columbus's certainty that he and his men had encountered barbarians. Columbus's romance would reverberate into the coming century as both Spanish and English travelers described their ability to overcome native resistance by offering trinkets and novelties.

The confidence with which they approached such moments of exchange was often rooted in a persistent assumption that a lack of alphabetic writing signaled savagery. In 1558 Pedro de Gante wrote to Phillip II of Spain that the natives of Mexico were fundamentally "people without writing, without

---

14 Ungerer, "Printing of Spanish Books," 178.
15 K. Hall, *Things of Darkness*, 25–61; and Hadfield, "Benefits of a Warm Study."
16 Spiller, *Reading and the History*, 16–18.
17 Quoted in Gomez-Mariana, "Narration and Argumentation," 106. This passage has also been translated as "made them so much our friends that it was a marvel to see." Columbus, *Journal of Christopher Columbus*, 37.

letters, without written characters, and without any kind of enlightenment."
Literary scholars have long argued that the colonial encounter can best be
understood as founded on the "tyranny of the alphabet": Europeans defined as barbarians those who did not use writing to communicate.[18] But as
we see here, the inability to comprehend allegedly transparent structures of
value—trinkets are worth less than land—is a similarly key node on which
Europeans would hang their confidence in their newly articulated colonial
relationships.

The work of Richard Hakluyt in the 1580s to vitalize English interest in
colonization and trade put translated Spanish narratives directly into English hands and sparked the interest of elite and educated English men and
women in reading Spanish navigation accounts. His *Principall Navigations,
Voiages and Discoveries of the English Nation* would become a crucial volume for the consolidation of the idea of English national identity and the
notion that both Africa and America were available to English merchants
and settlers.[19] For the English, the publication in 1589 of Hakluyt's *Principall Navigations* and George Puttenham's *Arte of English Poesie* points to
the simultaneity of geography and literacy in the emergence of a racially
demarcated sense of national identity. To be a barbarian was to be both
African and illiterate.[20]

Literacy isn't reducible to reading alphabetic symbols. Numeracy too
is a core part of what Walter Mignolo has identified as "the spectrum of
communicative interactions across semiotic and cultural boundaries" that
manifest colonizing processes.[21] Much scholarly effort has been devoted
to refuting the idea that early Europeans saw indigenous peoples through
a racialized lens from the very start.[22] However, attending to the ideological links between commerce and the racialized hierarchies that developed

18 Mignolo, "Literacy and Colonization," 66. For a foundational argument that conveys
    the importance of the concept of savagery for Elizabethan English readers, see Mon-
    trose, "Work of Gender," 4–5.
19 On the influence of Hakluyt's publications on the idea of Africa and Africans, see Bar-
    tels, "Imperialist Beginnings"; on Hakluyt as an advocate of colonialism, see Mancall,
    Hakluyt's Promise, esp. 93–94.
20 This argument is made by I. Smith, "Barbarian Errors," 170.
21 Mignolo, "Literacy and Colonization," 72.
22 For early work on the role of gender and wonder rather than race in the English
    encounter with the New World, see Greenblatt, *Marvelous Possessions*; and Montrose,
    "Work of Gender." For a foundational text on the history of race in early America, see
    Vaughan, "Origins Debate."

later is a crucial step in correcting the ways we have misunderstood the ideological processes Europeans developed to accommodate and justify new practices related to both trade and race. Claims about value, trade, and population constituted the evidence supporting accusations of barbarism toward newly encountered peoples. These ideas, explored by the travelers published in Hakluyt's volume and elsewhere, often preceded claims about the absence of character and other markers of civility as Europeans defined it. These new definitions justified the commodification and enslavement of human beings. New cultural ideas about value, accounts, and trade were crucial to this process.

As monarchs moved to signal that Spain's encroachment on native wealth was legitimate, they pointed to the underutilized wealth of New World inhabitants as proof of their savagery. As literary scholar Elvira Vilches has illustrated, the language of gold and civility occupied two distinct geographies for Spanish monarchs and traders in the fifteenth century. They saw gold in the East as discursively connected to the power of the great states of Khan and Cathay. But Columbus's failure to encounter such states in Hispaniola led to a shift in which gold and silver in the Atlantic would be ideologically located on lands inhabited by those he described as savages and monsters. Spaniards interpreted the people Columbus encountered as unable to comprehend the value of gold and other riches. For Europeans, this put them in the category of savages. From that starting point, it was just a small step to claiming that the wealth they encountered was "found" and "unclaimed" and that they themselves were the legitimate possessors of it.[23]

Decades later, the English too situated native inhabitants as illegitimate occupants of territories, which thus legitimately devolved to European control. For example, they claimed that Native American mortality rates proved that they were not constitutionally made for the Americas; their bodies betrayed their inferiority and the likelihood that God intended the Americas for Englishmen.[24] This notion of natural inferiority was rooted in Europeans' desire to legitimate their access to and claims on gold. This thought process produced a connection between monetary value and rational human subjects. To recognize money and assign it a value alleged to be universal (gold rather than shells) is to be civilized and rational. It constitutes a concept of value as property that always entails degrees of dispossession. In other

23 Vilches, *New World Gold,* 57.
24 Chaplin, *Subject Matter,* 116–98.

words, the form of subjectivity depends on those who are nonsubjects. The claim to natural rights is rooted in the legitimized seizing of wealth from those who have no such rights.[25]

The Columbus voyages took place on the heels of Portuguese contact with West Africa and Henry the Navigator's attempts to reach the fabled gold markets of Timbuktu in the early fifteenth century. Prince Henry's quest for wealth was realized in 1441, when Antam Gonçalves delivered slaves and gold to Portugal. With the capture of first a man and then a woman from Cabo Blanco, Gonçalves materialized his dream that he and his crew would "meet with the good luck to bring the first captives before the face of our Prince." This was a crucial event in many respects as it led to return journeys, one of which involved the exchange of an elite captive for "ten blacks, male and female . . . [and] a little gold dust and a shield of ox-hide and a number of ostrich eggs."[26] Zurara's account describes the numerous voyages Gonçalves and Gil Eannes made over the course of the decade and their constant efforts to obtain captives and trade goods. Here is just one example: "They entered the village and searched it thoroughly, to see if they could find anything in the houses. And in searching they lighted on seven or eight Moorish women, whom they took with them, giving thanks to God for their good fortune . . . and they rested and enjoyed themselves that night, like men that had toiled hard in the day."[27] The accounts are crucial for many reasons, not least of which is that they introduced male and female captives as legitimate objects of exchange and hinted at how the female captives might provide some rest and "enjoyment" for sailors in ways that did not warrant explication.

Textual moments like these provide a window into a set of changes underway both on the African coast and in Iberia. I reference them here as suggestive signposts of the transformations in how wealth and value were being conceived. In 1496 a Spanish slave trader requested a reward from the Crown for delivering a "shipload of Gold" to Spain from Hispaniola,

---

25 The production of European property-owning men as possessing universal rights has been the subject of much careful engagement by Black feminist theorists Hortense Spillers, Sylvia Wynter, and Imani Perry. As Perry has noted in reference to John Locke's construction of universal Man, the people white Europeans cast outside the property regime would always be "shadow" Western men and women. "The negation," she writes, "attends the form." Perry, *Vexy Thing*, 19. See also Spillers, "Mama's Baby, Papa's Maybe"; Wynter, "Unsettling the Coloniality of Being."

26 Zurara, *Discovery and Conquest of Guinea*, 40, 57.

27 Zurara, *Discovery and Conquest of Guinea*, 72.

even though his ship was actually laden with enslaved Native American men and women.[28] Rendering them as already gold suggests their intimate proximity to the monetary schemas that drove Europe's contact with Africa and the Americas in the fifteenth and sixteenth centuries. Captives and gold were equally fungible, marked with a fixed and legible value. This kind of symbolic and literal equivalency would continue. In the late sixteenth century, Spanish colonists smuggled vast quantities of silver out of Peruvian mines and illegally exchanged it for enslaved Africans—whose value offset a massive deficit.[29] Well into the eighteenth century, the value of bullion exported to Europe from Latin America exceeded that of sugar and other commodities similarly routed.[30] The crucial role of slave labor in extracting that wealth meant that the enslaved themselves would function as wealth-producing specie. In that regard, they were the biotic commodity that stabilized currency and thus would find themselves outside of the category of "population" as it was mobilized in Europe; even as they would become subject to enumeration rooted in the language of population, they would be rendered as commodities by the economies of value.

This is not to suggest that the act of reducing people to things was either simple or complete. Indeed, the refusal of the enslaved to be rendered into things is the most enduring aspect of the history of the Black Atlantic. The rhetoric of commodification at the heart of the transatlantic slave trade is both a consequence of that trade and a technology that facilitated its development. As historian Stephanie Smallwood has stressed, the stages of commodification required a series of reiterative maneuvers, over time and with different agents, that would culminate in the transformation of humans into cargo.[31] Long familiar with the fully human interactions that characterized encounters on the African coast, both African and European traders cobbled together worldviews to assist them in making the practices of racial slavery licit and legible. The notion that some members of any group might (or even should) be subjected to enslavement—and thus to a calculus that associated the slave with familial or even national wealth— had a long history. However, the conceptual relationship between gold and slaves played a crucial role in making entire populations part of a racial valuation that deemed them enslavable. Europeans believed that gold (and

28 Las Casas, *Historia de las Indies*, 1:326–28, 337, quoted in Vilches, *New World Gold*, 86.
29 Flynn and Giráldez, "Born with a 'Silver Spoon,'" 216–17.
30 Borucki, Eltis, and Wheat, "Atlantic History," 435.
31 Smallwood, *Saltwater Slavery*.

to a lesser degree silver) was a universally applicable and legible standard of value. Finding gold in the Indies was both a problem and its resolution. Gold was not as available as the Spaniards had hoped, and its value was not as constant or stable as they had assumed, but this was tempered by the "strangeness" of the residents of these lands. Spaniards transmogrified that strangeness into claims that indigenous peoples and Africans were so physically different from Europeans that they were enslavable and exchangeable. Ultimately, racial thinking worked to stabilize the category of value that enslavement was based on, moving the definition of *slave* so that instead of referring to a subset of a population that was legitimately subject to enslavement as a result of crimes or war, it applied to entire populations identified using the notion of race and its heritability.

Misidentified Values

In 1482 King Edward IV of England sought permission from the pope to "exchange baser merchandise for nobler" in Africa.[32] His language was steeped in the expectation that gold extracted from the area of the African coast near present-day Ghana could transform England, and his calculations of comparative worth have defined the desired terms of trade in the Atlantic ever since.[33] The idea that Europeans could trade trifles or trash for gold reflected a clear demarcation of different and degraded systems of value. This idea of difference evoked what anthropologist William Pietz has described as "a contempt for a people who valued" such trash.[34] Fueled by the search for precious metal, Europeans created a relationship with the continent that was dominated by a vision that gold and human beings would enter the balance sheets of European merchants as the raw materials of a beneficial Atlantic trade.

Thus, the English monarch's request for advantageous terms of trade tapped into another sort of alchemical process by which enslaved and enslavable men and women were becoming signifiers of value. It was not only Africans who would enter the ledger books of elite European households.

32 Hair and Law, "English in Western Africa," 245.
33 Wennerlind, "Credit Money."
34 Pietz, "Problem of the Fetish, II," 41. It should be emphasized that this idea, something that Curtin has called the "gee-gaw myth" in reference to the trade for enslaved Africans, has been refuted. Curtin, *Economic Change*, 312. See, for example, Alpern, "What Africans Got."

By the end of the fifteenth century, enslaved Native Americans whom the explorer Pedro Alonso Niño sent to Ferdinand and Isabella also served as signs of colonial wealth. They joined Africans and their descendants in many of Europe's port cities, where their presence as captives initiated the ideological process that moved Africans from trading partners to objects of trade in the minds of cosmopolitan Europeans.[35] For Europeans, Africans came to occupy the same symbolic and economic register as gold and silver did; they would become a form of specie, a reliable coin—Africans were rendered into financial instruments. This produced the material and ideological capacity needed to engage in the long-distance economic development that characterized early modern capitalism.

The process by which capitalism took root in early modern Europe involved new conceptualizations of labor and commodity. Enslaved men and women entered fifteenth-century European cities and courts as indices of the luxurious and the exotic, but they demarcated a very different economy of exchange by the end of the sixteenth century: one through which Europeans authorized the appropriation of African bodies to produce wealth for Europe. As literary scholar Amanda Bailey has argued in her examination of the political imaginary of credit, late sixteenth-century English juridical trials concerning debts introduced a notion of abstract value into the realm of the human: "Money, in the form of the bond ha[d] the power to create, destroy, and rearrange human beings."[36]

While the process by which the language of commerce eclipsed the language of family appears self-evident, it unfolded slowly. In the 1530s, almost a hundred years after Zurara remarked on the captives in Portugal, the Englishman John Hawkins voyaged to Senegambia and then to the West Indies with a shipload of enslaved African women and men. A gunner on one of Hawkins's ships characterized the Englishmen's slaving venture as

35 The process by which commodification took place is difficult to chart precisely because of the successful completion of that process. Smallwood argues that "we are only able to approach commodification from the vantage point of its end result—the thing already commodified, already represented as a commodity in the ledger, bill of sale, or political economic treatise." In asking us to refocus attention on the process, she argues that the question must be, "If people can be rendered convincingly as commodities where circumstances provide that competing systems of representation are silenced or disavowed, then how were such circumstances produced or discovered?" Smallwood, "Commodified Freedom," 294–95.

36 Amanda Bailey, *Of Bondage*, 17, 51–74.

a mission of mercy. He described taking five hundred men and women to the English ships just before three despotic, naked, and savage "kings of the negroes" did "with their power drive into the sea . . . about seven thousand men, women and children who all perished."[37] In the mind of this sailor and, presumably, those of his readers, the contrast was clear: the five hundred captives who would find themselves enslaved in the Spanish Caribbean became the lucky ones; they were saved from the despotic violence of their own rulers, who, not incidentally, were incapable of appreciating the potential value embodied in those they were killing. This notion comported with a much older understanding of slavery offered as a pardon in the face of a death sentence, but it is tinged with the framing work of savagery and misplaced value that would come to play a central role.[38]

European involvement in the slave trade unfolded slowly. The fifteenth- and sixteenth-century accounts of Portuguese and Dutch travelers who encountered people from the western and west-central coast of Africa situated slaves alongside the other potential trade goods that could be extracted from the continent; in a range of documents, slaves appear in lists of commodities that might include ivory, gold, cloth, wax, rice, millet, and pepper. European travelers also wrote that African rulers commonly accepted gifts of people as tribute and as a component of diplomacy; they presented this as evidence of the simplicity and culpability of Africans. The existence of slaves on the African coast was by no means shocking or unexpected to European traders, but the role of those slaves in the unfolding of new and unimaginable Atlantic economies would devolve over time.

European writers used African practices that they poorly understood as justification for the trade in human beings. In his 1594 report on the region, Portuguese trader Andre Álvares de Almada wrote that Christians traveling around the Gambia River understood not to trade for slaves who had been obtained by African slave traders through illegitimate kidnapping. He noted, "When our people refused to buy them, because this is forbidden, the blacks who brought them and offered them for sale killed them on the spot so that [their kidnapping of them] would not be discovered." Almada was "not sure that it would not have been better to have bought them, since this would have meant that they received baptism and became Christians."

---

37 Hortob, *Rare Travails of Job Hortop*, 3.
38 On enslavement as punishment for capital offenses, see Patterson, *Slavery and Social Death*, 126–29.

He demurred, however, saying that he would "not meddle further in this business, for it involves points which I am not competent to determine."[39]

When Manuel Alvares described the trade in slaves around Sierra Leone, he blamed the injustices of the trade on "the heathen" who "when getting rid of their own people . . . run contrary not only to nature and divine law but to canon and civil law." These were people, therefore, who saw no value in their own kin. He wrote of the "abominable abuses" of those who had obtained slaves for sale and blamed greedy Spaniards who had set "reason" aside and become slaves themselves to the "rattle and tinkle" of gold and silver.[40] It is clear that some chroniclers fully grasped the slippery moral terrain on which they stood, but this recognition failed to stem a tide that was gaining considerable momentum in the sixteenth century.

In Hakluyt's *Principall Navigations*, he described the process by which the trader and later comptroller of the English Navy John Hawkins, during his 1562 journey to Sierra Leone, "got into his possession, partly by the sworde, and partly by other means, to the number of 300 negroes at the least, besides other merchandises which that country yeeldeth."[41] At this juncture, Hakluyt's characterization of "negroes" as merchandise raised no eyebrows. The messy and fraught process that Zurara struggled with had, a century later, been neatly transformed into a simple transaction. Neither man's words are evidence, in and of themselves, of widespread agreement about the morality of slave trading. But the structure of Hakluyt's language conveys something important. The easy link between Africans as "merchandise" and the "country" that yields wealth originated in the English economic context with which Hawkins was familiar and in which such formulations were comprehensible. It assured Hakluyt's readers that there was no sovereign nation with which Hawkins had to contend: the country he wrote about simply yielded merchandise for the English market.

The language also erased decades of treaty and trade negotiations between European and African polities and situated the continent as a source of raw material for England's economic future.[42] In this future, access to markets would always be both ordained by God and ruled by Europeans

39 Álvares de Almada, *Brief Treatise* (1594), 276.
40 Alvares, *Ethiopia Minor*, chap. 5, 3.
41 Hakluyt, "The First Voyage of John Hawkins, 1562–1563," in Donnan, *Documents Illustrative*, 1:46.
42 On the history of European-African contact before the slave trade, see Bennett, *African Kings and Black Slaves*, 31–68.

based on their rational superiority. Published in 1621 and using language that coursed through the pamphlet literature on trade at the time, Thomas Mun argued that the new trade routes that brought England into contact with the Indies while avoiding trade with the Turks were a mark of God's favor to the nation.[43]

Writers such as Hakluyt and Mun thus presented slavery as logically assigned to the nation's marketplace. This was an argument, not a statement of fact, but it had productive roots. The casual description of men and women as "merchandise" might strike the modern reader as expected.[44] But in the sixteenth century, the practice of using the language of commerce to define relationships between Europeans and Africans was still unfolding. As historian Herman Bennett has argued, "As a social practice, commercialization [of the African slave trade] has a history still in need of a narrative."[45] Zurara's text implicitly questioned the violence embedded in the logical apparatus of slavery, the disavowal of the rights of mothers who clutched their babies to their chests, and the impartial logic that transformed these mothers and babies into easily extractable merchandise.

Reading the two texts together suggests the problem at the heart of *Reckoning with Slavery*: discerning how a commerce that depended on maternity erased both mothers particularly and kinship more broadly from view. While Zurara's text expressed horror and empathy, the description of Hawkins's successful voyage a hundred years later solidified the definition of certain human beings as merchandise. The rhetorical device depicting Hawkins's slave trading—situating people as a category of merchandise alongside others the land "yielded"—turned a horrific act into something quotidian and unremarkable. It was also a product of how numeracy was mobilized to situate the business of the slave trade as an overriding concern that erased the violation of affective relationships at its core. The emphasis on commerce signals a binary separation between sentiment and the market that came to define the Western political economy.

When it was first published and circulated in Richard Hakluyt's 1589 *Principall Navigations*, the Hawkins reference stood out: in a volume that

43 Mun, *Discourse of Trade*.
44 Should you encounter Hawkins's voyage through Elizabeth Donnan's volume of primary documents about the slave trade, it follows almost directly behind Gomes Zurara's wrenching description of families divided into "fifths," further suggesting that John Hawkins simply voiced the inevitable. Donnan, *Documents Illustrative*.
45 Bennett, *African Kings and Black Slaves*, 50.

ran some seven hundred pages, less than 5 percent pertained to Africa or Africans.[46] Hawkins's words were buried in a range of texts that highlighted England's potential role in the international arena. One might thus dismiss it as contributing very little to the ways English readers might begin to conceptualize race or slavery. But in tandem with a set of emerging notions about wealth, trade, and the commodifiability of human beings, it marks an important pivot in the language of trade and humanity. Hakluyt's inclusion of the Hawkins voyage is also important for what it would signal to readers in the coming decades. Reprinted widely in the seventeenth century, Hakluyt's "grammar of colonization" provided readers with a vocabulary for the expanding boundaries of the English empire.[47] For some readers, these boundaries were experiential, but for most they were stories about places they would never see but would encounter through the tobacco in their pipes, the sugar in their bowls, and, for the elite, the people who waited at their tables and the gold English guinea coins stamped with the insignia of the Royal Africa Company in their pockets.[48]

Slavery was not, of course, an entirely new concept for the English, nor was it only through the encounter with Africa that the English came to think of it. As historian Alison Games has argued, "large numbers of Englishmen acquired intimate experience with slavery [in the Mediterranean in the sixteenth century], both as a condition that might befall them and as a status of the laborers who attended them."[49] Slavery and hereditary racial slavery are two distinct forms of human hierarchy. Becoming a captive was something that could befall men and women everywhere, but becoming a slave came to mean something quite different in the Atlantic. In this era, English captives taken in conflicts on the north coast of Africa received much attention. The imperative to redeem them introduced the problem of white slavery to small towns and port cities across England as communities rallied to raise funds to bring home English captives who had fallen victim to slavery at the hands of North Africans.[50] This peculiar manner

46 Hair, "Attitudes to Africans," 48.

47 Mancall organizes chapter 7 around this idea of the grammar of colonization. Mancall, *Hakluyt's Promise*, chap. 7, 128–55.

48 The coin, minted beginning in 1663, was made from gold imported from West Africa and thus was called a guinea coin. The elephant and castle sometimes appeared on the face of the coin and sometimes on its reverse. Brewer, "Slavery, Sovereignty, and 'Inheritable Blood,'" 1050.

49 Games, *Web of Empire*, 71.

50 Colley, *Captives*, 73–81.

of enslavement was linked more to religious and cultural differences than to the language of commodity that would soon become inextricable from the practice of enslaving Africans. In other words, the language of commodities and merchandise that marks Hawkins's work signifies a set of new relationships that was cohering alongside those of hereditary racial slavery. Both racial difference and commodification were mobilized to create a new criterion for those who would be enslavable.

Soon after the Hakluyt collection was published, the English explorer Richard Jobson published *The Golden Trade: Or, A Discouery of the Riuer Gambra, and the Golden Trade of the Aethiopians* (1623), a text about his efforts to locate gold by following the Gambia River into the interior. He describes a transaction that occurred at a port on the river in which an African slave trader, apparently in an effort to avoid negotiating a bargain while recovering from drinking too much, offered "certain young blacke women" as slaves for Jobson to buy. Jobson demurred, saying, "We were a people who did not deale in any such commodity, neither did we buy or sell one another or any that had our owne shapes." The trader marveled at this statement and proclaimed that elsewhere this "merchandize" was "sold to white men, who earnestly desired them, especially such young women, as hee had brought for us."[51] Some scholars have interpreted Jobson's refusal as a broad repudiation of slavery. However, Jobson's full stance indicates something much more vexing than the righteous indignation of a man opposed to the traffic in slaves. It alerts us to a conceptual shift that was well underway in the first decades of the seventeenth century in which *commodity* could easily refer to young Black women and their monetary value for white men who "earnestly desired" them.

That Jobson and his men were offered only women might be rooted in regional conditions that produced women for trade. But in the context of the shifting assumptions about race and slavery that were emerging in the early seventeenth century, it also references both the sexual economy of slavery and the reproductive economy that would soon develop around it.[52] While Jobson's rejection echoes Zurara's recognition,

---

51 Jobson, *Golden Trade*, 112.
52 The offering of enslaved young women and girls for sex as matters of diplomacy and trade had been happening since before the fifteenth-century arrival of Europeans on the West African coast. Such gestures were embedded in a much longer gendered history of slavery and enslavement both in Africa and elsewhere. See Miller, "Women as Slaves"; Robertson and Klein, "Women's Importance."

it does so without concern about the position of those women. While it registers as a marker of English distinction from Iberians, a means to demarcate national identity, Jobson soon shifted from rejecting the practice to fully embracing it.

Specie and Values

As news of Iberia's contacts and conquests in Africa and the New World spread, English merchants, investors, and theorists scrambled to make sense of the vistas that were opening. The discovery of silver and gold in the New World caught the attention of European states. The metals were tricky, spurring wildly hopeful and harmful behavior in seemingly all who encountered them. Spaniards struggled to understand how and why their access to New World gold mines failed to translate into increased wealth, stability, and power for the monarchy (the Spanish Crown declared bankruptcy several times in the sixteenth century).[53] But English men and women were busy conceptualizing the new terrain of markets and exchange. On the heels of the Spanish conquests, the pope's excommunication of Elizabeth I opened up possibilities of trade between Protestant English merchants and Muslims, which ultimately led to trading ventures in the Levant, on the Barbary Coast, and elsewhere in the Mediterranean and in the Ottoman Empire. By the end of the sixteenth century, hundreds of English merchant ships were ferrying English goods to an expanded world and returning laden with consumer and luxury goods.[54]

As the possibilities for accruing wealth through trade expanded for the English, some feared that there was insufficient English coin for transacting business. At the end of the sixteenth century, Queen Elizabeth addressed the debasement of English coin that had occurred during her father's reign in the 1540s, but concerns about the presence of foreign coin and the notion that Spanish coin had corrupted English nobles continued to produce both anger and dissent.[55] The coinage issue involved more than problems with the availability of money; it touched on metaquestions about the power of the Crown and the definition of intrinsic value. Concerns about value

---

53 Vilches, *New World Gold*, 30, 220–70.
54 Games, *Web of Empire*, 50.
55 See Stephen Deng's discussion of John Donne and the Dutch Church Libel, which assigned Spanish gold the power to infect the English Queen and her subjects. Deng, "'So Pale, So Lame,'" 268, 272.

extended beyond the space of market exchange to include the social and cultural practices that shape the meanings attached to money. And thus the coinage crisis of seventeenth-century England must be understood as an index of shifting notions of worth, wealth, and value. The real and symbolic values of coins were by no means secure during this time.[56] In the first decades of the seventeenth century, concerns emerged about the dangers of exporting coin to European markets and squandering coin by turning gold and silver into decorative household objects or plate. The English upper classes appeared to view gold and silver as visual markers of their status rather than a means of securing wealth.

In 1622 Edward Misselden admonished men who were striving to "live above their calling" and craved goods from foreign markets. He argued that the nation was being depleted of its treasures by this wanton flow of money to other countries, especially "as money that is traded out of Christendom . . . never returneth again."[57] The use of silver money in foreign trade was a cause for alarm to many English writers, but the ability to bypass the Turkish "infidels" in the trade to the East balanced their concerns. Mun wrote that the English were "exporting of a lesse quantity of silver out of Europe unto the Infidells by many thousand poundes yearly than hath beene accustomed in former times."[58] And Mun mobilized quantitative data to support his claim that rounding the Cape of Good Hope and thus bypassing trade with the Turks was benefiting England rather than depleting the "gold, silver and Coyne of Christendome."[59] In addition to the growth of trade with other European nations, the Americas were beckoning. Thus, the movement of English coin was linked to religious and cultural similarities and to the hope that trade itself would consolidate, rather than disperse, European notions of legitimacy and hierarchy.

As English economic theory began to be generated in conversation with narratives of travel to Africa, claims that Africans were idolaters were routed through accusations that they did not value their possessions correctly—in

---

56 In "The Causes of Want of Money in England and Wales, 1621," the ninth explanation in a list of fourteen was "the consumption of gold and silver in England in gilding and silvering of beds, houses, swords, stools, chairs, etc." "The Causes of Want of Money in England and Wales, 1621," British Museum, Add MS 34, 324, fol. 181, reproduced in Thirsk and Cooper, *Seventeenth-Century Economic Documents*, 12–13.

57 Misselden, *Free Trade*, 11, 22.

58 Mun, *Discourse of Trade*, 9.

59 Mun, *Discourse of Trade*, 8.

effect, that they were not able to think rationally.[60] Attributing moral standing to rational thinking came to saturate much of Enlightenment thought. It was also wielded as a weapon in the relationship between European slave traders and settlers and would come to define many of the symbolic rituals of European appropriation of land and labor in the Americas.[61] The newly theorized categories of wealth—trade and colonialism—were always intimately bound up in discursive efforts to locate and define indigenous and African peoples. What emerged as distinct fields of knowledge—economy and culture—began as indistinguishable ideas.

Changes to the marketplace in the early seventeenth century produced fissures in moral certainty regarding usury, the role of the commons, and the relationship between landowner and laborer in the face of surpluses that could be translated into wealth-producing market exchanges. As Joyce Appleby has written of this time period, "a profound transformation of values was in the making, one in which the very source of order was being redefined."[62] As English writers navigated the terrain from which this new source of order would emerge, they produced a new realm of thought when they began to consider market activities as distinct from social relations. In the works of writers like Thomas Mun, Gerald de Maylnes, and Edward Misselden, "the economy" came into view for the first time, bringing a new way of thinking about value.

As has been widely stressed in work on seventeenth-century economic thought, one of the greatest ideological changes during the early part of the century was a move away from an understanding of labor as fundamentally social. Elizabethan statutes were designed to regulate laborers and the roving poor. They reflected a social order in which "each person's status and location [was] prescribed, duties and responsibilities [were] fixed, purposes clear, and commitments arranged hierarchically."[63] As English trade moved toward Europe and into the Atlantic, new relationships to markets crafted profoundly new ways of thinking about work, value, and society. Mun, Misselden, and Maylnes separated trade, markets, work, and money from their social contexts. They argued that the economy operated along lines that were distinct from nature and thus were quantifiable and predictable.

60 Pietz, "Problem of the Fetish, II," 41.
61 Seed, *Ceremonies of Possession*, esp. 16–40.
62 Appleby, *Economic Thought and Ideology*, 72.
63 Appleby, *Economic Thought and Ideology*, 37–38.

As Appleby notes, they "created a paradigm."[64] These ideas would be used against the New World and African peoples, who, like the chaos of new economies, needed to be properly tamed. In the European imagination, these people needed to be brought into order.

Early English advocates for trade, such as Hakluyt and Mun, situated wealth as in motion. They were pushing back against a cultural logic that understood wealth as something to be displayed rather than circulated. In a pattern that mimicked the relationship between the aristocracy and Black servants, gold and silver money was as likely to be displayed as plate or buttons as to be put in use in the service of "immediate impersonal monetary exchanges."[65] As we've already seen, the value of circulating coin did, however, bring danger, as coinage was tied up in a wide range of concerns that exceeded its materiality. As English writers debated the power of coin, they ascribed to foreign coins the power to infect the monarchy and had to grapple with the absence of coin in the colonies. For example, planters in Barbados and Virginia had to purchase slaves with the commodities they produced; they used tobacco, ginger, cotton, and ultimately sugar to pay for slaves.[66] Because what was used for currency was fluid during the sixteenth and seventeenth centuries, situating African people as currency required only a short conceptual leap.

As Kim Hall has argued, depictions of Black people in jewelry and portraits became "symbols for the accumulation of profitable foreign goods" during this period (figure 2.1). The presence of Black children and servants in English decorative and fine arts defined a whiteness "not only constructed by but dependent on an involvement with Africans that [was] the inevitable product of England's ongoing colonial expansion."[67] If certainty about value had been dislodged by the currency crisis, rendering intrinsic value a speculative prospect, other certainties were bound to be similarly unfettered. Thus, humans were alchemically transformable into, and displayed like, gold. An interpretation of the familiar image of Anthony van Dyck's *Princess Henrietta of Lorraine, Attended by a Page* (1634) (figure 2.2)

64 Appleby, *Economic Thought and Ideology*, 49.
65 Muldrew, "'Hard Food for Midas,'" 81, 109–11.
66 Deng writes that during the Elizabethan era, "upholding 'Englishness' both materially and symbolically partially required maintaining the purity of English coin while preventing the pernicious influence of foreign coins circulating in England." Deng, *Coinage and State Formation*, 170; on commodities as payment for slaves, see Menard, *Sweet Negotiations*, 64.
67 K. Hall, *Things of Darkness*, 211–53, 253.

FIGURE 2.1 *Cameo of a Black Woman*, workshop of Girolamo Miseroni, ca. 1600. Staatliche Münzsammlung, Munich, Germany. Reproduced in Spicer, *Revealing the African Presence in Renaissance Europe.*

through the lens of coinage and value augments our understanding of the visual economy as derived through the rubric of race alone.[68] It is not a simple matter of the enslaved child signifying the status that accrued to Henrietta; the child is the *embodiment* of silver or gold. As Elvira Vilches and Chi-Ming Yang have illustrated, the precious metal coming from the Indies triggered an anxiety regarding its provenance and a worry that when gold or silver were hoarded they lost their value.[69] Both concerns were routed through the distant lands and peoples of the Americas and China and were thus embedded in a set of meanings fully entangled with ideas

68 Bindman, "Black Presence in British Art," 240; see also 253 (fig. 136).
69 Vilches, *New World Gold*, 95–144; and Yang, "Silver, Blackness, and Fugitive Value," 144.

FIGURE 2.2 Anthony van Dyck, *Princess Henrietta of Lorraine, Attended by a Page*, 1634. Kenwood House, London, England. Art UK, accessed October 1, 2020. https://artuk.org/discover/artworks/princess-henrietta-of-lorraine-16111660 -attended-by-a-page-191703.

about discovery, provenance, savagery, and value. The African child in the portrait, whose movement is stayed by the hand of the European woman, is thus cemented into place; he is clearly a reflection of her wealth while also a contribution to it. Van Dyck has situated the child, clothed, attentive, and in service, as a sort of specie.

African Commodities

These new ways of thinking about value and trade did not stop at England's shores. Africa played an important role for Englishmen seeking to obtain wealth and to demarcate the parameters of their national identity. Africans are situated in these earliest narratives as products of the land rather than owners or even cultivators of it. As Herman Bennett has argued, as Europeans mapped the West African coast in the early sixteenth century, "knowledge about peoples and places only assumed importance in relationship to regional productivity, the desirability of the respective commodities, and the inhabitants' willingness to engage in trade."[70]

The earliest descriptions of West Africa, those penned by Portuguese traders at the Gambia River, wove discussions of commerce almost seamlessly into discussions of geography. Andre Álvares de Almada, for example, described the mouth of the river and the volume of fresh water it delivered into the sea, followed immediately by the statement that "it is a river which possesses a large trade in slaves, in black and white cotton cloths, in raw cotton and in wax." Further, he observed that "the whole land furnishes foodstuffs in abundance, rice, the milho called macaroca, and other ground crops."[71] The landscape takes on the shape of a character here, furnishing crops rather than supporting people's cultivation of crops. The effect is a dislocation of the continent from its spatial geography to an economic placeholder in the European imaginary.

Katherine McKittrick argues that the Middle Passage rendered Africans as placeless and that the people without a place in the early modern era were those with no legitimate claim to the land. In the eyes of Europeans, their enslavement was therefore deserved and legitimate.[72] The process McKittrick identified was actually underway on the continent well before the material realities of capture and transport congealed in the Middle

70 Bennett, *African Kings and Black Slaves*, 149.
71 Álvares de Almada, *Brief Treatise* (1594), 275.
72 McKittrick, *Demonic Grounds*, 4.

Passage. Thus, in the English imagination, the continent itself colluded to justify enslavability. Indeed, the English marked African bodies as wealth and, with a logic that circles back around upon itself, as racially different because they were commodifiable.

The sixteenth-century encounter between Europeans and West Africans was steeped in what the anthropologist William Pietz has termed the "mystery of value." As I have already noted, European writers often wrote that Africans traded "trinkets" for objects of "real" value.[73] Out of this mystery emerged an unsurprising circularity of racial logic. These texts reflect a crucial part of the process by which rationality became connected to a notion of European superiority and freedom that came to be racialized.[74] For many European writers, to describe the African continent was to evoke monstrosity, heathenism, and simultaneous attraction and repulsion. Underpinning all of these responses was a through line of concern about irrational trade practices that was related to the problem with which English and other European writers were grappling: how to fit new credit instruments and new trade practices into older ideas of economy. The only answer was to create a new conception of what *economy* meant, and the trade in African slaves was a key aspect of that creation.

By the middle of the sixteenth century, English writers were confident that a connection existed between African peoples and the trade of commodities. They evoked the Black body as one of many possible trade goods from the continent and imbued it with meaning in the context of early modern England's relationship to Africa and, of course, to settlement in the Atlantic. The language used by Hawkins and Jobson outlines a shared framework articulated for readers across decades. Even as Hakluyt cavalierly described Senegambians as "merchandise" in 1562 and Jobson refused "such commodity" in 1620, the association of Africans with commerce was clear.[75] The travel literature of the time engaged in a process of

73 Pietz, "Problem of the Fetish, I," 9.

74 Elsewhere I have explored the interplay between monstrosity and gendered notions of racial heredity and hierarchy, and while I stand by that work, here and in the chapter that follows, I revisit these texts with an eye to the question of the commodity and commodification.

75 In their 1999 edition of Jobson's narrative, David Gamble and P. E. H. Hair characterize the gesture that I have made here—refuting Jobson's claim with evidence of Hawkins's actions—as facile, noting that "Jobson did not buy slaves. The English voyages to River Gambia did not, the voyages of the 1618 Guinea Co. did not, and the many English voyages to Guinea between the 1580s and the 1630s almost without exception did not."

smoothing away the contradictions involved in the trade in human cargo through evoking a proximity among Africans, consumer goods, and the purportedly innate inability of Africans to engage in the complicated calculus of trade.

Early descriptions of people in Africa typically located them on a continuum from barbaric savages with no ability to count to simpletons who were easily distracted by the pretty goods sophisticated and savvy Europeans offered them. When the Portuguese arrived at the Pra River on the coast of present-day Ghana in 1471, they spent almost ten years trading with the Eguafo peoples for small quantities of gold. Gold dust, gold ornaments, and gold weights were all part of the language of contact and exchange. As they began building a fort there, at what they named Elmina, the textual record of what was happening began to shift. Setting aside the fact that elaborate trading patterns based on precise and minute measurements had shaped the trans-Saharan gold trade since the third century CE, the Portuguese were quick to substitute a language of irrationality in place of recognition.[76] For example, in the account of the founding of the Portuguese fort at Mina, the people's rage in response to the "utter ruin of their sacred rocks" was immediately assuaged through the delivery of bracelets and shawls, which were the "principal merchandise" and the "medium of exchange" in Guinea.[77] The fundamental relationships of value are here articulated—rationality was discursively located in Christianity, and irrationality was tethered to an understanding of spirituality rooted in the land. Any moral concerns could be soothed through a devalued compensation that made the Portuguese appear to have performed an act of reparation.

The gesture here would intersect with the work of writers who sought to erase the considerable evidence of African economic institutions and capacities. George Abbot's *A Briefe Description of the Whole Worlde* (1599) dismissed sub-Saharan Africa in a few short paragraphs and described the people only as "exceeding blacke" and without religion until the Portuguese

---

Gamble and Hair, introduction to Jobson, *Discovery of River Gambra*, 31. My point in linking Jobson and Hawkins here is not to mount an argument about the ubiquity of late sixteenth- and early seventeenth-century English slave trading but rather to suggest that Jobson's rhetorical flourish occurred in the context of a readership quite familiar with the potential for slave trading on the African coast and quite accustomed to mulling over the relative merits of engaging therein.

76 Garrard, "Myth and Metrology," 456; and Sheales, "African Gold-Weights."

77 Pina, *Chronica del Rey Dom João II*, in J. W. Blake, *Europeans in West Africa*, 76.

arrived, who "keep the people in subjection, to their great commoditie." In Senegambia, Abbot wrote, "our Englishmen have found traffique into the parts of this Country, where their greatest commoditie is Gold and Elephants teeth." From here to the Cape of Good Hope, "there is no matter of any great importance."[78] Africa was empty of anything built by Africans, and what was left were indeed things that Europeans wanted. But they imagined that their access to those raw materials was unimpeded by Africans, whom Europeans believed could not value them and thus had relinquished any claims.

In the 1600 English translation of Leo Africanus's 1550 *Descrittione dell'Africa* (Description of Africa), even in the intimacy of domestic life, Africans did not take proper account of things. Africanus wrote that in Guinea "they sell their children unto strangers, supposing that their estate cannot possiblie be impaired."[79] It was not simply Africans' inability to account for their estates that was the issue; their failure to properly value kinship was a key element of what set them "outside." By 1600, of course, slave owners in Spanish America were struggling with the impediment that kinship could mount to the logics of long-term slave ownership.[80] As the concept of perpetual and hereditary racial slavery cohered, a refusal to regard kinship as a universal property, one experienced by Africans in the same way that it was by Europeans, was at the foundation of hereditary racial slavery. A strategic dislodging of Africans from the family of Man would become crucial to rendering them as commodities.

Giovanni Botero's widely translated and reissued *Relatione Universali* (1589), first published in English as *The Worlde* in 1601, devoted over two hundred pages to describing Europe and only twenty pages to the rest of the world. He opened with the allure of the land of Prester John—the legendary Christian ruler of a city made of gold—somewhere on the African continent:

> To speake in a worde: there is no countrey under heaven fitter for increase of plants and all living creatures, but none lesse helpt by arte or industry; for the inhabitants are idle and unthriftie. They have flaxe, but make no cloth, they have sugar-canes and iron-mines, but knowe not the use of either: and as for smiths, they feare them as fiends.

---

78 Abbot, *Briefe Description*, fols. M2–3.
79 Leo Africanus, *Geographical Historie of Africa*, 42.
80 Dorsey, "Women without History"; and J. L. Morgan, "*Partus Sequitur Ventrem*."

They have rivers and streames, yet will they not take the paines in drouths to cut the banks to water their tillage or harten their grounds. Few give themselves to hunting or fishing, which causeth their fields to swarme with foule and venison, and their rivers with fish. But it seemeth that the true ground of their idleness ariseth from their evill usage: for the poore people perceiving their land-lords to pole and pill them, never sowe more than they needs must.[81]

Here is a predictable analysis of the coexistence of abundance and "sloth" that sees it as ultimately rooted in a disregard for the proper value of things.[82] Botero elaborates on two phenomena: that the disregard for value is traceable to the despotism of evil and ungovernable elites and that this inability to appreciate value is responsible for all manner of ignorance and illiteracy:

They keepe no method in their speeches, and to write a letter, many men (and that many daies) must lay their wits together. At meales, they use neither cloth, napkin, nor tables. They are utterly ignorant in Physicke. The Gentlemen, Burgers, and Plebeians dwell apart, yet may any man rise to honour by virtue and prowesse. The first borne is heir to all, even to the utmost farthing. Through the whole land there is not a towne conteining above 1600 households, and but few of that quantititie: or, for the most part they dwell dispersed in small villages. They have no castle or fortification, in imitation of the Spartans, maintaining that a country ought to be defended by the sword, and not by strength of earth or stone. They barter one thing for another, and to make reckonings even, they supply the want with corne and salt. For pepper, frankinsence, myrrhe and salt they give gold, and that by waight: as for silver it is in little request.[83]

These passages do multiple work by articulating a lack of innovation on the part of Africans that the English defined as idleness in the face of massive resources and by noting the unimportance of Africans, as evidenced by their reliance on barter, their willingness to trade gold for spices, and their general disinterest in silver.

81 [Botero], *Worlde*, 213. The work was published in seven editions between 1601 and 1630. Paul and Meshkat, "Johnson's Relations," 110.
82 As John Locke would soon articulate, the "improvement" of nature would become a decisive sign of both civility and the legitimate possession of territory. Locke, "Property," in *Two Treatises of Government*, sec. 32.
83 [Botero], *Worlde*, 214.

Elsewhere, as William Pietz has shown, Europeans used the language of the fetish—or what they saw as an "irrational propensity to personify material objects"—to articulate the claim that Africans refused "rational" trade relations.[84] One can only conclude that in the minds of the English, Africans' supposed lack of rational attention to value and industry consigned them to their natural place in "the worlde"—raw resources to be transformed into valuable commodities through European resourcefulness. It should not, of course, need repeating that this maneuver occurs despite what was then a centuries-old understanding in Europe that long-distance trading routes associated with the Wangara peoples delivered gold from the African interior to Europe.[85]

The one instance in which African industry is constantly evoked originates in the iconographic cannibal shop (figure 2.3). Cannibalism was a touchstone for claims that Africans were monstrously different; the cannibal delineated an absolute absence of European civil norms. In the European imagination, cannibals symbolized the dangers associated with the notion of colonial migration. As arguments in favor of colonial settlement mounted, the need to convert natives from pagan ways produced the cannibal as a figure that marked the inevitability of European colonial dominance.[86] Historians of the Americas have carefully noted how important the cannibal was to the construction of the New World for European travelers and readers. Such constructs were also applied to Africa but to different ends. In 1555 Peter Martyr's *De Novo Orbe* (On the New World, first published in 1500) was published in English; in it he described native New World cannibals simmering human flesh in their pots or roasting it on their spits, and he narrated that they kept women "for increase as we do hens to laye egges."[87] In the evocation of husbandry in the context of anthropophagy, we see the beginning of the idea of the cannibal shop.

Duarte Lopes's *Report of the Kingdome of Congo* (1597) is possibly the original source of many writers' descriptions of African cannibal merchants[88]:

84 Pietz, "Problem of the Fetish, II," 23.
85 On the gold trade into Europe, see Wilks, "Wangara, Akan and Portuguese . . . I"; and Wilks, "Wangara, Akan and Portuguese . . . II."
86 Seed, *American Pentimento*, 97.
87 Martyr, *Decades of the Newe Worlde*, 2.
88 For example, in Pory's translation of Leo Africanus he closes his discussion of "Places Undescribed by John Leo" by reproducing the quote that follows. Leo Africanus, *Geographical Historie of Africa*, 41.

FIGURE 2.3 *Cannibal Shop.* From Lopes, *A Report of the Kingdome of Congo* . . . 1597.

They keep a shambles of mans flesh as they do in these countries for beefe and other victuailes. For their enemies whom they take in the warres, they eate, and also their slaves, if they can have a good market for them they sell or if they cannot than they deliver them to the butchers to be cut in peeces and so solde to be rosted or boyled. It is a remarkable fact in the history of this people, that any who are tired of life, or wish to prove themselves brave and courageous, esteem it a great honor to expose themselves to death by an act which shall show their contempt for life. Thus they offer themselves for slaughter, and as the faithful vassals of princes, wishing to do them service, not only give themselves to be eaten, but their slaves also, when fattened, are killed and eaten.[89]

In Lopes's ascribing of industry to Africans only to illustrate monstrosity, the numeracy associated with an English shopkeeper vanishes amid the incredulity evoked by a cannibal butcher's shop. This serves as evidence of the opposite of rationality.

Lopes positioned this description close to a discussion of Luandan currency in a gesture that did further damage. He described the Lumache shells that female divers harvested and that Luandans valued based on color and size (the female being more valuable): "Here you must note that gold and silver and mettell is not of any estimation, nor in use of money in these countreyes, but onely these Lumache: so that neither with golde nor silver in masse or in coine you shall buy anything there, but with these Lumache you shall buy both golde and silver, or anything else." Lopes reviewed the range of items used for money in Africa and in China with a tone of astonishment: "It appeareth, that the money which is payed for everie thing is not mettall, all the worlde over, as it is in Europe and in many and sundry other countries of the earth." Just before his full discussion of the cannibal butchery, he touched on circumcision and "another foolish custome . . . to mark their faces with sundry slashes made with a knife."[90] His discussion of the cannibal shop thus closes a narrative arc that could have led to an acknowledgment of African numeracy and facility in trade, but the cannibal butcher shuts down any possibility of a rational vocation. Lopes's narrative mobilizes the absence of rational merchandizing as the crucial index for enslavability.

89 Lopes, *Report of the Kingdome*, 35.
90 Lopes, *Report of the Kingdome*, 22, 24, 35.

Lopes's *Report* was driven by his desire to situate the Congo as a source of merchandise. It told future European traders how to navigate the waters of trade in this region of the world. His careful description of currency began with a tone that was ethnographic rather than dismissive; understanding the currency of trade is, of course, a crucial detail for such a guide. He wrote at a moment when European traders and adventurers had understood and embraced Portugal's investment in the trade in cowrie from the Maldives. The association between cowrie gathering and women in the Maldives was certainly known among sailors and traders and in 1619 was confirmed in writing by François Pyrard de Laval, who described the process in great detail after spending five years in captivity on the atoll.[91]

In Lopes's account, the position of women "places" this shell money for his Portuguese readers. The irrationality of this currency, marked by women's participation in its acquisition, is only gradually revealed to the reader, as if Lopes is himself loath to go there. In his hands, *lumache* signals the foolishness of African systems of value and the potential for Europeans to trade with Congolese without loss of actual valuable currency. But by the time we arrive at self-mutilating cannibals and delusional natives who offer themselves up for free to the meat market as a mark of their regard for the king, Lopes cannot keep his incredulity at bay. What began with such promise ends in the chaos of those who must be enslavable.

The figure of the cannibal loomed large in the literature of early modern Atlantic contact. The cannibal feast is ubiquitous in early accounts of travel to the Americas, in which the consumption of human flesh augmented accusations of sexualized monstrosity that were central to the mapping of the Atlantic.[92] Such references drew on a much earlier iconography in which cannibalism indicated the monstrous and barbarous dangers lurking at the edge of the polis. But cannibalism generated specific meaning in the context of particular contemporary anxieties about commodification. Stephan Palmié has argued that Europeans had to learn to consume men, to develop the "acquired taste" for slave regimes.[93] While slavery was prevalent in the ancient societies early modern Europeans so revered, the taste in the early modern period was for the new mode of enslavement that situated Africans as perpetually and fundamentally different. Iberians initially forged

91 Pyrard's narrative concerned his 1601 voyage and five-year captivity in the Maldives. Pyrard, *Voyage*, quoted in Hogendorn and Johnson, *Shell Money*, 34.
92 J. L. Morgan, *Laboring Women*, 22–23.
93 Palmié, "Taste for Human Commodities," 46.

the connection between cannibalism and enslavement in the sixteenth century. As they searched for a legal reason to justify the enslavement of Native Americans, the need for labor was not enough. Beginning with Queen Isabella, monarchs decreed that enslavement was a legitimate punishment for those who attacked the Crown's military or for those who "eat human flesh."[94] In the transatlantic slave trade, of course, the slave owners, not the slaves, became the consumers of flesh.

Writings like those of Lopes and Botero, which were published in translation in England at the end of the sixteenth century, provide a literary and descriptive root for two strands of English thought, one about what *African* meant and one about the problem of value. These two strands cannot be separated. As England moved into the seventeenth century, the ways English men and women experienced and understood their economic identities began to fundamentally change. As Joyce Appleby has written, "the persistence of change had brought an end to that equilibrium between people and land, labor and repose, peasant and lord, king and kingdom, production and consumption," that had marked the Middle Ages.[95] In its place emerged new polarities between native and settler, sovereignty and dispossession, and trade and treasures. And yet the transformations wrought by the changes in the English economy were mere ripples compared to the seismic changes the transatlantic slave trade brought to captive and free Africans in the Black Atlantic world.

Populations

The concept of population came into being for early modern thinkers as a new way of considering community in relationship to governance. Although the modern understanding of the term *population* was not mobilized until the middle of the eighteenth century with the writings of David Hume, the notion entered English parlance in the early seventeenth century, primarily in relation to concerns about depopulation, at moments of plague or war, in an effort to understand population loss or what Michel Foucault called "dramatic mortality."[96] This might at times provoke assertions to the contrary, but the concept of collective population, for English writers, was initially associated with loss. In his 1978 lectures on population,

94 Seed, *American Pentimento*, 97.
95 Appleby, *Economic Thought and Ideology*, 11.
96 Foucault, *Security, Territory, Population*, 67.

Foucault linked the emergence of the concept to political economy, another new eighteenth-century form of knowledge. The idea of population was also firmly keyed to a notion of collective identity.[97] Lindon Barrett has argued that the "unprecedented proximities of populations" led to a number of dichotomies that emerged in this period: "European and African, consumption and production, supervision and subordination, reason and unreason."[98] In other words, for Europeans who had long been concerned about losses to their own population, the movement of people produced a moment when difference, articulated and recognized, became something to be reckoned with in ways that went far beyond bodily phenotype.

The metaphor of population growth and decline was mobilized widely not just in relation to colonialism or trade but also in relation to other ideas. For Robert Powell, the evils of enclosing common land were best conveyed through a vision of depopulation and a warning that "chocking the wombe . . . be a worse sinne then the hiding and hoarding up of her fruites after birth."[99] As early as 1571, when Thomas Smith received authorization from Queen Elizabeth to establish a plantation in the Irish county of Antrim, the notion that moving English men and women outside England would benefit the nation relied on changing ideas about population growth and stagnation. Smith wrote that "England was never . . . fuller of people than it is to this day." He ruminated that after the dissolution of the monasteries, the country was faced with "double the number of gentlemen and marriages, whereby cometh daily more increase of people. . . . There are many lacke abode, and few dwellings emptie."[100] Smith's capacity to imagine Ireland as a colony of England was shaped in part by his familiarity with the works of Richard Eden, Peter Martyr, and the contemporary translations of Leo Africanus's *Descrittione dell'Africa* that had rendered Africa as "peopled" in a very particular way by the middle of the sixteenth century.[101]

---

97 One of Foucault's core concerns in these lectures is the way in which population is rendered "natural." One of the processes that makes it so is data, or the concretizing of trends concerning birth and death rates. Given that such efforts emerge hand-in-hand with efforts to distinguish the English population clearly from populations that are enslavable and colonizable, the degree to which the notion of population is conducive to racialist thinking seems clear to me.

98 Barrett, "Mercantilism, U.S. Federalism," 106.

99 Powell, *Depopulation Arraigned, Convicted and Condemned*, 4.

100 T. Smith, "Letter Sent by I. B.," fol. 13.

101 Quinn, "Sir Thomas Smith," 545.

Colonialism carried with it a series of equations tied to population, a politics of mathematics that made possible the notion that human difference could be identified and quantified. Quantification, of course, had an underbelly of violence that was not always made perfectly clear. But in a foundational text of early modern mathematics published in 1658, Edmund Wingate transformed the Josephus problem into a computational challenge in which a boat overfilled with Englishmen and Turks requires a mathematical solution that yields survival for the English by drowning only the Turks.[102] In this example, it becomes clear that mathematics offered a solution to the messy problem of English vulnerability in the face of the presence of "others." Indeed, mathematics imparted a veneer of impartial logic that obscured deeply prejudiced thinking.

It would be difficult to find a better example of the link between seventeenth-century colonial thinking and political arithmetic than the writings of Thomas Hariot. After he went to Virginia as a surveyor with Sir Richard Grenville in 1585, Hariot developed revolutionary new work in algebraic symbolism. Modern editors of his *Artis Analyticae Praxis* note that through Hariot's work "a new world of mathematical existence has come into being, self-dependent and detached from the substantial base to which it is, nevertheless, connected."[103] While the mathematical work itself was purely an exegesis of symbolic algebra, the drive to think through these mathematical concerns was rooted in an environment dominated by ideas about population and colonial expansion.

In his unpublished mathematical papers, Hariot articulated a very early rumination on the relationship between colonialism and the mathematical analysis of population growth, distinguishing between cultural understandings of reproduction (prohibitions of incest, for example) and mathematical ones. The ability to couch moral judgment in secular rationality was a key feature of this kind of speculative exercise from the beginning and would become a key aspect of how numeracy begat race-based thought. To

102 The Josephus problem originated with the first-century historian Flavius Josephus, who described a group of forty men standing in a circle who are executed based on a numerical count. The problem asks where a man should stand in order to be the last survivor. In Wingate's shipboard version, the challenge is to place the men so that the only ones who are purposefully drowned are Turks. Wingate, *Mr. Wingate's Arithmetick*, 498–99. In Keith Thomas's lecture on numeracy in early modern England, he notes that children were being taught mathematics in the seventeenth century with this word problem. K. Thomas, "Numeracy in Early Modern England," 117.
103 Hariot, *Thomas Harriot's Artis Analyticae Praxis*, 15.

mobilize mathematical calculation was to introduce the notion that human communities could be rearranged for the good of the state. Hariot calculated that while standing shoulder to shoulder, 300 billion people could *fit* on England. But although the nation could and should be home to such a wealth of bodies, the landmass would have to be at least three times larger for such a populace to be comfortably *sustained*. The need to find room to sustain England's potential population brought the New World into focus, and Hariot's time in North America led him to speculate that Virginia might be the place where Englishmen might, in historian Joyce Chaplin's words, "find a place to stand."[104] This was more than simply a thought experiment; mobilizing the purported clarity of calculation allowed Hariot to suggest that subjects of the English monarch could logically be dislodged from the geography that created them as English and yet still retain their essential character as Englishmen.

In his *Briefe and True Report of the New Found Land of Virginia* (1590), Hariot provided further evidence of the interlocking origins of demography, numeracy, race, and colonialism. He divided his account of Virginia into three parts, each driven by a discussion of "commodities." In the final part of the report, he turned to the people of Virginia:

> In respect of us they are a people poor, and for want of skill and judgment in their knowledge and use of our things do esteem our trifles before the things of greater value. . . . Although they have no such tools, nor any such crafts, sciences and arts as we, yet in those things they do, they show excellence of wit. And by how much they, upon due consideration, shall find our manner of knowledge and crafts to exceed theirs in perfection and speed for doing or execution, by so much the more is it probable that they should desire our friendships and love, and have the greater respect for pleasing and obeying us. Whereby may be hoped, if means of good government be used, that they may in short time be brought to civility and the embracing of true religion.[105]

For Hariot, civility would derive from the use of and proper appreciation for things. Natives would acquire the ability to value things through adopting the logic of trade. Two years before Botero wrote about the scarcity of common sense among Africans, Hariot had thought carefully about the

104 Chaplin, *Subject Matter*, 126.
105 Harriot, *Briefe and True Report*, 48.

problems of population and concluded that large and dense populations benefited the nation-state because they generated considerable military and economic power. He concluded that monogamy elevated women and their reproductive capacity, while polygamy degraded them.[106] For authors who were writing accounts of English "discoveries," the connection between concerns about European populations and populations in Africa or the Americas was intimate. Hariot's ruminations reflect the desire to articulate two ways that a crowded nation could solve the problem of population growth: by generating military power or by accessing colonial lands. Both solutions reflected the new ways that people were being converted into populations for early modern English theorists.[107]

Peopling Nations

Because the kind of logic that was rooted in the emerging discipline of mathematics was a core feature of the Enlightenment, it is easy to overlook the extent to which this "making up of people" was linked to the idea of race and to racial hierarchies.[108] These hierarchies rendered the slave trade comprehensible as Europeans used race to produce human collectivities that were supposedly destined to relinquish both themselves and that which they produced to Europe. The movements of peoples across oceans in service of nations bolstered the drive to understand people as populations with fixed identities—imbued with an Englishness or Frenchness that would not dissipate under the American sun. It also produced a new kind of evidentiary data upon which the logic of nation building and colonial settlement depended.

Colonial settlers were not the only population subjected to accounting. While the move to quantification is a well-documented feature of early Enlightenment political thought, its relationship to the development of the slave trade is far less carefully considered.[109] The earlier conceptual vocabularies regarding legitimate subjects set the links among citizenship, population, and commerce into motion. These vocabularies were tied to the first efforts to gauge population in the English American colonies and were

---

106 As Alison Bashford and Joyce Chaplin point out, this was anti-Muslim antagonism. Bashford and Chaplin, *New Worlds*, 25.

107 Bashford and Chaplin, *New Worlds*, 26.

108 Hacking, "Making Up People."

109 For a critical engagement with the problem of race in early modern scholarship, see, for example, Erickson and Hall, "'New Scholarly Song.'"

simultaneously applied with brutal results in Europe's engagement with the transatlantic slave trade.

For the English, the need to compile demographic data in service to these developments was nowhere more pressing than in the North American colonies. They came to the New World on the heels of Spain. Their vision of extracting raw material wealth from the land was quickly supplanted by an ethos of settlement and cultivation, and thus they had particular reason to pay close attention to the composition of their settlements.[110] Tracking and accounting for population growth would be key to gauging the successes of colonial ventures, and thus attention to reproduction was logical and important.

"Population" was a new tool for articulating the relationship between colonial economies and the wealth of the nation, and as early modern English writers mobilized it, concerns about reproduction and legitimacy grew. The long-standing consensus that God had created Adam and Eve to "be fruitful and multiply" (Genesis 1:28) gave way to secular concerns about the extent to which the size of a given population drove economic successes and failures.[111] In 1625 John Hagthorpe wrote that among the benefits that would accrue to England from increasing trade would be "unburthening this our fruitful mother of her many, many Children by transporting yearly [to the Plantations] ten thousand poore people . . . unburthening this land of a million" over the next twenty to thirty years.[112] He was not alone in seeing the colonies as a solution to England's population problem. Writing in the context of Newfoundland and colonial plantations generally, Richard Eburne noted that "the price of all things are growne to such an unreasonable height" that common people are "even undone." The only solution to this problem would be "the diminution of the number of people in the land."[113]

By the middle of the seventeenth century, the assumption that the state should have not only data but also opinions about the intimate lives of the populace was becoming commonplace. Realizing that extracting wealth

110 As Chaplin writes, "If other nations had had greater national prowess, better ability to discover mines, and swifter military control over native populations, the English could make up for lost time by planting themselves in America and breeding there." Chaplin, *Subject Matter*, 117. On the evidence that counting the populace became an imperative in sixteenth-century England, see Glimp, *Increase and Multiply*, chap. 1.

111 On theology and reproduction, see Glimp, *Increase and Multiply*, 147.

112 Hagthorpe, *Englands Exchequer*, 26.

113 Eburne, *Plaine Path-Way to Plantations*, 10–11.

from the American colonies would depend on a robust quantity of English settlers, those writing from the speculative distance of a London escritoire and those more directly involved in colonial settlement became keenly interested in assessing birth and mortality rates. Seventeenth-century colonial settlers were sent with instructions to keep close count of populations, "including the 'Fruitfulness or Barrenness' of native women," wherever they visited.[114] Governors and legislative bodies produced regular censuses, which formed the basis for colonial policy.

James Harrington wrote in 1656 that New World bachelors should be taxed at twice the rate of their married male counterparts and that those who had sired ten children should be freed from paying taxes for the remainder of their lives.[115] Harrington clearly understood population as linked to Englishmen's fertility. Indeed, he defined population as linked to Englishness in a gesture that aligned with other English writers who speculated about the relationship between population, sovereignty, and a whiteness that would only devolve to the English. Richard Eburne wrote that young single men would hinder the colonial project if they remained unmarried or attempted marriage with a native woman, a course that was neither "profitable nor convenient (they having had no such breeding as our women have)."[116] In this regard, the notion of populating the colonies through sexual contact with indigenous women was rejected in favor of Englishwomen brought to the colonies—but the question was indeed of interest to some speculative writers.

What links these concerns about population in the colonies is a commitment to increasing the numbers of Englishmen, through whom land in the Americas could be claimed. These ideas about the reproduction of the English were linked to the issues of taxation and profitability, but kinship and paternity remained connected to the interests of the Crown (in contrast to how population would work against captive Africans). And thus, for theorists of policy and the acquisition of wealth from the settlements, no matter how degraded the English settler was, his reproductive capacity

114 Boyle, *General Heads*, quoted in Bashford and Chaplin, *New Worlds*, 33.
115 Harrington, *Oceana*, 97. See also Cassedy, *Demography in Early America*, 50.
116 Eburne was using the term *breeding* in reference to childbirth, not manners. He preceded the quoted lines with this: "Therefore are [young men] the lesse fit for a Plantation and old men fitter then they, not onely because of their better experience in the world, their gravitie and authoritie, as I said before, but also because they have families, and so children under them, which will helpe to fill the Plantation apace." Eburne, *Plaine Path-Way to Plantations*, 110.

signaled the health of the colonial settlement (and thus of the nation). In other words, as they pondered the relationship between population counts and national interests, they were also producing populations—"making up people"—to whom characteristics and uses could then be attached.[117] These populations included English settlers in the Americas and the children they fathered with indigenous women. They did not include enslaved Africans or the children Englishmen fathered with African women.

Almost a century after Hariot traveled to Virginia, English writers continued to refine arguments in which population, morality, and numeracy reinforced notions of the human hierarchy as implicitly and explicitly raced. On the surface, John Graunt and William Petty, the two writers most strongly associated with the rise of demography as a tool of the nation-state, were concerned primarily (and logically) with sex, as it pertained to population growth. In Graunt's *Natural and Political Observations Mentioned in a Following Index, and Made upon the Bills of Mortality* (1662), he lauded the wealth that accrues to a state "according to the number of their people" but couched his pronatalism in a long chapter on the logics of "encouraging marriage and hindering Licentiousness."[118] His contemporary William Petty approached the relationship between population growth and government from the position of incentive and punishment; he suggested that tax monies should be used to defray the costs of nursing and lying-in for Englishwomen in the colonies and that women over the age of eighteen who failed to bear children should be repeatedly fined.[119]

Petty and Graunt are associated with the rise of demography—what was then termed *political arithmetic*—as a technology of statecraft. As political arithmetic came into full view, its uses appeared to some to be self-evident. Graunt mounted what historians and political scientists agree was the first systematic use of demographic evidence to understand a contemporary sociopolitical problem. As he concluded his examination of the weekly mortality statistics, Graunt allowed that some might still ask what use it was to know the "numbers of people, how many Males and Females, [etc.]"[120] He concluded that to know the numbers was to know specific facts rather

117 Hacking, "Making Up People."
118 Graunt, *Natural and Political Observations*, 64–71, 70. For more on Graunt and Petty, see Buck, "Seventeenth-Century Political Arithmetic," 72.
119 "Concerning Marriages" and "Of Marriage etc.," in Petty, *Petty Papers*, 2:49, 2:50–52. On population schemes in the English colonies, see Cassedy, *Demography in Early America*, 50.
120 Graunt, *Natural and Political Observations*, 96.

than opinions. His work was an exercise in distinguishing the material from the social. As historian Michael Zakim writes, "Once social authority became a function of worldly accords instead of divine rights ... it needed to be anchored in an irrevocable logic, or set of proofs, accessible to natural reason."[121] It is, however, replete with the kind of nonempirical assumptions that are always built into the edifice of objective knowledge. Graunt argued that knowing a region's rate of material consumption would help identify "proper citizens" and that knowing the number of beggars—those without income or the ability to access the market—would enable the king to preserve the peace, as keeping that number low ensured that proper citizens were available to defend the Crown. Graunt argued that the number, marital status, rate of birth, and religious affiliations of the people were the data that transmuted people into citizens or that distinguished citizens from "such as live *ex sponte creates*, and are unfit subjects of Trade."[122]

The language here requires pause. To be "unfit subjects of Trade" grows from living in a state of nature. In Graunt's grammar of citizenship, the ability to trade goods was what made a person a proper subject. Any who might find themselves objects of trade were thus excluded from the universe of citizen-subjects Graunt constructed. The exclusion is incidental, but in the context of an increasingly complex mass of populations, its power should not be overlooked.

The overriding concern of both Petty and Graunt was to establish the idea that England was a source of wealth by virtue of its trade. Graunt began his study by articulating England's power to attract and supply consumers. He saw misinformation about the nation's population as an impediment to the growth of the national economy. Indeed, he wanted to know the parameters of England's population because his goal was "making ... England as considerable for Trade as Holland." In other words, Graunt's desire to increase English trade drove his demographic inquiry.[123] In the process, he naturalized the links among the knowable subject, the working consumer of goods, and the sovereign state. Petty too was committed to an expansive set of interventions in state policy based on reputedly transparent demographic evidence.[124] Petty aimed for a nation made visible and

---

121 Zakim, "Political Geometry of Statistical Tables," 456.
122 Graunt, *Natural and Political Observations*, 99. See also Endres, "Functions of Numerical Data," 250.
123 Graunt, *Natural and Political Observations*, 29.
124 Briggs, "John Graunt, Sir William Petty," 8.

wealthy through demography. Like Graunt, he believed that clarity about demographics would lead to peace. He argued that the "true greatness of a prince lies in the number, art and industry of his people." When Holland, for example, could see the "true greatness" of England, it would refrain from engaging in military hostilities with an obviously superior power.[125]

For Petty, Graunt, and the political theorists with whom they were in conversation, excessive populations that did not consume in the formal market were a threat. Faced with such a population in Ireland, Petty pondered the transportability of the Irish. He was not the first, as both the English and the Spanish monarchs had begun to consider expulsion or forced movement of the Irish and the Moors (respectively) as solutions to the problem of rebelliousness.[126] But for Petty, the solution had more than a simple religious valence. As Mary Poovey has observed, Petty was arguing that transportation would change poor Irish nonconsumers "into economic beings instead of religious, political, or even national subjects."[127] His plan for the forced transportation of the Irish depended on intermarriage between the two populations, which would transform the Irish into English citizens. It hinges, then, on a recognition of kinship and paternity as a vehicle for enhancing the power of the Crown.

This clarity about the potential of the Irish created (without naming) populations that were unable to bolster the state in this particular way and that were therefore increasingly marked as without the protection or value of kin.[128] As historian Ted McCormick has argued, there's an alchemy that adheres to Petty's notion of transmutation.[129] Its proximity to the movability of Africans should be accounted for. Petty converted the Irish from socially or culturally embedded people into something valuable because of their ability to augment the population and labor power of the English. They counted because of what they would bring to the state.

Labor was certainly quantifiable before Petty and Graunt wrote, but as Petty understood, it was defined by a field of meaning that was rooted in the land and community in which it was performed. Feudal relationships situated work as a value conferred by members of a family to landowners, who had obligations to those who worked their land. Feudal laborers were

125 Endres, "Functions of Numerical Data," 253.
126 Barber, "Settlement, Transplantation and Expulsion."
127 Poovey, *History of the Modern Fact*, 136.
128 Buck, "17th Century Political Arithmetic," 69.
129 McCormick, "Alchemy in the Political Arithmetic."

thus attached to the land, and their value was inextricable from the land on which they worked. This was initially a source of confusion for English legislators, who alternately included "Negroes" in lists including "Cattle, Horses, and other moveables" and defined them as real estate rather than chattel.[130] Such legislative indecision suggests that Petty's reimagination of labor rather than laborers as the unit of analysis was not entirely simple. Nonetheless, Petty gave voice to a shift in practices of quantification that had profound implications for those ensnared by its new terms.

Only occasionally did Petty explicitly refer to slaves and slavery, even though he was thinking through problems of population and mobility at precisely the moment when England had solidified its commitment to the slave trade.[131] In his unpublished work, he wrote that the shape of Africans' skulls accounted for differences in "their Natural Manners and in the internall Qualities of their minds."[132] In published work, he noted that an English laborer's value could be as high as £80, while that of an Irish laborer was only £15, "as slaves and Negroes are usually rated."[133] Irish laborers who transformed into Englishmen would thus increase the value of their labor to the nation fivefold. He wrote with confidence that his readers would understand "slaves and Negroes" as naturally occupying a degraded place.

At the time, of course, the value of enslaved laborers and the goods they were producing for the English market was rising sharply, but two fields of value were operating at the same time here: the market value of wages paid and the value of labor as currency. The gap between them operated like negative space, defining the purportedly natural higher value of English laborers. Petty used economic certainty to mask nascent ethnic and racial ideology. The distance between the Irish and "slaves and Negroes" was made tangible in Petty's notion of transport and the Irish's transformation into Englishmen. Racial ideology became an argument for the mutability of the Irish or the fantasy of the tractability of Africans. As became clear in the example the Spaniards set and English slave traders took up,

130 "An Act Establishing the Courts of Common Pleas . . ." (1661), 27–33, esp. 28, and "A Declarative Act upon the Act Making Negroes Real Estate" (1672), 93–94, in R. Hall, *Acts, Passed in the Island of Barbados*.

131 Scholars have, for the most part, failed to consider that contextual reality, focusing instead on intellectual and political trends in Europe as though they (and he) were hermetically sealed from Africa or the wider Atlantic world.

132 Chaplin, "Problem of Genius," 14.

133 Petty, *Political Anatomy of Ireland*, 1:152.

a population valued solely for its labor is a population that can easily be extracted from particular geographies and located elsewhere to benefit the state.[134] In the case of the transatlantic slave trade, Petty, Graunt, and myriad other political arithmeticians had also seen the corollary: that the well-being of one population could be mobilized to justify the shocking appropriation of another.

Racing Populations

How did the ideas that transformed African people into commodities connect to transformations in how Europeans thought of themselves? In his discussion of how different types of people come into being, Ian Hacking writes of the mania in the nineteenth century for "making up" people, a time when the labeling of human types "may have engendered vastly more kinds of people than the world had ever known."[135] While this may well be correct, the mania for constituting people into distinct groups that would determine their social and economic standing began in the sixteenth and seventeenth centuries. It emerged in the context of considerable anxiety on the part of political and economic writers about how people and the things they bought and sold would be harnessed for the good of the nation. The population growth that took place in England in the sixteenth century gave way to a continent-wide stagnation and drops in prices and production in the seventeenth century.[136] Whether this was a full-on economic crisis is a matter of some debate, but crisis or not, Jacobean economic policy in England marked a crucial moment in the development of English Atlantic markets that was driven by a strong sense of crisis among the elite with regard to both population and wealth.

What emerged was a foundational commitment to the pursuit of imperial expansion rooted in a colonial commodities market that depended on slave labor.[137] Embracing this plan for economic stability relied on many

134 Sussman, "Colonial Afterlife of Political Arithmetic," 117. According to Poovey, the logical connection between the desirability of relocating populations to new territories outside the nation and the idea of populational abstraction is crucial because abstractions "tend to emphasize the well-being of an aggregate rather than of individuals." Poovey, *History of the Modern Fact*, 137.
135 Hacking, "Making Up People," 226.
136 De Vries, "Economic Crisis."
137 For an introduction to the impact new consumer goods produced in the colonies, see Zahedieh, "Making Mercantilism Work." For an argument about the relative value of

political, material, and ideological convergences: a monarchy open to new kinds of growth, a portion of the population willing to resettle, shipbuilding technology that put West Africa and the American continent within reach, and an ideological shift in how people and things acquired facticity in the service of secular governance.[138]

That final ideological shift is exemplified by a new understanding of the marketplace "as a mechanism, not of discrimination or exploitation, but rather of social and economic inclusion."[139] To be English was to produce and acquire goods, whose exchange in the marketplace ultimately enhanced the state. But this notion of social and economic inclusion relied on a notion of a cohesive population, a concept of "us." It required a clearly articulated sense of the social unit whose inclusive logic functioned by marking the boundaries of the categories of humans and markets or, indeed, markets in humans who were excluded.

As the growth of overseas trade began to shape seventeenth-century European commerce, the vast majority of imports to European ports were commodities produced by forced labor.[140] Indeed, among English essayists, sugar, like other new foodstuffs, posed a problem that was inseparable from those who produced it: "What agreement or affinity is there between our *Fruits, Grains, Herbs*, and *Seeds*, and those that come from the East and West Indies? Not so much as that between the complexion of a Fat-nosed Lubber-lip'd Blackamore, or Swarthy Bantanman, with a head like a sugar loaf, and our most *Florid Beauties*."[141] In England, as sugar and tobacco became ubiquitous and inexpensive commodities, the abstraction required to ignore or accommodate their origins also became widespread. Sugar and other New World imports were not neutral items in an ever-widening marketplace that functioned in service of the nation. Because these goods were perhaps too intimately associated with the abject bodies who were forced to produce them, they and the bodies they brought to mind posed problems of corporeal identity that were difficult to settle. Race and racial hierarchy would play an essential role in

---

goods produced by indentured servants versus slave labor, see Menard, *Sweet Negotiations*, 29–48.

138 This is, of course, the intervention that Poovey makes in *A History of the Modern Fact*.
139 Briggs, "John Graunt, Sir William Petty," 20.
140 Zahedieh, "Overseas Expansion and Trade," table 18.7, 410.
141 Tryon, *Good Housewife*, quoted in K. Hall, "Extravagant Viciousness," 98. For discussion on changes in food consumption, see Shammas, *Pre-industrial Consumer*, 119–56.

resolving those problems by separating those who produced from those who consumed.

Much of the copious scholarship devoted to the problem newly encountered populations posed for the English has been devoted to clarifying the emergence of race as an ideological stance that responded to the problem of slavery. I am suggesting that the two phenomena cannot be untangled: that slavery as an economic practice and race as an ideological conviction emerged simultaneously in a field of meaning that propelled early modern capitalism in ways that were crucial and brutal. Charting the development of conceptual vocabularies that sought to place Native and African populations locates the articulation of race and racial difference in discussions of numeracy and logic rather than in expressions of "irrational" or "unthinking" prejudice. Overlooking the connection between race and rationality in these foundational moments ill equips us to comprehend its powerful sway over those who made that connection to justify profoundly damaging violence.

As certain people were defined in relative proximity to the English, others were pushed farther and farther away. A key element of this realm of political economy and nascent demographic science is that the work of differentiation was so often accomplished through the bodies of women. Thus, at the same time that the Virginia House of Burgesses declared that children born to Englishmen and African women would follow the condition of their mothers, becoming slaves, Petty advised English planters to "buy Indian girls of under 7 yeares old and use them as wives."[142] At the beginning of the eighteenth century, Robert Beverly criticized earlier English settlers for refusing to intermarry with Native American women. He wrote that "had they embraced this Proposal . . . the Colony, instead of all these Losses of Men on both sides, would have been encreasing in Children to its Advantage. . . . The Country would have been full of People."[143] Beverly laid the responsibility for the lack of population squarely on the shoulders of unwilling Englishmen. Writing almost two decades later, Virginia slave owner and tobacco planter William Byrd answered what appeared to him to be a logical question: "How populous would the country have been and consequently, how considerable [had only white men married Native women]? Nor could the shade of skin have been any reproach at this day, for if a Moor may be washt white in three Generations, Surely an Indian might

142 Petty, *Petty Papers*, 2:49–53, quoted in Cassedy, *Demography in Early America*, 50.
143 Beverly, *History and Present State of Virginia*, quoted in Cassedy, *Demography in Early America*, 87.

have been blancht in two."[144] Native American women's bodies became the conduit for conquest, the imagined site of easy and fluid cultural transformations. While the differences in how Native Americans and Africans came to be depicted by European settlers are crucial, those differences were routed through women's bodies in similar ways.

While the theoretical Moor could be whitened, at no point did colonial settlers seriously consider African populations to be assimilable in the ways they assumed the Irish or Native Americans were. There is a singular absence of any speculative ruminations about African women as wives for Englishmen in the Americas although they inhabited English colonial settlements in significant numbers. As historian Carol Shammas has argued for colonial Virginia, and Russell Menard for colonial Barbados, the transformation of labor regimes in the Americas from a reliance on indentured servants to a reliance on enslaved African laborers replaced male servants with male and female slaves.[145] The African women the English (and other colonial settlers) enslaved were completely vulnerable to sexual exploitation, and white men saw them as always available sexual outlets. But white people never understood them to be potential peoplers of English settlements. While some Englishmen were willing to speculate about population growth through sex across one color line, none were interested in characterizing African women as useful in this endeavor.[146] This distinction between Africans and other populations should be understood as emerging from a range of rationalist projects of the early modern Enlightenment that included the particular use of demographics to define Black women as both enslavable and able to physically transmit enslavability.

During the seventeenth century, more so than at any other time in the history of the slave trade, relatively balanced sex ratios predominated in most of the English colonies. The presence of enslaved women in the New

144 W. Byrd, *History of the Dividing Line*, quoted in Cassedy, *Demography in Early America*, 88.

145 Shammas, "Black Women's Work"; and Menard, *Sweet Negotiations*, 47. This is not to suggest that there were no colonial situations in which Europeans strategically married African women. As Pernille Ipsen has most recently illustrated, the marriages between Europeans and African women on the West African coast were crucial to the trading alliances that formed there in the seventeenth and eighteenth centuries. Ipsen, *Daughters of the Trade*, 20–53.

146 See Spear, "Colonial Intimacies," on sex as a tool of colonial settlement. Peter Bardaglio charts the "depth of feeling against racial intermixture" in his study of colonial statute law. It should be emphasized what is prohibited here is Black/white Englishness, not Native American/white Englishness. Bardaglio, "'Shamefull Matches.'"

World, on plantations and in ports, certainly could have suggested a political arithmetic for the Americas that included African women in the peopling of the monarchy. In the eighteenth century, Spanish slave-owning settlements did, in fact, offer a place for Black women and Spanish men to form families and for their children to move from slavery to freedom. The Spanish tradition of racial classification, which was displayed in massive *casta* (mixed-race) paintings (see figure 2.4), is one of many things that distinguished Spanish and English patterns of slave ownership. But even there the urge to classify should be read as indicating that mixed-race children could only incrementally acquire Spanishness.[147]

English theorists and settlers harnessed African women's reproductive capacity to the growth of the population even as they increasingly linked the notion of population to white Europeans. They described enslaved men and women in terms that used the language of commerce, the market, and cargo. Describing Black women as "breeders" of slave property put them outside the boundaries of the women who could contribute to legitimate—white—population growth. That population was of course also rooted in kinship.

Embedded in the rationalist turn toward discourse about demographics and population was a degree of dehumanizing violence—even for white women—that sat uncomfortably alongside the assurances that national strength would be augmented through population growth and colonial settlement. Both Petty and Graunt referred at various times to Englishwomen as "breeders."[148] The breeding woman became fodder for Jonathan Swift's outrageous 1729 proposal that in the context of overpopulation and poverty, "a young healthy child well nursed is at a year old a most delicious, nourishing and wholesome food, whether stewed, roasted, baked or boiled, and . . . will equally serve in a fricassee or a ragout."[149] Swift mobilized cannibalism

---

147 Early settlers persistently assured themselves and those at home that they would remain untouched by American savagery—that they and their descendants would retain their identity as Englishmen, despite being born across the Atlantic. The initial English reluctance to engage in sexual alliances with Native Americans is located in this concern rather than in a vaguely articulated notion of bodily difference. Ultimately, that reluctance gave way to an increasing confidence in English resilience in the face of savagery and to a willingness to engage in cross-cultural sex for a range of reasons, including domination, diplomacy, and population growth.

148 Briggs, "John Graunt, Sir William Petty," 9.

149 Swift, *Modest Proposal and Other Satires*, 259. In a discussion of Swift's connection to these earlier theorists, Peter Briggs argues that Swift was attuned to the "deliberate nar-

FIGURE 2.4 Ignacio Maria Barreda y Ordoñez., *casta* painting, 1777. Real Academia Española de la Lengua, Madrid. Reproduced on Dana Leibsohn and Barbara E. Mundy, *Vistas: Visual Culture in Spanish America, 1520–1820*, 2015. https://vistasgallery.ace.fordham.edu/items/show/1659.

here in order to drive home a crucial point: political arithmetic might well be the Englishman's discursive savagery.

English readers of the early eighteenth century were quite familiar with the trope of the savage cannibal, so seeing it mobilized here to indict themselves would have been quite a shock. By the beginning of the eighteenth century, Swift felt compelled to take on the implications of abstract ideas about population. He built on the writing of Graunt, who, for example,

---

rowing of social vision and human sympathies that might allow a thinker to pursue a train of ideas into absurdity without quite noticing." Briggs, "John Graunt, Sir William Petty," 11.

rationalized high mortality rates among men with the explanation that their deaths from disease and accidents spared society from the horrors of male competition over insufficient numbers of women. Swift understood that Graunt's rationalizing converted violence that had previously been unspeakable into palatable speculative planning. But even in Swift's masterful hand, the potential violence embedded in demographic data is made only partially visible. Such violence is perhaps best encapsulated not by Swift's "absurd" offering of a baby "fricassee or ragout" but rather in the inability of both contemporaries and modern scholars to see that, by 1729, such an offering was, in fact, already on the menu in the tens of thousands of bodies that had already been transmuted into sugar to satisfy European appetites.

In many ways, the roots of Swift's parody can be found much earlier, in colonial record books and demographic reports to the Crown. At first glance, it might seem that Englishmen who could not contemplate Black women as producers of Englishness had reached the logical limits of their political arithmetic. Surely the act that determined that the status of children born to enslaved women would follow that of their mother in colonial Virginia suggests the failure of numerical thinking. If producing Englishness in the settlement context was of paramount importance to colonial successes, then intermarriage with African women would have made sense. However, the logic of political arithmetic was not simply about producing census data; it also produced categories of people in both thinkable and unthinkable relationships to one another.[150] Women of African descent could certainly be used for sex and for offspring, but the children of such unions had a decidedly different place on the household ledger than a legitimate son or daughter. As early as the mid-seventeenth century, demographic rationality had produced the clear distinction between those who counted and those who were *only* always counted.

There was a significant conceptual gap between the population schemes of the English that involved the Irish or the "natives," both of whom were transformable into whiteness, and those that involved Africans, who could only be commodities. The process by which Africans and their descendants in the Americas were indelibly marked as excluded from the body politic is clarified by discerning the connections between racial thinking and numeracy. Europeans and their descendants came to be inextricably associated with liberties precisely at the moment when unfreedom and

150 Trouillot, *Silencing the Past*, 73.

slavery were not just on the rise but were absolutely crucial to Europeans' attaining the economic power that bolstered political freedom.

The writings of Petty and Graunt point us toward a key set of ideological shifts in which demography and the rational figurations that accompanied it—used in a range of conversations about trade, population, and the greater good—enabled a process that naturalized the outlines of sovereign subjects. The identity of the Irish became sublimated to the collective well-being of the English state, and that sublimation was amplified with horrifying clarity for Africans and their descendants as they were pulled into the Atlantic marketplace. By the time of the Glorious Revolution in 1688, elite Englishmen understood that political arithmetic could be invasive: to be subjected to enumeration was to risk being marked as outside the category of legitimate subjects. Well before the end of the seventeenth century, Englishmen who were called to testify in court refused to comply with the routine demand that they enumerate their worth. They often couched their refusal in claims that they were "gentlemen" and that their word should be taken as already trustworthy, but they did so in numbers that far outstripped the proportion of gentry in the population.[151]

The notion that status should shield one from being subjected to valuation gained currency at the moment when being identified as a subset of the population through enumeration became tinged with racial hierarchy. Property-owning Englishmen insisted that only the poor, the conscripted, the emigrants, and the Irish were legitimate objects of governmental queries about the size and composition of a population.[152] They were rightly concerned that the encroachment of the Crown into matters they understood as private and familial threatened to transmute them in much the same way as the Irish had been transmuted. The potential danger of being reduced to matters of exchange was already a topic for alarm in the seventeenth century—the very period when England fully staked its claim as a slave-trading, colonizing power.

Thus, the English rationalized their elimination of African women's progeny from the population by instituting an overriding understanding of them as products. We understand this, and yet we need more clarity about the repositioning of a white man's offspring from kin to inventory. Something far more than abstraction was at play for enslaved women on the

151 Shepard, *Accounting for Oneself*, 67.
152 See Sussman, "Colonial Afterlife of Political Arithmetic," for an elaboration of this argument.

English colonial frontier. As they were systematically being assigned value as commodities, their capacity to situate their children as kin was being stripped away. The presence of women like Elizabeth Keye in the courts testifies to their prescience, their understanding that enslavement, race, heredity, and kinship were amalgamating in ways that boded very badly for them and for their children. The enactment of such thinking undergirded the relationship between hereditary racial slavery and Atlantic modernity.

The story of the early modern slave trade and the story of racial formation in the Atlantic world cannot be understood as a simple journey from "savage to slave to black."[153] Such a framing divorces the making of Blackness from the world in which numeracy, the credit economy, and demographics were interwoven. Africans were not immediately rendered savage, moved to the category of enslavable, and finally marked as racially distanced and indeed condemned. While historians of the Iberian Atlantic have done much to disrupt this narrative arc by clarifying the mutual recognition of sovereignty that characterized much of the first decades of contact, the intellectual and discursive tools that white Englishmen used to move Africans from sovereign to savage, and the relationship between those tools and the slave/race slots that followed, remain opaque.[154]

Economic historian Carl Wennerlind concluded his study of seventeenth-century credit with a focus on the willingness of English finance ministers, investors, and propagandists to simply ignore the human dimensions of the slave trade. Backers of the South Sea Company relied on "the public favorably imagining the prospects of the Atlantic Slave trade."[155] For the company's shareholders, mobilizing that imagination was crucial in the context of the expanded role of an "investing public." Moreover, even though the company ultimately failed, during its first years public confidence in the slave trade as a means of addressing the nation's financial crisis was strong enough to repeatedly inflate the share prices of the company. The widespread ability to ignore the mortality of slaves and the possibility of slave rebellion or revolt aboard ships strikes Wennerlind as a core component of what he terms *credit fetishism*—the power of "credit's general capacity to obfuscate its underlying social reality."[156] How, then, had the connection among Africans, currency, and colonial extrac-

153 For a critical overview of this gesture, see Baker, *From Savage to Negro*, 5–13.
154 Green, *Rise of the Trans-Atlantic* ; and Bennett, *African Kings and Black Slaves*.
155 Wennerlind, *Casualties of Credit*, 197.
156 Wennerlind, *Casualties of Credit*, 199.

tion predated the South Sea Company and enabled the ideological underpinnings of the venture to begin with? By the end of the seventeenth century the link between the promise of Atlantic wealth and the economic health of the nation was seamlessly made through the silenced bodies of African men, women, and children. I would argue that the fetish of credit was joined to another equally phantasmagorical manner of thinking. The degree to which racialist logics were mobilized to transform violence into the rationality of financial instruments and the fiscal health of kingdoms in Europe suggests that race and capitalism were caught in circuits of reinscribing logics from the onset. Indeed, the degree to which hereditary racial slavery authorized conceptual notions of what was marketable and how colonial markets should or could rationally function remains a provocation in the history of the Atlantic world.

THREE. "To Their Great Commoditie":
Numeracy and the Production of African Difference

As Europeans tried to control new relationships of exchange in the six-teenth and seventeenth centuries, they produced accounts of Africa full of ellipses and omissions. Driven by the need to identify sources of extractive wealth, these writers constructed representations of Africans that reflected their own location in the profoundly changing epoch that the voyages of Christopher Columbus had inaugurated.[1] African men and women and the societies they lived in emerge in these documents as boundary markers for Western rationalism rather than as ethnographically located subjects. These logical gaps have been read as evidence of the origins of race think-ing, and, of course, in many ways they are precisely that. But these accounts also hint at the way emerging notions of rational objectivity were crucial to the erasures and violations at the heart of these texts.

Numeracy played a central role in the production of a record of slav-ery from which all manner of things were omitted. As race congealed as a technology, disavowing evidence of numerical rationality among Africans became increasingly important to Europeans. Attending to the shifting valence of numbers and the commercial language of trade helps establish

1 See Sylvia Wynter's crucial discussion of *Propter Nos*—the idea that the world was made for "us" and the clarification of who is excluded from "us"—and the images that serve as the boundary markers for Western rationalism in the aftermath of Columbus's reconceptualization of the globe and of Christianity. Wynter, "1492," 20–28.

the epistemic context in which captive women and men were configured and abstracted as commodities, the objects of the Atlantic slave trade. At the same time, the language of European travelers, traders, and investors does contain traces of the women who are my primary concern. As travelers described women as sexual favors, as sellers of goods, and as chaotic and unaffected parents, we catch a glimpse of some of the ways African systems of value may have crossed the Atlantic with them. The echoes of the African past that scholars have found in African-descendant women's participation in formal markets in the Caribbean and the American South are one manifestation of this phenomenon. There are others, but they too are buried beneath the edifice of the European need to situate the continent as a place of irrational thought. Women's sexual and reproductive disorder became wedded to the idea of populational excesses that suggested a never-depletable population for Europeans willing to stem chaotic fecundity with the orderly rigor of hard labor.

In the early modern Atlantic, ideologies of race came into being alongside newly consolidating ideas about wealth, nationhood, and population. The origins of these concepts are mutually embedded. As we work to peel back the origin stories of the Atlantic world, it becomes clear that the web of ideas out of which "Europe" and "Africa" emerge was mutually produced.[2] Universalizing concepts of reason were congealing in the period when Iberians and other Europeans were setting their sights on West Africa and the Americas with an eye toward trade and conquest. They constructed a rationale to legitimate their access to both continents that was rooted both in religion and in claims that they alone had access to reason. As the English considered their role in the Atlantic, the stability of their own economy, their need to calculate populations, and their belief that wealth could legitimately be obtained through enslaving others, they also consolidated nascent ideas about racial difference and racial hierarchy.

The language used in travel accounts—both those written and those read by Englishmen—to describe the continent and its people deployed a range of strategies to assign newly encountered lands and people to an

---

2 As the literary scholar Lisa Lowe has argued for the history of liberalism that emerged in the wake of the early modern, "the uses of universalizing concepts of reason, civilization, and freedom effect colonial divisions of humanity, affirming liberty for modern man while subordinating the variously colonized and dispossessed peoples whose material labor and resources were the conditions of possibility for that liberty." Lowe, *Intimacies of Four Continents,* 6.

order that made sense to the writer. The primary purpose of these accounts was often to situate the lands of the continent within a newly honed sense of geography. But in doing so, they offered commentary on economies and sex that would become embroiled in emergent ideas of race and racial hierarchy. As stories of Europeans' political, military, and economic encounters with Africans on the West African coast were crafted and circulated, Europeans drew on numeracy and its habits of thought to position Africa in a field of value.

As we have seen, new ideas about quantification, population, value, currency, and credit became crucial elements of the transition that made it possible for Europeans to regard Africans as commodities. But the significance of numeracy is not limited to the strategies Europeans used to make sense of trade or markets. While Africa and Africans had long occupied a place in European thought and indeed in Europe, their place and that of commerce began to shift in the sixteenth century. Europeans began to locate the African continent and its people in a rapidly expanding web of ideas about the globe, religion, mastery, and colonial settlement.

Accounts of travel to sub-Saharan African circulated widely among English readers in the sixteenth century. They found their way into lyric poetry, plays, novels, and other forms of popular culture. They were widely translated into a range of European languages. Texts written elsewhere reverberated for English readers and merchants intent on situating England as a force to be reckoned with on the global stage.[3] By the end of the sixteenth century, curious English readers had encountered increasingly detailed, though often chimeric, glimpses of the African continent. Long-told tales of the golden cities of the mythical Christian ruler Prester John circulated in tandem with eyewitness accounts of Senegambia, Guinea, Congo, and the Cape of Good Hope written primarily by Flemish or Italian travelers associated with Iberian households. The language Europeans used to describe Africa and Africans marshaled a range of descriptive tropes related to concepts of monstrosity and chaos. But the linkages European writers made between numeracy and rationality were key aspects of new notions of hierarchy that soon became part of the concept of race and racial difference.

As we have already seen, geographic accounts of "the worlde" ascribed uneven importance to the African continent. European writers described

---

3 For discussions of how Englishness emerges in contradistinction to foreign "others," see K. Hall, *Things of Darkness*; Spiller, *Reading and the History of Race*; and Hadfield, "Benefits of a Warm Study."

Africa as vast and abundant but included just a few pages on the continent in volumes that devoted reams to Europe, Asia, and the Americas. Those pages constituted the narrative of Europeans' gradual refusal to accord African states sovereignty and a desire to situate Africa only as a source of wealth and resources for burgeoning European empires. The few descriptions of people in Africa almost always situated them along a continuum that began with sophisticated and savvy traders and ended with barbaric savages who had no ability to count. These accounts offer a window onto the process by which Europeans narratively rendered sovereign peoples enslavable. They also suggest possible interpretations of how African women and men understood the terms of their capture and enslavement.

In the next chapter, I will more fully consider the experience of the Middle Passage, but here, as I linger in representations of the African past, I want to explore the chimeric place of Africa in the Black Atlantic. Despite the careful work of African historians and the efforts of scholars of the Black Atlantic to fully consider African history, when our scholarly attentions begin with the ship—either as a metaphor or as a material reality—we fail to situate captives as full and complex historical actors. The Middle Passage has been primarily understood, and rightly so, as a moment of "catastrophic rupture."[4] Efforts to narrate a social history of the African past can flounder in the wake of the ship because we are at a loss for evidence and at a loss for words. In lieu of an archive of disaster, the transatlantic passage becomes the starting point for the African diaspora, a talisman for the violent dislocation that inaugurates Black Atlantic cultures, and the African past becomes vestibular. In the hands of artists, filmmakers, and writers, even the slave forts of Elmina in Ghana and Senegal's Goree Island are transformed "from originary sites of the slave trade to an ancestral memorial to which only African diasporic blacks have 'the right of return.'"[5]

To be captive on the Middle Passage is to be unmoored, oceanic, and thus without identity. Literary scholar Hortense Spillers writes of captives who were moving across the Atlantic but were "also *nowhere* at all."[6] They embodied the antithesis of place, which signaled their commodification. Historian Stephanie Smallwood explores commodification as a critical process rooted in the disorientation of the endless Atlantic horizon.[7] Tracing

---

4 Gilroy, *Black Atlantic*, 4, 197.
5 Tillet, *Sites of Slavery*, 118.
6 Spillers, "Mama's Baby, Papa's Maybe," 72.
7 Smallwood, *Saltwater Slavery*, 124–25.

the experiential links between lives lived before and after capture has been the challenge taken up by scholars of the diaspora—most fruitfully, though not exclusively, by historians working on the eighteenth century.[8] Still, Africa gets positioned primarily as that which was lost and thus, unintentionally, that which remains unchanged. As histories of slavery are approached from the perspective of the Americas, questions are organized around how to make sense of that which follows. How do we account for all that was lost among those involuntary migrants, and how do we honor what they were able to maintain?

Because the scholarship on enslavement is concerned with disaggregating the overwhelming structure that is the slave trade, work on the experiential dimensions of enslavement often circles around phenomena that are the antithesis of trade: culture, religion, or family. Thus, there are studies of creolization and African retention, Santeria and Candomblé, and naming patterns and fictive kin. These aspects of cultural formation are rarely connected to histories of African economies, nor are the histories of trade (both in goods and in people) seen as connected to the cultural life of numbers and value. As is the case across the disciplines, the field of knowledge out of which African history emerged—one dependent on the very narrative structures meant to define Africans as enslavable—was itself embedded in the Enlightenment categories of humans that structure the subdisciplines of human history. What of the impact of the cultural aspects of trade, markets, commodification, and currency on Africans who endured the Middle Passage and arrived in the Atlantic world—both materially and in the ways they, and we, craft the stories that become their pasts?

In order to rationalize and represent what would become a massive trade in humans, European slave traders mobilized a series of ideas to clarify the structures of transatlantic slavery—the reduction of human beings to articles of trade—and to accommodate vicious actions. Some of these are visible as outrages of racism and inhumanity, but many remain buried in the records of capitalist numeracy: logbooks, receipts, account ledgers, tables of valuation that include human beings, tables of the loss of life aboard slave ships, and accounts of the monetary loss slaveholders incurred when men, women, and children died on plantations. Such archival traces can produce only so much that will help us retrieve the lived experiences of

8 For examples of this kind of work, see A. Byrd, *Captives and Voyagers*; V. Brown, *Reaper's Garden*; Smallwood, *Saltwater Slavery*; Sweet, *Domingos Álvares*; Mustakeem, *Slavery at Sea*; and Bennett, *African Kings and Black Slaves*.

African women caught in the seventeenth-century slave trade. These records do speak to transactions and events that alter both the ledger and the economic histories of the slave trade. The extent to which the records of the slave trade depend on the erasure of African people as historical subjects is obscured, as are the experiences that attend the process of reducing human beings to objects of commerce. The ship captain's ledger is no place for sentiment; such moments of discernment are the antithesis of the rational economy.

As the slave trade unfolded, the interplay between commodification and racial hierarchy produced an archive from which African women rarely emerged. Efforts to understand their lives often end with a lacuna. The drive to comprehend the particular experiences of women and girls is foiled by data and sources that place women outside the frame of inquiry. Economic histories of trade, value, and commodity exchange examine worlds that appear to be neither inhabited nor influenced by women and girls. And yet they are there in bills of sale, in the complaints of ship captains who were thwarted from satisfying sexual urges, and in the accounts of merchants who haggled over the value of suckling children.

A focus on these kinds of records reveals more than the presence of women in the early modern slave trade; it also reveals their role in a taxonomy of value linked to the emergence of race as a tool of hierarchy and capital accumulation. Well before their capture and transport to the Americas, women and girls who lived on the West African coast were exposed to concepts of value and exchange that rendered comprehensible the violences to which they were increasingly vulnerable. They participated in extensive long-distance markets, they attempted to elude capture and sale by warring polities, and they experienced being offered to visiting traders or diplomats as sexual objects. These experiences were of interest to European observers only insofar as they could be recast as part of the extensive rationale mounted to produce the continent as a marketplace for their own ambitions.

Amoral Economies

As enslavement shifted from the consequence of war to a commercial practice dependent on peacetime trading relationships, European writers found themselves engaged in a complicated dialectical process that required them to both articulate and neutralize the practice of buying and selling human beings. Much of the travel literature from the start of the sixteenth to the beginning of the seventeenth century seems to have been engaged in smoothing away the contradictions involved in the trade in human cargo by leveling accusations that Africans were innately unable to engage in the numeracy that trade required.

When the English traveler Richard Jobson refused the offer of female slaves on the African coast in 1620 by claiming that the English "were a people who did not deale in any such commodity," he constructed a myth.[9] By 1620 English settlers in the Americas had begun to buy and sell Africans and had identified many ways they could use African women's bodies. Jobson's claim was rooted firmly in an effort to use the bodies of Africans to establish that Protestant England was distinct from Catholic Spain.[10] Jobson did so alongside other English writers and traders who came to understand commerce—both that which engaged in and that which rejected slavery—as a site of rational acts that marked a break from old religions. Of course, the fact that the purported rationality of commerce was grafted onto the quagmire of the trade in human beings is itself evidence of the irrationality and violence that were at the core of the birth of the Enlightenment's universal subject.

By the middle of the seventeenth century, if not before, the relationship between the enslavement of human beings and rational trade was so solidified that entries in the ledger that account for England's payments to compensate the colony of Jamaica for its service related to Oliver Cromwell's Western Design could be rendered in human bodies: "One hundred Eighty two Negroes and twenty two pounds sterl . . . which will pay the Commission Officers twenty two weeks and one day. . . . One hundred and Seven Negroes and eight pounds sterl . . . which will pay officers and Soldiers about twenty nine days pay."[11] But well before this articulation of bodies and debt, Iberian and northern European traders and travelers alike had to render the messiness of corporeality into figures that could be neatly confined within the accountant's ledger. They had to forge and

9 Jobson, *Discovery of River Gambra*, 89/90 [140].
10 Slavery and despotism were, in the hands of the English, a way to distinguish themselves from the Spaniards. They often did so through accusations of impurity as well. Edward Daunce reminded English readers that "the *Mores* in eight monthes conquered *Spaine* . . . and . . . the Spaniards were eight hundred years before they recovered that losse: during which time, we must not think that the Negroes sent for women out of *Aphrick*." Daunce, *Brief Discourse*, 31, quoted in Griffin, "From Ethos to Ethnos," 101.
11 "Invoice of Good Sent by His Majestie," Brathwayte Papers, mssBL 1–461, box 1, 1660, Huntington Library, San Marino, California.

solidify an equivalency. The role of women in those ledgers is more than just an afterthought.

The extent of any available commodity had to be firmly articulated and established before it entered a balance sheet. It would not have made sense to begin to think of Africans as a commodity to be circulated widely without clarifying that there was a significant supply to be tapped—a supply based on which a price could be set and an equivalent value tabulated. Alvise da Cadamosto's 1455 account of his voyages to Senegambia is among the earliest of a genre that took pains to establish the possibilities of exchange both with and of Africans.[12]

Establishing the continent as a site of excessive natural resources sometimes happened through a sleight of hand that both centered women and their bodies and defined them categorically as oddities. When Cadamosto discussed the "Land of the Blacks" in his early chapters on the Canary Islands, he opened the chapter this way: "That woman who has the largest breasts is considered more beautiful than the others: with the result that each woman, to increase their size . . . binds around the breasts."[13] For Cadamosto, the excesses of the continent apparently began with women's breasts. This was part of his discussion of a community that he marked as "brown men," whom he saw as intermediaries between Arabs and Blacks.

His text moved on to state that Africans believed that Portuguese ships were phantoms because they didn't understand the "art of navigation"— ignoring the fact that the salt and gold trade brought commodities to markets across hundreds of miles of desert terrain. He concluded his discussion of the salt trade with a description of an irrational and anonymous exchange of salt for gold in which a "race of blacks who do not wish to be seen or to speak" leave gold opposite piles of salt that those who have carried

12 The Venetian trader Cadamosto sailed to Senegambia in 1455. (He styled himself Ca do Mosto, the name of the Venetian palace where he was born, but twentieth-century editions of his work and references to the man use the modern spelling, Cadamosto.) His narrative was published in Italian in 1507, then translated into Latin, German, and French before 1515. It was widely circulated, though not included in the monumental travel narratives presented by Richard Hakluyt in *Principall Navigations* (1589) or Samuel Purchas's continuation of Hakluyt's work in his four-volume *Purchas His Pilgrimes* (1613). Cadamosto's attention to the possibility of exchanges between Africa and Europe was in line with the earliest ethnographic accounts by European travelers to Asia, who were primarily concerned with economy and markets and less interested in cataloging human difference. See Hodgen, *Early Anthropology*, 78–104.

13 Cadamosto, *Voyages of Cadamosto*, 19.

the salt to the coast accept or reject. "They carry on their trade without seeing or speaking to each other," he wrote, and his description of this exchange is framed by the assumption that Africans were incapable of fully comprehending matters of commerce.[14]

As his narrative unfolded, he described flora, fauna, and geography, and he referred to the slaves he was trading for along the way. His observations regarding the Jalof people farther up the Gambia River focused on the number of wives allotted to rulers and the request of the king, who, "having been given to understand that Christians knew how to do many things, [asked] whether by chance I could give him the means by which he could satisfy many women, for which he offered me a great reward." Cadamosto immediately amplified this account of sexual excess with a claim that the king's jealousy was such that he did not allow even his own sons to enter the quarters of his wives.[15] Finally, he described the ritual gestures of humility that vassals had to show when they approached the king: "All this appears to me to proceed from the great fear and dread in which these people hold their lord, since for the most trivial misdeed he seizes and sells their wives and children. Thus it appears to me that his power exacts obedience and fear from the people by selling their wives and children."[16] His narrative marked the Jalof people as barbarous because of the "wives and children" a king sold as slaves. His account of the Barbacenes and the Sere who lived along the coast of the bay emphasized that "they will not recognize any lord among them, lest he should carry off their wives and children and sell them into slavery, as is done by the kings and lords of all the other lands of the negroes. They are exceedingly idolatrous, have no laws, and are the cruelest of men."[17]

Although Cadamosto's efforts to trade along the Gambia River were thwarted by locals, he returned in 1456 to try again.[18] He wrote that although the people at the port of Mansa, in present-day Gambia, along the river traded "articles of little value in our eyes" for "negro slaves and a certain quantity of gold," the quantity of trade was very small. He concluded that those who approached his ship by canoe "do not commonly venture

14 Cadamosto, *Voyages of Cadamosto*, 23.
15 Cadamosto, *Voyages of Cadamosto*, 38.
16 Cadamosto, *Voyages of Cadamosto*, 40. Herman Bennett examines Iberian attention to the rituals of humility as a marker of political diplomacy. Here I am interested how Cadamosto engages in a symbolic act of erasing that political exchange, using the bodies of women and children to do so. Bennett, *African Kings and Black Slaves*, 110–21.
17 Cadamosto, *Voyages of Cadamosto*, 54.
18 On his return trip, he claimed the Cape Verde Islands for Spain.

far outside their own country, for they are not safe from one district to the next from being taken by the Blacks and sold into slavery."[19] That Cadamosto's ambition to establish trade relations was thwarted by Africans' concerns about capture is a theme that runs through the text. He presents his own desire to procure slaves as seemingly unconnected to his sympathetic understanding of their vulnerability. By the final pages of his narrative, the fundamental truth his text has conveyed about Africa is that the people treat European ships and men with caution or awe and that it is widely inhabited, full of people whose enslavability was marked by the vulnerability of women and children.

Drawing on medieval literatures, other writers circulated claims that best characterized the population of the continent as a swarm. In *The Fardle of Facions* (first published in 1520 and translated from French into English in 1555), Johann Boemus inaugurated the genre of ethnological description of customs.[20] Boemus argued that the descendants of Ham spilled out of Arabia in swarms that proved the extent of the "greate mischief [of] the untimely banishmente of one manne."[21] He characterized North Africa as "well enhabited" in contrast to the wasteland that was the Saharan region, but he described Africa's social order and corporeal customs as inverted, to foreclose the possibility of rational subjects. He wrote that African women engaged in trade, traveled abroad, and "kepte lustie chiere" in taverns while men stayed home spinning fibers and making lace. Men urinated sitting down while women stood, and male children had to care for their parents.[22] Finally, children, the products of utterly unregulated coupling in which men took as many wives as they wanted, were raised "with so lytle coste as a man would scantly believe," were fed on roots, and went shoeless and naked in the overly temperate countryside.[23] Boemus described a world of inverted norms that invited the conclusion that enslaving the people who inhabited it was simply imposing order on nature. Boemus's text is important not only for its originary articulation that to chart the customs of peoples was to understand national polities and exchanges but also for the way he used reproduction and gender relations to situate Africans as, at best, strangers who lived in nature without culture.

19 Cadamosto, *Voyages of Cadamosto*, 70.
20 On Boemus, see Hodgen, *Early Anthropology*, 111–61.
21 Boemus, *Fardle of Facions*, 28.
22 Boemus, *Fardle of Facions*, 45.
23 Boemus, *Fardle of Facions*, 60.

The notion of an abundance of people as a result of the perverse or disordered treatment of women appeared in a number of narratives. For Pieter van den Broecke, who wrote in 1609, the excesses of Angola were best illustrated through the bodies of women and children. He described a king with 1,500 wives and a multitude of dishonorable children—"the sons are mostly thieves and the daughters whores." "Each man has as many wives as he can feed" because the "female population here is, on the average, lovelier than any other place in all of Africa." He concluded that the women were held "under terrible constraint" because "the wives must provide a living for the men by seeding, planting, working the land with hoes and doing much other very hard labour. Meanwhile the man lies idly on his side (more or less like the lazy women in Spain)."[24]

The swipe at Spanish women was more than a nod to international rivalries, although it did highlight Dutch industry. It articulated the importance of regularized gender relations and suggested that the alleged excesses of the king's court were the undoing of the entire polity. In Van den Broeke's account, the contradictions of the region cohere in women's bodies. They are beautiful drudges who are both attractive and dangerous. Their work is degraded and has the effect of degrading or emasculating the men. He cautioned against having sex with Angolan women, who, he claimed, had venereal diseases, before launching into a detailed description of the ease with which these women gave birth, emphasizing their strength and endurance during the birthing process and their rapid recovery.[25] What is most telling here is that Van den Broeke situated his remarks about their skill and success in childbirth—a crucial element of the rationale for enslavement and for the emerging speculative finance associated with slave ownership—directly before a discussion of Africans' inability to properly comprehend wealth. Following that description, he then noted that the area was full of silver, tin, and copper mines, "which are not being worked because the people are so lazy and are not accustomed to labour."[26] The connection Van den Broeke made between unregulated population growth and (in his estimation) a failure to recognize value is foundational in the transformation of the continent from the location of a range of sovereign trading partners and infidel enemies to a source of human chattel.

24 Van den Broeke, *Journal of Voyages*, 97–98.
25 I have discussed this claim regarding pain-free childbearing in J. Morgan, *Laboring Women*, chap. 1.
26 Van den Broeke, *Journal of Voyages*, 98–100.

By the start of the seventeenth century, Africa was a conundrum for European writers. Its abundant population, flora, and fauna served as a provocation for theorists who were trying to understand changing notions of state power, national wealth, and population growth. In 1626 John Speed evoked ancient authority when he wrote that Africa had both scarce population and scarce habitable terrain, although he still managed to evoke excess: "[Africa] in most parts hath scarce plenty sufficient to maintain her Inhabitants, and where there is, we shall meet with multitudes of ravening Beasts, or other horrible Monsters, enough to devour both it and us. In a word, there is no Region of the World so great an enemy to man's commerce . . . so Pliny reports."[27] For Speed, people's inability to properly occupy a territory was proof that they were not God's intended inhabitants.[28] This argument would prove crucial as Englishmen legitimized their seizure of the lands of indigenous peoples in North America. Here Speed used it to justify the seizure of Africa's wealth, which he described as undervalued and unoccupied. A people incapable of assessing the value of what nature had provided was unworthy of claiming it. Thus, Africa became opened to European rational economies. And where settlement was impossible, Africans themselves became the extractable value.

The relationship European writers constructed among women's procreative practices, the general absence of regulated marriage, and what they insisted was demographic chaos set in motion a conflicting sense of overpopulation that did not support the tradition of negotiations with sovereign polities that had previously characterized the relationship between Portuguese, Dutch, and English traders and their West African counterparts. While the men who lived and traded with the inhabitants of western Africa in the fifteenth and sixteenth centuries may have understood them to be formidable peoples with complicated and individuated histories and cultures, something was changing. An inescapable sense was seeping into their narratives and letters that a teeming mass of heathens produced by outlandish women whose value lay in their commodification, not in their humanity, were transforming the Europeans' goals of identifying trading partners to obtain gold and spices that had originally compelled them to go to the coast. The possibility that the true source of wealth on the coast would be human beings—not Prester John's imaginary kingdom of gold—began

27 J. S., Map and Description of Africa, 1626, CO/700 African Photograph, National
    Archives, Kew, England.
28 Chaplin, *Subject Matter*; and Seed, *Ceremonies of Possession*.

to change the way Europeans described and experienced African polities. This is a very early example of tethering the idea of population as a political category to the idea of population as an extractable resource.

Although the idea that the African trade could be accomplished with trinkets and shawls was contradicted by many of the writers' own experiences, that notion did important work for the readers of travel literature. Stories about trade and commerce were the backbone of exploration and discovery. The goal of acquiring knowledge about the geography and cultural landscape of the continent folded into the desire to situate Africa as a source of trade goods that could be taken from people who had no capacity to understand their value. Africa became legible to European readers as a site of raw commodities—the most valuable of which were its people.

In this regard, on his 1562 slaving voyage, John Hawkins followed in the footsteps of the many Englishmen based in Iberia who had been treating Africans as merchandise for decades by the middle of the sixteenth century.[29] Hawkins's raid, which was essentially a series of assaults on towns and villages, was no model for European interaction with the inhabitants of the African coast. As historian P. E. H. Hair wrote, "The Portuguese knew better. They appreciated that civil relations with African coastal peoples were a *sin qua non* for profitable trading."[30] But civil relations were situational, and establishing a profitable trade in people increasingly relied on separating the coastal people, with whom the Europeans could establish trading relationships, from the masses just inland.

Cadamosto opened his discussion of the continent with a description of Arab traders in Argin—Arguin, in present-day Mauritania—who "come to the coast to trade for merchandize of various kinds, such as woolen clothes, cotton, silver and . . . cloaks, carpets and similar articles and above all, corn, for they are always short of food. They give in exchange slaves whom the Arabs bring from the land of the Blacks, and gold [dust]."[31] Cadamosto's attention to the particularities of early forms of human commodity exchange set the tone for narrative conventions that would follow. He mixed accounts of curious (to

29 Drawing on the Spanish sources in the *Archivos General de Indies*, Gustav Ungerer documents the involvement of English merchants in the late fifteenth- and early sixteenth-century Spanish slave trade, both in Spain and to the Americas. He notes that the first English slave trader was not Hawkins but rather Thomas Malliard, who secured a license to sell two enslaved Africans to Santo Domingo in 1521. Ungerer, *Mediterranean Apprenticeship of British Slavery*, chap. 1.
30 Hair, *Africa Encountered*, 213.
31 Cadamosto, *Voyages of Cadamosto*, 17.

him) culture and physiognomy. He wrote with an often conflicting sense of both censure and admiration for the wealth generated by trading in slaves. In one paragraph, he wrote that the Azanaghis were "the best slaves of all the Blacks," in the next that they were "a very poor people, liars, the biggest thieves in the world, and exceedingly treacherous."[32]

In many ways, Cadamosto's text inaugurated a conventional narrative structure that much of the early modern travel literature would follow, namely, that of simultaneously describing and dismissing elaborate trade networks and experiences with traders. Cadamosto followed an account of the complex negotiations he and an African trading partner conducted when trading gold and salt with the statement that "in this land of the brown men, no money is coined, and they have never used it. . . . Their sole method is to barter article for article." Then he described the use of cowries as currency and explained that "the gold they sell they give by the weight of a *mitigallo*; according to the practice in Barbary, this *mitigallo* is of the value of a ducat, more or less." Later in the narrative, he repeated that "they do not use money of any kind, but barter only, one thing for another, two for one, three for two." Such exchanges took place at a twice-weekly market. In his description of the market, he repeatedly emphasized that both men and women were there: "men as well as women came to sell."[33] The ability to both recognize and erase evidence of African numeracy and sophisticated calculations is the hallmark of these narratives. The contradictory impulses of these writers reflect a growing awareness that the shift from commodity trade to a trade in persons engendered a need to negate previous narratives that had affirmed Africans' local economic practices.

Cadamosto's treatment of trade and sex similarly offered readers a new way to comprehend the relationship between Europe and Africa. His first trade negotiation took place with the Jalof lord Budomel, who promised slaves in exchange for horses. Budomel signified his good intentions with the body of a "handsome young negress, twelve years of age, saying that he gave her to me for the service of my chamber. I accepted her and sent her to the ship."[34] Cadamosto's acceptance of this girl inaugurated his ability to conceive of himself as a slave trader, and though we cannot trace her experience, the fact that her "twelve-year-old" body was understood as giftable would certainly have been clear both to her and to the girls and women

---

32 Cadamosto, *Voyages of Cadamosto*, 18–19.
33 Cadamosto, *Voyages of Cadamosto*, 25, 48.
34 Cadamosto, *Voyages of Cadamosto*, 36.

left behind under Budomel's control. Cadamosto remained evasive about his further interactions with the girl, but he did not feel compelled to articulate any moral opposition to a transaction that turned her into an object of trade.

In 1447, in a letter sent to Genoa, Antoine Malfonte (about whom nothing is known beyond his name and his letter) more explicitly conflated the market in slaves with sexual depravity. Following his claim that slaves were sold "at a very low price" after being captured in internecine wars among "the blacks," Malfonte wrote that "these peoples, who cover the land in multitudes, are in carnal acts like the beasts; the father has knowledge of his daughter, the son of his sister. They breed greatly, for a woman bears up to five at a birth." He then turned to cannibalism and illiteracy: "Nor can it be doubted that they are eaters of human flesh, for many people have gone hence into their country. . . . They are unlettered, and without books."[35] His letter returned again and again to the vast populations of the land of the Blacks and thus the role of female fecundity in producing a population that was vast and without knowable boundaries—"a heathen king with five hundred thousand men." He wrote that "there are so many peoples that there is almost [no trade good] but is of use to them." As he linked the spheres of population, markets, and sex, Malfonte offered an early look at how individual Europeans were invested in discursively producing an understanding of these human beings as overly populous, owing to women's uncontrolled sexual prowess, and as without rational practices.

Gomes Eannes de Zurara wrote of Antam Gonçalves's 1441 voyage to western Africa in a far more straightforward way. Gonçalves began his expedition by taking a single man and a single woman. Zurara wrote that a compatriot of Gonçalves said to him, "You are carrying off these two captives, and by their means the Infant [Prince Henry] may come to know something about this folk."[36] As the primary intent of cultivating the prince's knowledge was to introduce him to the possibilities embodied by the legions of captives described in the remainder of the narrative, the reproductive pair and what they enabled the prince to "know" might together be understood as initiating Europe's ability to rationally engage in the trade in human beings, who were meant to increase their captors' wealth through sexual reproduction.[37]

35 "The Letter of Antoine Malfonte from Tuat, 1447," 85–90, in Cadamosto, *Voyages of Cadamosto*.
36 Zurara, *Discovery and Conquest of Guinea*, 46.
37 Zurara, *Discovery and Conquest of Guinea*, 39–43.

The connection between gender and commerce was made explicit early on. In much of the fifteenth- and sixteenth-century travel literature, women were portrayed as engendering both disorder and value. For Boemus, gendered disorder was quite specifically rooted in commerce. In a description of Egyptian social order, he wrote that "their women in old tyme, had all the trade of occupying and brokage abrode, and reuelled at the Tauerne, and kepte lustie chiere: and the men sate at home spinnying, and woorkyng of Lace, and suche other thynges as women are wonte."[38] Women's work as traders and brokers indicated the alarming breakdown of social order, in which men did all sorts of things that women should be doing. This comment is situated between Boemus's astonishment at the fecundity of the land and his amazement that children—even those born of a "bought woman slave"—were always understood to be legitimate and were never a great cost to their parents. Thus, Boemus's larger point about the bounty of raw materials is borne out by a disordered yet abundant population that was unhampered by the constraints or expectations of formal marriage and orderly lines of descent.[39]

European men criticized African men's role in the sexual economy that they imagined as situating African populations as legitimate sources of slaves. In 1606 Pieter van den Broeke wrote that men's access to wives was unlimited and that this access both explained African slavery and legitimated European participation in the slave trade. Van den Broeke's sexual titillation is immediately buried in the productive consequences: "They keep wives as their slaves. They must plough the land with hoes, which is heavy labour, and then seed and weed. . . . I have seen there that women came out of country with 12–16 hides on their head and a child tied to their back, on top of which they were in late pregnancy and the men going beside them carrying nothing other than his weapon."[40] The idle warrior carried only his weapon, but his sexual prowess and wantonness were on display through the presence of the fertile and seemingly always pregnant wife. In 1623 Richard Jobson speculated that African men bore the curse of Ham because they had excessively large penises.[41] Here again, a European writer linked perverted masculinity and unregulated sexuality to a demographic argument that has failed to garner much attention from historians

38 Boemus, *Fardle of Facions*, 45.
39 Boemus, *Fardle of Facions*, 60.
40 Van den Broeke, *Journal of Voyages*, 38.
41 Jobson, *Golden Trade*, 52.

precisely because it is so buried in titillation. In fact, these two phenomena performed important and coordinated work.

The connection Boemus drew between men's sexual abnormality and women's productive and reproductive lives soon became a crucial part of the evidence European writers used to prove that Africans lacked a civic culture. It is widely known that travel narratives became a vehicle for the claim that Africans had no recognizable social norms and that this claim was used to justify Europeans' practice of racial slavery. But the purpose women served in this maneuver warrants particular attention. Europeans often dismissed the idea that Africans had social norms by claiming that African parental bonds were ultimately (and easily) subverted. The dismantling of African kinship, which would become the foundation of hereditary racial slavery, was narrativized and rationalized here.

Van den Broeke initially tempered his critique of the supposed lack of these bonds with sympathy, writing that "this year was such a dire time that parents were forced to sell their children for their subsistence and maintenance."[42] But he later abandoned this sympathetic tone: "During my stay I bought a lovely young girl of about ten years of age from her mother for the price of 130 lbs. of rice, and the mother acted so coolly, as if it were not even her child. Various parents came to offer me the virginity of their children, aged 7 or 8 years, for a couple of handfuls of rice."[43] The accusation that African women and men were indifferent parents became crucial; it marked Africans as vectors of kinlessness, as the accusation of parental disregard became part of the claim that African women produced children only for the marketplace. This manner of kinlessness would function as the core of hereditary racial slavery; it disregarded the crucial barrier that symbolically separated family from the marketplace and thereby firmly placed Africans outside of the collectivities that defined European belonging.

This trope was important from the beginning of the slave trade, even as it unfolded unevenly. Zurara also made claims about the looseness of parental ties. He wrote of a community along the Senegal River that was trying to evacuate in the face of the encroaching Portuguese: "And the Moors rising up about dawn had sight of [the Portuguese sailors] when they were coming, and like men without heart and deprived of hope, they began to fly, every one where he perceived he could best take refuge, leaving behind goods, wives and children, as men who perceived that they had

42 Van den Broeke, *Journal of Voyages*, 28.
43 Van den Broeke, *Journal of Voyages*, 39.

quite enough to do to save their own lives."[44] Zurara was creating a complicated moral economy in which abandoning children and mothers signified that African men did not value their own communities. The claim that that parental and communal bonds dissolved in men's desire to save themselves seems to establish for the reader that Africans were not of the same moral community as the Portuguese. Ultimately, the entire chronicle testifies to the importance of capturing Africans:

> I cannot behold the arrival of these slips with the novelty of the gain of those slaves before the face of our Prince, without finding some delight in the same. For me seemeth that I behold before my eyes that pleasure of his, of what kind it would be. . . . O holy prince . . . seeing the beginnings of some recompense, may we not think thou didst feel joy, not so much for the number of the captives taken, as for the hope thou didst conceive of the others thou couldst take?[45]

The joy of the prince is the overriding principle, and the small number of captured Africans, men and women, boys and girls, is a sign of much more to come.

Ruminations on kinship ties among Africans do not occupy a steady or static position in these early narratives. Indeed, it is their instability that I believe warrants our attention. After this discussion of parental abandonment (which is admittedly tinged with empathy), Zurara wrote that Gonçalvez and his men came across a woman and her children, whom they tried to subdue and take on board. Her strength at resisting her assailants surprised them. The three men who had failed to force her into the boat realized that they could simply "take her son from her and carry him to the boat; and love of the child compelled the mother to follow after it." Only then did they capture her.[46] The kinship between this mother and child saturates this story, and yet for both the men who enticed her and the writer who told of her, that kinship is quickly sublimated to the larger goal of obtaining captives for the joy of the prince.

Remember that Zurara wrote a wrenching description of the first group of captives sold in Lisbon in 1444. There he wrote of the agony caused by the callous separation of mothers from children, and brothers from brothers, as the captives were divided into parcels and distributed among

44 Zurara, *Discovery and Conquest of Guinea*, 106.
45 Zurara, *Discovery and Conquest of Guinea*, 51.
46 Zurara, *Discovery and Conquest of Guinea*, 259.

the ship's investors.[47] That passage captures, brilliantly and empathetically, the profound violence of rendering human beings into commodities. Yet in the passages describing the mother's capture, one is struck by the functionality of the connection between the woman and her child—the usefulness of that connection for catching her. In the face of the prince's joy and the myriad descriptions in the text of capture unmitigated by women's anguish at finding maternal love used against them, the agony of seeing a child taken onto a strange ship and the willingness to place herself in danger in an effort to provide protection take on a decidedly ephemeral quality.

Women and girls do not inhabit these texts in large numbers. The concept of the slave was intimately linked to that of war captive and only over time began to be applied to whole populations, including women and children. But when they appear, they do important work for European readers and, presumably, writers. These women help to normalize and secure the context that made a large-scale trade in slaves morally plausible. Van den Broeke's entire experience of the Senegambian region was marked by the "service" of African women. In his description of reaching Cape Verde, he wrote, "We brought our trade-goods ashore. The factor rented a house with a black woman to serve me for two iron bars per month."[48] As his later commentary suggests, the service she provided potentially exceeded housekeeping. The service of Black women here, and the rejection of that service elsewhere, marked African traders and rulers as savage. Their offering of virgin girls for handfuls of rice would be yet another piece of evidence showing African difference. Its association with the intimacy of sex and household was not incidental, as it evoked African indifference to family and to alleged European bonds of decency. We should not lose sight of this Black woman "serving" Van den Broeke. While keeping house for him, she would have witnessed a traffic in men, women, and girls. Through her we might begin to understand the meaning-making that was as important a commodity exchange on the coast as was the trading of cloth for slaves. For, without this naturalization of female commodification, the capacity for European wealth through trade would have been considerably diminished.

Most European writers assumed that contact with sovereign peoples on the West African coast came with the sexual services of African women and girls. Richard Jobson was in a significant minority when he refused the

47 Zurara, *Discovery and Conquest of Guinea*, 81.
48 Van den Broeke, *Journal of Voyages*, 28.

services of an African girl.[49] Other writers were far more likely to argue, as Valentine Fernandes did of the Mandinka at the Gambia River, that "if any of our whites arrive at a house of a black, even the king's, and ask for a wife or daughter, he sends anyone the man chooses to sleep with, and he does this for good friendship and not from force. A father himself hands over any girl the man chooses and if he wants her sisters, these too. If anyone sleeps with his own sister or daughter, as often happens, this is no crime."[50]

These descriptions of inconsequential paternal bonds, sexual availability, and perversion were embedded in discussions of trade. In Fernandes's writing, the discussion of sexuality is immediately followed by a list of commodities: "What these lands produce are green parrots, gold but not much, male and female slaves, cotton cloth, mats, hides, a little musk, and monkeys with tails."[51] Sandwiched between green parrots and a little musk, these men and women are effectively evacuated from their culture or customs precisely because those customs failed to be legible to European readers. Fernandes's reader then immediately encounters a long description of the ways "men in this land do not marry but buy their wives." In this way, Fernandes transformed a population that was worthless as a sovereign trading partner into one whose worth is measured and valued as a commodity. In such an economy, the objections of writers like Manuel Alvares, who wrote that when Christians refused to purchase slaves on the West African coast, despotic rulers slaughtered the slaves, or Jobson, who refused to engage in the slave trade at all, begin to fade and become archaic at best.

In his *Briefe Description of the Whole Worlde* of 1608, George Abbot wrote that although the Portuguese had "wonne few of the people [of West Africa] to imbrace their religion ... the Portingales passing along Africa to the East Indies have settled themselves in many places of these countries, building Castles and Townes for their own Safeties, and to keep the people in subjection, to their great commoditie."[52] Here the ability of

---

49 This refusal came at considerable erotic cost, according to his twentieth-century editors. David Gamble and P. E. H. Hair write that his refusal was "perhaps based on a lack of understanding" and that while Jobson was silent on the sexual conduct of the English on the river, "he himself was patently attracted by the physical appearance of the Fula women whose outward carriage is such that we may well concede [licentious libertie]." Gamble and Hair, introduction, 31.

50 Fernandes, "O Manucrito," 268.

51 Fernandes, "O Manucrito," 268.

52 While Abbot was undoubtedly using the word *commoditie* to mean "comfort," sixteenth-century usages also include a "natural resource or material" or "income or

the Portuguese to subjugate the peoples of Senegambia is framed as critical to their ability to extract wealth from the region. In the absence of direct competitors, however, authors were quite clear about crafting Africa as unimproved: ultimately, "to speake in a worde: there is no country under heaven fitter for increase of plants and all living creatures, but none less helpt by arte or industry."[53] Africa thus took shape as the context against which England might prove itself economically and religiously superior, in part because it was a continent that Englishmen and other Europeans defined as underutilized.

The English translation of sixteenth-century Berber traveler Leo Africanus stated, "Being almost twise as bigge as Europe, albeit for inhabitants it is not halfe so populous . . . the lande of Africa is in many places unhabitable," thus marking it as geographically strange.[54] For what does one do with such abundance? Translated and published in London in 1600, the narrative had circulated before that in Arabic and Italian. His descriptions tend to focus on the land and fauna of the continent, although he uses both the concept of value and women's behavior to signify the ways that the continent is lacking. He refers to people everywhere, so Africa was uninhabitable only for Europeans. He stressed the abundance of resources, noting that there were "great store of mines of gold, silver, iron, and copper; but they know not how to digge and refine the same: for the people of this country are so rude and ignorant, that they have no knowledge for use of any arte or occupation."[55] And yet Leo Africanus's characterization of sub-Saharan Africa imparts a sense of demographic abundance that leads to a kind of emotionally untethered disorder rooted in faulty mathematics. He wrote that in Guinea "they converse together in great families; and they fight oftentimes for water and for pastures; neither have they knowledge of learning or liberall arts. . . . They sell their children unto strangers, supposing that their estate cannot possiblie be impaired."[56] This analysis of African family life profoundly contradicts Zurara's account of a mother who was willing to be enslaved so she could be with her son.

---

revenue." *Oxford English Dictionary*, online ed., s.v. "commodity, n.," accessed April 2, 2019, http://www.oed.com/view/Entry/37205?redirectedFrom=commoditie. Abbot, *Briefe Description*, Section K, n.p.

53 [Botero], *Worlde*, 213.

54 Leo Africanus, *Geographical Historie of Africa*, 2.

55 Leo Africanus, *Geographical Historie of Africa*, 15.

56 Leo Africanus, *Geographical Historie of Africa*, 43.

Similarly, the early modern English cartographer and historian John Speed wrote that the inhabitants of the Cape of Good Hope "kill their own children in the birth to avoid the trouble of breeding them and preserve their Nation with stolen brats from the neighbouring Countries."[57] Both Leo Africanus and Speed indicted the peoples of Africa for a failure to recognize the value of their population, accusing them of failing to regard the bonds of kinship as important. Tales of the sale or murder of children are implicit indictments of mothers. Leo Africanus's accounts of women normalize the capture and transport of children who would otherwise be doomed to death at the hands of their inhuman mothers. These fantasies of African cultural practices invariably appear in tandem with remarks about the abundance of raw African populations, and these authors typically contrast that abundance with the dearth of other raw materials on the continent. Immediately following the tale of children sold at birth, Leo wrote that from Senegambia to the Cape of Good Hope, while "our Englishmen have found traffique into the parts of this Country, where their greatest commoditie is Gold and Elephants teeth, there is no matter of any great importance."[58]

Wiping the continent clean of anything "important" was a strategic act. Before the writings of Leo Africanus or the map of John Speed, economic and diplomatic relationships between Iberian countries and their trading partners in sub-Saharan Africa in the fifteenth century had situated African polities as sovereign states whose authority in matters of trade and conquest was indeed a matter of great importance.[59] As travel writers and advocates of trade worked to construct an Africa ripe for the taking, they set about undoing decades of experience with politically and economically astute Africans. When the Portuguese arrived at the Gambia River in the fifteenth century, they described the care with which Mandinka merchants weighed and measured gold, using finely balanced scales suspended from cords of twisted silk and balanced with brass weights.[60] In the early sixteenth century, Jon Lok wrote, "They are very wary people in their bargaining,

---

57 J. S., Map and Description of Africa, 1626, CO/700 African Photograph, National Archives, Kew, England.

58 Leo Africanus, *Geographical Historie of Africa*, 2.

59 On trading alliances, see Green, *Rise of the Trans-Atlantic*; on diplomatic relations, see Bennett, *African Kings and Black Slaves*.

60 Álvares de Almada, *Brief Treatise* (1594), in Gamble and Hair, *Discovery of River Gambra*, 277.

and will not lose one sparke of golde of any value. They use weights and measures, and are very circumspect in occupying the same."[61] Portuguese travelers understood these African merchants to be analytically skilled and steeped in an economy that required both technology and a comprehension of value.

This recognition of the sophistication of African trade gave way to narratives that presented Africans as utterly ignorant about accounting. In his 1677 *Merchants Map of Commerce*, a text explicitly organized to identify markets and trade goods for English merchants, Lewes Roberts wrote of the inhabitants of the West African coast:

> Their ignorance in trade may be judged by their ignorance in Accompting and Reckoning, for when they have past the number of Ten, they rehearse so many words one after another for one number, that they are so puzzled and combred therewith, that they cannot tell how to get out, and so sit buzzing so long, till at last they have lost their Tale, and forgot their number, and so are forced to begin to tell again; but since they began to trade with the English, and were to reckon above the number of Ten, for they use no more amongst them, they reckon on till they come to Ten, and then take one of their fingers into their hands, and then tell to Ten again; and then take another finger into their hand, and so proceed till they have both their hands full, which in all maketh one hundred, then they mark that up, then begin to tell as at the first, and use the same order as before.[62]

Here Roberts constructs an image of ignorance that reflects many Iberian and English writers' devastating dismissal of African economy. This kind of specifically inflected accusation did a far more complicated bit of work than the blunt tool wielded, for example, by the fifteenth-century Muslim historian Ibn Khaldun, who wrote that "the Negro nations are, as a rule, submissive to slavery, because (Negroes) have little that is (essentially) human and possess attributes that are quite similar to those of dumb animals."[63] The introduction of an alleged intellectual defect carried a slew of accusations about civility, capacity, and culture. It circles back to Columbus's

---

61 "Richard Eden's Account of John Lok's Voyage to Mina, 1554–5," 326–47, in J. W. Blake, *Europeans in West Africa*, 343.

62 L. Roberts, *Merchants Map of Commerce*, 78.

63 Ibn Khaldun, *Muqaddimah*, 117. The words in parentheses are part of the modern translation. Also quoted in Sweet, "Iberian Roots," 147.

excitement that native peoples could be subdued with trinkets and to Europeans' view that the ability to correctly compute value reflected a society's capacity to retain its autonomy.

These accusations were not uniform. The deficits of some were thought to be temporary or environmental. In 1690 John Locke wrote that he had spoken with Native Americans who "could not, as we do, by any means count to 1000: nor had any distinct idea of that number, though they could reckon very well to 20."[64] Locke leveled accusations about the supposed limitations of the mathematical abilities of Native Americans in a slightly gentler tone than Ibn Khaldun because he felt that the phenomenon grew from a "needy simple life." He separated these failings from those of some Englishmen, noting that their failure to "number in words" was connected not to their capacities but to their lack of the proper language to talk about numbers.

In the context of Africa, something far more insidious was going on. This shift to the view that Africans lacked mathematical skills proved very useful to merchants and traders, who used the assertion that African people had neither God nor king to protect them as a way of justifying traders' work to establish a regularized trade in slaves. The claim that the abundance of Africa rightly belonged to Europeans was often sandwiched between claims that Africans did not have the capacity to understand value, whether it be that of gold, shells, or children. Such claims mobilized evidence of an African "superstitious misunderstanding of causality" as evidence of the absence of reason.[65] When the writer Cadamosto claimed that Africans believed that ships were the work of the devil "because they [did] not understand the art of navigation, the compass, or the chart," he was, as anthropologist William Pietz has argued, mounting an argument about African irrationality.[66] Accusations about numerical ignorance articulated with those concerning the lack of civic norms and would have a long and promiscuous afterlife.

By the middle of the seventeenth century, facts, as articulated by members of England's Royal Academy, were inseparable from civil norms, as invoking them would combat civil disputes.[67] As literary critic Henry Louis

---

64 Locke, *Essay Concerning Human Understanding*, 161.
65 Pietz, "Problem of the Fetish, II," 42.
66 Cadamosto, *Voyages of Cadamosto*, 51, cited and discussed in Pietz, "Problem of the Fetish, II," 42.
67 Poovey, *History of the Modern Fact*, 110.

Gates Jr. has argued, Africans' alleged lack of literacy was a crucial weapon in the arsenal that political theorists of the eighteenth and nineteenth centuries used to deny them both culture and history.[68] In the minds of early modern Europeans, the lack of reckoning and rational thought were of equal importance in marking the continent as a legitimate resource for European extractive economies. Gendered notions of civility and disarray are woven through that project as early as the fifteenth century. Such claims produced connections between currency and children; this speaks to the production of a rationale for enslavement rooted in a reproductive economy wherein African women's alleged disregard for their kin moved their children out of the conceptual landscape of families and onto the balance sheets of slave traders.

Such claims ultimately found full fruition in a pseudoscience that situated Africans adjacent to apes on a great chain of being. When Andre Donelha wrote about western Africa in 1625, he argued, "When this country is peopled with Christians it will be the richest in all Ethiopia, with the greatest trade and commerce, since no other equals it for natural advantages." "Peopling" was quite different from identifying teeming populations. Europeans would not mobilize African women's fertility to produce Christians or other legitimate subjects who could properly take account of and trade Africa's commodities to advantage. That those advantages were insufficiently mined by its inhabitants went without saying, though shortly later Donelha drives that point home via a discussion of monkeys and their use of tools, concluding, "They say if it meets a woman alone, it makes a match with her."[69] Readers familiar with the history of racist ideology will recognize these accusations, which were wielded most aggressively by the late eighteenth-century proslavery propagandist Edward Long.[70] Long wrote, "I do not think that an oran-outang husband would be any dishounor to an Hottentot female; for what are these Hottentots?"[71] Both writers produced Africans as enslavable by virtue of women's behavior. In Donelha, the link signals a moment much earlier than Edward Long's, though both use the connections between value and computation to undergird the accusations about the ways women carried sexual disorder with them. Women's

68 Gates, *Figures in Black*, chap. 1, esp. 18–24.
69 Donelha, *Account of Sierra Leone*, 81, 93.
70 I have discussed Long in chapter 2. For more on the depth of his racist interest in polygenism, see Seth, *Difference and Disease*, esp. chap. 6.
71 Long, *History of Jamaica*, 364.

alleged sexual congress—be it with apes or simply outside the bonds of marriage—stood for a multitude of irregularities that would prove crucial in the long-term relationship between Europeans and the natural resources of the African continent.

African Economies

Those who wrote and read these accounts of what we now call the Atlantic world did so in the midst of new concepts of population, commodification, currency, and value in relationship to the African continent and its people. Situating women as sexually available conduits of excess fertility erected a set of tropes that linked race, sex, and enslavability in the minds of slave traders and slave owners well into the nineteenth century.[72] These tropes created an enduring and powerful means of conveying the logic of racial slavery. As we know, this normalized excessive and systemic violence. But the claims can also be mined for information about how women were situated in local economies of goods and of the enslaved. That victims of the trade found themselves in a situation whose violence and parameters were fundamentally incomprehensible has helped to convey the enormity of the slave trade's violations. Ancillary to that discussion is a reliance on an archive that, at best, characterizes the continent as premodern and void of complex economic ideologies. It is not entirely surprising that even those of us who are most devoted to centering the experience and the humanity of the enslaved should emphasize their disorientation.

And yet buried beneath the dismissive descriptive language of travelers to the continent, we also find evidence of long-standing complicated markets and economies. These have been carefully examined by economic historians of Africa but have had less impact on the writing of histories of the slave trade and enslavement. The degree of economic complexity on the western and west-central African coast in the decades and centuries leading up to the transatlantic slave trade arguably produced a population of enslaved persons who were fully capable of comprehending the

---

72 There is a growing body of work on the enduring connection among gender, sexuality, and slavery. The foundational texts include Beckles, *Natural Rebels*; Bush, *Slave Women in Caribbean Society*; and Gaspar and Hine, *More Than Chattel*. Work that builds on these earlier studies includes Berry, *Price for Their Pound*; J. L. Morgan, *Laboring Women*; Paugh, *Politics of Reproduction*; Spear, *Race, Sex, and Social Order*; Turner, *Contested Bodies*.

economic claims laid upon their persons and their progeny. Europeans' urgent need to refute the idea that inhabitants of the West African coast possessed economic rationality testifies to its core importance as a marker of Western notions of civility, autonomy, and unenslavability. It also raises questions about the role of racialist discourse in the construction of early Enlightenment commitments to the rationality of market relations. And, finally, it points to the quite potent cultural histories of economies these same sources illuminate—albeit just beneath their surface.

To fully engage with the ways Atlantic Africa responded to European mercantilism is beyond the scope of this text, but as anthropologist Jane Guyer cautions, studies of that response must situate it as both a reaction and an autonomous voice.[73] The particular ways European observers understood African economies to be inscrutable or irrational were based on Africans' efforts to oppose the European mercantilist policies that sought to utilize African resources without paying a fair price. That opposition took many forms, both defensive efforts to protect communities from slave raiders and commercial efforts to preserve balanced trade relations.[74] Further, despite the effort to denigrate African systems of trade, there were also important alignments between West African systems of trade and European ones. For example, African economies' use of cowries or cloth as specie actually accorded quite nicely with the mercantilist project. For some early modern economic theorists, buying slaves with English coin would have represented a net loss as that currency would not have made its way back to London markets. Bartering for slaves with iron bars, guns, or cowries solved that problem even as it set in motion a range of unequal exchanges of the kind with which modern Atlantic economies still struggle. Thus, while it would be overreaching to say that European traders had a systematic plan to situate African economies as outside the rational and the knowable, their claims should not be regarded as mere chauvinism but should instead be linked to the project of assigning rational primacy to European mercantilism.[75]

73 Guyer, *Marginal Gains*, 173, 14.
74 For discussion of the range of strategies employed by West African communities and states, see the essays collected in Diouf, *Fighting the Slave Trade*, esp. Hawthorne, "Strategies of the Decentralized," and Inikori, "Struggle against the Transatlantic Slave Trade."
75 It is difficult to obtain good information on the extent to which West African economies were monetized in the early modern period. But it remains too easy to imagine that there is something inscrutable about African monetary systems or that the extent to which early African economies were monetized is out of reach for the historian.

Such primacy adheres to (and explains) the common assertion that Africans sold their brethren for cheap consumer goods or for "gewgaws."[76] Early modern writers often asserted Europeans' superiority by referring to terms of exchange. In the late fifteenth century, the Portuguese chronicler Ruy de Pina exemplified this discursive move in his description of the ease with which the Portuguese assuaged the local inhabitants at the construction site for the Fort of São Jorge da Mina in Senegambia. He wrote that "it was necessary to demolish some houses of the negroes, and to this they and their women consented easily and without taking offence in return for large reparations and the gifts which were given to them." Because Pina had already minimized the cost of those gifts earlier in the narrative, his mention of "large reparations" should be taken as tongue in cheek; the whole exchange was meant to highlight the supposed ease with which the Portuguese were able to construct a permanent fort on the coast.[77] Although European writers emphasized their ability to obtain gold for "articles of little value in our eyes," the terms of trade were, in fact, costly for Europeans and reflected the influence African traders had in exchanges.[78] Gold dust, meticulously calculated against the Islamic *mithqual*, was traded for other currencies along the western coast, such as cowries, salt, and cloth.[79] Despite the impulse of early modern writers to minimize the importance of these other currencies, early African economies were "more monetized than outsiders realized."[80]

While shell currencies were in circulation on the West African coast before Europeans' arrival, including cowries that arrived from the Maldives via Cairo and the Mediterranean, the Portuguese acceleration of the trade of cowries from the Indian Ocean to the West African coast set in motion the relationship in which "the cowrie became the shell money of the slave trade."[81] In the sixteenth century, the Portuguese secured their dominance of the cowrie trade and, with it, the illusion that Africans lacked a rational

---

Overly narrow definitions, certainly rooted in the very European economic theories that don't fit African markets, ensure a narrow conclusion in which money equals gold.

76 Curtin, *Economic Change in Precolonial Africa*, 312.
77 "The Foundation of the Castle and City of São Jorge da Mina, 1482," from Ruy de Pina, *Chronica del Rey Dom Joao II* (1500), in J. W. Blake, *Europeans in West Africa*, 77.
78 Cadamosto, *Voyages of Cadamosto*, 68. On the terms of trade, see Richardson, "Cultures of Exchange," 155–56.
79 Henwick, "Islamic Financial Institutions," 87.
80 Curtin, "Africa and the Wider Monetary World."
81 Hogendorn and Johnson, *Shell Money*, 1.

currency. For the Portuguese (and later Dutch and English) traders who brought cowries to the West African coast at little to no cost and collected returns on their investment of up to 500 percent, this noncurrency proved to be a very valuable commodity.[82] The contradictions between the material ways in which trade was carried out and the violence done through the claim that no such rational materiality existed are at the heart of the commodification of human beings on which the transatlantic slave trade was built.

The slow turn toward the slave trade in these first decades of European contact with (and presence on) the West African coast has been well documented. While the development of the transatlantic trade drew on long-standing connections outsiders made between Blackness and enslavability, it also built on a range of labor and kinship structures in local polities that included slavery and slave labor. African historians agree that women in precolonial West African societies performed considerable hard labor both in freedom and as slaves.[83] The sexual division of labor often fell harder on women than men, which meant that women were no strangers to the notion that their capacity for hard work was part of what defined the rhythms and parameters of both their present and their future. Geographer Judith Carney has mounted a careful case for the possibility that women in Senegambia were kept from the Atlantic slave trade in part because of their crucial role in processing millet and sorghum for local consumption.[84] Historian Claire Robertson notes that "the successful expansion and prosperity of a society often depended on how much female labor could be mobilized, and slavery was an ideal vehicle for doing so, even more when the slaves could produce children, free lineage members, to increase the population further."[85] Both historians and seventeenth-century English travelers have articulated a keen awareness of women's role in cultivating these grains with skill, strength, and precision.

Europeans benefited from the long-standing role of women as marketers from the moment they set foot on West African shores. The Portuguese garrison of Mina was provisioned by bread, fruits, and vegetables that local

---

82 Hogendorn and Johnson, *Shell Money*, 36.

83 For an early articulation of this, see Robertson and Klein, introduction to *Women and Slavery*. See also Meillassoux, "Female Slavery," 49.

84 Carney and Rosomoff, *In the Shadow of Slavery*, 74; Jobson, *Discovery of River Gambra*. Carney's earlier work establishes both male and female expertise in rice cultivation in Senegambia. Carney, *Black Rice*, 9–30.

85 Robertson, "We Must Overcome," 68.

African women cultivated or made and sold. A hundred years later, Dutch trader and explorer Pieter de Marees discussed women's role in the markets. In one illustration for his text, they arrive at the European fort ready to sell the food they carry on their heads to the Dutch.[86] But the presence of women in proximity to Europeans was also a point of contention. In 1514 King Afonso of the Kongo wrote to his Portuguese counterpart to complain that slave traders were purchasing Kongo women instead of the men they had permission to buy. Historian Linda Heywood points out that his objections were rooted in the concern that Portuguese priests were using Kongo women for sex, turning them into "whores."[87] In areas of western Africa from which European slavers extracted captives, women's labor was critical to the development of markets in agricultural products and other goods that crisscrossed the continent. The internal trade that developed in these spaces spurred economic transformations in domestic economies up and down the coast that economic historian Morten Jerven argues both "precede the slave trade and go beyond the Atlantic trade."[88]

In a region with a highly developed agricultural system, the role of women as workers and producers was crucial. The connection between women's labor and the wealth that labor might bring to a family or kin group would have been rationalized knowledge for all who inhabited the region. As the seventeenth century unfolded and the region became increasingly pulled into the transatlantic slave trade, women's work was transformed. Historian Boubacar Barry describes the development of "kin-based 'democracies'" in inwardly focused communities "threatened with extermination" in the face of the increased demand for captives from both European slave traders and African captors. In areas bent on supplying captives for the slave trade, women increasingly turned to agriculture and other sources of food, while men built and manned boats, which "they then turned into fleets of war canoes with which they spread terror throughout the Southern Rivers."[89] In the century when the Portuguese reached the Senegambian coast, for example, agricultural work dominated the lives of even the women who had not previously been responsible for this kind of work.[90] The slave trade

---

86 Carney and Rosomoff, *In the Shadow of Slavery,* 49.
87 Heywood, "Slavery and Its Transformation," 6.
88 Jerven, "Emergence of African Capitalism," 438.
89 Barry, *Senegambia,* 33, 43.
90 There is a considerable literature on the various ways in which elites accumulated wealth in African polities; both "wealth in people" and landownership are important,

transformed women's economic lives locally even when they were not captured and taken from their homes.

We know that from the moment Europeans first made contact with West African polities, some women were accustomed to their bodies being commodified and used to negotiate the boundaries of trade and diplomacy. In Europeans' records of exchanges when African men offered women to European traders, the women had no choice but to accept their situation. Yet we can surmise that well before Europeans began to write of women being offered to visiting traders as symbols of welcome and lubricants of goodwill, women along the African coast understood themselves to embody a multiplicity of exchanges. This understanding and their knowledge of the importance of their role in agricultural production up and down the West African coast would have been the mental context for the excruciating experience of being captured, transported, and sold into hereditary racial slavery. As they endured that process, African women became unwitting participants in the transformation of the Atlantic into a region defined by the notions of trade, commodity, and racial hierarchy, which wrenched the Americas and Europe into the modern crucible of racial capitalism.

---

even when land is emphasized over people. As Barry argues, the structures that produced stratified social relationships based on the accumulation of wealth were steeped in a recognition that "productive and reproductive relationships" were the social context that gave land its economic and use value. Barry, *Senegambia*, 32, 30.

FOUR. Accounting for the "Most Excruciating Torment":
Transatlantic Passages

The first sub-Saharan African person to be enslaved and transported to Europe by European traders was a woman. She was taken in a Portuguese raid against the local Idzāgen in 1441 at the Río de Oro in Senegambia.[1] Nothing further is known of her or of what her captors imagined they had accomplished by seizing her. She represents an origin story, of sorts, and the impossibility of knowing more about her is itself a reflection of how she came into being. She is emblematic. Like the woman the same year whose strength almost protected her from capture until "love of [her] child compelled the mother to follow" onto a slaver's ship, she suggests something much bigger than her own tragic dislocation.[2] These unnamed women, who entered ships with little comprehension of where they were headed, disembarked with some capacity for predicting how their lives would now unfold even if the particulars of what the Portuguese city held were unknown. The use of children as a lure, the recognition that their identity as women and mothers changed the strategies that slavecatchers used to capture them, their probable exposure to the sexual predation of the crew on the journey—all these factors confirmed the outlines of their enslavement

1 Saunders, *Social History of Black Slaves*, 5.
2 Zurara, *Discovery and Conquest of Guinea*, 259.

and the value form that their bodies would take as they were transformed into commodities.

What does it mean to frame an examination of the Middle Passage with the story of these individual female captives? These two women were transported as unwilling passengers on ships rather than as cargo. When they reached Portugal, they likely encountered others from Africa whose status ranged from slave to servant to property-owning lord.[3] Starting with them forces us to think about how gender shaped their experience of enslavement, how they might have interpreted their experience, and how their interpretive frames compel a reassessment of the larger histories of the Black Atlantic world. This chapter is framed by questions about how women were enslaved and transported, what happened to them on ships, why they became blurred in the contemporary stories of the slave trade, and what they understood about their capture and their future.

In 1566 the ship *Santiago* left Sierra Leone for Puerto Rico. The captives on board, likely the victims of Mane incursions from the east, would not have been the first members of the Sapes lineage to find themselves enslaved in the Americas. Indeed, for almost a hundred years, communities in the region of Sierra Leone were exposed to incursions, capture, and sale. They understood that enslavement to the Europeans was a consequence of warfare and that the ships plying the coast were there to collect the victims of these wars.[4] For some, that knowledge was sufficient to warrant extreme action. Before heading west across the Atlantic, the *Santiago* stopped at the Los Islands off Conakry in Guinea for fresh water. While there, the captives on the ship watched with hope or fear as people on the island—themselves refugees from the Mane wars—attacked the ship and killed one of the crewmen. Unfortunately, their rage could not reverse the fate of the captives on board, and the ship soon raised sail and pulled off, heading toward Puerto Rico. Those who survived to disembark would navigate a multiplicity of losses, including that of other captives on board. Mortality rates on similar slave ships in the first part of the 1560s ranged from 10 to 40 percent, and thus the total number of captives loaded in Sierra Leone could have been much higher than the ninety-two who disembarked.[5] That same year, for example, almost half of the 268 captives on another ship that left the

3 Saunders, *Social History of Black Slaves*; and Phillips, *Slavery*.
4 Hawthorne, *Planting Rice and Harvesting Slaves*, 55–89.
5 H. Klein et al., "Transoceanic Mortality."

Sierra Leone coast died before the ship landed in Cartagena.[6] Death during the transatlantic crossing would be just one aspect of the brutal calculus of the voyage. Ships were dangerously overpacked even in the early years of the transatlantic slave trade.[7] While mortality rates and the efforts of Africans to overthrow slave ships demand our attention, they may distract us from other crucial aspects of the experience of the passage. The captives on board the *Santiago* had to process their captivity through their identity as women. When the *Santiago* arrived, only fifteen of the ninety-two people on board were male. The rest were female.

The seventy-seven women and girls, whose lives would now be defined by a newly unfolding Atlantic, were the successors of that first woman captured by the Portuguese more than a hundred years earlier—epistemologically located by their identity as captive women and by the risks that their valuation as such exposed them to. Despite the rather startling sex ratio on the *Santiago*, this voyage was unremarkable in many other ways. For the previous sixty years, ships had been making their way across the Atlantic loaded with captives bound for enslavement in Spanish America. For them, the journey would have been steeped in the anguish of dislocation, fear, and privation. However, some aspects of their expectations about their labors—both manual and sexual—would have become quite clear to them.

Like those before and after them, the women and girls on the *Santiago* would have comprehended the transformations that their time on the ship portended. In the case of this voyage, the assumption that their capture was shaped somehow by their sex would have been inescapable. The small number of men on this ship is perhaps cause for surprise but only for modern scholars; as we have seen in chapter 1, women often constituted majorities on sixteenth- and seventeenth-century ships, and even when they did not, they were not vastly outnumbered. Women in large and small numbers were taken up by Portuguese slave traders from 1441 onward, and their experiences en route to European ships, on the Atlantic, and at sales in ports and settlements throughout the Americas ought to be a commonplace part of the story of the Black Atlantic world. Yet the assumed subject of the story of the slave trade and the Middle Passage has too often been male. He is, at best, a warrior—she is rarely a woman.

6 Voyage 28058, *Santo Antonio* (1566), http://slavevoyages.org/voyage/database.
7 Rodney, *History of the Upper Guinea Coast*. On the likelihood of ships being both overcrowded and underdocumented in the early years of the trade, see Duquette, "Ship Crowding and Slave Mortality," 544.

As a result, there are gaps in our ability to comprehend how gender framed the transformation of individuals into commodities. We must close this gap when we are considering the interplay between ideas of race and those of commerce. Both in their socially inscribed positions close to markets on the African coast and their status as those whose reproductive capacities produced the racialized populations exposed to the markets on the other side of the Atlantic, women help us see the experience of comprehending enslavability as the terms of that process changed. It bears repeating: a number of ships left the Senegambian coast in the sixteenth century with significantly more women than men. The communities who were exposed to the ravages of the slave trade at this time would have been well aware that women's gender did not protect them from sale. A Flemish merchant who traveled with a Portuguese ship to West Africa in 1480, Eustache de la Fosse, wrote flatly that in the late fifteenth century on the Grain Coast, "they brought us women and children for sale" and that the Portuguese sold them easily and profitably later that year at the Gold Coast.[8]

The explanation for these sex ratios remains elusive, not least because scholars of the slave trade have not focused on female captives except as indices of the relative strength of African polities or the crisis among African men. Thus, historians note both the refusal of the obas in Benin to sell any male slaves to the Portuguese after 1530 and sex ratios like that on the *Santiago* only in relation to the strength or weakness of a patriarchal African state. Historian Toby Green, for example, interprets his findings concerning the sex ratio on ships from Sierra Leone in the 1560s as an index of the destruction the Mane people meted out in that region during recurrent invasions.[9]

Attention has been paid to the demographic impact of the slave trade on areas like eighteenth-century Angola, where the exceptionally high proportion of male captives led to female majorities, which significantly transformed kin and community dynamics at home, and the Bight of Biafra in present-day Nigeria, where predominantly female captives entered the Atlantic market, which reflects gendered practices of cultivation in the region.[10] Starting from the assumption that women's economic productivity in African states insulated them from sale, some scholars have concluded that offering women for sale to European traders "might indicate a society

8 Fosse, *Crónica de uma viagem*, quoted in Fage, "Slaves and Society," 298.
9 On the obas, see H. Klein, "African Women," 36; on Sierra Leone, see Green, *Rise of the Trans-Atlantic*, 240, 252.
10 Miller, *Way of Death*, 161–62; and Nwokeji, *Slave Trade and Culture*, 144–77, esp. 148–49.

in which economic reasoning was little developed."[11] Aside from the possibility that these women had clearly developed economic reasoning of their own, linked not least of all to their self-valuation, our knowledge of what capture, transport, and sale meant for women remains a profoundly neglected area.

New work devoted to filling in the considerable gaps in our understanding of the scale of the Iberian slave trade to the Americas before 1650 has provided new evidence on sex and age ratios, but that evidence has not yet been taken up as a core concern.[12] In this early period, patterns of capture and sale differed from later patterns, which suggests different demographic contours and supports a new set of inquiries into gender and captivity for scholars of West African history and historians of the slave trade. Here I want to center women on slave ships in order to engage with gender, captivity, and the documents of enslavement as crucial aspects of the origins of reproductive racial capitalism as well as Black radicalism, as manifested in the self-awareness of African women.[13]

Recall from chapter 1 that captains of slave ships often didn't record the number of women who were part of their cargos, while other sources suggest that African women played an important part in the way that Europeans understood the continent and the business of trade. While the presence of African women on board early ships has not attracted significant attention among scholars who are concerned with aggregating the demographics of the slave trade, it may be that fifteenth- and sixteenth-century contemporaries found these women to be unremarkable because of their ubiquity rather than their absence.

Indeed, for some Iberians, West African women were a visual embodiment of the coast and its possibilities for trade. On the Cantino planisphere of 1502, the earliest map of Portuguese geographic discoveries, women signified Portuguese aspirations in West Africa (figure 4.1).[14] In black silhouette, curvy figures move about outside the Portuguese fort that dominates the interior of this map of the West African coast. The women are nude

11 Fage, "Slaves and Society," 306n76.
12 Wheat, *Atlantic Africa*; Green, *Rise of the Trans-Atlantic Slave Trade*; and Richardson and Silva, *Networks and Trans-cultural Exchange*.
13 This framing extends the work on Black radicalism by Cedric Robinson in *Black Marxism*.
14 The map is housed at the Biblioteca Estense, Modena, Italy. A PDF of the map can be found at http://bibliotecaestense.beniculturali.it/info/img/geo/i-mo-beu-c.g.a.2.html. Accessed November 30, 2020.

except for tools at their waists and a white cloth around the hips of one. Their bodies suggest an assumption that women provided crucial labor in West Africa and would do so in the New World. The Cantino map charted the African coast with "unprecedented accuracy and detail" and proved to be of crucial strategic and political use for Iberian traders and navigators.[15] These female figures convey a sense of confident knowingness as they cluster around the Portuguese fort (in marked contrast to the fantastical mysteries indicated by mythical animals found on many maps of the period—animals that symbolized the unknown).

The slave trade to Iberia was some fifty years old when the Cantino map was produced; an estimated 80,000 to 150,000 African captives had been brought to Portugal by that time.[16] After they had been marched through the streets of Lisbon in chains, African women encountered Portuguese female "clerks," whose job it was to ensure that Portuguese men did not force sex upon them before their sale—afterward, of course, such subjugation would be part of what positioned them as enslaved.[17] It is not clear that having female clerks present was widespread in Iberia. We do know from the official record of taxes on slave sales that throughout Spain women brought a higher price than men.[18] A German observer wrote in 1495 that the women offered for sale in Valencia were "well proportioned, with strong and long limbs."[19]

The sale of Black women also features in early modern Iberian popular culture. In the 1640s the Spanish poet Antonio Enríquez Gómez wrote, "Don't command me to steal anything except women of Guinea, daughters of the Congo and Mandiga, which are to be sold and bought."[20] For playwrights and cartographers alike, the sale of African women and children

---

15 It was not, of course, without errors. J. Gaspar, "Blunders, Errors and Entanglements," 184.

16 A. C. de C. M. Saunders estimates that there were 32,000 enslaved persons in Portugal by 1550. Robin Blackburn sees this as a conservative estimate and notes that "female slaves were nearly as numerous as male, a very different pattern from the norm on the [Atlantic] islands." Saunders, *Social History of Black Slaves*, 27; and Blackburn, *Making of New World Slavery*, 112–13. For a brief overview of the presence of Africans in Spain in the sixteenth century, see Weissbourd, "Race, Slavery."

17 Phillips, *Slavery*, 67–69. William Phillips writes that the clerks were there to "prevent them from being used as prostitutes," but this strikes me as euphemistic. One wonders who would be paying whom in the scenario of a raped and caged woman.

18 Phillips, *Slavery*; and Blumenthal, *Enemies and Familiars*.

19 Muzer, "Relacion del viaje," 1:328–417, quoted in Phillips, *Slavery*, 53.

20 Gómez, *Amor con Vida*, quoted in Schorsch, "Blacks, Jews and the Racial," 117.

FIGURE 4.1 Detail from Cantino planisphere, 1502. Biblioteca Estense, Modena, Italy. Estense Digital Library, accessed October 1, 2020. https://edl.beniculturali.it /beu/850013655.

had become part of normal Iberian culture. The cartographer who made the Cantino map chose women's bodies to symbolically place the West African coast in the Portuguese geographic imaginary; they were iconographically useful as a way to indicate the source and possibility of African wealth.

The important point here is that the Portuguese assumed that women were natural laborers alongside men and children. The presence of African families who were divided and put to work in Portuguese and Spanish households and fields did not provoke particular concern among most observers. Women were understood to be valuable investments and were noted as such without concern about femininity or sentiment.[21] These women's presence in the labor force was simply a daily reality of fifteenth- and

21 Their presence was raised only in ruminations on the importance of familial bonds as the Portuguese counted African converts to Christianity against Jews and Muslims. See Costa, "Portuguese-African Slave Trade," 47, 50.

early sixteenth-century slavery. Not until mines and sugar fields became potential sources of wealth in the Americas after the first decades of the sixteenth century did slave owners and slave traders begin to articulate a need for more male than female slaves.[22] Even so, they continued to use female labor without complaining about women's alleged inferiority in strength or endurance. They simultaneously consumed popular accounts of Africa that constructed racial difference through the notion that African women failed to meet expectations of femininity produced in the European imaginary.[23] While it is perhaps only symbolically relevant that the first enslaved sub-Saharan captive brought to Portugal was female, it is also an indicator that, right from the start, slave traders in Iberia and in the Iberian Atlantic would not balk at capturing and enslaving African women.[24]

And so, 120 years later, although the seventy-seven women and children who disembarked from the *Santiago* onto the shores of Puerto Rico in 1566 could not have known precisely what they would face on the island, women's use as both laborers and vectors of enslavability was predictable for slave traders and those who purchased human property. By the middle of the sixteenth century, ships loaded with captives had been leaving the African coast for Iberia, Cape Verde, the Gulf of Guinea islands, and, ultimately, the Americas for over a century. During those hundred years, some Europeans, especially those living in or traveling to port cities on the Mediterranean or in the southern Atlantic, would have been increasingly comfortable with the notion that African women were likely laborers for European property owners.

Had these women and children been captured a few decades earlier, they would likely have become laborers in Mexican and Peruvian mines. But mining had begun to diminish in the 1530s, and the sugar mills of Puerto Rico and Hispaniola had begun to fuel the demand for slave labor instead. At its height, the population of enslaved laborers in Puerto Rico reached fifteen thousand in 1565.[25] Thus, the women on the *Santiago* would have been compelled to do the rigorous work of cultivating sugar. They also would

22 On balanced sex ratios in Iberia and the desire for ship captains to obtain two-to-one ratios of men to women by the sixteenth century, see Green, *Rise of the Trans-Atlantic*, 239. For my argument that the orders to ship captains were entreaties rather than directives, see J. L. Morgan, *Laboring Women*, 50–68.
23 J. L. Morgan, "'Some Could Suckle.'"
24 Sweet, "Iberian Roots," 163, 156.
25 Stark, "African Slave Trade," 493–95.

have begun contending with the effects of that work on their bodies and their futures. Even though their capacity to reproduce was a benefit to their owners, from the moment they arrived in the sugar colony, their identities as mothers became primarily symbolic. Their ability to raise any children who had survived the transatlantic passage would have been severely hampered by the toll that cultivating sugar took on their bodies. Further, the likelihood that they would have any further children diminished.[26] As historian David Richardson has noted, "Females entering the Atlantic slave trade were destined . . . to live and die producing sugar and other crops rather than children."[27] The women who disembarked from the *Santiago* and other ships like it entered an Atlantic economy in which owners were fully prepared to unload them onto sugar fields, not into their kitchens or nurseries.

But before we leave them consigned to the brutal rhythms of cane cultivation in Puerto Rico, we need to consider their passage across the Atlantic. Was their experience of the Middle Passage markedly different from that of women who traveled in smaller numbers? Or of those who were captured and confined in the hold of a European ship with fewer women and more men? Would such differences matter? How, if at all, did the Middle Passage change on a boat full of women? Did their numbers protect them from the sexual rapacity of the crew, or did they attract further depravities? Did their identity as mothers—to either children on the ship with them or children they had been forced to leave behind—make them more or less aware of their altered futurity? Even when they were transported in smaller numbers, had the lives they had left behind given them tools or frameworks for understanding the realities of their commodification? Or did they experience that particular violence as forged entirely in the disorienting violation of the hold of a disastrously overcrowded ship somewhere in the middle of the Atlantic Ocean?

The metaphors historians have used when discussing the Middle Passage have tended to link it to either capital or challenges to capital. Historian Marcus Rediker describes the slave ship as a machine that delivered laborers to insatiable owners, while anthropologists Sidney Mintz and Richard Price use the notion of fictive kin as a metaphor that interrupts the machine of forced labor.[28] Kinship comes into sharp focus when we consider the experiences of women on slave ships. The concept of race requires

26 Tadman, "Demographic Cost of Sugar."
27 Richardson, "Cultures of Exchange," 172.
28 Rediker, *Slave Ship*; and Mintz and Price, *Birth of African-American Culture*. The notion of fictive kin—for example, of shipmates as chosen cousins—has driven considerable

a notion of kinship to make it legible. Infidels, heathens, and savages were seen as such because of their refusal to recognize the word of God or a similarly obstinate unwillingness or inability to avail themselves of the benefits of civility. While communities or nations may have been trapped in such dismal circumstances for generations, exposure to Christianity and civility conveyed at least the possibility of transformation and the legitimacy of damnation if change was rejected. Race, however, provided an entirely different corporeal certainty in which the generation and regeneration of subjection was produced by and through families.

Historians' perspective on the oppositionality between kin and the machine is rooted in nineteenth-century formulations of the distinction between public and private realms, a distinction already deeply marked by the claims of whiteness and civility when it emerged. Here, in the machinations of the early modern slave trade, we have something quite different. The machine of the early transatlantic slave trade did not simply feed on family—consuming as it did people who came to the trade enmeshed in kinship ties and communities amplified by them. It was sustained by creating a fiction in which the meaning of kinship was subsumed by racial hierarchy, the very thing that rendered familial ties dispensable in the eyes of slave traders.

Further, the notion of fictive kinship has had at least two unintended consequences in the scholarship on Atlantic slavery: "kinship" rather than "family" continues to mark Africans as outside of European hierarchies of humanity. Moreover, the emphasis on "fictive" marks biological family ties as impossible for captives, even though they included mothers and children, as we know from the fifteenth-century records.[29] Slave traders and slave owners were unwilling to locate themselves as perpetrators of violence. Instead, as exemplified by the convoluted writings we have already explored, they mobilized concepts of savagery and drew on gender, sexuality, and rationality to articulate racialized enslavability. Faced with the scant attention paid to the lives of fifteenth- and sixteenth-century West African women and children, which produces them only as evidence of the manliness of those who captured them or of the social disorder they were presumed to evoke, what route can we take toward understanding the

---

scholarship on the contours of slave resistance and has presented the idea that family ties served to interrupt the isolation that commodification attempted to impose.

29 See Brian Connolly's nuanced discussion of what he terms the "vernacular epistemology of kinship." Connolly, *Domestic Intimacies*, 166–209, esp. 169–95.

gendered experience of the Middle Passage and the impact it had on slaves' lives afterward? How is it possible to account for them?[30]

Recording Middle Passages

In my effort to unearth the symbolic arc of kin and economy in the context of Atlantic enslavement, I want to begin with some of the rare visual records of the slave trade. These eighteenth-century images have long been important to the social-historical project of comprehending the Middle Passage. But I'd like to read them for something more elusive and hard to grasp than the materiality of confinement on board slaving vessels. Even though these records were produced more than two hundred years after the voyage of the *Santiago*, they are useful in the effort to translate the meaning that has come to be attached to the Middle Passage both for historians and for the women, men, and children who endured it.

The plan of the *Marie Seraphique*, from a 1769 voyage from present-day Luanda, Angola, is unique because it was produced by an eyewitness to the trade, a second lieutenant on board the ship who offered a glimpse of the materiality of the voyage (figure 4.2).[31] Still, the challenge of imagining the victims of the Middle Passage as other than predominantly male is bolstered by the visual archive's hold on historical memory. Here we see women throughout the ship, and at least one woman clasping her baby at the stern of the boat. Other small figures throughout indicate that the nursing infant was not the only child on board. Yet one is primarily struck by the uniformity of the figures depicted. The viewer struggles to discern any marks of sex, age, or infirmity that distinguished one captive from another. Documents of the experience of the Middle Passage were deeply steeped in the political economy of the moment of their production. These images constitute an "imagistic memorial site," perhaps more memorial than evidence.[32] At the same time, as is the case with so much of the Black

---

30 In framing this chapter and, indeed, the larger intervention it bolsters, I owe a considerable debt to Stephanie Smallwood's *Saltwater Slavery*, in particular her brilliant and generative second chapter, "Turning African Captives into Atlantic Commodities," in which she attends to the fact that for captives on the Middle Passage, "'accountable' history was only as real as the violence and racial fiction at its foundation." Smallwood, *Saltwater Slavery*, 34.

31 On the identity of the image's painter, see Radburn and Eltis, "Visualizing the Middle Passage," 544.

32 M. Wood, *Blind Memory*, 16.

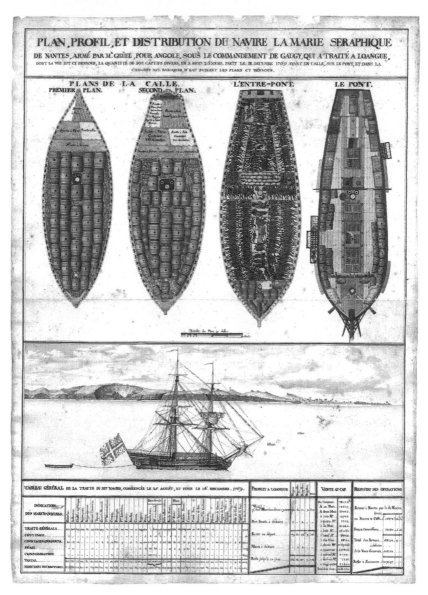

FIGURE 4.2 *Plan, profile, and layout of the ship* Marie Seraphique, 1769. Nantes History Museum, France. *Slavery and Remembrance,* accessed October 1, 2020. http://slaveryandremembrance.org/collections/object/?id=OB0026.

Atlantic archive, they become the visual touchstone for future efforts to depict the history of that trade. Our visual archive is tethered to the numeracy of the merchant record. There too the enslaved are rendered as a tabula rasa, people without the distinguishing marks of culture or civic identity that could have interrupted their fate.

Efforts to capture the dehumanization of the trade, like the widely reproduced cross section of the slave ship *Brookes* (ca. 1788), offered a gesture of sympathy that simultaneously denied the people depicted any possibility of autonomy (figure 4.3). Titled *Description of a Slave Ship*, it was meant to convey the horrors of overcrowding on board a typical slave ship. Whether it does so is a matter of dispute, as it misrepresents the numbers and conditions of those on board this ship.[33] It does, however, provide a visual argument that the enslaved were in a state of natural dispossession.[34] To write a history of the Middle Passage is to write with and through the image of the *Brookes*, as it instigated an antislavery imaginary that bolsters current scholarship. As art historian Cheryl Finley has recently argued, *Description of a Slave Ship* became the "slave ship icon," an image with a powerful and deeply resonant hold on how diasporic scholars and artists wrestle with the histories of the Middle Passage.[35]

In this eighteenth-century illustration, the subject is slavery, not the enslaved. The illustrator used the people in this image to condemn guilty slave owners. Captives are to be mourned, but they are not the subjects; the visual economy here centers slave traders and the British public. Women are present on the *Brookes*. We see them separated from the men in the illustration, their location on the upper deck reflecting the protocols of the slave trade and indicating that ship captains and crew did plan for the presence of women on board their ships. But that intentionality does not convey much more than the fact of their presence. Even in a later French version of the image that includes a woman on the upper deck giving birth, this is a sympathy that offers no real possibility of futurity (figure 4.4). The woman in childbirth is crammed among women whose bent knees signal their debilitating present. Her head rests in the lap of one woman, while another woman reaches between her legs to assist in the birth of the child, a child already marked for the market. The image presupposes the viewers'

33 Radburn and Eltis, "Visualizing the Middle Passage," 536.
34 M. Wood, "Celebrating the Middle Passage," 124; see also his full discussion of *Description of a Slave Ship*, in M. Wood, *Blind Memory*, 17.
35 Finley, *Committed to Memory*, 19–56.

DESCRIPTION OF A SLAVE SHIP.

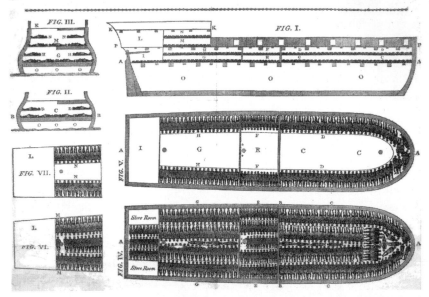

FIGURE 4.3 *Description of a Slave Ship*, 1801. The British Library, London, England. The British Library, accessed October 1, 2020. https://www.bl.uk/collection-items /diagram-of-the-brookes-slave-ship.

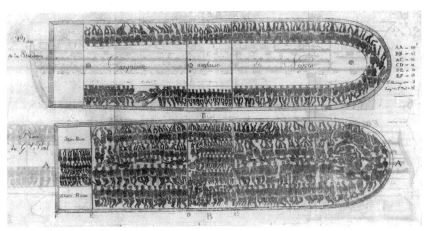

FIGURE 4.4 *Diagram of the Decks of a Slave Ship*, 1814. From *Slavery Images: A Visual Record of the African Slave Trade and Slave Life in the Early African Diaspora*, accessed July 28, 2020. http://slaveryimages.org/s/slaveryimages/item/2004.

recognition that the child signals nothing more than value and vulnerability. To catch sight of birth on board the slave ship, then, is to see how reproduction arranged enslavement and how the "radically different temporality" of death and birth into slavery is itself at the heart of the modern world.[36] This image calls forth the hideous development of the birth of a commodity that would underpin global markets, not the birth of a child enmeshed in a web of affect and kin.

One can only assume that the illustrator inserted the image of the woman giving birth as a device intended to shock his viewers into action. One can almost be forgiven for not seeing her at first and then being stunned in the moment of recognition. But the ability to include such a moment on a slave ship depends on generations of evidence, of circulating stories and experiences retold. The birth on that ship was likely no more a surprise to the nineteenth-century viewer than the news that the sugar on English tables and the tobacco in English pipes depended on the hundreds of bodies crammed into ships like the *Brookes*. The shock came only from the way the intimacy of kinship production forcefully interrupted the machinery of the slave trade. The reality was that the entire economy of the colonies depended on the *claim* that African women gave birth to slaves, not to daughters or sons, not to kin. While increasing their property through childbirth was not the dominant economic strategy of slave owners in the Americas, these prerogatives attached to the logic that linked race, property, and kinlessness are foundational. To fully reckon with that reality, we must restore enslaved women in our understanding of what the Middle Passage entailed and how their lives were embedded in the unfolding structures of the slave trade from its earliest iterations.

Gendering Middle Passages

Women who gave birth during the Middle Passage would have been captured in an early stage of pregnancy. Their condition would have dawned on them during the stages of their capture—forced overland marches, confinement in a slave fort, a long wait on a ship from which the coast was tantalizingly visible, and then the realization that the view of the coast and all it held was slipping permanently away. For these women, pregnancy would thus mark the commencement of a journey into a future in which protecting or parenting their children would grow increasingly impossible. Rather

36 Clifford, *Routes*, 265.

than succumbing to the shock of their travails, we need to consider both the ubiquity of their presence in the slave trade and the unimaginable experience of pregnancy and delivery on board a slave ship for what it might tell us about the structures of kinlessness and enslavement.

The reality of their location in kinship networks would obviously endure for the women and men who found themselves captured and transported to waiting ships. Other aspects of their pasts would also constitute the grounds on which they would attempt to understand the violence that delivered them to the Americas and to build new frameworks for understanding their present. The acquisition and sale of slaves in Africa for the transatlantic trade used local concepts of value.[37] As an example, the Kabre in the Togo hinterlands have an unsettling and enduring reputation for selling their own kin to African traders. While grappling with the extent to which such a reputation sets them outside "the Western analytical (and popular) dichotomy between persons and things," anthropologist Charles Piot centers Kabre structures of value and ownership in order to identify indigenous economic principles that help situate the meanings embedded in what appears to be a long-standing practice of children being sold by their mother's brother before the age of initiation.

These acts of sale occurred in the nexus between staking ownership claims to the children and maintaining control over the mechanics of loss in the face of vulnerability to external raids or debt peonage. They were more complicated than evidence that Africans would expose those they knew to the alienation of the marketplace. Instead, the sale of kin was part of an effort to retain power through assessments of risk, value, and commerce that the Kabre mobilized in concert with notions of kinship and community. But at the same time, the communities in which these strategic enactments of the sale of kin took place would have been well versed in the wrenching economies of human commodification.[38] Those subjected to such sale at the hands of their uncles would understand the entanglements between kinship and commodification even before their passage across the Atlantic.

When European travelers wrote either that Africans could be lured by their children or that they sold children, they recognized family ties among

---

37 Piot, "Of Slaves and the Gift," 48nn34–35. African historians have paid significant attention to how slaves were acquired for both internal and external slave markets. This attention to supply and demand is rooted in the conviction that clarity on these questions will illuminate the extent to which Europeans or Africans shaped the terms of trade. Such research is designed to clarify the power dynamics between trading polities.
38 Shaw, *Memories of the Slave Trade*, 40–45.

captives. They absolutely knew that kinship ties existed among those they enslaved, and yet they insistently erased this knowledge from their accounting. They provided, instead, evidence of inconsistent knowing that Africans were indeed members of families even as they mounted a system of hereditary racial slavery that required the conceptual framework of kinship and inheritance. At the end of the eighteenth century, the enslaved woman Belinda remembered her fears of moon-faced men with bows and arrows "like the thunder and lightning of clouds" during her childhood on the Volta River on the Gold Coast. The terrors of her girlhood were made more poignant by the agony of her actual capture. She rendered her separation from her parents in the language of rape: she was "ravished from the bosom of her country . . . cruelly separated from her [aging parents] for ever." And she wrote that she and her fellow captives endured, during the Middle Passage, "the most excrutiating torments."[39] Belinda's words evoke a terror and wrenching recognition of separation that had by then gripped women and girls captured on the coast for more than 250 years.

Many African children would have similarly found themselves facing an uncertain future in the hands of European slave owners who seemed to be incapable of seeing them as children. Quobna Ottobah Cugoano wrote of his first sight of white people on the Ghanaian coast and his fear that they would eat him, "according to our notion as children in the inland parts of the country."[40] These remembrances are evidence of how knowledge of slavery and capture had saturated the Gold Coast by the first decades of the eighteenth century and suggest the landscape of loss and suffering the transatlantic trade left in its wake.[41]

But when Belinda petitioned the Massachusetts legislature in 1783 for compensation after living in slavery for some fifty years, her language reflected her acumen about the value of her labor, which "augmented" the "immense wealth" of her owner, the loyalist Isaac Royall. The vast array of experiences that bolstered her ability to petition the legislature are lost to us now, but the processes that shaped her sense of her value cannot be

39 "Belinda Sutton's Petition," 1783, Massachusetts Archives Collection, Boston, accessed October 1, 2020, https://dataverse.harvard.edu/dataset.xhtml?persistentId=doi:10.7910 /DVN/0GMCO. See also Sutton, "Petition," 142.
40 Cugoano, "Thoughts and Sentiments," 149.
41 Paul Lovejoy writes that "an understanding of the living conditions of people from western Africa must assess the extent of death and destruction and the impact on those reduced to a service status, whether or not they stayed in Africa or were sent to the Americas." Lovejoy, "Daily Life in Western Africa," 4.

segregated from her very early awareness that she was not protected by kinship from the violent dislocation of the Atlantic market. It is Belinda's clarity that is most significant, for it demonstrates the very different work that kinship and capitalism had come to perform for the enslaved and for slave owners. Belinda clearly articulates the ways in which her work built Royall's wealth on the painful ground of her own severed kin ties. Those ties continued to define her and her relationship to her past and her present even though in some ways her enslavement was rooted in the fiction that such ties didn't exist. Belinda's petition thus clarifies that the work of erasing kinship was always incomplete. Because Belinda and other African women like her received no protection from their identities as members of families, their lack of control over their reproduction only amplified their sense of loss. A clear understanding of that loss existed on the African coast as a direct result of the slave trade. That sense of understanding, that critical comprehension, was sedimented from the violence wrought by a trade that depended on alienating human beings from the very communities that knew them to be human beings.

The records of the trade reflect that alienation, albeit from very different vantage points. If we return to the incomplete records from ship captains and slave traders regarding women on their ships, we find an interesting echo in the very few instances when survivors of the slave trade wrote of their experiences. The erasures ship captains performed might be usefully contrasted with the silences of the few autobiographical accounts of capture and sale to the Atlantic market and the even fewer first-person accounts of surviving the passage. Although both sources leave unanswered questions about the Middle Passage in their wake, their silences perform exceedingly different work.

Survivors of the forced crossing rarely offer a glimpse of what the transport actually entailed. Olaudah Equiano's narrative provides the fullest account of the conditions on the slave ship. His account reports that the "loathsome smells . . . the filth of the necessary tubs . . . the shrieks of the women, and the groans of the dying, rendered the whole a scene of horror almost inconceivable."[42] Whether he was writing from experience or from the stories passed down to him from those who did endure the passage, Equiano narrates an experience that most writers allowed to fade from view.[43] Narrative arcs begin with an African home, but the rupture caused

42 Equiano, *Interesting Narrative*, 41.
43 On the claims regarding Equiano's birthplace, see Carretta, *Equiano the African*, 1–17; and A. Byrd, "Eboe, Country, Nation."

by the captives' first view of "houses with wings" is usually followed by a fundamental silence about what happened on those ships.[44] There is an enduring opacity about the nature of the passage pierced only by an author whose experience of the passage itself isn't fully verified.

Most autobiographers either skipped the passage altogether or gave strikingly minimal accounts of it, preferring to focus primarily on their lives either before or after the forced transatlantic crossing.[45] Writing in the vein of gratitude for Christian conversion and traveling as a special "beloved" slave of the ship's captain, James Gronniosaw recalled the transatlantic passage only as the source of temporary seasickness that "wore off" as he became accustomed to it.[46] There is no space in his testimony for the agony of those who traveled under vastly different circumstances. Similarly, Venture Smith devoted a third of his narrative to a description of his multiple captures and transfers to the Ghanaian coast and only one sentence to the Middle Passage—that it was "an ordinary passage, except great mortality by the small pox, which broke out on board"; he noted that "out of the two hundred and sixty that sailed from Africa, not more than two hundred [arrived] alive."[47]

These short accounts suggest that the Middle Passage was unrepresentable for those who survived it. It is certainly not hard to fathom that to speak of the pain of that experience might have been to reinsert oneself into a moment of brutality that was all the more disturbing because of its attachment to one's present alterity. Perhaps the singularity of that pain inaugurated a life that was so powerfully reconfigured that to speak of it risked too much. Including that account in testimony designed to refuse what the Middle Passage was supposed to have wrought might have brought back the specter of the agonies of commodification. That slave narratives exist at all is proof that the claims that the commodification of the Middle Passage triumphed over kinship were false. Those who wrote such narratives did so to bear witness to the falsity of the claim, but the risks attendant on speaking of it were considerable and were not to be taken lightly.[48]

While there is no doubt that a curtain of sorts fell between the African present and the future as it would unfold on a slave ship, the West African

44 Gronniosaw, *Narrative* (1780), 14.
45 Handler, "Survivors of the Middle Passage," 39.
46 Gronniosaw, "Narrative" (1772), 38.
47 V. Smith, "Narrative," 375.
48 For the foundational discussion of the role of writing in the history of slavery, see Gates, *Figures in Black*, 3–58.

coast was peopled with those who struggled to make sense of their losses. On a slave ship in the mid-eighteenth century, a seven-year-old boy lamented his capture. He had been "caught up" while out tending goats, and he feared that his mother and younger siblings would starve in his absence as he was the eldest and believed in his singular role as provider because "his father was taken away before, therefore there was no one to help her now."[49] His anxiety could only have been surpassed by that of his mother, who may not have known the fates that awaited both her son and his father but certainly understood that their bodies had been devastatingly altered by the market.

Many narratives of slavery evoke the "bitter wailings of a bereft mother, the deep anxiety of an afflicted father, the tender lamentations and suffused eyes of brothers and sisters," but few allow that expressions of sorrow and loss might contain with them an analytic of economic suffering.[50] That bitter wailings convey only affect and not calculus is a divide that is contradicted by the women who were positioned to understand the violence that underpinned the rationality of the marketplace. Here the focus on kinship illuminates what the political scientist Cedric Robinson calls the origins of Black radicalism. Kinship offers a counternarrative in which maternity and political economy occupy the same field of meaning. It suggests that enslaved women's grief clarifies something other than the simple existence of family life among the captives: it rather suggests the growth of a critical comprehension among captive Africans about the relationship between the disruption of family and the production of children for a marketplace.

While Africans could not have anticipated or prepared for the particular brutalities of the transatlantic voyage, they could clearly comprehend the appropriation of kinship for a new and brutal kind of profit. Although I do not intend to suggest parity or continuity between the use of slavery in West Africa and its use by white Europeans, it is crucial to grasp that many women on the West African coast occupied subordinated and, in some cases, exploited statuses even before the European trade in slaves wrought havoc in local polities. The recognition that their subordination would, in a sense, continue could not possibly have brought any kind of comfort. Indeed, it could amplify the agony of recognition, as they understood the degree to which a framework of subordination could deliver one into a realm of suffering previously inconceivable. And, of course, the emotional

49 Brinch, *Blind African Slave*, 74.
50 Webb, *Memoir of Mrs. Chloe Spear*.

consequences of recognizing that one kind of suffering echoed another cannot possibly be apprehended from this distance. It is quite possible that doing so simply compounded the psychic cost of capture and transport.

But we should attend to the possibility that this kind of horrible recognition of economic violence laid the groundwork for a politics of gendered recognition, a critique of power rendered more visceral because of women's capacities to birth both a marketable commodity and a market gain.[51] We must continue to reckon with the capacity of enslaved women to understand that their reproductive lives were embedded in the calculated logic of the slave trade and its aftermath. That recognition was steeped in so much agony as to be rendered almost incomprehensible. But there are glimpses of what it meant to route commodification (and its refusal) through kin. We can apprehend it in the work that "mother" does when, a world and centuries away, faced with the agony of her sons' and daughters' return to slavery at the hands of slave catchers in Ohio, Margaret Garner pled, "Mother, help me kill the children."[52]

Once ships pulled away from shores, calculations of risk and possibility took on a desperate importance. For women, who often retained a greater freedom of mobility (with all the vulnerabilities and possibilities that went with it), calculating those risks could lead in a number of directions. For many of the women who were on the ship with Cugoano in the mid-eighteenth century, the possibilities ahead were so bleak once it left the coast that they planned to set fire to the ship; they preferred mass suicide to whatever lay ahead. All of the women had remained unchained so that the "dirty filthy sailors [could] take the African women and lie upon their bodies." But for one of the women, the anguish of repeated sexual violation was preferable to being engulfed in flames. She betrayed the plan. Her calculations added up to a different conclusion. In the aftermath of the attempted revolt, many of the women perished because the "discovery was likewise a cruel bloody scene."[53] The "likewise" distressingly reveals the persistence of the "cruel and bloodied" usage they were subjected to by filthy sailors.

51 The argument that enslaved women were close observers of power is one that I make in J. L. Morgan, "*Partus Sequitur Ventrem.*"

52 Reinhardt, *Who Speaks for Margaret Garner?*, 59, 221. Paul Gilroy writes that Margaret Garner's story, like Frederick Douglass's, articulates a "contribution towards slave discourse on the nature of freedom itself." Freedom is a desire for death over the perversion of maternity that her story reflects. Gilroy, *Black Atlantic*, 66–69, esp. 68.

53 Cugoano, "Thoughts and Sentiments," 149.

Historian Sowande Mustakeem has documented the ubiquity of sexual violence on late eighteenth-century and nineteenth-century slave ships. That experience was augmented by the more profound isolation that female captives experienced on ships where they were significantly outnumbered in the later decades of the trade.[54] Here I want to locate the exposure of female captives to sexual predation and violation as foundational to the production of race and racial hierarchy, rather than as its horrifying culmination. This kind of evidence in the Black Atlantic archive only faintly outlines the ubiquity of women's violation on slave ships, countering the erasures performed in captains' ledger books. In this realm of accounting, women's movements and roles are visible, even if only partially so.

The prevalence of rape on slave ships hovers in the background even when it isn't spoken of directly. When discussing the fear of rebellion off the coast of Whydah in 1702, a slave ship captain wrote, "To avoid a similar incident, we put the largest part of our Negroes in irons, and even among the Negresses those who appeared to us the most resolute and the most dangerous. . . . Although because of their beauty they were very dear to the chief officers and sailors who had each given their names to chosen ones, there was nothing left to do but put them in chains."[55] The captain's statement of resignation reveals a host of outrages that reflect the extent to which the discursive realm he traveled had firmly situated these women as bounty. This view had congealed by the start of the eighteenth century. Although this captain sometimes inserted outrage into his offhand tone, rape of captive women on slave ships persisted regardless of how captains felt about it. For captive women, the terms of their enslavement were always conveyed on and in their bodies. Rape has always functioned as a tool of war, and for the women exposed to the sexual predation of crewmen, perhaps it was experienced as such. Narrative descriptions of women's experiences during the passage were part of a stylized visual economy in which the violence directed at them was always sexualized for the European reader and viewer (figure 4.5).

The prevalence of rape may have been a significant factor in some women's willingness to further endanger themselves by organizing revolts on slave ships.[56] In 1735 a rebellion on a ship captured the work that gender and race

---

54 Mustakeem, *Slavery at Sea*, 86–90.

55 *Voyages aux côtes de Guinée* (1719), quoted in Munford, *Black Ordeal of Slavery*, 2:344. See also Taylor, *If We Must Die*, 32–35, for a full discussion of sexual violence on board ships.

56 Richardson, "Shipboard Revolts," 76.

FIGURE 4.5 Pretaxat Oursel, *Transport des négres dans les colonies* (Transportation of negroes to the colonies), 1800s. Musée d'Histoire de la Ville et du Pays Malouin, Saint Malo, France. *Slavery Images: A Visual Record of the African Slave Trade and Slave Life in the Early African Diaspora*, accessed July 28, 2020. http://slaveryimages .org/s/slaveryimages/item/3000.

could perform in the eighteenth-century trade. Before the rebellion, an African called Captain Tomba had been enslaved on Bance Island. Enraged by Tomba's role in organizing local Baga villagers to defy English slave traders, the factor at Bance had made a pointed effort to find and capture him. Tomba's commitment to fighting the slave traders continued on the *Robert*, and he, together with three other men and a woman who brought him weapons and crucial strategic information, attempted to take over the ship. When they were discovered, the ship's captain decided that the conspirators' value precluded executing them but not whipping them. The woman who had joined Tomba's effort was the only conspirator the captain executed (although he also executed two other slaves to teach the rest a lesson). The unnamed woman was "hoisted up by the Thumbs, whipp'd, and slashed . . . with Knives before the other Slaves till she died."[57] Her death was neither more nor less brutal because of her sex, but the captain may have made a greater spectacle of it because she was female.

From the perspective of ship captains, women posed particular challenges to order—not just to the structural organization of the ship but also to the captains' larger sense of hierarchical certainty regarding deeply held beliefs about gender, sex, and the concept of difference. Women's contradictory

57 Atkins, *Voyage to Guinea*; Rediker, *Slave Ship*, 14–16.

location in the nascent hierarchy of race and sex was never more forcefully articulated than on a slave ship. When crew members "chose" women, their vulnerability was highlighted. Yet because they were given greater range of motion owing to the alleged docility of their gender, women were at the heart of every successful insurrection. Revolts were more likely to occur on ships with fewer men and more children, suggesting that maternal ties during capture and enslavement produced a range of radical responses.[58] Women's presence on slave ships and auction blocks evoked the problem of their contradictory reproductive potential; they were listed in family units even as the logic of the slave trade sought to erase the concept of filial relation. The work of race and capitalism is embedded in this simultaneous ascription and erasure, in this intermittent knowing regarding the motherhood of enslaved women. Even the accounts of the death and suffering of African women point to the shifting terrain they were meant to occupy.

It is difficult to calculate women's mortality rate during the Middle Passage compared to that of men and children, although evidence suggests that women succumbed in equal proportion to men.[59] The meaning ascribed to that mortality, however, became attached to European gender conventions. Many eighteenth-century slave traders thought that men felt the "fixed melancholy" that killed so many captives more keenly than women and children. Traders believed that the weakness of character of women and children made them quick to recover from the nostalgia that led captives to desire and often bring about their own death.[60] Assigning a cause to slave deaths was an important part of the record keeping of slave traders, and in their logbooks they positioned women contradictorily, as both more vigorous than men and more inclined to madness. This contradiction raises the question whether women's madness during the Middle Passage was connected to their feelings about the devastating consequences of their past and future reproduction.

Slave ship captains were reluctant observers of captive women's reproduction. They were, in fact, reluctant observers of much that transpired in their work as slave traders. The literary theorist Hortense Spillers writes that that although the traders' lack of curiosity about their captives— their "inveterate obscene blindness"—should astonish us, we know that

58 Richardson, "Shipboard Revolts"; and Behrendt, Eltis, and Richardson, "Costs of Coercion."
59 J. L. Morgan, *Laboring Women*, 51–56.
60 Mallipeddi, "'Fixed Melancholy,'" 241.

it existed.[61] Such blindness seems to have been at the heart of the race making underway as ship captains and slave traders worked to normalize the violations they were setting in motion. To nineteenth-century critics of slavery and the slave trade, the notion of birth on these ships of death was by no means anomalous. Also, women's bodily presence was a reminder of their reproductive possibilities, which were a key component in how slave owners and slave traders imagined their racialized difference. Motherhood had to be replaced by something more functionalist, set apart from affective connections.

From the very beginning of the slave trade, European observers wrestled with the contradictory space of maternal longing. In the incident from 1441 that Zurara described, such longing was key to capturing a woman by using her infant son as a lure. Yet Europeans simultaneously dismissed the connections among African kinfolk as foolish or nonexistent. So how do we comprehend the space of maternity on a slave ship? Is the brutality of the slave ship best captured by the agonizing image of a woman giving birth on board, a woman who endured the dawning reality of her pregnancy and her enslavement simultaneously?

The eighteenth-century Black Englishman Ignatius Sancho, born on a slave ship and the author of a series of letters on his life and the problems of slavery published posthumously in 1782, described the story of his birth.[62] The onset of his mother's labor came amid the roiling rhythms of a fetid ship. His birth must have generated profoundly mixed feelings for her. Whatever the nature of those feelings, she did not experience them for long; she died of fever shortly after the ship carrying them arrived in the Spanish colony of New Granada (Colombia). Sancho's father could not bear the conditions he found himself in and committed suicide, leaving infant Sancho to a slave owner who risked the toddler's life on another Atlantic crossing before delivering him into enslavement in England. Sancho's nameless mother, forever consigned to an obscurity that was interrupted only by her son's rise to literacy and public prominence, embodied the reproductive logic of hereditary racial slavery even as the particularity of giving birth on the slave ship amplified its grammar.[63]

61 Spillers, "Mama's Baby, Papa's Maybe," 70.
62 Sancho, "Letters of the Late Ignatius Sancho," 100. For more on Sancho's life and influences, see Sandhu, "Ignatius Sancho."
63 In her groundbreaking "Mama's Baby, Papa's Maybe," Hortense Spillers laid the theoretical groundwork for considering race as a grammar that structured both the slave

Her experience was not singular. On the ship *James* in 1675, one woman died days before the ship left the African coast, where its crew had been loading men and women for months. Her misery must have been excruciating as she "miscarreyed and the child dead within her and Rotten she dyed two days after delivery." The agony of the experience shimmers through the columns of the ship captain's "Account of the Mortality aboard the *James*." The link between her and another woman lost during the passage may not have been obvious to the crew, but they seem intimately connected: little more than two months later, another mother on the ship succumbed after what the captain saw as maternal madness: "Being very fond of her Child, Carrying her up and downe, wore her to nothing by which means fell into a feavour and dyed."[64] The register of grief is erased from the captain's accounting, even if its traces can still be apprehended. But as the theorist Judith Butler has argued, "without grievability, there is no life, or, rather, there is something living that is other than life."[65] Here there is an account. Here maternity and madness overlap, and the role of the captain as a distant observer leaves a trace that evokes both the presence of pregnant women and the perversion of what a pregnancy could portend.

In whatever way it saturated the chaotic violence of the Middle Passage, motherhood was part of the rationalizing equation of capture and sale. It supported the market. According to agents of the Royal African Company stationed in Barbados, when the ship *Delight* arrived in 1683, a third of the captives were "very small most of them noe better then sucking children nay many of them did suck theire Mothers that were on boarde." The captain responded to this complaint, for complaint it was, with the argument that bringing them "cost not much and the shipp had as good bring them as nothing she being paid by the month."[66] His reasoning was indeed correct, though the rational calculus covered far more complicated equations than he was capable of considering. In 1750, on the *Duke of Argyle*, the captain rejected one woman and her "young child" because she was "very long

---

trade and, subsequently, American life.

64 "Voyage of *The James*, 1675–76," in Donnan, *Documents Illustrative*, 206–9.

65 Butler, *Frames of War*, 15.

66 PRO T70/16 f49, Edwyne Steede Stephen Gascoigne to Royal Africa Company, Barbados, April 1683. National Archives, Kew, England. Also quoted in Galenson, *Traders, Planters, and Slaves*, 110–11. The ship they refer to is voyage 15076, *Delight* (1683), http://slavevoyages.org/voyage/database.

breasted." It must be assumed that another trader would not have been so choosy. Another woman was purchased with her "small child" without comment. Other women were loaded alongside small boys or girls with whom they may or may not have shared blood ties.[67]

The assumption that enslaved women would provide some kind of care for the children consistently made its way into the narratives of survivors of the trade. But ultimately the care women provided for children was only a source of increased vulnerability. Here, perhaps, we can see kinship on display in its most tortured form, as women were tasked with protecting infants and children for a future that loomed in shadow and violence. Indeed, for some, it may have occasioned even further violation, as with a woman—known only by the number 83 assigned to her in the captain's record of his complement of slaves—raped "brutelike in view of the whole quarter deck." The captain's unwillingness or inability to protect this woman rebounded into an empty promise recorded primarily for his own eyes: "If anything happens to the woman I shall impute it to him, for she was big with child." Of course, something quite profound had already happened to the woman. Her rape and her pregnancy both demarcated her descent into hereditary racial slavery. While she could not fully comprehend her new status at that point, should she and her child have survived the journey, we can imagine that there would be many moments in which the starkness of her body's new value would cause her to jerk back into the visceral memory of her violation on board the ship. She and other women on that ship and many other ships would have had to grapple over and over again with the perverted futurity that their pregnant and captive bodies foretold.[68]

On January 7, 1750, on the coast of Sierra Leone, a steward for the *Duke of Argyle* purchased a woman in a bit of a bidding war with a French trader. From the captain's journal, we learn that the loading of his ship had been adversely affected by the autonomy of African traders on the coast, who would no longer bring slaves to the ship, instead forcing traders to come to them. He understood that "she [was] a good slave" and thus sent his steward to purchase her. Once he obtained her, he saw that she "had a very bad mouth" and had cost him more than he would have liked. She died on

---

67 John Newton, entries dated January 25, February 10, and March 20, 1750, on board the *Duke of Argyle*, in J. Newton, *Journal of a Slave Trader*.

68 John Newton, entry dated January 31, 1753, on board the *African*, in J. Newton, *Journal of a Slave Trader*. For further discussion of sexual violence on board eighteenth-century slave ships, and of this case in particular, see Mustakeem, *Slavery at Sea*, 86–88.

June 13, a mere two weeks after the ship finally left the coast for the Atlantic passage but more than five months after being brought on board. He wrote, "This morning buryed a woman slave (no. 47). Know not what to say she died of for she has not been properly alive since she first came on board."[69] The inevitability of her death is highlighted by the captain's inattention on a later journey to the potential mortality of the women on board. Faced with the unsettling prospect of having to go to the American mainland from Montserrat rather than to Jamaica, he wrote, "I should be extremely loath to venture so far, for we have had the men slaves so long on board that their patience is just worn out, and I am certain they would drop fast had we another passage to make."[70] He wrote nothing about the patience or vulnerability of the women on his ship.

But it is the words of ship captains who were unmoved by the immorality of the trade that provide us with glimpses of what enslavement meant for women. The English slave ship surgeon turned abolitionist Alexander Falconbridge published his accounts of the slave trade in 1788. Designed to raise opposition to the trade, Falconbridge mobilized the pain of the women he encountered so as to produce sympathy in his reader. Through interpreters, a woman captive on board a ship off New Calabar, near present-day Port Harcourt, Nigeria, told Falconbridge that "she had been kidnapped and, notwithstanding she was big with child, sold for a slave."[71] In his discussion of madness brought on by the Middle Passage, Falconbridge described only women. He wrote of a woman so "dejected" that she wanted "nothing but to die" and of women chained to the decks of slave ships because they had gone mad—a madness that did not prevent their sale "during a lucid interval" to the owners of the sugar fields of Jamaica. It appeared also in descriptions of women's refusal of food or their persistent efforts to commit suicide by jumping overboard or by hanging themselves. (Women used their mobility on ships to procure rope and hang themselves in the night while laying on their sides "using great exertion."[72]) Evidence gathered toward the end of the eighteenth century, when female captives were significantly outnumbered by males, consistently suggest that

69 John Newton, entries dated January 7 and June 13, 1750, on board the *Duke of Argyle*, in J. Newton, *Journal of a Slave Trader*, 28, 56.
70 John Newton, entry dated June 3, 1753, on board the *African*, in J. Newton, *Journal of a Slave Trader*, 81.
71 Falconbridge, *Account of the Slave Trade*, 17.
72 Falconbridge, *Account of the Slave Trade*, 38–42.

women's efforts to escape the Middle Passage were as intense as those of their male counterparts.[73]

The narrative histories of female captives aboard the slave ships that sailed the Atlantic in the early modern and modern periods come to us as a pastiche of demographic records, distant witnesses, polemic images, and autobiographies asphyxiated by their narrative structure. Casting about for a fragment of evidence that best conveys the specificity of violence and its generative economy demands a methodological capaciousness. The literary scholar and social theorist Saidiya Hartman has suggested that we need a "critical fabulation" in the face of the impossibility of recovering the histories of those whose absence from the archive is a systemic manifestation of the violence perpetrated against them; this is a call for a methodological strategy by which we can hear the "mutters and oaths and cries of the commodity."[74]

73 W. Blake, *History of Slavery*, 129, 141. Evidence of suicide rates during the Middle Passage is sparse and, as Terri L. Snyder has argued, difficult to quantify. Snyder, "Suicide, Slavery, and Memory." For a very limited period toward the end of the eighteenth century, about 5 to 7 percent of all deaths in and leading up to the Middle Passage were considered self-inflicted. Eltis, *Rise of African Slavery*, 157n73.

74 Hartman, "Venus in Two Acts," 11.

FIVE. "The Division of the Captives":
Commerce and Kinship in the English Americas

For those who survived the Middle Passage, startling new identities would come into existence in the New World, defined by the interplay of unrelenting market relations and violent subjection at the hands of Europeans. Such intrusions on the capacity to understand themselves as kinfolk existed side by side with their efforts to maintain their ties to one another, and to their origins in communities, during their transport and capture. Their location as the foundation on which extractive colonial economies would be built across the Americas was an abstraction that couldn't have been clear to many—but the myriad small exchanges in which their identities in families or their forged connections as kinfolk were disrupted and destroyed by the market in and for their bodies were anything but abstract.

As they navigated this new terrain, the material experiences and comprehensions that captives brought with them into their captivity met the market exchanges that would now define them. As they disembarked from slave ships up and down the western Atlantic coast, they brought with them a clear understanding of the dangers of capture and captivity as well as knowledge of markets, commodities, currency, valuations, and, of course, kinship. Disorientation and questions abounded, but as they tried to brace themselves for what would come next, survivors of the Middle

The quotation in the chapter title is from Gomes Eannes de Zurara, *The Chronicle of the Discovery and Conquest of Guinea* (1896), 81.

Passage faced the first immediate articulation of their new identity—their sale. The myriad sales of slaves were part of the fabric of everyday life. They offered repetitive object lessons to those being sold and to those buying slaves that market relations were embedded in the bodies of this particular category of human being. They made it clear that, whatever else one might hope for and dream of in these lands, the market would forever undermine Black people's social connections.

Across the seventeenth-century English Atlantic world, sales of people took place in the open. The lesson Zurara learned while watching the sale of captives in Portugal, the one he attempted to convey on paper, would reverberate for both captives and buyers again and again on the other side of the Atlantic. The captives, the buyers, and the sellers were publicly locked in a practice of monetizing human beings that was both banal in its quotidian nature and unprecedented. As the philosopher Sylvia Wynter notes in her elaboration of the *pieza*—the term given to the ideal slave, the African man who functioned as the standard of value for Portuguese slave traders—the act of sale "reduced the African from the specificity of his/her multiple identities to quantifiable Negro labor."[1] The narrative slippages that had rendered Africans as currency for a hundred years would now be expressed in full view of those being commodified. As the enslaved were subjected to the transaction that passed them from one white man to another, the import of what was happening would not have been lost on them. In eighteenth- and nineteenth-century slave societies, the infrastructure of the slave trade—slave markets in city centers or roadways full of coffles—condensed the experience of slavery in ways that historians Walter Johnson and Marisa Fuentes have carefully elaborated for radically distinct historical moments.[2] In the seventeenth century, before the erection of such physical infrastructure, the profusion of slaves as marketed goods would also enact a distinct lesson for all those who observed. New social and economic relations were being established through the coupling of people with commerce in formerly inconceivable fashions.

The foundational economies of hereditary racial slavery were mounted on the presumption that ties of kinship—which were allegedly nonexistent—would not interfere with the market for human beings. By the time the English entered the slave trade in the seventeenth century, slave traders

1 Wynter, "Beyond the Categories," 82.
2 On the nineteenth-century New Orleans slave market, see W. Johnson, *Soul by Soul*; on eighteenth-century Bridgetown, Barbados, see Fuentes, *Dispossessed Lives*.

had of course been landing on African shores for more than 150 years. Thus, while the particulars of enslavement shocked and profoundly affected each individual victim of the transatlantic slave trade, by the seventeenth century the violence of their capture would, for some, have been something entirely possible. The selling of slaves to European buyers on the African coast must have engendered consideration of what could happen as the result of capture. In the moment of sale, these possibilities would have become horribly concrete.

Sales, and the involuntary and voluntary movement of captives across the landscape, educated both slave owners and the enslaved about the new parameters of kinship and alienation. Questions concerning how moments of sale might have resonated for captives and what those moments of sale produced as they became embedded in racial meaning are at the heart of this chapter. What frames of reference did captives use to understand the sales of men and women? How did the terms of New World slavery interrupt and recast those terms? What frames did slave owners use?

Enslaved women and men in the English colonies were subjected to a range of processes that were ostensibly designed to teach them to be slaves— branding, the coffle, public display and examination, separation from shipmates, renaming—which also taught them about the degree to which these new economies were saturated with the commodification of human beings. These processes also made it clear that Europeans refused to endow kinship among Africans with the same characteristics of feeling, social order, and connection that they attributed to their own kinship.[3] Capture and captivity in West Africa, in contrast, were in large part defined by the incorporation of captives into existing kinship networks—networks defined by hierarchies and brutalities but within which the captives would understand themselves and their new circumstances through a transformed sense of kinship.

The networks built on board slave ships, which anthropologists Sidney Mintz and Richard Price characterized as the origins of New World kinship, show that social connections among the enslaved would be routed through metaphors of kinship and newly constituted genealogies.[4] As a result, the categories of kinship and property appear inextricable in the processes that

3 Ira Berlin opened his foundational article "From Creole to African" with the example of eighteenth-century slave owner Robert "King" Carter explicitly mobilizing the renaming of captives as a tool for "stripping newly arrived Africans of the signature of their identity." Berlin, "From Creole to African," 251.
4 Mintz and Price, *Birth of African-American Culture.*

produced racial slavery. The negation of African kinship and then Black kinship that was set in motion at the moment of capture became the basis for how slave owners articulated hereditary racial slavery and for how the enslaved refused it in the Americas. The moment of sale, which dissolves kin ties based on the logics of the market, condenses the legal and racial regimes mounted over time in the Atlantic world into a single instant—one arguably legible on both sides of the transaction and one inscribed into and by the law for the Englishmen.

Sales

From the onset of the slave trade, observers recognized that the moment of sale conveyed an awful power—one opposed to social connection and kinship. Stories of the efforts of the enslaved to interrupt the moment of sale are as old as the slave trade itself, as Zurara observed on the shores in Lagos in the fifteenth century, when captives protested against being separated from their kin.[5] As they refused their commodification, captives fruitlessly struggled to force buyers and sellers to recognize the destruction wrought by the moment of sale. Sale was an originary moment in the destabilization of and violent disregard for Black family life.

Yet, in our symbolic registers, sale has been rendered by the auction block as a moment of stillness and pathos rather than a dynamic moment rich in productive violence. The auction block stands as a persistent and powerful symbolic image in the history of slave life.[6] Through it, pathos, violence, and subjection get attached to a silent, waiting, scrutinized body. Fixed by the gaze of the consumer, tallied and divided, Black life on display and on offer becomes exemplified by a figure of passivity inscribed by the stasis of the block. This stasis situates the objects for sale as still and dispassionate and demarcates the moment of sale as void of compassion or connection across the gulf of the economic transaction. It hides the productive moments out of which moments of sale were constructed and renders the processes of the market invisible as it condenses the movements and decisions of all those involved into a single still moment in time. Instead, the many moments of sale added up to a theater of sorts—"performances of nonrecognition," according to the theorist Imani Perry—in which those

5 Zurara, *Discovery and Conquest of Guinea*, 81–82.
6 On the auction block, see McInnis, *Slaves Waiting for Sale*; McKittrick, *Demonic Grounds*; and Anne Bailey, *Weeping Time*.

who possessed legal personhood demarked it through their reiterated entry into the marketplace for nonpersons.[7]

Auction blocks and houses predominated in the geographic interiors and in the secondary or tertiary sales of men, women, and children who were distanced from the slave ship by time or generation. The auction block's impact derives from both the weight of a nineteenth-century experience and an oppositional abolitionist imaginary. But, as shown by the experiences of those discussed in chapter 4, sales in fact took place in a wide range of settings, few of which were as permanently demarcated or as structurally isolated as the auction block. Sales and all the structures that attended them were embedded in the messy colonial society that greeted the captives when they disembarked after months of stultifying and disorienting travel. They were sold on piers, on board ships, after long marches through towns and into the countryside, on corners, in the back of shops, in the post office or the public house, on wharves, from the backs of wagons, inside urban living rooms, with a stranger, with a child, with a spouse, alone or in full view of those whose sale would come next. They were sold to men or women, sold by strangers or by those who had known them long enough to call them by a name. They were sold by those who spoke their language or by those whose words were gibberish to them, sold to those who looked like them, those who looked a bit like them, or those who looked nothing like them.[8] The places of sale were haphazard, makeshift, mobile, and pedestrian.

To be sold into the chaotic spaces of daily life should suggest a landscape peppered by myriad explosions, moments when pity, compassion, or connection were set aside again and again in favor of the quite different moral economy of the slave sale.[9] To linger on the range of early modern experiences of sale is to reckon with the extent to which these foundational moments of Atlantic slavery produced a reiterative articulation of commodification. These moments did not just convey the complicated status that skin color marked but also the extent to which they and the families they might construct were enmeshed in the violent fiscal relations they had been caught by on the other side of the Atlantic. The particular moment of sale itself conveyed a beginning for the captive and, as such, functioned as an experiential foundation for assessing the terms of one's enslavement.

7 Perry, *Vexy Thing*, 27.
8 Desrochers, "Slave-for-Sale Advertisements."
9 Fassin, "Critique of Moral Reason," 485–88.

Slave ship captains organized the initial sales of their captives in various ways. Sales were often announced some days in advance, giving slave owners and their representatives time to plan. Captives would be brought to the deck of the ship and, huddled in the glare of daylight with their shipmates (likely together for the last time), would be auctioned off alone or in small groups. Those whose turn came later in the process would slowly comprehend that they would soon be led away from the ship by a white man, or, perhaps furthering the disorientation, his Black servant.

In the late seventeenth and early eighteenth centuries, auctions came under attack because they benefited wealthier purchasers; they were replaced throughout the English West Indies and in South Carolina by the more democratizing form known as *scrambles*. Descriptions of the fear that gripped captives subjected to a scramble are powerful. Their ship would have anchored days earlier, and then they would have been washed, oiled, and fed in preparation for something. A sense of foreboding must have circulated among the survivors. Herded together in a large group on deck, perhaps amassed in a group not delimited by sex or age for the first time, the captives must have responded to the smaller gathering of white men with an alarm that only escalated when those men rushed toward them, grasping at them with chaotic roughness, perhaps tussling with an opponent who also meant to claim a particular woman or man, marking them in some temporary way (with a ribbon or a smear of paste), and shoving them into smaller groups. Olaudah Equiano described the terror of captives, loaded on board a ship, whose comprehension of what was unfolding lagged behind the rapid pace of the event.[10]

Once the sale was completed, the captives were removed from the ship, separated from their family members or familiars, marched through the filth and chaos of early American cities, and finally made to set themselves down on a mat in the dwelling that would constitute their new home. If the symbolic importance of a ribbon tied roughly and tightly around their wrist did not immediately compute, its weight would later have been seared into their flesh with a brand: hearts or crowns topped with the initials of the man who had first claimed them with a piece of fabric.[11]

---

10 Equiano, *Interesting Life*, 70.
11 In a runaway ad in the *Jamaica Courant* in 1718, for example, the "Madagascar Negroe-Boy" was "Marke'd on his Left Breast M. B and on his Right [image of a small crown with the capital letter P beneath it]." The same edition included an ad for a group of runaways, two girls and three "Negro-Men boys" all marked "D. A Hart and P. On

It is hard to imagine any kind of stillness amid the chaos of a shipboard sale, as captives were grasped, shoved, and pulled. But perhaps there may have been a moment of clarity, a recognition that the collective experience on the ship, as vicious and sickening as it had been, was ending; instead of experiencing the death and consumption many had feared, they would now live under the dominion of a stranger who had marked them as his or her property. Comprehending the various ways captives assessed this process is, of course, impossible. We cannot know what this process was, or how and when it took place. But equally impossible is the conclusion that no such process of assessment occurred. Moments of sale would set in place a framework for understanding the parameters of their enslavement, and seeing the sales as such enables us to understand the act of transferring commodities as connected to moments of comprehension.

Much was for sale. With each act of sale, those who had the capacity to purchase were situated as distinct from those who were exposed to sale. The majority of English settlers arrived in the colonies under various forms of bonds: they were not wealthy, and they were not free.[12] But over the course of the seventeenth century, as clarity about the importance of slave labor to the colonies and about those who could legitimately be sold came into view, whiteness became a source of protection, a further result of the market in slaves. Like the capture and transport of Africans to the market, the purchase of enslaved people in the seventeenth century required some incomplete knowing, a refusal to recognize that those being purchased were witnesses to the violence that was underway.[13]

Survivors of the Middle Passage and those who purchased them were locked into a relationship that was incommensurate on all levels, not least in the greater ability of the enslaved to fully comprehend the truth: the transactional process that was meant to reduce an enslaved person to

---

her Breast." "Advertisements," *Jamaica Courant*, August 5, 1718, 4, America's Historical Newspapers.

12 Eltis, *Rise of African Slavery*.

13 Cheryl Harris's work on whiteness as a form of property that coheres in the aftermath of abolition provides the crucial framework for my thinking here, as I chart the multiple ways in which slave sales educated free whites on the tangibility of their status. Walter Johnson's important study of marketplace transactions in antebellum New Orleans clarifies the productive nature of purchases; further, Daina Ramey Berry focuses on the experience of being sold, emphasizing the degree to which sale saturated the life span of the enslaved. C. Harris, "Whiteness as Property," 1707; W. Johnson, *Soul by Soul*; and Berry, *Price for Their Pound*.

thingness would always fail. Even without a clear vision of the future, the recently arrived captives would have already endured a range of transactions designed to distance them from their social and cultural milieu. The refusal of slave owners to engage with the emotional and intellectual processes enslaved individuals were undergoing formed a key entry to the erasures at the heart of the logic of racial slavery. The presence of women and children, or pregnant women, only accentuated a captain's or a purchaser's possibly desperate need to claim that they could not see enslaved people as human.

Legalizing Sale

The work to distance the enslaved from the kinship ties that marked them as rooted in human communities was at least partially enabled by the legal instruments that defined them, and their descendants, as enslavable. We know a great deal about the legal foundations of slave ownership in the Americas and the role of race in defining the status of slaves. Questions about the origins of slave law, about the relationship between Roman law and common law in delineating the status of the slave, and about the presence or absence of slavery as a legal concept before the advent of the American colonies have been carefully explored in an effort to historicize the development of race as the justification for enslavement.[14] This work serves to disrupt overly simple conclusions about natural racial prejudice as an explanation for the system of hereditary enslavement that overtook the Americas.

English settlers arrived in the Americas without a legal tradition of slavery to transport and thus had to craft legal codes, which have been interpreted as responsive rather than productive. As historian Thomas Morris has argued, the legal contours of enslavement were drawn from the law of property, and thus it is in property law that one must ground explorations of the unfolding intersection of race and slavery. In other words, as we seek to understand the legal standing of the first generations of enslaved Africans in the Americas, we must look to the laws designed to rationalize

---

14 For a comprehensive discussion of law and slavery, see Tomlins, *Freedom Bound*; Higginbotham, *In the Matter of Color*; Watson, *Slave Law in the Americas*; Finkelman, *Slavery and the Law*; Morris, *Southern Slavery and the Law*; and Morris, "'Villeinage." Alan Watson reminds us that Romans were among the world's greatest slave users and had a highly developed law of slavery. Watson, "Seventeenth-Century Jurists," 368.

property, not to laws designed to solidify the status of human beings as slaves.[15] It is not that legal formulations constituted the ground on which social realities unfolded; rather, the legal instruments that authorized the sale of human beings in the market are at the heart of how the enslaved encountered the property claims made upon their persons. The violations caused by such logics of property, and the ways in which enslaved people worked to invert them, are at the heart of the matter.

African people who found themselves in the American colonies, both enslaved and free, used a variety of strategies and a range of legal frameworks to make claims regarding their freedom and rights.[16] In the English Atlantic world, statute law that regulated the status and behavior of those designated as Negro or mulatto followed relatively late after property law, which impinged most violently and systematically on the legal personhood of those individuals. This lag is illustrated most clearly by the law of descent passed by the Virginia House of Burgesses in 1662: "Whereas some doubts have arisen whether children got by any Englishman upon a negro woman should be slave or free, Be it therefore enacted and declared . . . that all children borne in this country shall be held bond or free only according to the condition of the mother."[17] This statute designed to clarify the outcome of behavior was routed not through the bastardy laws in England, which would have centered the personhood of the interracial child, but rather through the laws of increase as applicable to chattel property, which were rooted in English common law.[18]

In the very limited spaces where marginally free Africans were able to maneuver in Virginia in the seventeenth century, the courts became a vehicle through which they could oppose property claims that were damaging to their children. They used petitions that sought to transfer property rights in children from white owners to Black parents or guardians as they

15 Morris, *Southern Slavery and the Law*, 42.
16 For a review of the comparative legal tradition that grew up around the publication of Frank Tannenbaum's *Slave and Citizen*, see Bennett, *Africans in Colonial Mexico*, 33–50; and Fuente, "Slave Law and Claims-Making in Cuba."
17 The law decreed that the children of "negro" women fathered by Englishmen would follow the condition of the mother. It is commonly referred to by modern scholars as the *partus sequitur ventrem* act. Hening, *Statutes at Large* 2:170; M. Newton, "Returns to a Native Land," 115–16; and J. L. Morgan, "*Partus Sequitur Ventrem*."
18 Morris, *Southern Slavery and the Law*, 45. Rebecca Anne Goetz clarifies that the 1662 statute mobilized "religious criteria to codify perceived differences between English bodies and African bodies." Goetz, *Baptism of Early Virginia*, 79.

grappled with the reach of the marketplace into their family lives.[19] They did so well before the early eighteenth-century turn in Virginia from a labor system that relied on indentured servants to one that primarily exploited the labor of the enslaved, and thus their actions reflect a comprehension regarding the dangers of their situation that significantly preceded the moment at which they would have been embedded in a widespread land-scape of racial slavery.

Before the colony fully embraced slavery as a labor system, some Black women and men in Virginia recognized that property law was being ap-plied to them and their children. Elsewhere in the American colonies, enslaved men and women similarly attempted to forestall their children's enslavement through recourse to the law and colonial authorities. In Dutch New Amsterdam in the 1640s, before legal clarity about the status of en-slaved people existed, the claims to freedom of those who had been en-slaved by the Dutch West India Company were hemmed in by the language of property. Adult men who petitioned the Dutch West India Company for freedom as compensation for military service and manual work were granted it—on the condition that they paid a yearly sum to the company and that their children remained enslaved.[20] As we shall see in the follow-ing chapter, the Dutch West India Company thus used family ties to confer a delineated freedom in which parents were unable to claim ownership of their children. Property rights—rather than claims to status—became the grounds on which enslaved Africans in Anglo-Dutch legal environments made claims about their right to family relationships.[21]

Because of the intersections of property law, nascent racial formations, and kinship, the reach of the market into family life was palpable, for newly enslaved Africans in the early colonial Atlantic as well as for those who were acquiring clarity about the relationship between African descent and vulnerability to forced labor. Their wide-ranging experiences of being sold clarified to African men, women, and children the ways in which their value rested on the quite tangible logics of exchange. To be sold was, of course, just the beginning of the long lesson of subjugation. But it was a lesson whose contours reflect much about the simultaneity of imposed kinlessness,

19 On the use of the courts by Black people in early Virginia, see Breen and Innes, "Myne Owne Ground"; Goetz, Baptism of Early Virginia, 86–111; and J. L. Morgan, "Partus Sequitur Ventrem."
20 For a discussion of the freedom petitions, see Foote, Black and White Manhattan, 37–40.
21 Freedom claims in New Amsterdam are discussed at length in chapter 6.

kinship, and racialized thinking. In the context of an emerging labor system in which unfreedom and hereditary enslavability were collapsing onto racialized persons, abstract notions of property and valuation were having extraordinarily material consequences for people who were African and who were rendered Black and enslavable by the marketplace. For scholars attentive to the unfolding of early modern racial capitalism, then, thinking through the repeated acts of sale becomes a method by which we can apprehend that process.

Marketing Families

In 1682 Jean Barbot published an account of the time he spent trading slaves along the Gold Coast near Cape Coast Castle in present-day Ghana. His description of an African family exemplifies the problem of family life disrupted and reconstituted under slavery: "Among my several runs along that coast, I happened to have aboard a whole family, man, wife, three young boys, and a girl, bought one after another, at several places; and cannot but observe here, what mighty satisfaction those poor creatures expressed to be so come together again, tho' in bondage."[22] The circumstances that tore this family apart, exposing them individually to sale along the coast, are forever lost. But even in the context of a self-congratulatory narrative of his own largesse, Barbot's description of their satisfaction at being reunited highlights the depth of what they had believed to be their loss.

In the journal entry that may have been the backbone of this story, Barbot wrote of purchasing a pregnant woman in the morning, a little boy and a little girl in the afternoon, and a husband and father several days earlier. The woman endured the Middle Passage while pregnant and gave birth to her fifth child after the passage, once the family was sold in Martinique. Barbot watched their tender reunion, described their tears of happiness and their continual "embracing and caressing [of] one another," and rewarded them, and himself, with the order that "they should be better treated aboard then commonly we can afford to."[23] He added this comment on his treatment of them on board to the later edition of his writings, having presumably reflected further on how the story might influence his reputation for largesse.

22 Excerpt from *John Barbot's Description of Guinea*, in Donnan, *Documents Illustrative*, 1:289. For further elaboration on the first and second editions of Barbot's text, see Hair, Jones, and Law, in Barbot, *Barbot on Guinea*, 2:550, 2:558.
23 Barbot, *Barbot on Guinea*, 2:557n29.

The family thus endured the Atlantic crossing together, and one can only speculate as to how they processed this "good fortune." Their anomalous situation might in fact have only heightened their terror.

At some level, Barbot understood that the traffic in human beings continually dissolved families, and thus he situated this particular family as if they were singular in order to imply that other captives were commodities with no familial ties. We must be fully attentive to this sleight of hand as we consider the ways that kinship erupts from the archive of slavery and capitalism. "I did not care to separate them when I reached the Islands and I sold them to a single master," Barbot wrote. In the later edition of his narrative, he added that selling them as a group had garnered a lower price than he would have received had he sold them individually, framing this with the information that he had been "informed of that gentleman's good-nature, and [took] his word, that he would use that family as well as their circumstances would permit, and settle them in some part by themselves."[24] The overlay of the market on the affective ties of those buying and selling human beings within it should not be seen as anomalous. Rather, the self-congratulatory tone that situates Barbot and the Martinican "gentleman" in opposition to the slave market reflects a tool of racial dominance: as this family and many others would come to understand, exceptional Black people were mobilized as proof that the majority deserved enslavement and brutality. This became a technology of this system of racial slavery that both mobilized and disavowed the family as an institution among the enslaved.

Zurara's description of the scene at Lagos situated a recognition of kinship as the tool through which he could convey all that was wrenching about slavery. For slave traders, the tensions around the kinship of captives would endure. The relationship of the unnamed wife and mother to her children and their father became embedded in their exchange value on the market, which was made manifest in the instant when she caught a glimpse of her children being loaded onto the ship at anchor off Cape Coast Castle. Affect and economy were inextricable in her and her family's experience on the slave ship and in the value assigned to its members as a group. If they survived their subsequent enslavement in Martinique, the mother and the father would have retrospectively understood (at the very least) the role their kin ties had played in maintaining their proximity to

---

24 *John Barbot's Description of Guinea,* in Donnan, *Documents Illustrative,* 1:289; and Barbot, *Barbot on Guinea,* 2:557n29.

one another. They may also have discerned that being together as a family made them vulnerable. Most slavers, Barbot included, offered infants and children for sale on the market *through* family in a most perfidious and normalized manner.

It is a mistake to overlook the importance of reproduction in the conceptualization of early modern markets simply because of the generally low rate of natural increase among those enslaved early in North American colonies or those doomed to live short and brutal lives on West Indian and Latin American estates. Both slave traders and the enslaved would learn that the terms of enslavement were in no way interrupted by affective economies of maternity, regardless of the effect on birth rates. Maternity was both present on the transatlantic crossing and visible to those who encountered captives immediately upon their arrival in the American colonies. Neither femininity nor maternity offered protection from commodification, as slave traders identified infants and children first and foremost as commodities.

As planters from the West Indies to the Chesapeake transitioned from utilizing indentured English and Irish laborers to fully embracing slavery and slave ownership, their compunction about assigning women to fieldwork evaporated. While such a shift may well be characterized by "a more rational and efficient use of the available workers," it also brought with it an intimate engagement with reproductive potentiality that fell squarely into the purview of accumulative strategies for maximizing wealth.[25] Given the intimacy of their entanglement, the murky calculus of racial slavery became clear at the moment that an enslaved woman's thickening midsection indicated a pregnancy. Calculations of returns on investments were worked out on and through enslaved women. While reproductive rates in these places were low and infant mortality rates were high, women's multiple labors contributed not only to the process by which their commodification was ensured but also to the broadest aspects of human commodification in the Black Atlantic, including its intellectual and economic rationale.

In 1626 Dutch settlers imported eleven men from Africa to serve as the first slaves of the Dutch West India Company in New Amsterdam. Two years later, the company brought in three women for "the comfort of the company's Negro men."[26] The unbalanced sex ratio and the identification of the enslaved women only as sexual outlets for working men together

25 Menard, "How Sugar and Tobacco Planters Built," 318.
26 L. Harris, *In the Shadow of Slavery*, 21.

set a tone that has reverberated from the colonial period well into the contemporary construction of colonial historical narratives. Outnumbered almost four to one, the women whom the Dutch West India Company transported to New Amsterdam experienced an isolation that would soon dissipate when the company imported more enslaved laborers. In 1664, the final year of Dutch settlement, Peter Stuyvesant sold a "lot of Negroes and Negresses" to the highest bidders. Among those who purchased more than one laborer, all but one purchased groups that included women.[27] These are moments when slave owners are caught up by the contradictory violence at the heart of sales. In addition to the larger "lot" of people, Stuyvesant sold an enslaved man whom he recognized as married and then "urged" the purchaser to buy the man's wife as well; he is involved in an episode of exchange that speaks fervently to the emotions attached to these market relations.[28] A few months later, the *St. Jacob* arrived in the colony with 160 men and 140 women, a slight imbalance, to be sure, but one that still allowed enslaved men and women to form families in the colony and allowed slave owners to imagine that the stark act of buying and selling people was mitigated by a largesse similar to that which Barbot exercised on the island of Martinique.[29]

Having been purchased to provide a kind of balm, the meanings ascribed to these women's labor were not always rendered visible in the marketplace. The persistence of unequal pricing patterns for male and female laborers is another chimera. While scholars have emphasized the broad and long-term patterns of market pricing to affirm that the premium prices slave owners were willing to pay for male laborers comport with patriarchal values that assumed that males were stronger than females, other factors were also at work. Focusing on aggregates does not allow for an analysis of competing systems of value in which women's reproductive potential—alongside the crucial contributions they made to Atlantic economies through their work in sugar, tobacco, and rice fields—was part of the economic decision-making that undergirded the prices paid for women who survived the Atlantic crossing. While value might well be indexed in the

---

27 "Conditions and Terms on Which the Director General and Council of New Netherland Propose to Sell to the Highest Bidder a Lot of Negroes and Negresses," May 29, 1664, in Donnan, *Documents Illustrative*, 3:427–28.
28 L. Harris, *In the Shadow of Slavery*, 21.
29 The Council of New Netherland to the Directors at Amsterdam, August 17, 1664, in Donnan, *Documents*, 3:433; and L. Harris, *In the Shadow of Slavery*, 22, 15.

prices buyers were willing to pay for the men and women they enslaved, those sums reflect gendered and racialized presumptions about labor that were still in flux in the seventeenth century.[30]

Thus, an overly reductive focus on the different prices owners paid for women and men might cloud the relatively early emergence of purchasing patterns among English slave owners in the Atlantic that reflect an awareness of the economies of reproductive labor. It must be emphasized that in this early moment in the history of Atlantic slavery, *slave* was not synonymous with *male*. Indeed, in these makeshift and pedestrian markets where humans were bought and sold, women were omnipresent. Buyers saw, interacted with, and purchased women constantly. In the Barbados Ledger that the Company of Royal Adventures kept from 1662 to 1664, the purchasing practices of Barbados slave owners illuminate this disturbing practice—one that involves a manner of speculative investments in the reproductive possibilities afforded to a slaveowner who balanced the sex ratios among his laborers.[31] On a single day in February, for example, the planter Shill Hussick purchased twelve women and eight men. The women were bound for his sugar fields, but it is likely that the English planter also had the report of his contemporary Richard Ligon in mind. In 1657 Ligon had written of the men and women purchased in Barbados that "we buy them so as the sexes may be equal; for, if they have more Men than Women, the men who are unmarried will come to their masters, and complain, that they cannot live without Wives . . . and he tells them, that the next ship that comes, he will buy them Wives, which satisfies them for the present."[32]

Ligon's assessment demands to be read from the perspective of those twelve women. Arriving at a plantation and summarily assigned either to a man with whom they had survived the crossing or to one they had never

30 David Eltis, Frank Lewis, and David Richardson write that "from the planter's perspective, newly arrived slaves were largely undifferentiated except by anticipated productivity, and possibly by a culturally shaped gender bias on the part of both African sellers and American buyers." Eltis, Lewis, and Richardson, "Slave Prices . . . in the Caribbean," 677.

31 Barbados Ledger, 1662–1664, fol. 10, T70/646, National Archives, Kew, England. The only vessel listed in the Trans-Atlantic Slave Trade Database with an arrival date that comports with these purchases is the *Susan*, which arrived on February 20, 1664. There is no further information about the vessel other than that 230 enslaved persons survived the voyage (57 died en route). Voyage 21417, https://slavevoyages.org/voyage/database. See also my discussion of the ledger in J. L. Morgan, *Laboring Women*, 82–83, and in the accompanying notes.

32 Ligon, *True and Exact History*, 46–47.

laid eyes on, these women would have been subjected to a quick and clear education about the outlines of their future. In this instance, rather than providing her with a husband who would connect her to a new family and children that would enhance her status in a new community, the initial sexual encounter would be rooted in a set of economic relations whose full corollaries would come slowly but certainly into view. As had been the case for the mother Barbot bought and sold in 1679, these women would have realized that the terms of their labor were not distinct from their sexual availability and reproductive future. While clear accounts of African women's sexual exploitation are sporadic for the seventeenth century, we have every reason to believe that the glimpses of sexualized violence and violation we see in the extant accounts are narrow windows onto an expansive vista.[33]

Whatever they were walking toward, at least the twelve women and eight men purchased by Hussick, having come from the same boat and traveled together overland to Hussick's plantation, recognized something of their collective pasts in one another's presence. A very different and more complete isolation awaited six girls who also appear in the Barbados Ledger. On that same February day, five different Englishmen accrued debt to the company for the purchase of "1 girle" or "2 girles."[34] These young women, likely below the age of sixteen, would have felt their isolation acutely. The multiplicity of their exploitation announced itself in the record book: as company officials leafed through the pages of this ledger, the implication that these men were purchasing sex would have been impossible to escape. Perhaps easier to overlook would have been the assumption that the future reproductive lives of these girls were also in the hands of their new owners. Their destination may or may not have been enslaved men "unable to live without Wives," but even in the burgeoning sugar economy of Barbados, the recognition that enslaved women embodied sexual and/or reproductive and productive wealth was, by the middle of the seventeenth century, a commonplace, one borne out by the archival tracings available to us in the Barbados Ledger. Men and women, boys and girls, are purchased together in almost every sale and on almost every page. The account book indexes the intimate violence of sale and purchase; the accounting protocols that identify sale and gender cause the specificities of gendered identities to be lost to us in these records. The dangerous potentialities that were built into the sale of the six girls in Barbados could not have been lost on them

33 I elaborate on this point in J. L. Morgan, "*Partus Sequitur Ventrem.*"
34 Barbados Ledger, fol. 10, T70/646, National Archives, Kew, England.

or on the women and men who watched these youngsters as they were led away.

Accounting practices in the English Atlantic during the early modern period hint at a milieu in which the productive possibilities of African women's bodies were readily accessed. The Barbados Ledger contains an almost relentless reiterated coupling. Robert Smith buys two men and two women, Theodore Lou buys four men and four women, Ferdinando Bushell buys thirteen men and sixteen women, and William Johnson buys one boy and two girls and then, two months later, one boy and one girl.[35] The pattern is as impossible to ignore as the likelihood that the pairings these planters created in the marketplace were rooted not in affection that may have developed among those so purchased but rather in the purchaser's strategic investment strategies. The purchase of paired men and women is an almost unspeakably violent intrusion of the market into the intimate lives of the enslaved. While an increasingly explicit practice of encouraging enslaved laborers to reproduce or attempting to force them to reproduce is found only in the later records of plantation economies, we see the roots here.[36]

While the reproductive rates of enslaved women and men on English Caribbean slave plantations remained crushingly low throughout the slavery period, these seventeenth-century patterns of purchasing appear to reflect a consistent effort by slave owners to construct a gender-balanced workforce. Even as owners began to purchase more men than women in the second part of the eighteenth century, they likely did so to compensate for higher mortality rates among adult men.[37] In historian David Barry Gaspar's study of eighteenth-century Antigua, he notes a series of correspondence in which British slave owners advise the purchase of women and girls. Writing in the 1730s and 1740s, Walter Tullideph explicitly recommended buying "Ten Young Girls and Five Young Men" or "10 Men boys & 10 Women Girls" to maintain plantations' workforces. Gaspar speculates that such purchasing "could also mean he considered possibilities of natural increase."[38]

35 Barbados Ledger, fols. 45–48, T70/646, National Archives, Kew, England
36 For eighteenth- and nineteenth-century discussion of "breeding" and the market around reproduction, see Turner, *Contested Bodies*; Paugh, *Politics of Reproduction*; Berry, *Price for Their Pound*; and Sublette and Sublette, *American Slave Coast*.
37 Burnard, "Evaluating Gender in Early Jamaica," 87.
38 D. B. Gaspar, *Bondmen and Rebels*, 85.

The project of unearthing the extent to which European men and women purchased enslaved women and girls for the purposes of exploiting them sexually or reproductively faces challenges related to the evidence. We know that eighteenth-century slave owners and abolitionists alike situated their politics regarding slavery in conversations about the practice of encouraging reproduction among the enslaved. When slave owners faced the end of the legal slave trade to British and American markets, they were confident that they could influence population growth; this indicates that the connection between reproduction and slavery was already solidified.[39] Still, evidence of the breeding policies of slave owners is tentative, although new studies make clear that reproduction was always on the minds of those who purchased human capital, whether or not they were able to actively shape its contours.[40]

The connection between breeding and the horrors of slavery was a rhetorical foundation for antislavery activists of the nineteenth century, who understood the power of narrating the "lurid abuses of slavery."[41] For historians, the link between accusations of breeding and abolitionism has posed considerable problems as it raises a specter of hyperbole in the face of resounding archival silences, particularly for the period preceding the nineteenth century.[42] The search for evidence of slave owners explicitly interfering with the intimate lives of the enslaved (as they did with the mating and reproduction of livestock) is compromised by the silences and ellipses of slave owners. Working through the question of breeding has been a project of historians for more than forty years. The economic historians Robert Fogel and Stanley Engerman worked to dispute the evidence of forced breeding at the hands of American slave owners, and their work continues to echo into the twenty-first century. In their 1974 work *Time on the Cross*, they argued that the "thesis that *systematic* breeding of slaves for sale in the *market*" took place was faulty and unsubstantiated.[43] Their tone here, with

---

39 Paugh, *Politics of Reproduction*, 4–17.
40 Turner, *Contested Bodies*. Berry's work on the impact of sale on those being sold, and their careful efforts to refuse their commodification, is a crucial contribution to this discussion. See Berry, *Price for Their Pound*.
41 Smithers, *Slave Breeding*, 20. See also Pierson, "'Slavery Cannot Be Covered Up,'" 391–92; and Lasser, "Voyeuristic Abolitionism."
42 Across a range of studies of reproduction and gender under slavery, historians are forced to gesture toward the practice of slave breeding without being able to fully document it. See, for an example, Barclay, "Mothering the 'Useless,'" 119.
43 Fogel and Engerman, *Time on the Cross*, 78–86, 78. They wrote, "Systematic breeding for the market involves two interrelated concepts: 1. Interference in the normal sexual

its italicization of the words *systematic* and *market*, suggested that, in the absence of "stud farms," the abolitionist rhetoric was nothing more than prurient fantasy.

But their model ignores the language of speculative finance that we now understand was well within the purview of the culture of capitalism. This is to say, the absence of a stud farm does not negate the connection between hereditary racial slavery and slaveholders' understanding of the reproductive futures of the women and girls they purchased. Further, while the articulation of that understanding may well be found only in the late eighteenth century, the crude attempts of seventeenth-century writers like Ligon to mask the alienating violence of slave owners' interference in the intimate lives of the enslaved suggests that the financial speculations that mark modern capitalist investment strategies are rooted in speculations regarding enslaved women's bodies. We are charting, after all, the development of a labor system in which "slaves were treated not only as a type of commodity but as a type of interest-bearing money."[44] Investments in slave labor, like all investments, were rooted in notions of futurity that were always bound up in the physical bodies of the enslaved. It is a mistake to overlook the foundational importance of reproduction in producing hereditary racial slavery as a logical means of controlling enslaved people economically and socially.[45]

Even in a sugar island saturated with death, slave owners worked to balance the sex ratios on plantations, and enslaved men and women struggled constantly with the emotional and psychic toll that sex, pregnancy, and birth took on them.[46] Fogel and Engerman's conclusions that slave owners did not systematically manipulate the intimate lives of the enslaved is plausible only if one thinks in the most functionalist terms about what constitutes interference. In those terms, it is indeed unthinkable that slave owners could have had both the ability and the desire to so profoundly pervert the personhood of enslaved men and women. But it is equally unthinkable that slave owners whose only preoccupation in the American

---

habits of slaves to maximize female fertility through such devises as mating women with especially potent men, in much the same ways as exists in breeding of livestock; 2. The raising of slaves with sale as the main objective, in much the same way as cattle or horses are raised" (78).

44 Baucom, *Specters of the Atlantic*, 61.
45 This is my core argument in J. L. Morgan, *Laboring Women*.
46 Burnard, "Evaluating Gender in Early Jamaica," 87; Dunn, *Tale of Two Plantations*, 23–73; V. Brown, *Reaper's Garden*.

colonies was the production and extraction of wealth would not have carefully attended to women's reproduction and worked to protect the profit that accrued to them when enslaved women had children. Enslaved women played foundational roles in colonial economies, as evidenced by headright proposals that offered equal amounts of land in exchange for the transport of either Black men or women to the new colony of South Carolina, or the fact that Black women constituted a taxable form of wealth in the colony of Virginia.[47] In the evidence of purchasing patterns, we see new slave owners—those whose property in persons was most vulnerable to the ravages of ill health, mortality, and frontier uncertainties—laying the groundwork for a labor system that always took into account the reproductive possibilities of the enslaved.

In line with this seventeenth-century context, the evidence that slave owners used coercive violence to encourage reproduction among workers they deemed particularly suited to labor comes into focus. "Forced coupling," as Thomas Foster argues, becomes increasingly evident to historians of late eighteenth- and early nineteenth-century American slavery.[48] In court cases involving rape and illegitimacy, in newspaper accounts of discipline and punishment, in the prurient obsessions of clergy, and in the testimony of enslaved and formerly enslaved people, the extent to which the abuse and manipulation of enslavement was saturated in sexual violence is clear, as are explicit (indeed, sometimes state-sponsored) acts intended to "encourage" enslaved women's childbearing and punish them in its absence. These exploitive acts—most brutally illustrated by the records of Thomas Thistlewood in the eighteenth century—reveal the many ways slave-owning women and men subjected enslaved women and men to sexual abuse.[49]

As early as the seventeenth century, planters clearly assumed that purchasing both women and men and then managing reproduction were part

---

47 On headrights, see P. Wood, *Black Majority*, 15–18; on the taxing of Black women, see K. Brown, *Good Wives, Nasty Wenches*, 116–28.

48 Foster, *Rethinking Rufus*; and Foster, "Sexual Abuse of Black Men," 454–58.

49 Using a Latin code, Thistlewood recorded in his journal his repeated rapes of the enslaved women he both owned and managed as an overseer on a sugar plantation in eighteenth-century Jamaica. They are the most explicit evidence available to historians of the daily sexual violences that enslaved women were exposed to. Sasha Turner is engaged in a study of the women who bore the brunt of Thistlewood's violence. See Turner, "Abba." Douglas Hall's and Trevor Burnard's studies of Thistlewood are the two extant full-length monographs devoted to his life. D. Hall, *In Miserable Slavery*; and Burnard, *Mastery, Tyranny, and Desire*.

of managing a plantation. When Henry Drax left instructions for the management of his Barbados sugar plantation in 1679—instructions preserved and circulated in Barbados and then published in the eighteenth century—he told his overseer to "recrute" ten to fifteen new "Choyce Young Negros . . . fit for plantation service" each year in order to maintain the labor force. The language here is important, as the seventeenth-century usage of *recrute* indicated augmentation of an existing body, usually a military one. It works here to convey a rational growth, one at arm's length from the slave ship and the stench of the Middle Passage. Drax enslaved 327 men, women, and children and was thus accounting for an annual death rate of almost 5 percent, including in the years when "contagious distemper happens a great mortality."[50]

Death and birth were always linked in the conceptual and literal balance sheets of the slave owner. Drax's instructions for accommodating the mortality rate followed an extensive discussion of the importance of breeding animals for meat and for dung to fertilize the already depleted soil. Drax used the language of family in a number of places in his document: he told the overseer to feed all "those of my family . . . either whites or blacks" at a full table. He described his enslaved driver, Moncky Nocco, whose wife and mother were with him on the plantation, in terms that both attended to and disregarded his family. One can read the document as an early example of the paternalism of Drax and of the many people who read this much-copied and widely circulated set of instructions.[51]

Following the lead of Peter Thompson, who urges historians to recognize the self-interest that produced Drax's soft language, I'd like to suggest that the omission of an explicit recognition of the violence of life and death for the enslaved on a sugar plantation be resituated as one of the tools slave owners used to rationalize economic choices that by their very nature were embedded in a reproductive economy. One of the later recirculations of Drax's *Instructions*, transcribed by William Belgrove and published in 1755, suggested that planters would need three hundred slaves to run a five hundred–acre plantation. The recommended configuration of that population included "50 Improving Boys and Girls at 30 L. Per." Drax included an estimate of what it would cost to maintain that community of workers: "To Repairs of Negroes at 5L. Per Ct. Upon their Prime Value, or 5 per Ct. Or

50 Drax, *Instructions*, 3, transcribed in Thompson, "Henry Drax's Instructions," 585.
51 The manuscript was published in multiple editions in England and in North America. See also my discussion of Drax and Nocco in J. L. Morgan, *Laboring Women*, 120–21.

15 per annum," amounting to annual expense of £600.[52] He explained why that expense would be so high:

> Suppose those Slaves don't dye; it is reasonable to imagine that they, as well as the Cattle and Horses must be so much the worse: For if every Planter would take an Inventory of the Value of his Slaves the first Day of February, and again the first Day of November, he would discover that difference [in their health and productivity] at least in the Countenances of 300; and so it will admit in Proportion a difference in the Value of the Horses and Cattle between the first Day of March, and the last Day of September. For if we see inanimate Things, such as the Utensils of the Plantation become worse, though used with the greatest Care in the Hands of the Artificers, how much more must the Constitutions of the Human and Animale Creatures be impaired: The Slaves in reaping the ripe Crop, nursing the Young, and planting the ensuing one, and the Stock by the Labour of reaping and carrying it to Market?[53]

It may seem self-evident that an advice manual for the aspirational plantation owner would include attention to the life and death of the labor force. Indeed, the literature on slavery and capitalism often emphasizes the role of planters as rational actors whose financial and political machinations were crucial parts of the modernist project.[54] However, an exclusive focus on the logical reasons behind planning for mortality among the labor force does not take into account the relationship between the causes of mortality and the ways in which slave owners rationalized them. For Drax, as for so many other English plantation owners, the connection between death and a low birth rate was so obvious that it did not warrant discussion. Yet the hopeful possibilities lying dormant in the phrase "Improving Boys and Girls" must be situated alongside the mistreated and dead individuals that were the reason a planter would need to purchase new laborers every year.

"Breeding," then, must include slave owners' opportunistic responses to family formation that fully eclipsed enslaved women's ability to produce kinship outside the marketplace. When they assessed the multiple

52 Thompson, "Henry Drax's Instructions," 580–81; and Belgrove, "Treatise upon Husbandry," 41–43.
53 Belgrove, "Treatise upon Husbandry," 46.
54 Roediger and Esch, *Production of Difference*; and Rosenthal, *Accounting for Slavery*.

possibilities for wealth and profit represented by the bodies of the men and women displayed for purchase, English men and women articulated a range of presumptions concerning their long-term property rights to the children who issued from Black women's bodies. These ideas were planted in the seventeenth-century Atlantic and emerged in the eighteenth century in the economies of extraction that required the normalized and systematic abuse of fellow human beings. Relegating their explicit engagement with reproductive wealth to the realm of the unthinkable does more than erase a key ideological component of hereditary racial slavery (the market rewarded heritability); it simultaneously removes a key aspect of the experience of enslavement and a critical tool that enslaved people could use to comprehend the parameters of their enslavement and the racialized power dynamics of the societies in which they found themselves detained.

That pregnant women and children were present on slave ships and at slave sales in the seventeenth century did not mean that slave owners always saw Black children as a good investment. There is ample evidence that early slave traders and purchasers were ambivalent about the cost-benefit ratio when they purchased small children. While some slave owners eagerly calculated the value of enslaved women's future "increase," others offered women on the market at a discount because of their propensity to bring small, worthless children into already overcrowded urban spaces.[55] One overseer in Granada believed that plantation owners would "far rather the [enslaved] children should die than live," as their presence hindered the productive work of their mothers.[56] At the same time, children were routinely put to work on English Atlantic plantations in "grass gangs," and on many large plantations their labor could be significant.[57]

In early December 1681, two large slave ships docked in the Nevis harbor carrying a total of 725 enslaved persons, described as "mostly women." (Interestingly, these arrivals were characterized as "mostly women" even though women constituted only 48 percent of the captives on one ship and 38 percent on the other.) As the representatives of the Royal African Company reported to company officials, the presence of the women wasn't

---

55 L. Harris, *In the Shadow of Slavery*; and J. L. Morgan, *Laboring Women*.
56 "A Committee of the House of Commons, Being A Select Committee, Appointed to Take the Examination of Witnesses respecting the African Slave Trade," 1791, in *House of Commons Sessional Papers of the Eighteenth Century*, 82:89, accessed November 30, 2020. ProQuest. See also Teelucksingh, "'Invisible Child.'"
57 Teelucksingh, "'Invisible Child,'" 238, 243.

itself a problem; they were concerned about the forty children "under the age of eight yeares" on the first of the two ships. This was "contrary to [the Captain's] Charter," and the Nevis representatives were not satisfied with the captain's explanation that he "could not buy soe many men and women without that number of children."[58] The ship captain thus fully inscribed these African families into the English economy. Children constituted 34 percent of the enslaved population on this ship; they accounted for 18 percent of the enslaved passengers on the second ship, the *Alexander*, which arrived from the Bight of Benin two days later.[59] Historian Jerome Teelucksingh reports that the extant data indicate that from 1673 to 1725, 14 percent of all the captives taken from the West African coast to the British West Indies were children.[60]

Correlating the concern over the numbers of women and children on board with the numbers of these two populations on the manifests of ships does two things. First, we see evidence of their presence. Second, we also see that there is a threshold, a percentage of children that would have triggered alarm and concern on the part of the captain in the face of censure from the company officials. As he confronted his anxiety that he would be unable to sell them all, he would have engaged in a series of calculations about which children were old enough to be sold without an adult woman to serve as their parent. In other words, he would already be thinking of how he might best break up families. Children, whether desired or not, were fundamentally embedded in the equation of colonial slavery. They were there well before the first half of the nineteenth century, which has been identified by scholars of the slave trade as the period when the number of children captured and sold peaked.[61] The emphasis on avoiding the importation of children clearly emerged from an economic imperative: children under the age of eight could not work as hard as older captives could. Traders and owners would view them as temporary drains on the economies of the plantations or urban households where they were held. That was a risky calculation in environments where diseases could decimate a household well before an owner might reap the profit from a long-term investment in

58 Henry Carpenter and Robert Helmes to Royal African Company, December 24, 1681, in Donnan, *Documents Illustrative*, 1:275.
59 Voyages 9891 and 9892, https://slavevoyages.org/voyage/database.
60 Teelucksingh, "'Invisible Child,'" 238.
61 Eltis and Engerman, "Was the Slave Trade Dominated?"; and Eltis and Engerman, "Fluctuations in Sex and Age."

laborers. Moreover, the women with whom children disembarked would be charged with caring for them, which would also delay slave owners' return on their investment.

Slave owners simultaneously complained about and benefited from the bearing and raising of children by the enslaved. But even when children died before reaching an economically productive age, that they took on their mothers' status undergirded the larger logic that upheld the system of property and the rationale of capitalism. Notwithstanding a general sense that children and their care were risky investments, slave owners were responsive to shifts in the economic landscape that put women's reproductive potential back into the realm of speculative finance. Slave owners' relationship to women's reproductive lives shifted in response to the interplay among demographics, cultivation, and access to the Atlantic slave trade. Historian Karol Weaver writes that in eighteenth-century Saint-Domingue, when access to the slave trade was disrupted by the Seven Years' War, French slave owners were suddenly attuned to birth rates, "not because they envisioned enslaved women taking on the motherly traits expected of white Creole women, but because they viewed female slaves as breeding units that were not living up to their full (re)productive potential."[62]

Historians Sasha Turner and Katherine Paugh have identified similar phenomena among slave owners in the English West Indies: when faced with the looming deadlines of amelioration (1807) and emancipation (1833), they began to institute explicitly pronatalist policies, hoping to squeeze as much labor out of bonded workers as possible.[63] Purchasing patterns in the antebellum years in the American South also reveal that slave owners became aware of the value of assigning the care of small children to women. Historians Charles Calomiris and Jonathan Pritchett have suggested that keeping families together—which almost always entailed a discounted price in the market—was in fact economically beneficial for slave owners.[64] In particular, it was advantageous to keep young children with parents to decrease the cost of caring for those children. But the economic rationale coexisted with economic imperatives that arose from quotidian matters that challenged slave owners' sense of control over the people they enslaved.

---

62 Weaver, "'She Crushed,'" 98.
63 See Turner, *Contested Bodies*; and Paugh, *Politics of Reproduction*, 154–90.
64 Calomiris and Pritchett, "Preserving Slave Families," 1009.

Throughout the English Atlantic colonies, slave owners were quick to disparage the reproductive work of enslaved women as a drain on the assets of their plantation economies, and historians have been overly quick to assess their complaints as rational. Scholarship on the question of slave breeding hinges on the explicit rather than the reactive and as a result fails to adequately engage with the reality that slave-owning men and women fully comprehended that they were expropriating the labor power of men, women, and children whose connections to one another were part and parcel of their lives as slaves. Further, it fails to problematize the impulse and experience of family formation among enslaved populations, both those whose birth rates rose above the death rate and those for whom birth was always associated with the likelihood of infant mortality.

Whether infants were born into seventeenth-century American plantation economies or death rates depleted the population of laborers, they represented a cost to the slave owner. The prices owners paid for men, women, and children would have been yet another site of brutal education for survivors of the Middle Passage. The economies of the West Indian and American colonies were deeply affected by changes in the prices paid for enslaved men, women, and children. Economists have attended to the discernible patterns in prices paid for enslaved men, women, and children based on age, sex, and infirmity.

Historian David Galenson has carefully analyzed sales records from the Royal African Company for Barbados in the late seventeenth century. During that period, shiploads of enslaved men and women were sold to planters over the course of several days; the most valuable men and women, those who cost the most, were sold first. Galenson, who breaks down the prices owners paid for enslaved men, women, and children at various points during the sale, illuminates the importance of order of purchase as a way to understand changing criteria of value as they applied to human property.[65] While men generally commanded a higher price than women, both men and women purchased at the end of a sale "yielded only about half the prices of their counterparts sold at the sale's beginning."[66] In other words, some men sold for significantly less money than some women. Also, the slave owners who made purchases in the final stages of the sale were not just latecomers but were disadvantaged in the marketplace; they owned far fewer acres of land than those who purchased on the first day of the sale.

65 Galenson, *Traders, Planters, and Slaves*, 64, 71–92.
66 Galenson, *Traders, Planters, and Slaves*, 76.

Of less interest to Galenson and other economic historians is the impact of these pricing trends on the men, women, and children who were navigating the slave market from the other side of the equation. Indeed, the experience of being sold is so profoundly removed from the scholarship on slave pricing that economic historians have reproduced the calculations of the early modern slave traders who reduced human value to economic value though the universal equivalent of the *pieza de india*. Under the logic of the pieza, young, healthy enslaved men were the measure based on which all other laborers—women, children, the elderly, the infirm—were assessed. Thus, a child might be valued at half a pieza, or an older man could be valued at three-quarters of a pieza. Similarly, buyers and sellers converted "mixed groups of slaves" into "prime male equivalents" for the purpose of assessing the aggregate impact of slave value on Atlantic economies.[67] In such a framework, the experience of being sold falls completely out of view as individual men, women, and children are reduced to currency values.

Being sold would have been an absolutely pivotal moment for those who survived the Middle Passage. Watching how buyers selected particular captives could not have failed to make an impression on all those offered for sale. A purchaser's resentment at having purchased a slave the market categorized as "refuse" would slowly and painfully reveal to the enslaved person that age, injury, or illness had consigned them to a reluctant master. These lessons in value and assessment were not limited to the particular value owners assigned to the bodies of slaves. Much has been made of the reluctance of colonial slave owners to purchase enslaved persons from elsewhere in the colonies. They mistrusted the impetus behind the transshipment of enslaved persons from one colony to the other, confident that it was "Criminalls or otherwise of Little worth who are So Transported."[68] Indeed, with few exceptions, the mainland English colonies imposed higher import duties on slaves from other colonies than on those who came directly from West Africa. They did so at the moment when their reliance on the slave trade was growing, at the end of the seventeenth century.[69]

67 Karl Marx writes that "only the action of society can turn a particular commodity into the universal equivalent." Marx, *Capital*, 180; see also Richardson and Eltis, "Prices of African Slaves," 185; and Smallwood, "Commodified Freedom," 143.
68 Isaac Norris to Prudence Moore, December 8, 1731, Isaac Norris Letter Book (1730–1734), Historical Society of Pennsylvania, Philadephia, quoted in Wax, "Preferences for Slaves," 376.
69 Wax, "Preferences for Slaves," 379; O'Malley, *Final Passages*.

Those who transported and purchased men, women, and children who had already endured enslavement elsewhere were convinced that they would yield unreliable returns on the investment, so much so that it seems impossible that this mixture of disdain and disappointment was hidden from the enslaved.

Acts of Sale and Theft

For many men and women, the moment of sale on the deck of the ship was only the first of many. For captives who survived the Middle Passage in the seventeenth century, the multiplicity of future sales was compounded by geography as the likelihood of secondary or tertiary sales changed depending upon where and when they found themselves in the Caribbean islands, South Carolina, the Chesapeake, or New York. In various stages of development, these colonies provided different settings for the enslaved as they grappled with their own individual commodification and the collective commodification into which they and their descendants were locked with each or any sale. In the newspapers of the colonial English Atlantic, notices of slave sales, ads about runaways, and the news of the week existed side by side. These ads offer a window into how the transactional economy of slave sales was made mundane and legible for literate whites while simultaneously being rendered outlandish and legible for those being bought and sold. Advertisements usually ran on the last page of a newspaper and were frequently bundled, as seen in figure 5.1, with news of horses and mules "stray'd or stolen." They also were often placed next to mundane or humorous tidbits that editors offered. Both juxtapositions served to buffer the reader against the human drama that gripped these men and women.[70]

Throughout the American colonies, the connection between newspapers and advertisements for enslaved runaways was so close that one

70 See, for example, a runaway slave ad on the same page as an ad for a horse that had wandered off: "To Be Sold," *South Carolina Gazette*, February 12, 1756. Accessible Archives, accessed November 30, 2020. https://www.accessible-archives.com/collections/south-carolina-newspapers/; for examples of ads similarly positioned, see "Negroe Slaves," *Jamaica Courant*, July 30, 1718, 4, Readex: Caribbean Newspapers; and "To Be Sold," *Kingston Journal*, November 29, 1760, 2, Readex: Caribbean Newspapers. These ads have been carefully and extensively examined for a range of information about the lives of the enslaved. Most recently, historian Sharon Block has mined the runaway ads for data on skin color and other descriptive aspects of the bodies of enslaved men, women, and children. Block, *Colonial Complexions*, chap. 2 and app. 1.

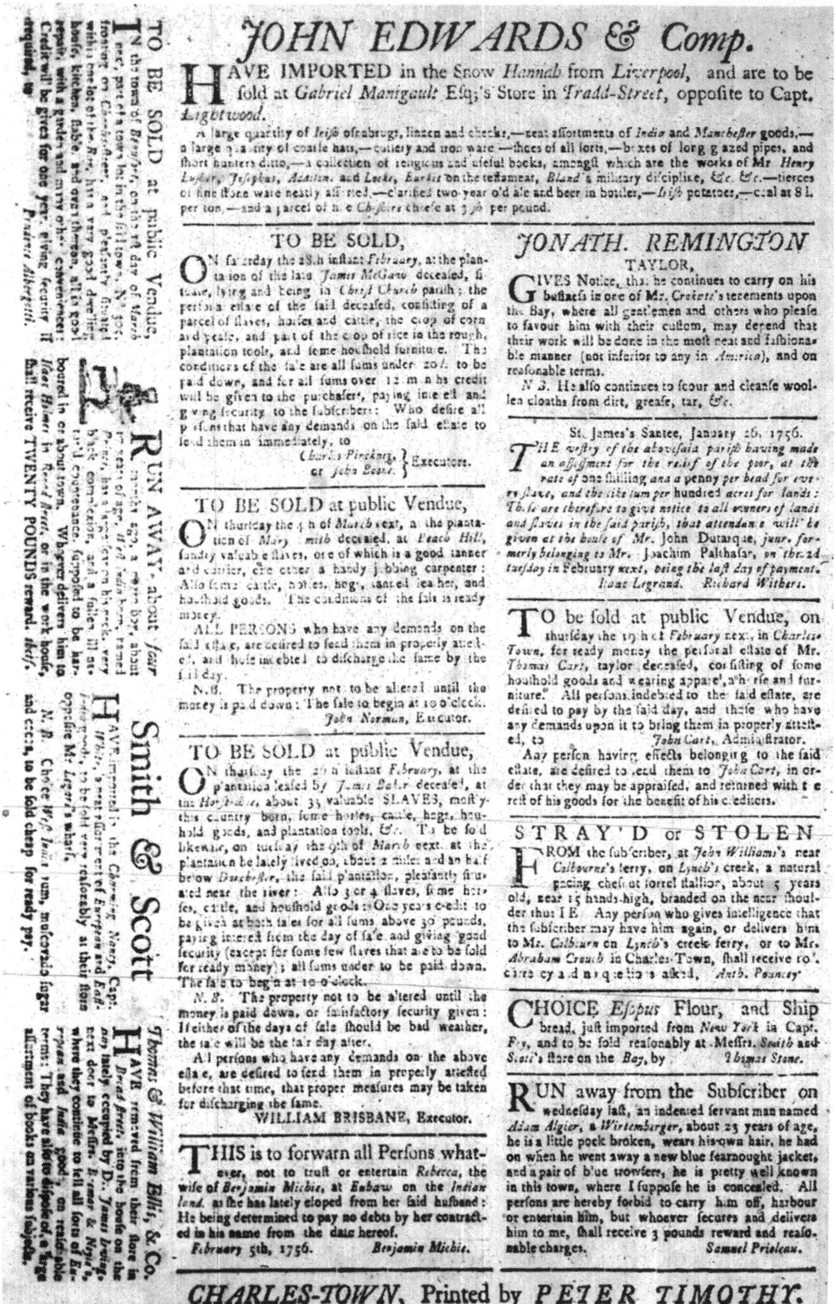

FIGURE 5.1 Advertisement page. *South Carolina Gazette*, February 12, 1756. Accessible Archives, https://www.accessible-archives.com/collections/south-carolina-newspapers/.

scholar has noted that "slavery and the newspaper grew up together."[71] Replete with efforts to retain human property, colonial newspapers house the sometimes contradictory evidence of slave owners' surveillance. It is the efforts of African captives, those who had not been born into Atlantic slavery, that situate the runaway ads as a counterpoint to the slave-for-sale ads. Escaping into an entirely or relatively unknown landscape might be read (as it often was by slave owners) as an act of disoriented desperation, one moreover doomed to fail without the assistance of acculturated and culpable creole counterparts. It must also be read as a strategic effort to shift the logic of property, which even newly enslaved Africans were well positioned to understand. In the texts of advertisements seeking to recapture Africa-born enslaved persons, one can detect a note of astonishment on the part of the slave owner: How could such a disoriented captive manage to escape? The tone might be read as dismissive, but it may also indicate the profound disruption to the socioeconomic order that these particular escapees embodied and therefore the active work it took to fail to understand that escape was both desirable and possible.[72]

Runaway ads contain a range of details regarding the slave or servant who had "stolen themselves" and offer crucial individuated observations about what enslaved men and women wore, what injuries they had survived, and the communities that slaveowners believed they ran to or from.[73] Here I am interested in how the ads testify to slave owners' persistent efforts to recapture wealth in the form of runaways. The publication of colonial newspapers lagged behind settlement, so the advertisements emerge in the eighteenth rather than the seventeenth century. But this does not suggest that the sentiments expressed by those who placed ads only appeared then. As slave owners used newspapers to find runaways, they displayed an assumption that the enslaved required constant instruction in the reality of their enslavement. While that assumption itself must be called into question, the environment it created meant that enslaved women and men did indeed acquire a clear sense of their market value and, alongside it, a range

71 Desrochers, "Slave-for-Sale Advertisements," 623.
72 This is precisely the point made during the lead-up to the Haitian Revolution, which Michel-Rolph Trouillot characterizes as the unthinkable. Trouillot, *Silencing the Past*.
73 These kinds of details have been extensively discussed in the historiography of enslaved runaways. See for examples Meaders, "South Carolina Fugitives"; M. Johnson, "Runaway Slaves"; Waldstreicher, "Reading the Runaways"; Bly, "'Pretends He Can Read.'"

of possible strategies to interrupt that value by insisting on their capacity to behave in ways that commodities never do.

Occasionally, the ads themselves offer a window onto that sense of market value experienced by those being sold or sought. In Boston in the early eighteenth century, an unnamed woman was repeatedly offered for sale in the local paper. For months, from October 1705 to April 1706, she was made aware of the impending change to her circumstances. Her enslaver, the postmaster John Campbell, advertised repeatedly for her sale. There is no indication why she proved so difficult to sell, but she did. Perhaps Campbell charged too much; perhaps she was infirm or was reputed to be intransigent. Campbell placed multiple ads telling prospective buyers that she could "be seen at his House next door to the Anchor Tavern in Boston." Although she remained unsold, she endured being repeatedly perused for purchase and thus constantly being resituated in the market. In early February she might also have been made aware that he didn't situate her as a unique commodity because he offered "a parcel of very good Flax" alongside her. By March the flax had been sold, but she remained.[74] Markets were markets. The bundle of flax and the enslaved woman at the postmaster's disposal were simply a microcosm of an Atlantic-wide articulation of commodities with reproduction. That had implications for those who bought and those who were sold. It reduced the transaction in human property to the quotidian, transforming the process of being sold into an experience that condensed the disruptive nature of market relations into the outrage of being prepared for market. Situating the flax and the woman alongside each other in the ad blurred the pain of her exposure to the marketplace—though not, of course, for her.

There are interpretive possibilities embedded in the practice and experience of sale on both sides of the equation that normalized it. This is an example of print capitalism as defined by political scientist Benedict Anderson. One consequence of print capitalism was the production of a sense of collective belonging. In this case, the proximity of ads for people and ads for products suggests that an important part of that collective belonging was the ability to remain unsold and free to purchase both goods and people.[75] Readers of the Boston News-Letter were hailed as those who understood that both the enslaved woman and the flax were defined by a new regime of rationality in which she appeared as an object that could be seen at any time a free white person desired.

74 Boston News-Letter, October 10, 1705–April 15, 1706, America's Historical Newspapers.
75 Anderson, Imagined Communities, 37–42.

The connection between sales and runaways has long been evident—historian Peter Wood's foundational characterization of runaways as "slaves who stole themselves" reminds us that the first consequence of running away was an interruption of ownership.[76] But even when the enslaved stole themselves, they were still objects of market value. Running away may have interrupted ownership, but it did not interrupt commodification, even as it struck at the heart of the way that property relations were being structured. A runaway woman removed herself from the claims made on her in the name of capitalist accumulation. Neither she nor her progeny could be sold, bought, inherited, or claimed in perpetuity by another. Being sold and running away were entirely different phenomena; nonetheless, they were bound together in the advertisements section where the newspaper reader encountered them. Notices of sales and notices for runaways became linked in the minds of readers, who were themselves beginning to comprehend the economic relationship between enslavement and the wealth produced in the colony. This site of production of racial ideology joins the traveler's observations and the ship captain's logbook, all of which collectively constitute the print capitalism of racial slavery: the written "evidence" that enslavement was logical and legible and that it produced a class of unenslavable persons who could use the narrative of capital to write themselves into legibility.

In considering the men and women who were subjected to all the sedimented aspects of power and hierarchy in the colonial sale or purchase, we find in the act of running away evidence of comprehension. Advertisements for runaways illustrate the extent to which alertness defined the everyday lives of slave owners. The runaway advertisement is thus also a window onto the quotidian practices of surveillance enacted by slave owners and other free white settlers in the early modern Atlantic. Those who wielded power were unable to let their guard down. Historians Gwenda Morgan and Peter Rushton note that "alertness was an inherent part of everyday social relations in households or communities."[77] At the same time, the experience of being under surveillance was equally omnipresent. To run away, particularly for "new" Africans, was to signal the futility of surveillance.

In the first extant runaway slave advertisement in colonial Virginia, two "new Negro" men ran from "Roy's Warehouse in Caroline County" in 1736. The subscriber provided very little contextual detail about the men, merely a subjective description of their "yellow" and "very black" complexions

76 P. H. Wood, "Runaways: Slaves Who Stole Themselves," chap. 9 in *Black Majority*, 239–68.
77 G. Morgan and Rushton, "Visible Bodies," 51.

and the information that they had taken with them "Cloths and Frocks . . . which they had when I bought them."[78] The following month the *Virginia Gazette* published an ad that concerned at least one enslaved person who had survived the Middle Passage. A "young Angola Negro" had run away some three months earlier and was assumed to be "in Company with an old Negroe Fellow from another plantation."[79] The act of running away broke the web of surveillance by announcing that the careful notation of the height, weight, or appearance of a man or woman for sale could not reduce them to a static and docile piece of property. Escaping exemplified the possibility of autonomy and thus unleashed fear in the community of readers that their needs for labor would be interrupted by the refusals even of those who had only just landed on the shores of these new plantation economies.

Reading the advertisements for slave sales and runaway ads skews our attention away from the plantation and toward the port cities where ships landed and newspapers were printed. Indeed, those who advertised for the recapture of a female runaway often speculated that she might be traveling in the direction of a colonial town.[80] The port towns of the Atlantic world provided rare cover for Black women. There they might disappear into areas where women's participation in domestic work and the sexual economy meant that the sight of a woman walking alone along a street was not in and of itself cause for alarm. The newspaper accounts of sales and runaways centered on colonial cities and thus offer information about urban life for Black women in the Atlantic world.

Tens of thousands of enslaved persons arrived at the port cities of Bridgetown, Kingston, Charleston, and New York, the entry points for the slave ships that plied the Atlantic Ocean. Clearly the slave trade drove economic growth in these cities, but the slave trade was not the only mechanism by which slavery was integrated into urban life. As we have seen, the buying and selling of people could not be cordoned off from the buying and selling of other merchandise. The case of a middling-level purveyor of

78 Runaway ad, *Virginia Gazette* (Williamsburg), October 15–22, 1736, http://www2.vcdh .virginia.edu/gos/search/relatedAd.php?adFile=rg36.xml&adId=v1736100001.

79 Runaway ad, *Virginia Gazette* (Williamsburg), October 29–November 5, 1736, http://www2.vcdh.virginia.edu/gos/search/relatedAd.php?adFile=rg36.xml&adId =v1736100003. The other man referenced in the ad was said to speak English fairly well, which suggests that he either came from another slaveholding country or was also born in Africa.

80 For a study of the relationship between urban spaces and gendered fugitivity, see Fuentes, *Dispossessed Lives*, 13–45.

dry goods in Bridgetown, Barbados, in the early eighteenth century makes this point. His record book indicates that, along with the clothing, shoes, hose, candles, saddles, furniture, flour, and other perishables he offered, the item that he sold most often was red caps, an item of clothing that was distributed most frequently to enslaved women.[81] At another point in his record book, this merchant mentioned a debt being paid with cash that was brought to him by the man the debtor had enslaved. The coming and going of enslaved men and women who carried coin to pay off debts and the procurement of garments that enslaved women wore in the sugar fields paint an unremarkable picture of an economy profoundly rooted in slavery. It is a moment potentially overlooked in the extraordinary violences rendered by the slave economy, but it also encapsulates the mundane work done by and through the presence of enslaved women and men, whose comings and goings were embedded in economic phantasmagrams that worked to situate them as merely objects in a busy urban landscape.[82]

In ways both big and small, then, the anonymizing consequences of markets were forced into the intimate lives of enslaved women and men. With the word *intimate*, I mean to evoke the potentially solitary world of the woman in the home of the Boston postmaster as well as the more collective confines of enslavement experienced by a man carrying coins to a shopkeeper on an island populated by tens of thousands of enslaved laborers. The market seeped into spaces that both Europeans and Africans felt were not just antithetical to commerce but hostile to it. The market put a price on ethics and human values in ways that early modern English thinkers from Thomas More to King James I to Thomas Hobbes all objected to.[83] The objections of Africans can also be discerned, not from written tomes, but from the myriad efforts to escape enslavement, whether by appealing to the courts, as Elizabeth Keye did, or by running away, engaging in marronage, or otherwise attempting to destroy the property relations that kept them in a state of subjection. Africans articulated the distinction between the market and kinship despite the ways in which European slave owners

81 S. D. Smith, "Account Book of Richard Poor," 612.
82 This is a moment that historians Trevor Burnard and Emma Hart might characterize as evidence that "slavery and modernity were two sides of the same coin." Burnard and Hart, "Kingston, Jamaica, and Charleston," 222.
83 For a discussion of seventeenth-century tensions expressed by Englishmen regarding the impact of merchants and the marketplace on society, see Finkelstein, *Harmony and the Balance*, esp. 15–25.

increasingly depicted them as lacking interiority—any space that collectively or individually opposed the market.

Enslaved African women's reproductive capacity meant that they embodied the contradictions at the heart of the development of Atlantic markets. As literary theorist Alys Weinbaum has argued, our ability to see objections rooted in the body as occupying the plane of political theory requires a philosophy of history that grows out of those women's lives.[84] Indeed, as we have seen in chapters 3 and 4, the oppositional potential of kinship claims is threaded through early modern accounts of the West African coast in ways that shed light on the experience of family for the enslaved before and during capture and also indicate how unprepared the enslaved were to subsume the smooth running of market capitalism under family.

For the captives who came from West African communities where households were organized to maximize wealth in people rather than wealth in property, the concept of family would have been rather distinct from that of their English or European captors. For them, personhood devolved from relationship to a community; it was a process, not a fixed state of being, and thus the experience of being wrenched from that community and transported alone to the Americas would have led to a particularly acute kind of alienation and pain. During the torturous months of the Middle Passage, creating relationships would have constituted more than a balm; it would have enacted a process of suturing one's self back into the fabric of time and space. Flexible understandings of kinship, what historian James Sweet calls the "politics of belonging," were rendered into strategies that transformed isolation at the "precipice of social death" into a sense of sociality and connection.[85]

At the end of the eighteenth century, Olaudah Equiano articulated his freedom claims in and through the marketplace. To escape the commodification of his body, he purchased himself. As literary scholar Ross Pudaloff notes, Equiano used "the relationships of exchange as the means of creating freedom."[86] Equiano's complicated relationship to commodification is an entry point into a discussion that sees the relationship among enslavement, freedom, and commodification as far more generative than the expected opposition between slave commodity and human being. Although he wrote as a strident abolitionist, offering his life story as testimony to both

84 Weinbaum, *Afterlife of Reproductive Slavery*, 61–87.
85 Sweet, "Defying Social Death," 257; and see also V. Brown, *Reaper's Garden*.
86 Pudaloff, "No Change without Purchase," 376.

his humanity and that of the men, women, and children like him who had been unjustly enslaved, Equiano came close to arguing that enslavement, while an evil, was an inevitable consequence of his ability to use exchange as a way to stake a claim to a legitimate public identity. Decades after Equiano, Harriet Jacobs experienced profound grief when she obtained her freedom through purchase. For Jacobs, allowing someone to purchase her freedom and offer it to her as a gift was akin to complicity in the violation of enslavement.[87] Her agitation was a distinctly nineteenth-century articulation of the relationship between freedom and the marketplace.

Commodification as the antithesis of humanity emerged at a particular juncture in the late eighteenth century and thus needs to be dealt with carefully when considering the seventeenth- and early eighteenth-century world. Conceiving of human commodification as an end point on the spectrum of dehumanization fails to account for the moments when property claims to one's own person would in fact bolster rather than diminish one's claims to human fellowship. Further, thinking of commodification as the ultimate space of dehumanization suggests (perhaps because of the completeness of their reduction to "thingness") that those being commodified were unable to perceive that the property claims made upon them were, in fact, entirely exterior to their personhood. Historian Walter Johnson reminds us that the notion of dehumanization is sticky because "it leaves a trace of abjection on those it (sincerely) seeks to celebrate, advance, and protect."[88] Mobilizing this concept risks obscuring that the claim that a slave was a thing was always rooted more in the status of the slave owner than the status of the slave.

The experience of being marketed for sale in the American colonies was an initiation that was every bit as brutal as surviving the Middle Passage. As tens of thousands of African men, women, and children arrived on the Western shores of the Atlantic, the experience of being sold and then transported in and through port towns and cities marked their new status. It is a mistake to imagine that this process was contained or cordoned off from daily life in the towns and plantations of New World English colonies or in the many other spheres of colonial economies. As newly arrived English men and women carved out the turf on which they hoped they and their

---

87 Jacobs wrote of her effort to obtain her freedom without a price being paid. When her friend purchased her freedom, Jacobs wrote that she was grateful to be free but that she "despised" the fact that her freedom had been bought. Jacobs, *Incidents in the Life*, 288.
88 W. Johnson, "Racial Capitalism and Human Rights," 107.

descendants would prosper, they acquired new skills related to assessing and meeting the needs of the marketplace. Whether doing so required calculating the relative monetary value of an adult childbearing woman and a prepubescent boy or stocking the shelves of small shops with the kind of red caps that slave owners preferred women to wear in the fields or accepting that enslaved people might function both as capital and as customers, the pathway to economic modernity was indeed inextricably linked to slavery.[89]

In light of the various ways human beings became persons with a price, men and women whose freedom became clear in contrast to the enslaved's lack of freedom became increasingly comfortable with the notion that human beings could be used as a form of currency. In 1637, after crew members died on a slave-trading voyage, their surviving relatives on Providence Island, a newly established English colony two hundred miles off the coast of Nicaragua, petitioned for relief. Goodwife Williams asked "for allowance for three dozen knives, employed by her son in buying negroes."[90] Williams's action in approaching the court for recompense after her son's death barely makes an impact on the archival record. Yet in its quotidian normality it speaks volumes. Her identity as a grieving mother is made manifest in the articulation of the exchange of goods for human beings. In the lack of information about the exact way those knives were "employed," the violence of extractive economies is temporarily laid bare. In the refusal to locate the "negroes" in time or space, the reduction of persons into property is clarified. All of this occurred in the space of a moment in a dwelling that temporarily housed the business of state on a tiny island in the Caribbean Sea. As Goodwife Williams claimed her kin ties, she erased those of the slaves her son bought during his lifetime. Refusing to accord kinship and community to the enslaved was a key way in which slave owners clarified their own collective identities. In the act of testifying to the value of those people that her son bought—unmarked by kinship or geography— Williams defined the sanctity of her own blood ties and erased those of the women and men upon whose labor her son depended.

89 Burnard and Hart, "Kingston, Jamaica, and Charleston, South Carolina," 228.
90 Minutes of a Court for Providence Island, July 4, 1637, CO 124/2, pp. 304–5, Colonial State Papers, National Archives, Kew, England.

SIX. "Treacherous Rogues":
Locating Women in Resistance and Revolt

To find yourself on the other side of a sale, led away by an English man or woman who professed to own you, leaving behind the modicum of familiarity you had developed with those who had shared an unspeakable voyage with you, is a moment that strains the historical imagination. At a time when English and other European settlers had situated African women in a field of meaning where their labor was inevitable and their capacity to birth slavery was increasingly coming into focus, the ramifications of race as commodification—even in the absence of words to describe it—were coagulating around them. While the particularities of where they were going and who would constitute the communities in which their new status would crystallize ranged widely, the gulf that opened up between the slaver and the enslaved could not possibly have been clearer, regardless of whether they were led away with gentleness or brutality. This divide emerged from a wide range of phenomena—race, status, language, and religion paramount among them. But it is also a manifestation of the early modern distinctions between kin and the market and of the meanings ascribed to Enlightenment claims of rationality and civility on the part of the Europeans and their descendants.

This final chapter takes up the question of refusal. It does so by thinking through the categories of resistance and the ways that historians have understood enslaved women in the seventeenth- and eighteenth-century English colonies to either inhabit or fail to inhabit those categories. Doing so depends on considering the affective meanings of kinship and reproduction, both as they were felt during enslavement and as they shape the historian's effort to locate rebellious women. The conceptual spaces that kinship occupies are attached to women's bodies in ways that produce unasked questions, that erase women from the records of rebellion but that ultimately suggest how we can reconsider the phenomenology of enslavement, race making, and refusal.

Black women bore witness to the newly emergent discourses of race, commodity, and kin that shaped the early modern Atlantic world. Through the processes of capture, transport, and sale, they acquired critical perspectives on the new world in which they were situated. Enslaved women carried a set of experiences that attuned them in particular ways to the perverse logics of early modern Atlantic slavery: these experiences began on the slave ships, where their relative freedom of movement exposed them to the sexual violences of European crewmen and at the same time enabled them to be conduits of information and occasionally of rebellion, and continued in slave sales, when women's fecundity became part of the calculation of their value and, in the case of those with children in arms, also part of their anguish. This is not to say that enslaved men failed to understand these perversions; rather, it is to emphasize that while the documentary record may produce women as outside the nascent political culture of the Black radical tradition, the embodied experiences of rape and childbirth, or the possibility of such experiences, produced an analytic perspective in them that we must account for.[1]

Whether they stepped off those ships into slave societies like Barbados, where Black majorities labored to cultivate the main export crop, or into a society with slaves like Boston, where they worked alongside white laborers in smaller numbers, seventeenth-century African women's lives in slave societies and in societies with slaves exposed them to the bare realities of birth and death. In 1987 Hortense Spillers argued that the unknowability of paternity and the crucial vulnerability of the slave mother to sexual victimization formed the key to the history of American violence and racial taxonomies. She further suggested that in this economy of meaning, the enslaved woman's body functioned metonymically as "a praxis and a theory, a text for living and for dying," a way of understanding the profound violence upon which the nation was founded.[2] Without mobilizing an overly simplistic

---

1 It bears repeating that this also describes a process crucial to the shaping of white identity and European notions of Enlightenment freedoms.
2 Spillers, "Mama's Baby, Papa's Maybe," 68; see also Weinbaum, "Gendering the General Strike," 446–52.

reliance on the body, here I want to insist that the specter of reproductive capacities offers that metonymic text, a way to expansively consider the impetus and praxis for resisting the commodification of kinship under the terms of early modern enslavement. The implications of Spillers's text are clear; we can see how modern predicaments are clarified by understanding the foundational appropriation of African women's labors. But questions remain about their own assessments of that violence, their own comprehension of its origins, its parameters, and the possibilities available to them to try to refuse or evade it.

Putting women of African descent, those whose experience of the shifting racial climate was most intimate and corporeal, in the center of the narrative situates enslaved women as historical subjects who offer key theoretical models about and insights into the parameters of hereditary racial slavery. Enslaved women who were pregnant or had children to care for were the first to grapple with the ways that the alienation of their progeny and their reproductive potential placed them at the crux of unprecedented individual and systemic violence. That violence was in the service of extracting labor through a newly emerging language of race and racial hierarchy. Given what is clear about the structure of archival knowability, it is no surprise that on the topic of the most visible and potentially radical eruptions against slavery, the archive offers silence. Because most of these women are utterly erased from the colonial archive, their decisions, strategies, terrors, or friendships are primarily left to the imagination.[3] Yet the historian might catch glimpses made visible through slips of the pen or of calculation. These slips, or glimpses, which have illuminated this entire study, offer suggestions about how to understand the erasures and how to place them at the heart of our inquiries.

Historical documents have little to say about the role of enslaved women in revolts and rebellions.[4] Finding those women requires, as historian Aisha Finch has argued, a reading that "privileges utterances meant to be small and insignificant," that rejects the notion that women were passive or unconscious observers of men's radical resistance.[5] Relatedly, historian Marjoleine Kars implores us to think of those who "dodged" rebellions as a way to take seriously not just the "role of women in rebellion, but the role

3 See, for example, the work of Toni Morrison, in particular *A Mercy*.
4 For a generative discussion of the production of archivally driven knowledge about the African and African American past, see D. Thomas, "Caribbean Studies."
5 Finch, "'What Looks Like a Revolution,'" 124.

of rebellion in the lives of women."[6] Finch and Kars are among the most recent scholars to offer new methodological approaches to the gaps in the archival evidence concerning enslaved women's resistance to the institution of slavery. With few exceptions, the leaders of and participants in the uprisings that were most disruptive and are best documented were men. Well aware of the multiplicity of constraints on women's roles in revolts, historians have emphasized the quotidian dimensions of women's opposition to slavery and the ways their support for rebellion falls out of the archive of slave resistance.

In many ways, this chapter follows a similar strategy: it centers the range of embodied behaviors available to women in order to contribute to a new perspective on the problem of tracing ideologies of resistance. At the same time, I want to seriously consider the relationship between the archival silence on this issue and the proximity of such silences to a range of evidence that speaks to slave owners' and legislators' knowledge of and accounting for enslaved women, in particular their presence and their economic value to plantation economies. Here, as elsewhere, the omissions might best be understood as an ideological production that was itself crucial in the arsenal of ideas slave owners constructed to justify the moral economy of slavery.[7] A slippery logic is involved in the assumption that the role of women in family life explains their absence from rebellion. I want to insist that because African and African-descended women were embedded in the economies of early modern capitalism, the concept of boundaries between public and private spheres cannot retroactively explain women's absence from archivally recorded acts of rebellion. At the risk of stating the obvious: enslaved women were not choosing to stay home from rebellions because they anticipated that their fathers and husbands would act for them.

In the seventeenth and early eighteenth centuries, Black women's presence in the fields and homes of white families laid the groundwork for the ideological spaces that emerged in the nineteenth century as a separate sphere; it did so because their own claims to the privacy associated

6 Kars, "Dodging Rebellion," 42.
7 Here I am deeply indebted to Didier Fassin's engagement with the etymology of *moral economy*. Drawing on both E. P. Thompson's and Lorraine Daston's use of the term, Fassin reworks it to offer a theoretical tool to "comprehend profound social changes often rendered imperceptible, precisely because they are morally invested." Fassin, "Moral Economy Redux." See also Fassin, "Critique of Moral Reason."

with family life were already under assault, if not unimaginable. Neither can the ideological processes that produced racial hierarchy, reproduction, and motherhood become the explanation for the only way that enslaved women's resistance is made visible. Enslaved women had no relationship to the private and the domestic, to the realm outside the market; such a relationship was fundamentally impossible. Enslaved women's and men's family life existed inside the marketplace. It was always vulnerable to sale and separation, always encoded in structures of value that were unrelated to affect. Because of this, the family lives of enslaved people always served to demarcate the boundaries of the emergent terrain of bourgeois affective private relations through their exclusion from this terrain.

When enslaved women and men claimed the prerogatives of private life, those claims were necessarily rendered as sites of conflict and were therefore deeply political. They were politicized and volatile because they fundamentally disrupted the distinct oppositional spaces of commerce and family on which whiteness was coming to rest. The inability to protect private life—whether understood as the most intimate space of sexuality and corporeal integrity or as the more communal spaces of cultural practices— is indeed the hallmark of enslavement and enslavability. But the means by which the body was rendered private property was indeed a process. The ideas that produced the woman's body as fungible and her infant as both fungible and separable from her were embedded in the tricky discourse that would become race and would require an epiphany to be seen clearly. Such an epiphany produced the strategic and definitional practices of resistance, built on the violence so starkly rendered by enslavement. Thus, we cannot use family life or affective ties as a self-evident explanation for why enslaved women do not appear in accounts of rebellions. The work of expanding the categories of rebellion to include enslaved women needs to be grounded in a clear understanding of how and why slave-owning observers routinely failed to see enslaved women in the particular public space of rebellions.

The silence in the records suggests at least two explanations. One is that the risks that women incurred when they strayed from the slave owners' labor regimes were enormous. The overlap between labor control and sexual violence was profound in Atlantic slave societies as the authority slave owners wielded licensed a range of abuses. Antebellum records abound with evidence that the punishment of enslaved women was often an opportunity for slave owners to take prurient sexualized pleasure as women were stripped naked before whippings. Slave owners often went farther than prurient passive pleasure; they raped enslaved women in public view or allowed such rapes to happen as they attempted to reassert authority over the women and over the community as a whole.[8] Here the paradox of gendered enslavement was made manifest: in the slave owners' minds, women's resistance was unthinkable and simultaneously warranted an extreme and excessively violent and gendered response.[9]

The second is that it was always in slave owners' interest to understand enslaved women as embodying a pacifying influence on enslaved populations. Such claims are part of the earliest references to African women in the Atlantic archive. When slave-owning legislators referenced women only as "company for our Negroe men" or worried that a dearth of enslaved women would "occasion a revolt among the Negro men," they constructed African women as a panacea.[10] This ideological space is adjacent to that wherein African mothers' devotion to children became the vehicle of their capture, or a signal that the marketing of people is indeed a space of terror; we are reminded of the complexity of kinship in the history of the transatlantic slave trade. The notion that enslaved women might produce a context in which unruly men would docilely comply with the labor regime added to women's market value. The association of enslaved women with domestic tranquility exemplified the malleability of racialist ideology in a slave-owning society and the ease with which slave-owning settlers and legislators lived with paradox. In the arsenal of ideas that defended hereditary racial slavery for slave traders and slave owners, the claim that enslaved women in the Americas primarily served as helpmeets for enslaved men was an important conceit. Slave owners' assertion that they were compelled to purchase women because of their responsibility to enslaved men and to the larger society was self-serving in the extreme. In these superficial gestures toward recognizing the inner lives of enslaved men, slave owners aligned their own sense of manliness and conjugality with that of the enslaved. They did so by implicitly mobilizing the importance of kinship for enslaved people by suggesting that they would purchase or retain women

8 For a discussion of rape and enslaved women, see Block, *Rape and Sexual Power*, 64–74.
9 The context of a woman tethered and whipped is what led Spillers to the notion of female flesh, not the female body, as a "text for living and for dying." Spillers, "Mama's Baby, Papa's Maybe," 67.
10 Quotes from the New York and South Carolina governing bodies respectively. Both instances are discussed further below. On enslaved women as "company" for enslaved men in colonial New York see Harris, *Shadow of Slavery*, 21; on the absence of women causing revolt, see J. L. Morgan, *Laboring Women*, 93.

"for" men. However, that alignment was fleeting; they immediately severed it by purchasing women and men in the market in an act that denied them control over their own sexual access or conjugal practices and situated African women and their female descendants as irrevocably outside the category of the feminine.

For women, whose reproductive and productive capacities supported the edifice of hereditary racial slavery from the very beginning, the experience of enslavement was rooted in both their reproductive capacities and the newly hardening language of race and racial hierarchy. The claims that Black women's childbearing took place outside the realm of family life, that it was painless, that it was inconsequential, and that it did not involve emotional intensities served to sharpen the connection of birth and domesticity with privileged European women and their descendants. These claims thereby produced motherhood as always white and in service to the stability of the colony or the nation. Slavery associated enslaved women with a range of negative behaviors that served to clarify white femininity through opposition to Black women's gendered identities. In the minds of white men and women, enslaved women were indifferent and easily distracted mothers; however, they were fit for brute and uninterrupted labor and sexually available and avaricious. Within this mythical terrain, ignoring the possibility that enslaved women posed a danger to the state commensurate with that posed by enslaved men protected slave owners from grappling with the protective edifice they had constructed through a racial ideology that was rooted in gender ideology and market ideology.

As slave-owning legislative bodies considered the threats enslaved laborers posed, they rarely discussed women. When they did, they named them as "wives"—sexual partners whose presence pacified rebel men. Here kinship is wielded to dismantle any inference that husbands and wives constituted autonomous households under the terms of hereditary racial slavery. Historians have observed this language but have not fully registered the ideological work it did. Writing concerning a plantation in Antigua, one owner advised another to buy females: "You really want them, indeed the Negroe Men are craving for wifes and therefore would advise Girls to be bought for that Estate."[11] When the Virginia legislature asked the Carolina House of Assembly for enslaved women as compensation for Virginians' military assistance, the Carolina house refused because taking women away

11 Walter Tulledeph to George Thomas, Antigua, June 19, 1749, quoted in Sheridan, "Letters from a Sugar Plantation," 19.

"might have occasioned a Revolt also of the Slaves."[12] The erasure here of women from the category of those who might revolt is so common as to be foundational. "Slaves" will revolt without "wives." The illogic is as profound as it is ubiquitous.[13] For historians, it produces a connection between the assumption that enslaved women would not participate in uprisings and the failure to fully consider the actual material and affective conditions that could deter such participation. They are distinct arenas and yet are tethered to one another both in the moment of the utterance and in the archive that records it. Unwilling to exchange women for military assistance, the Carolina legislators spared those women the dangers and upheavals of transport north to Virginia. Those women, unaware of their pivotal role in legislative negotiations, were left in place. How the intersection between their forced labors and their intimate connections with enslaved men would actually define their everyday lives remained presumably outside of both the interest and the comprehension of legislative bodies.

The conclusion that enslaved women would not or could not participate in organized collective revolt to the same degree as men may well be borne out by the archive. Yet this needs to be concluded only after careful engagement with how archival evidence is produced in the making of the Black Atlantic, perhaps more so than for any other aspect of women's experience of enslavement. Here the connection between early modern numeracy and the formalizing of racial hierarchy is made clearest because it renders the presence and experiences of Black women hazy, unknowable, or simply erased. Colonial legislative bodies were constantly engaged in acts of accounting: they reported financial gains and losses; transcribed the value of units of corn, tobacco, indigo, sugar, and rice into pounds sterling, reals, and *pieza de india*; counted population growth and loss; argued about tax revenues; bemoaned the numbers of fighting men relative to the numbers of unruly Indians and Africans; and calculated the value of enslaved

---

12 Joseph Boone and Richard Beresford, Agents for the Commons House of Assembly in South Carolina, to the Council of Trade and Plantations, December 5, 1716, Sainsbury and Great Britain Public Record Office, *Calendar of State Papers*, 29:216, qtd. in J. L. Morgan, *Laboring Women*, 94n94.

13 A quick survey of the historiography of slavery shows that historians took up this language and used *slave* as a universal that was only rarely modified with *female* to indicate otherwise. Not until Deborah Gray White's groundbreaking 1985 study *Ar'n't I a Woman* did historians slowly begin to acknowledge the ways in which the term was presumptive and erased the particularities of both male and female experiences of enslavement.

Africans based on their age and sex. Colonial legislatures were steeped in numeracy and in the specific skills and language required to articulate gains and losses in the colonial marketplace. When enslaved women emerge in the accounts, those textual eruptions are more than simple anomalies. Rather, they are markers or placeholders for the work these eruptions performed for slave owners in maintaining the tenuous balance between claims that enslavement was logical and the recognition that it perverted the very moral economy on which their own autonomy rested.

It required considerable ideological work to render African men, women, and children as legitimately enslavable and fungible. Doing so produced an ideological currency, a shorthand that we recognize as racism, both for slave owners and for those who aspired to be slave owners. Enslaved women, of course, had to navigate the symbolic and material consequences of this currency. The specific ways legislators and slave owners referred to them on paper were, of course, not visible to the women experiencing the symbolic and material consequences of such language. Nonetheless, enslaved women's embodied and ideological practices at times explicitly contravened the best efforts of slave owners, slave traders, and legislators to position women in a way that would make them permanently and unremarkably invisible.

Plundered Mothers

In the context of the larger Anglo-Dutch War of 1665–1667, hostilities broke out on the Caribbean island of Saint Christopher between the English and the French, who occupied different sides of the island. An Englishman who described the conflict in 1666 reported that "the French negroes also came all armed, being promised each man a white wife and freedom, as well as plunder."[14] He thus mobilized the fantasy of slave rebels fueled by the promise of sex with white women to foment disgust at the behavior of the French. He did so even though the presence of women among an earlier band of Maroons who had escaped the French by running into the hills occupied by the English had already made it clear that the "rebels" were not all "men."[15] Concerning a band of twenty-seven runaways on Antigua that included at least ten women, the Council of Antigua was deeply frustrated

14 Francis Sampson to John Sampson, June 6, 1666, CO 1/20, 97, Colonial State Papers, National Archives, Kew, England.
15 D. B. Gaspar, *Bondmen and Rebels*, 173.

when "a negro woman . . . promised to act as a guide against the runaway negroes and herself ran to them." The council concluded "that she is worthy of death as soon as captured."[16]

The Englishman's suggestion is rooted in the reality that the French forces armed enslaved men, a practice common across European slave-owning colonies and not, in this case, itself a cause for alarm.[17] The fantasy that all slave rebels intended to rape white women, to humiliate them by taking them as wives, is both predictable and as old as Atlantic slavery itself—even though the accusation was not once borne out in fact.[18] As we shall see later on, this language mirrors that of English authorities, when they offered the "women, children, and plunder" from Maroon communities to any white settlers who killed a Maroon warrior in their conflict with what they called "Spanish Negroes" on Jamaica in 1655. Englishmen on Jamaica used women and children from the Maroon community to enact the same humility and shame on Maroons that they feared the rebels would enact on them.

On both Jamaica and Saint Christopher, white men mobilized women's sexual availability to inflame whites' outrage and passion for war, either through the specter of violation or through the intersection of sex and the accumulation of wealth in the form of plunder offered to military allies. Such a maneuver would have been contradictory if slave-owning settlers' claims were made manifest. But plundered Black and white women conveyed two distinct meanings. The exposure of white women to the allegedly rapacious desire of marauding Black men was a signal for outrage. The offering of Black women as a reward to white men protecting their kinsmen from marauding Maroons was a sign of strategy. The boundaries between Black and white on which racial slavery rested were, in fact, quite porous when it came to the gendered notions of passivity and femininity that produced these strange alignments in the language of danger and protection. There is a formulaic quality to enslaved women's presence and absence in the archival records that is particularly evident in discussions of slave uprisings or revolts. Women are included in vague ways, and, at first glance, their roles appear to comport with gendered notions of women as

16 Minutes of Council of Antigua, March 31, 1687, Calendar of State Papers Colonial, America and West Indies: Volume 12 1685–1688 and Addenda 1653–1687.

17 On the widespread practice of arming the enslaved, see C. Brown and Morgan, *Arming Slaves*.

18 Genovese, *From Rebellion to Revolution*, 104–5.

vulnerable. Enslaved women are discursively aligned with white women, who are usually evoked in these discussions in conjunction with the idea of plunder.

In both of these locations colonial authorities rejected the idea of women's active participation in militarized conflicts between settlers and the enslaved. They connected women and children to plunder both through the language used to describe them and through the structures that positioned them—to goods or wealth taken from an enemy by force—in ways that complicate the rigid structures of racial hierarchy even as we recognize that enslaved African women occupied a very different position on that hierarchy than did free or indentured Englishwomen. The alignment between Black and white women exemplifies the fluidity of "women and children," the way in which they evoked a position that moved across boundaries of race and status. However, when this connection between women and the spoils of war is resituated in the context of racialized revolt, it takes on a different meaning. Here the relationship between women and plunder is affirmative. It reflects a process by which African women and their descendants had already been situated as naturally and reasonably commodified. And so we need to pose the question again: Why is it primarily through absences or lacunae that enslaved women have a place in the historiographies of enslavement? By what logical route should we end an exploration of the lives of enslaved women with ruminations about their erasure from efforts to reject their enslavement during the early Black Atlantic period?

Before we return to the question of women in grand marronage or other forms of active rebellion, we need to consider the consequences of how hereditary racial slavery situated African women as possessing bodies that marked them as passive producers of enslavement. Historian Londa Schiebinger has used the term *agnotology* to describe the history of ideas or questions that remain unasked.[19] In the history of Atlantic slavery, the question of whether women might have been key formulators of resistance and revolt against the despots who exposed them to the most venal subjugations falls into this category. Scholars of gender, resistance, and enslavement in the eighteenth and nineteenth centuries have reshaped how we understand the presence and absence of women as rebels. From Angela Davis's foundational scholarship on enslaved women's efforts to carve out time and space to attend to their communities to Stephanie Camp's examination of women's movement and bodily pleasures as a way to expand what

19 Schiebinger, "Agnotology and Exotic Abortifacients," 320.

she named the "geographies of containment," the forms of women's resistance to enslavement have been amplified by feminist scholars of gender and slavery.[20] From them we have learned that a gendered analysis enables something far more transformative than simply discovering and inserting the female maroon leader Nanny's foremothers into the narrative of slave resistance. Instead, it expands the category of resistance by focusing on the intimate spaces of family and worship, of dance and dresses, as well as looking at the systemic transformation of kinship into the highly politicized space of oppositional ideological formations.[21]

By centering the efforts of enslaved women to expand the geographies of containment that characterized their enslavement, we make visible how their embodied experience of that enslavement produced a particular critique of power. Yet we remain hesitant to ascribe radical thinking to enslaved women and men. A scholar of race and rebellion writes that "there remains the possibility that the slaves who entered into rebellion better understood the power of capital and its corrosive effect on the plantation regime, than did their masters."[22] Indeed. The enslaved had to be "theorists of freedom," perhaps none more so than the women whose bodies were wrenched into the marketplace. If, as political scientist Neil Roberts argues, the technology of racial slavery is predicated on the effort to ensure that "the slave must never know what it means to be a person," then women whose reproductive potential laid bare the racialized logic of heredity and hierarchical claims to authority gained a critical perspective not only through their proximity to marketplaces but also through the ways the market was made manifest through their bodies.[23]

For enslaved women and men, the effort to transcend the logic of price and value transformed the meaning of many quotidian activities into resistant pleasures. Mobilizing a category of resistance expanded by scholars who have engaged gender as a frame enables a reconsideration of the parameters of racial slavery and its encroachment into the intimate or quotidian spaces of consciousness. The pleasures of a dance can be heightened by the recognition that dancing in the woods on the outskirts of a plantation is a radical act of reclamation and a substantive strategy to heal the body when one has been violently and insistently cast in the role of brute and ugly

20 Davis, "Reflections," 7; and Camp, *Closer to Freedom*, 12–34.
21 Camp, *Closer to Freedom*; and Finch, "'What Looks Like a Revolution.'"
22 Egerton, "Slaves to the Marketplace," 637.
23 N. Roberts, *Freedom as Marronage*, 15, 51–138, quote on 69.

cotton-picking machine.[24] At the same time, if historians see any and all efforts at locating pleasure while enslaved as oppositional, we run the risk of minimizing the violence of slavery and the ways its damages were lived.[25] At the heart of the work to see both the destruction caused by slavery and the efforts by enslaved women to resist that destruction is a conviction that in slave rebellions, the many-headed hydra that was racial hierarchy and racial ideology met with a similarly multivalent set of responses. Thus, both armed revolt and the refusal to accept the sartorial limits of osnaburg clothing belong on a continuum—politicized rejection of the violence that enslavement engendered took many forms. The use of clothing as a bulwark against commodification is an important example. Camp has argued that "women's style allowed them to take pleasure in their bodies, to deny that they were only (or mainly) worth the prices their owners placed on them."[26] Similarly, to claim a child as an emblem of parental connection instead of releasing them to the economy was a refusal of the logic at the heart of women's enslavement.[27] In attending to familial or corporeal pleasures, enslaved women and men enacted a critique of the edifices of containment. From this starting point, one can understand the range of interventions that may be understood as resistance and account for the gendered dimensions of those interventions.

One cannot discuss enslaved women's responses to enslavement without carefully thinking about reproduction as it was experienced, denied, and intentionally thwarted. The core of Camp's intervention bears reiterating—a somatic approach to resistance and politics illuminates the fact that the enslaved "possessed at least three bodies": the body as a "site of domination[,] . . . as [a] vehicle of terror, humiliation, and pain . . . [and as] a thing to be claimed and enjoyed, a site of pleasure and resistance."[28] Enslaved women's reproductive potential bridged their three bodies as it became enmeshed in the range of corporeal experiences of strategic responses to enslavement. Situating the reproductive body as the site of somatic resistance is deceptively simple; it runs the risk of mounting an argument on essentialist grounds that evoke a universal and ahistorical motherhood. To

24 For generative work on the implications of casting enslaved workers as machines, see Baptist, *Half Has Never Been Told*; and W. Johnson, *River of Dark Dreams*.
25 This is an argument made most persuasively by Painter, "Soul Murder and Slavery."
26 Camp, *Closer to Freedom*, 83.
27 J. L. Morgan, *Laboring Women*, 128–43.
28 Camp, *Closer to Freedom*, 66–68.

be or to become a mother while enslaved was always to face the evidence of slavery's core contradictory violence—that the child you understood as family was instantly embedded in the property accumulation of the person who owned you.

The commodification of personhood was inescapably generational, and it taught a violent lesson to enslaved women about the fungibility and individuation of themselves and their children. Thus, even for the first generations of enslaved women in the Black Atlantic, the experience of reproduction and the meanings attached to it were reshaped by the dawning recognition that enslavement and the mark of racial hierarchy were made manifest by the symbolic and material work of women's bodies. In other words, maternity opened up a world of pain, even as it could also convey affective pleasures that worked to counter the brutality of the labor regime. Similarly, the absence of maternity—the infertility wrought either by the labor regime or by women's interventions—took on entirely new meaning in the context of hereditary racial slavery. To refuse to bear children, or to find oneself unable to do so, was an opportunity to claim one's humanity by refusing genealogy: a contradiction, yes, but a potential to assert kinlessness rather than passively accept it.

The body, then, is an important point of entry into the discussion of women's opposition to enslavement. This is elusive, not certain. In the context of the body as a site of pleasure and resistance, reproductive potential might rationalize the relative absence of women in traditional spaces of resistance. At the same time, women's vulnerability to sexual abuse at the hands of slave owners and overseers has been understood as a point of entry into the radicalization of enslaved men. Frederick Douglass's awakening to the terror of enslavement while watching Aunt Hester's violation is the most iconic expression of that link, one that has been taken up repeatedly and productively by scholars of slavery and race.[29] There is no question that enslaved men and children experienced the violence meted out on the bodies of Black women as deeply traumatic and instructive with regard to racialized power. Yet no matter how carefully one situates Aunt Hester, focusing on her subjection belies her own desire or capacity to respond to the structures that positioned her in that kitchen, pinioned and

29 The call-and-response between Saidiya Hartman and Fred Moten around the torturing of Aunt Hester exemplifies the complexity of both Douglass's narrative and contemporary readings of it. Hartman, *Scenes of Subjection*, 3–4; and Moten, *In the Break*, 1–24.

viciously abused while her young nephew looked on. Her punishment becomes productive of a core narrative of resistance in African American life, but it is a narrative from which she herself is omitted. Turning to Douglass's awakening through the abuse of Aunt Hester in the nineteenth century attunes us to the far reach of the violence perpetrated on the bodies of enslaved women.

The challenge in unearthing the range of material responses to enslavement, particularly in the early modern Atlantic world, lies in the effort to balance the paucity of source material with the certainty that women's reproductive capacities were part of the myriad ways in which those who were subjected to enslavement could and did push back against the violence and violations that rooted hereditary racial slavery in their bodies. Further, explorations of women's material responses to enslavement need to be carefully situated in the recognition that the ideological structures that contained and rationalized racial slavery are precisely those that produced enslaved women as outside the category of the rebel or, in the case of Douglass, the "theorist" of slavery.[30]

In the context of what historians have described as day-to-day resistance, women's actions and oppositional stances are more likely to emerge in the historical record. Here slave owners are more inclined to include complaints about enslaved women's sullenness, clumsiness, or false illnesses.[31] While slave owners across the Atlantic world accused enslaved men and women of all manner of stupidity, refusal to work or learn tasks, carelessness, and malingering, when they mentioned women specifically it was primarily to register their conviction that enslaved women were particularly prone to feigning illness and neglecting or murdering their own children. The accusations have been understood as evidence of enslaved women's and men's systematic acts of pushing back, a refusal to comply with the regimes of labor that led slave owners to situate them solely as valuable in an account book. But slave owners' particular view of African women as antimothers without the capacity or desire to nurture or protect children should attune us to the equally particular work that women were called on to do in efforts to dismantle slave owners' project of rationalizing racial slavery. The production of maternity as a space of care and domesticity for white families had as its Janus face the dysselection of Black women

30 N. Roberts, *Freedom as Marronage*, 15.
31 For the first association between women and malingering in the historiography, see Bauer and Bauer, "Day to Day Resistance," 410–12.

as mothers—this act of violent negation happened in broad daylight, producing in enslaved women a consciousness of what was being mounted on their subjection.[32]

Moving the relationship between women's bodies and the markets that attempted to ensnare them to the center of our vision produces a history of emerging slave societies that is rooted in the lived experiences of enslaved women. If we imagine the market as a geographically bounded space and market transactions as temporally bounded spaces, we miss the ways a woman's reproductive potential ensured that her capacity to gestate a child meant that she carried the market inside her body. In that context, the efforts that enslaved women undertook to maintain control over their corporeal integrity need to be understood as occupying two distinct but related spheres—a personal or individual response and a collective or political critique. While evidence of reproductive control as a means of resistance or revolt remains elusive, women's fertility and fertility control under enslavement must be understood as a fundamental conduit for the production of an oppositional consciousness among the enslaved. As historian Liese Perrin has argued, when women avoided conception under slavery, they understood that their reproductive capacity was linked to the accumulation of capital in the hands of their owners. Fertility control—resisting the work of reproduction—then becomes a "form of strike."[33]

Drawing on the work to situate enslaved women's resistance in Black feminist geographies helps clarify the particular tensions wrought by slavery on the bodies of enslaved women and what those tensions produced.[34] With regard to enslaved women's resistance in the antebellum period, historian Darlene Clark Hine discussed women who actively rejected slave owners' efforts to turn them into breeders, situating their decisions as

32 Sylvia Wynter mobilizes selection/dysselection as a way to mark a neo-Malthusian pairing of life and death. I use it here to evoke Wynter's generative work to unpack the processes by which some are negated in the act of producing lives for others. Wynter and McKittrick, "Unparalleled Catastrophe for Our Species?," 36.

33 Perrin, "Resisting Reproduction," 256; see also my discussion of contraception and abortion in J. L. Morgan, *Laboring Women*, 113–14, 231nn15–19. Finally, on the question of W. E. B. Du Bois's articulation of the "General Strike" and his evacuation of reproductive labor from that formulation, see Weinbaum, *Afterlife of Reproductive Slavery*, 67–71.

34 Here I am thinking of Stephanie Camp's reworked notion of geographies of containment alongside McKittrick's "black women's geographies." Camp, *Closer to Freedom*; and McKittrick, *Demonic Grounds*.

"made consciously and with full awareness of the potential political and economic ramifications involved."[35] Enslavement does more than deny the fundamental interiority of gestation; it reverses it. Enslavement in the Atlantic depended on the alienation of Black women's reproductive labor, the transformation of family or kin into marketed goods. In such a climate, efforts to retain home, family, kith, or kin outside the marketplace took on a highly charged and politicized role. Such efforts constitute claims to freedom in the face of enslavement.[36] But they are also deeply personal experiences that express individuated pain and pleasure. For every woman who endured endless confinement in loopholes of retreat so as to protect her ability to parent her children, there is a woman for whom a thin needle slipped into a newborn's spongy fontanel was the only legitimate response to the brutality of mothering the enslaved. Most women fell in the space between these two responses, and there too is where we must struggle to grasp the meanings of resistance and reproduction. If we are not diligent, the terms *resistance* and *reproduction* threaten to shut down our historical imagination. Each evokes a singularity of purpose that fails to reflect the perversion of purpose on which racial slavery rested.

North American labor conditions were such that enslaved women there were able to give birth to children, and those children were likely to survive infancy. This led to population growth through birth rather than through the importation of more enslaved persons as in most of the Caribbean and Latin America. Thus, by the middle of the eighteenth century, for the enslaved the institution of slavery developed in tandem with family formation. Scholars of slavery and the slave trade are careful to emphasize the singularity of natural increase in North America among the slave societies in the Americas. But because the comparison is normally used to emphasize the death and infant mortality rates elsewhere, the emergence of a naturally increasing enslaved population in the plantation South suggests that women in these communities accepted their pregnancies and births without struggle. This could lead to the assumption that contradictions between kinship and enslavement were less prominent outside the West Indies. In fact, women whose bodies were caught up in the investment strategies of slave owners would soon find themselves immersed in an economy that was fundamentally at odds with the concept of family.

Before the mid-eighteenth century, enslaved women in North America, like their counterparts in the West Indies and Latin America, faced

35 Hine, "Female Slave Resistance," 126.
36 Patterson, "Slavery, Alienation," 164–65.

a more opaque set of relationships between reproduction, enslavement, and resistance. During the period when birth rates were hampered by the physiological consequences of sugar production on the islands and new disease environments throughout the colonies, enslaved women and men in seventeenth-century English settlements perhaps came to understand the possibility of childbirth as less assured—one more consequence of their newfound captivity. As they watched, or experienced, stillbirths, maternal mortality, or simply the absence of conception, the increasingly dangerous toll of pregnancy and childbirth under New World enslavement would have been made visible. Certainly former notions they had had about the inevitability of childbearing and the context in which it would take place were indelibly altered for any girl or woman who survived the Middle Passage. To return to Camp's three bodies: pregnancy and birth rendered an enslaved woman's body a site of domination and a vehicle of terror, but in the pregnant body's echo of a lost futurity, claiming the possibility associated with pregnancy might well have been a crucial site of pleasure and resistance. The ideological and material edifice of hereditary racial slavery did not produce only the three bodies of the enslaved; it also produced a critical knowledge about the workings of power on and against those bodies.

This is the field of meaning in which we must situate accusations about enslaved women's efforts to prevent conception or destroy a pregnancy. In her 1705 *Metamorphosis of the Insects of Surinam*, the naturalist Maria Sibylla Merian wrote of the *flos pavonis* (peacock flower; *Caesalpinia pulcherrima*), "The Indians and Africans, who are not treated well by their Dutch masters, use the seeds to abort their children, so that their children will not become slaves like they are. . . . They told me this themselves."[37] We know from the writings of European travelers that this particular plant was found in Barbados, Jamaica, and Saint-Domingue and in seventeenth-century Surinam. While the provenance of the plant itself isn't known, a similar one, with similar qualities, was found in Senegal, and "it is clear that [enslaved women] knew abortifacients before they entered the Caribbean's fraught sexual economy."[38]

In the immediate aftermath of emancipation, birth rates rose significantly among the formerly enslaved in Jamaica, indicating that in the context

---

37 Merian, *Metamorphosis insectorum Surinamensium*, plate 45. See Schiebinger's discussion of Merian in Schiebinger, "Agnotology and Exotic Abortifacients," 319; and Schiebinger, "Exotic Abortifacients and Lost Knowledge," 718–19.

38 Schiebinger, "Agnotology and Exotic Abortifacients," 340.

of the withdrawal of (already meager) medical attention and the imposition of severe economic hardship, having children remained something over which the now-free women could exercise some control.[39] Debates around reproduction were at the heart of the transition from slavery to freedom in the British West Indies as abolitionists, slave owners, and enslaved women fought over the transformations in the meaning of childbirth.[40] The desire to forestall conception and the possibility of infanticide are obviously linked politically and conceptually.

The first studies of everyday resistance on plantations in the southern United States located abortion and infanticide on a continuum of individual acts of resistance, cementing historians' early assumptions that women's capacities to resist enslavement were limited to the corporeal.[41] It is too easy to imagine that such bodily practices were evacuated of political meaning, that they were affective and somatic and thus spoke of an interiority steeped in pain and the desire to avoid pain, not a clarity about collective resistance. But if we accord the same consciousness to these women that we do to slave owners, the larger implications of these interior actions come into view. In the eyes of the slave owner, the women who removed her reproductive potential from his accounting had essentially already committed infanticide. To then engage in the actual murder of an infant was simply to extend an act of economic sabotage from one level to the next.

Infanticide law in the colonies had an important precedent in England; there it was the only capital crime for which one was assumed to be guilty instead of having to be proven guilty. The 1624 law Against Murdering Infant Bastards found a woman guilty of murdering her child if the child died and the woman had concealed the birth. The earliest reference to infanticide in the English-speaking New World is in Cotton Mather's 1702 account of a massacre in which "furious Tawnies ... dash'd out the Brains of [an] Infant, against a Tree."[42] Early modern writers used infanticide to mark barbarism or madness, ascribing the latter to Englishwomen and the former to everyone else. By the eighteenth century, frequent references to

39 For a discussion of birth rates in the aftermath of emancipation, see Dadzie, "Searching for the Invisible Woman," 31; and De Barros, *Reproducing the British Caribbean.*

40 In *Contested Bodies*, Sasha Turner provides ample evidence for the ways in which abolitionists and slave owners alike routed the end of slavery through the captive reproductive bodies of enslaved women between 1780 and 1834 in Jamaica.

41 In Bauer and Bauer's discussion of resistance, women's activism is reduced to the possibility of abortion. Bauer and Bauer, "Day to Day Resistance."

42 Mather, "Magnalia Christi Americana," quoted in Chapman, "'Happy Shall He Be,'" 238.

infanticide in English law, philosophy, and political economy texts served as a conduit for discussions about the capacity for sympathy and reason in civilized society.[43] In such an ideological context, the accusation of infanticide became crucial in the arsenal of racial hierarchy and the rationale for racial slavery. Its meaning was legible to both slave owners and enslaved women, though it carried very different meanings—to prevent a birth under the regime of hereditary racial slavery was both to inflict damage on the regime and (in the eyes of the slave owner) to clarify the legitimacy of enslavement to begin with. The ancillary damage such an act inflicted on the self was immaterial.

In Atlantic slave societies, the image of the malevolent and depraved enslaved mother circulated as a salve to exonerate slave owners from their responsibility for the low fertility and high mortality rates among the people they had enslaved, who were suffering the consequences of brutal extractive labor, inadequate food, and unhygienic living conditions. In this context, the accusation that enslaved mothers and midwives were responsible for the deaths of infants served an important purpose for proslavery writers, who claimed that infanticide allowed enslaved women to "live without moderation."[44] Close proximity to infant death was dangerous for enslaved women, whether they were guilty by association or by conviction. In 1708 a "negro woman" and an "Indian man" in New York murdered a man and a woman and their five children. It seems likely that the loss of the children at least in part explains the differential punishment of the man and the woman—he was hung, and she was burned.[45]

The possibility that some women were driven to infanticide must be taken seriously, but it must also be placed alongside evidence of high infant mortality rates. Both women and the men alongside whom they labored in the sugar, tobacco, rice, and cotton fields were surrounded by infant death. The pregnancies that came to term only emphasized the precarity of life and the vulnerability of women and children to the market. The eighteenth century was marked by an increasing recognition among slave owners in the British Atlantic colonies that childbirth on the plantation worked to their advantage. Slave owners' recognition of women's reproductive value

43 McDonah, "Infanticide," 216.
44 *Memoire sur l'esclavage des negres*, quoted in Weaver, "'She Crushed the Child's Fragile Skull,'" 104.
45 Governor Lord Cornbury to the Council of Trade and Plantations, February 10, 1708, CO 5/1049, n91, Colonial State Papers, National Archives, Kew, England.

fueled the willingness of colonists in North America to oppose the British plan to levy a prohibitively high tax on the slave trade by opposing British rule altogether.[46] They saw the tax on the slave trade as something they could avoid by relying on the reproductive work of the women they had enslaved in North America. Elsewhere in the colonies, slave owners embraced the 1807 ban on the slave trade. In North America the birth of Black children fed an internal trade that transported over a million Black men, women, and children to the cotton fields of Alabama, Arkansas, Louisiana, and Texas.[47]

In the sugar islands, even reluctant slave owners had to recognize that the loss of women's labor during pregnancy might be a cost they were willing to bear as wars disrupted the slave trade and they faced the inevitability of the 1807 ban. Eighteenth-century abolitionists and slave owners alike were deeply committed to policies that relied on population growth through enslaved women's fecundity.[48] After purchasing balanced numbers of women and men for a Jamaican plantation in the late eighteenth century, a plantation manager and an owner revealed their interpretation of the failure of the plantation to achieve natural increase: "[The] thing that hurts the Women breeding is owing to their Whoring about walking at nights to plays dancing til day light and a custom they have of suckling their children for two and a half [years] and venerials. . . . [It is] not that the Women do not breed, either owing to hard labour or inhumanity, for they do, but four children out of five die within the first nine days after they are born."[49] They clearly recognized the dual economic value they hoped to reap from enslaved women of childbearing age.[50]

This bit of speculative biopower is stunning in its breadth: the writer managed to expose his racism, shed light on how women were creating rival geographies around the plantation and practicing nursing habits of their own choosing, blame women for not having enough children, and then, in the next breath, imagine that infant death is outside anyone's control. Two aspects of the writer's screed stand out: the duration of breastfeeding

46 Paugh, *Politics of Reproduction*, 37–46.
47 Deyle, *Carry Me Back*, 283–89.
48 Paugh, *Politics of Reproduction*, 7.
49 Simon Taylor to Chaloner Arcedeckne, Kingston, Jamaica, January 17, 1791, quoted in B. Wood and Clayton, "Slave Birth, Death and Disease," 109.
50 The phrase "dual economic value" is from B. Wood and Clayton, "Slave Birth, Death and Disease," 103.

and the large number of dead infant bodies. Even in the wake of the brilliant work of historian Vincent Brown, it is challenging to fully understand how living in the midst of death transformed life in slave societies. Who tells us more about the way that slavery distorted the relationship between mothers and infants: the woman who has held many an infant in the death throes of tetanus and who refuses to stop nursing the one who survives, or the woman driven to smother her newborn before lockjaw, yellow fever, or the financial perversions of the man who counts her birth only on a balance sheet did the job for her?

Accounts of mothers who harmed enslaved infants clearly cannot be taken at face value. However, because these archival eruptions are the few spaces where slave owners and legislative bodies directed attention to women's lives, they cannot simply be dismissed. Rather, when we frame violence against newborns with a context that includes our awareness of how deeply contested motherhood was in the marketplaces that defined those women, we can recognize that although infant death may well have occurred in the manner slave owners described, it was not done in the spirit the owners ascribed to it. With regard to fertility control, abortifacients, or infanticide, we must consider how the meaning of resistance was deeply shaped by all that African men and women brought to their experience of slavery in the seventeenth-century Atlantic world. Here, in the degree to which slave owners were capable of understanding enslaved women as a source of danger, we see the clearest possible enunciation of the problem space the proximity of commerce and kinship created in hereditary racial slavery. Faced with the alarming recognition that women's opposition to enslavement might lead them to destroy their children or prevent their conception, slave owners needed to reroute their attention from the depravity of the slave market to the depravity of Black life. A recognition of the depravity of the market would have been rooted in recognizing the legitimacy of an enslaved women's desire to refuse the conditions of her enslavement and, as such, certainly could not be articulated.

Marooning Women

There were other, equally alarming spaces of refusal. One of these began with the presence of women as rebels in seventeenth-century Saint Christopher. Rebel and Maroon women were indeed present throughout slave societies in the Americas, even if colonial officials didn't accord them the same title that they did to rebel men. That women were part of organized uprisings against slave owners was clear to colonial settlers from the very beginning. In the beginning, there was marronage. African men and women who had recently arrived in nascent colonies took to the hills, collaborating with indigenous communities, forging protective encampments of their own, and often waging war on their former captors. The sixteenth-century origins of marronage clearly involved both women and men, as the practice began at a moment when significant numbers of women were arriving on the slave ships. Sometimes documents refer to women's presence in the leadership of Maroon communities, as in the case of Leonor, "Chief of the palinque of El Limon" in Cartagena.[51]

But throughout the region the presence of women among those who were recaptured, punished, or executed, while impossible to ignore, was situated in ways that excused careful consideration. Shortly after the English took the island of Jamaica from the Spanish in 1655, for example, they entered into a series of negotiations with Maroons who had strategically joined them in their fight against the Spanish. In the aftermath, peace treaties recognized the freedom and autonomy of these Maroon communities in exchange for a pledge of military support in the case of future, presumably imperial, conflicts. Complaining a decade later about the "Varmahaly negroes" who continued to make incursions against the English from the center of the island, the governor offered rewards to anyone who captured or killed these "sneaking and treacherous rogues." The language of the governor's statement does not gender the "rogues." He refers to them as "negroes" throughout the proclamation until its end, when he declares that "any person finding out the pallenque of said negroes, shall have and enjoy to their uses all the women, children, and plunder for their reward."[52]

The settlers who encountered the order would have understood that in the eyes of the governor, those who counted as rogues were men. In the minds of white colonialists, those men could be killed with impunity, and indeed should be killed, as doing so would reap the killer a considerable monetary reward and help protect the colonial venture. In this equation the women and children were valuable booty who had already been linguistically rendered as property in the Maroon encampment as a result of their proximity to "plunder" in the proclamation. In such a formulation, the assumption was that women would not be among the rogues, that they

51 Gómez, *Experiential Caribbean*, 67.
52 Order of the Governor and Council of War in Jamaica, CO 140/1, 138–40, September 1, 1665, Colonial State Papers, National Archives, Kew, England.

were neither fomenters nor leaders of rebellions but rather inconsequential inhabitants of the settlements. At best, white colonialists would have understood Maroon women as providing the food and shelter that nurtured the rebels.

However, the proclamation also indicates that whether or not they were dangerous rogues in the eyes of colonial authorities, the Varmahaly Negroes included men, women, and children. Women had made lives in this autonomous community and had worked to support the integrity of their settlement. They may have done so through provisioning, but there is no reason to suppose that they failed to do so militarily. Stories abounded of European troops being surprised by warriors hidden in trees and behind hillsides, ambushing disoriented soldiers who would hardly have been in a position to discern the sex of their hidden assailants. Further, childbirth here was normalized, as it was in other locations where Maroon communities thrived, in the West Indies, Brazil, Suriname, or Cuba. Thus, in the governor's proclamation, the birth of children, or at least their presence, is taken as a given. Birth rates among Maroon communities are very difficult to track, but in the records of conflict that colonial officials generated, children appear frequently, albeit as bounty or as victims of "depravity." Eighteenth-century chroniclers of the Caribbean wrote passionately about the "brutality" that "Maroons always displayed toward their wives and their children." They evoked the common trope of infanticide, claiming that it was common for Maroon fathers who were annoyed by an infant's cry to "dash it against a rock" and that "every gentleman" knows that Maroon fathers "offered their own daughters . . . for prostitution."[53]

If running away was the most fundamental refusal of the infestation of daily life by the market for the enslaved, it was also a way of reconfiguring the spatial confines of New World plantations. The combination of the relatively balanced sex ratios in the sixteenth and seventeenth centuries and the likelihood that enslaved women were excluded from the jobs that allowed some freedom of movement means that early sugar, rice, and tobacco plantations were likely peopled by a preponderance of women. As slave owners domesticated the land and built homes and dwellings to shelter themselves and the women and men they enslaved, they produced

---

53 Edwards, *History, Civil and Commercial* (1793), 539. As Richard Price points out in his reproduction of Bryan Edwards's discussion of the Maroons, these sections were taken verbatim from Edward Long's *The History of Jamaica* (1774). Price, *Maroon Societies*, 231, 241.

spaces of their own domesticity that rested uncomfortably on the backs of enslaved laborers. If we see the plantation as a space where women were particularly confined, then we can understand how the presence of women among runaways—sometimes alone, sometimes in small groups, sometimes with their children or with other women's children—posed a particular problem for the slave owner who understood himself or herself to be in a position of mastery over the enslaved. In some senses, runaway men were predictable. Their opposition to enslavement could be understood in masculinist terms as reflecting a kind of untethered savagery and a proximity to nature. Enslaved women who left their quarters pointedly rejected the terms on which the edifice of racial slavery rested, and thus, I argue, that act carried a deep symbolism.

Marronage developed in tandem with colonial settlement. Almost as soon as Spanish settlers brought enslaved Africans to the Americas, some men and women escaped to the edges of colonial settlements and established free encampments. Always understood as posing a danger to European authority in the Americas, Maroons engendered a range of responses, including militarized hostility and, when whites were unable to defeat Maroon fighters, reluctant acknowledgment of sovereignty and grudging respect for the Maroons' geographic and economic territory. The assumption has long been that Maroon bands were predominantly male. While male majorities were likely the norm, statistical evidence of how many women chose to join Maroon communities is hard to come by here, as elsewhere in the archive of the Black Atlantic. Early estimates placed female members of Maroon villages at 18–25 percent, a figure that mirrors many estimates of female runaways across the colonial Atlantic world.[54] Given the degree to which our understanding of sex ratios among runaways has shifted with a gendered analysis that recognizes, for example, the rates of truancy and support for truants among enslaved women, it must be assumed that much of our demographic understanding of the population of Maroon camps is mired in narrative and demographic practices that fail to account for women.

The early scholarship on Maroon communities emerged in the wake of the 1960s and was forged in a discussion of the nature of resistance, revolt, and radicalism that had not yet begun to consider the role of gender as a category of analysis. Early studies that historicized marronage imagined Maroons as men, as indeed they imagined all slaves as male. They took it

54 This is the figure that Price arrives at in *Maroon Societies*, 18–19.

for granted that colonial slave societies were, on the whole, marked by a "severe shortage of enslaved women."[55] Drawing primarily on evidence produced by colonial officials, historians reproduced claims that Maroon communities were riven with conflicts over the shortage of women that were amplified (or so the reports claimed) by natural inclinations toward polygamy. For example, reports claimed that Maroons were so desperate for wives that they constructed elaborate schemes for sharing women in an orderly way so the paternity of progeny could be determined. Even recent scholars have situated women as plunder that was taken rather than as coconspirators who had been liberated by those who shared a vision of freedom. Most scholars have not understood that women were part of Maroon communities unless the word *Maroon* is modified by the adjective *female*. To write, as one historian did as recently as 2006, that "the Maroons periodically raided plantations for food and women ... during lean harvests or as wives were needed" results in the unavoidable conclusion that women are not Maroons but rather supplies and, as such, necessary commodities.[56] This recommodification of African women in the hands of historians echoes their treatment by colonial observers but omits a crucial recognition: sometimes women were Maroons.

The symbolic meaning of marronage has shifted for scholars of slavery and freedom who have ruminated over whether or not establishing independent communities organized around ethnicity and hierarchical models of sovereign authority should be understood as revolutionary. For Cedric Robinson, Maroon communities index a crucial rejection of the terms of Atlantic slavery and are the roots of Black radicalism.[57] But this interpretation hasn't dominated the field. The masculinist nature of marronage is one of the first things colonial authorities conveyed in reports that narrated stories of guerrilla warriors and polygamist despotism. Such reports planted the seed of historical interpretations that emphasize the restorative nature of marronage: a desire to reproduce ethnic African poli-

---

55 Price, *Maroon Societies*, 18.

56 Fortin, "'Blackened beyond Our Native Hue,'" 8. In her 2004 dissertation, "Not Killing Me Softly," Rebecca Hall considers the history of women's participation in organized slave revolts and uprisings. In that work she provides a useful discussion of the discursive erasure of women from accounts of military conflicts between Maroon communities and US troops. She writes that scholars have narrowly conceived of maroons as either 'passive negresses,' or as male soldiers who fought and died for their freedom" (29).

57 Robinson, *Black Marxism*, 130–40.

ties in the New World.[58] It should not be a surprise that in marronage—arguably the most emphatic and profound rejection of the totalizing logic of hereditary racial slavery—women were fundamentally erased. Efforts to reinscribe women into this particular practice of resistance might focus on the role of women in cultivating land and caring for children in Maroon communities and thus provisioning the warriors. But to stop there would be to fail to fully consider the role of women in crafting a praxis of freedom-as-movement that is crucial to Black Atlantic counternarratives of modernity. As persons who fundamentally understood the nature of enslavement, who were among the first to see the particularities of hereditary racial slavery theorized through their bodies, women who ran to Maroon communities enacted a foundation of freedom that was arguably born from their own experience of reproduction.[59] The birth of children whose status was fundamentally changed by their mothers' flight testified to these women's importance in crafting the meaning of marronage and its refusal of hereditary racial slavery.

Even taken at face value, stories of women who escaped from plantations with rice and wheat seeds hidden in their hair attest to the importance of their agricultural skills in the camps and the intentionality of female runaways and rebels.[60] For the philosopher Joy James, these women give birth to a philosophical tradition rooted in the capacity to birth a new way of understanding freedom and reliance.[61] Interactions between colonial states and Maroon communities were deeply gendered because they were shaped by the challenge skilled guerrilla warriors posed to European troops. Despite being significantly outnumbered and outgunned, Maroon fighters were able to forestall European troops throughout the Caribbean and force colonial governments to concede military losses and

58 Genovese, *From Rebellion to Revolution*, 46–65, esp. 47.
59 Drawing on Hannah Arendt's notion of the distinction between liberation and the foundation of freedom that rests on the human experience and enactment of natality, Neil Roberts argues that marronage offers an articulation of freedom as movement that is rooted in the marronage community as a site of natality. For Arendt, action, or "the political experience par excellence," is produced by natality, which is, in turn, "the miracle that saves the world." Natality's importance is defined in its ontological relationship to human action. The "birth of new man and new beginnings" are signified by the action instigated by birth. Arendt, *Human Condition*, 9, 247; and N. Roberts, *Freedom as Marronage*, 23–24.
60 Groot, "Maroon Women," 161.
61 James, "Afrarealism and the Black Matrix."

negotiate treaty terms. With the exception of Nanny, a female Jamaican Maroon leader, colonial officials rarely discussed women as anything other than background noise. In the case of Nanny, her leadership and military prowess are usually reduced to lore about her ability to use her buttocks to catch bullets—a description "retold with such frequency that she has acquired a kind of materiality" that serves to confirm rather than critique the corporeal excesses with which African-descended women are associated.[62] In these contexts colonial officials' routine exclusion of women from the category of rebel (or even rogue) is best understood as embedded in the web of ideas about race and slavery that formed the ideological economy from which enslaved women struggled so powerfully to extract themselves.

The Dutch were, of course, not alone in ascribing pacification to enslaved women and children. In negotiations with Maroon communities throughout the region, Europeans brought gendered presumptions of power, plunder, and reproduction to the table. In 1663, after negotiating a treaty with the Maroon leader Juan Luyola, the English governor of Jamaica, Charles Lyttelton, stipulated that the "negroes of his Palenque, on account of their submission and services to the English, shall have grants of land and enjoy all the liberties and privileges of Englishmen, but must bring up their children to the English tongue."[63] In his description of the settlement that Juan de Bolas led in 1656, an English writer speculated about the growth of a large Maroon community that had retreated to the mountains, "where they not only augmented their numbers by natural increase, but, after the island became thicker sown with plantations, they were frequently reinforced by fugitive slaves."[64] If natality marks the foundations of freedom, Maroon communities were building freedom dreams as early as the seventeenth century.[65]

These early Maroon communities were defined along ethnic lines and were willing to engage strategically with slave owners against other enslaved people, so we cannot say that they necessarily signal the onset of a collective racial identity. Nonetheless, they were sovereign territories where men, women, and children crafted a social and political life in opposition to the colonial slave-owning authority. We should understand that at

62 Cummings, "Jamaican Female Masculinities," 144.

63 "Proclamation of Sir Chas. Lyttelton," February 1, 1663, CO 140/1 75–79, Colonial State Papers, National Archives, Kew, England.

64 Edwards, History, Civil and Commercial (1793), 303.

65 Robinson, Black Marxism, 130–40.

the very least, adult women would have been active members of communities built on kinship ties and the control of land and would thus have understood themselves to be part of Maroon communities rather than simply part of the supplies that the community mobilized.

In April 1656 an English captain wrote that his soldiers "fell upon some negroes as they were in Council and killed eight, ye rest fled only one woman taken alive."[66] Here the eight Negroes killed are assumed to be men until we learn that the one rebel captured was a woman. This woman in council was a provocation to the English militia, as she is to the historical record. She is the lone adult who was not killed as the document later describes that she, along with a boy, was "taken up." Her fate at the hands of English soldiers was gendered—servitude that would tilt toward the domestic (without the interiority that the word evokes), certain rape, and probable death.

In all this, the English were predictably late to the table. Spanish colonial authorities had been grappling with the realities of female Maroons and Maroon leaders since before the end of the seventeenth century.[67] By the end of the 1680s, Spanish officials had begun issuing formal decrees manumitting enslaved men and women who came from rival Protestant colonies and who converted to Catholicism, thus producing a significant interimperial maritime marronage.[68] Throughout the region, men and women braved the waters of the Caribbean and Atlantic to establish freedom in Spanish territory in a process that left considerable archival evidence in the form of petitions, baptisms, and documentation of other official proceedings. Although women are outnumbered among those who appear in the official record, they are there.

The women who found their freedom in marronage on English territory may have lived lives that strayed far from the assumptions of colonial governors and military leaders about female identity. This is an archival problem we must wrestle with here and throughout our engagement with the history of the Black Atlantic. Over time, the incapacity of the English state to see women as rebels only grew more entrenched. By the time Jamaican slave owners crafted their report on Cudgoe's War (sometimes referred to

---

66 Capt. Mark Harrison to the Admiralty and Navy Commissioners, April 30, 1656, CO 1/32, 60–61, Colonial State Papers, National Archives, Kew, England. On the next page of the same record, Harrison notes that "a party of soldiers also fell upon some plantations negroes, killed eight and took a boy and a woman," 62.

67 Landers, "Founding Mothers," 7–11.

68 Rupert, "Marronage, Manumission and Maritime Trade."

as the First Maroon War) in the 1730s, their language clearly betrayed the layers of gendered norms that are at the heart of archival silences. In describing a plantation that had been taken by "rebellious negroes," Governor Robert Hunter wrote that "there were at Hobby's two gangs of 100 men in each and several women which they had brought to help carry off the spoil."[69] Again, despite the importance of the female rebel Nanny in the story of resistance in Jamaica, in this case the women who accompanied the "rebellious negroes" are set outside the community of resistance, rendered passive, and, indeed, exploited by dangerous men who either used them as bearers or treated them as potential booty in the hands of the enemy who thus needed to be guarded.[70]

The gendered language of marronage in Jamaica had calcified by the time Edward Long and Bryan Edwards wrote their descriptions of Maroon communities at the end of the eighteenth century. In their hands, the female Maroons were reduced to drudges forced to perform the agricultural labor that these "savages" found "repugnant." According to Edwards, "the Maroons, like all other savage nations, regarded their wives as so many beasts of burthen" and displayed brutality toward their multiple wives and hostility toward their daughters, whom they offered to visitors as prostitutes.[71] Throughout Edwards's discussion of the history of the Maroons, he either treats women in the communities reductively as part of the landscape or cites them as evidence of male Maroon savagery and incivility.

Marronage constituted a very particular kind of revolt that was rooted in the reproduction of communities based on ties of kinship and ethnicity. In that context, the acknowledgment on the part of legislative and military bodies in slave-owning regions that women existed (even if only that) was predictable, albeit reluctant. In the context of revolts and conspiracies, it was much easier for colonial officials to completely omit discussion of women, whether because they actually did not participate or because acknowledging the presence of female rebel leaders was simply too destabilizing.

There is another piece to this, of course, and that is the process by which slavery introduced a monumentally important model of capitalism's ability

69 "Confession Made by Scyrus," Governor Hunter to the Council of Trade and Plantations, August 25, 1733, CO 137/20, ff. 178–79, Colonial State Papers, National Archives, Kew, England.

70 The report goes on to say, "They left one gange in the Negro Town to guard the women and children."

71 Edwards, *History, Civil and Commercial*, 321.

to appropriate and transform basic human relationships into commodities. In this regard, the archival obstacles to writing full histories of enslaved women without grappling with numeracy are mirrored in the inability to write full histories of capitalism without grappling with race. Across the Americas, European colonial settlers had been actively constructing slave ownership (materially) and slavery (ideologically) through women's bodies. The precarity of the linked enterprises was all too real as early as the seventeenth century, and it was essential for white people to erase what might otherwise be the humanizing acknowledgment that enslaved women were intimately embedded in kinship groups, families, or communities.

Appropriated Kinship

Elsewhere in the Atlantic, in ports or on lands with little terrain in which to hide, women were structurally situated as secondary in another way. As their reproductive lives are the primary path through which they are visible in the archive, their identity as mothers or wives needs to be scrutinized so that we can see past the pacifying and commodifying rhetoric in which they are embedded. As the English continued to navigate their interaction with so-called Spanish Negroes on the island of Jamaica, their records both betrayed the presence of women Maroons and pushed them to the margins of history.

In February 1644 a group of enslaved Africans in what was then New Amsterdam petitioned for a change in their status. Arguing that they had faithfully served the Dutch West India Company for the previous eighteen years, the petitioners asked for their freedom. They provided compelling reasons why they needed to be free: "they are burthened with many children so that it is impossible for them to support their wives and children, as they have been accustomed to do, if they must continue in the Company's service." In response, the Council of New Netherland conferred what historians have called "half-freedom" on the named petitioners "and their wives." In his 1978 study of colonial slave law, A. Leon Higginbotham pointed out that the terms of this semifreedom were indeed quite harsh and did not support the claims of earlier historians that half-free Blacks were treated equally with free whites.[72] What is absent from his (or other historians') analysis of enslavement under the Dutch in colonial New York is a critical engagement with the gendered ideology that drove Dutch colonial policy

72 Higginbotham, *In the Matter of Color*, 107.

regarding enslaved persons. The response of the director and the Council of New Netherland to the petitioners acknowledged and supported the concept of family formation among the Africans they enslaved along lines that were recognizable to European Protestants. "Husbands" and "wives" were granted considerable economic and social autonomy even as their reproductive lives remained tethered to the state. In exchange for freedom, the petitioners were required to make an annual payment to the Dutch West India Company in the form of wheat and a hog valued at twenty guilders, and the council decreed that "their children at present born or yet to be born, shall be bound and obligated to serve the Honorable West India Company as Slaves."[73] This intrusion into familial autonomy had implications that reverberated down through the generations.

The men identified in the 1644 petition were known by names that indicate their subject position and their familiarity with the complexities of the early Atlantic world. Paulo Angola, Simon Congo, and Anthony Portugis had surnames that reflected their complicated past—simplified in evocations of Portugal and its African slave trade. They, Jan Fort Orange, and the others would have spoken at least a modicum of Dutch and Portuguese, would have set foot on at least two other continents before arriving in North America and were culturally fluent enough to have initiated their petition to the Dutch authorities. There is no reason to suppose that the women they represented would have differed radically in their identity as Atlantic Creoles.[74] Yet the women recede completely from the record and from accounts of the petition. The invisibility of the petitioning women is evidenced in their anonymity and is further inscribed in the terms of their freedom.

While the Dutch West India Company was willing to confer quasi-freedom on loyal workers, it declared that the children of those workers would have to meet financial obligations if they too desired freedom. Their mothers would have understood the contingency of their own value. Dorothe Angola, the adoptive parent of an orphaned boy named Anthony (the child of half-free parents), and Maria Portogys, who apprenticed her daughter as a household servant to a Dutch family, negotiated themselves into the historical record while trying to protect children whose identity resided primarily in their use value. Placing the children in apprenticeships tied the adults to the colony as well. By this means, the Dutch

---

73 "Act of the Director and Council of New Netherlands," reproduced in O'Callaghan, *Laws and Ordinances*, 36–37.

74 For the origin of the term *Atlantic Creole*, see Berlin, "From Creole to African."

controlled parents. This contrasted with how owners controlled parents on colonial plantations to the south, where they speculated over unborn children, presuming that their financial futures would be enhanced as they added children to the workforce by enslaving men and women together.[75] Across the Atlantic world, the children of enslaved Africans were mobilized to convey clarity about the legitimacy and longevity of hereditary racial slavery, even in the context of freedom reluctantly conferred by colonial legislators.

Those who conferred half-freedom to enslaved men and women in seventeenth-century New Amsterdam mobilized a strange awareness of gender, race, and forced labor. In language that perhaps reflects an implicit devaluation of enslaved women in the face of their growing numbers, the correspondence between Amsterdam and New Netherland in 1664 about the cargo of slave ships sent to the colony complained bitterly about the females on board. Three out of four letters pointedly protest the condition of the women. One letter writer said, "Five of the Negro women who were, in our opinion unsalable have been kept back and remain unsold." Another wrote, "This is a very poor lot; indeed the women so poor that we fear the most of them will remain on our hands."[76] These complaints were written in the context of an important demographic shift in the colony. By 1703, forty years after the English laid claim to the colony, enslaved women outnumbered enslaved men in the city by almost two to one.[77] Well before that, English colonial officials were aware that in the city of New York, enslaved women of African descent outnumbered enslaved men. With the exception of the first generations of arrivals to the mainland Dutch colony, women always constituted a substantial proportion of the enslaved population. Ultimately, they outnumbered men in the city, while in the surrounding rural areas in New York and in New Jersey, men constituted the majority of enslaved laborers.[78]

75 L. Harris, *In the Shadow of Slavery*, 26.
76 Director Stuyvesant to the Directors at Amsterdam, June 10, 1664, and Council of New Netherland to the Directors at Amsterdam, August 17, 1664, in Donnan, *Documents*, 3:429, 433.
77 "By 1703, black women outnumbered men by 397 to 233, setting a pattern that continued for over a century." Hodges, *Root and Branch*, 41.
78 The first settler on Manhattan Island was a sailor of African descent, a freeman named Jan Rodrigues who was dumped there after a conflict on board his ship. Rodrigues became an essential conduit for trade between Native Americans and subsequent European arrivals. L. Harris, *In the Shadow of Slavery*, 13.

While the preponderance of women in the colonial city was a central component of slave life and of the life of the urban community writ large, the other critical demographic factor for free and enslaved persons was that a large number of them were Africa born. By the end of the Dutch period (1613–1664), the proportion of Africans and their descendants ranged from 10 percent of the colony's total settler population (approximately 800 out of 8,000) to 25 percent of the population in the city (approximately 375 out of 1,500).[79] After the colony fell into English hands in 1664, the growing numbers of Africans imported through the ports of New York City and its environs swelled the ranks of the enslaved. While the census of 1703 reported a Black population of 11 percent, by 1723 it was over 15 percent.[80] By the mid-eighteenth century, upward of 35 percent of all immigrants who passed through the port of New York City were enslaved.[81]

Eighteenth-century slave import records indicate that 30 percent of the enslaved who arrived at the port of New York were from Africa, while another 66 percent came from the West Indies.[82] Of the involuntary migrants who remained in the city, significantly more were women than men. Women enslaved in New York City during this period were likely Africa born because the birth rate remained low until the 1760s. Infant mortality rates were exceptionally high in the colony; many infants succumbed to serious illness before the age of two. What manner of strange grief must have settled on women who were accustomed to raising children among other women but who encountered one another only infrequently in the crowded and filthy streets of lower Manhattan without the children who would normally have occupied the female spaces of their past?

On June 23, 1712, Governor Robert Hunter (who would later preside over the Island of Jamaica during Cudjoe's War) submitted a long report to the British Lords of Trade that addressed a number of issues of importance to the New York colony, including the discovery and vanquishing of a slave revolt. He began with population growth, first apologizing that he still had no figures for a number of counties. Among those for which had numbers, he reported a 35 percent growth from 1703 to 1712 among white settlers and a 36 percent growth among slaves.[83] The perfect equivalency in population growth hid,

---

79 Hodges, *Root and Branch*, 31.
80 Kammen, *Colonial New York*, 181.
81 McManus, *Black Bondage in the North*, 15.
82 Foote, *Black and White Manhattan*, 65.
83 Governor Hunter to the Lords of Trade, June 23, 1712, in O'Callaghan, *Documents*, 5:339–43.

of course, very different realities; the increase in the number of the enslaved was linked to the slave trade rather than to birth rates. Indeed, the precarity of life and birth is amplified in the report of the violence meted out against slave rebels, even as Hunter's report soon led elsewhere, with a lengthy discussion of the "bloody conspiracy of some of the slaves of this place"[84]:

> By . . . strickt searches in town we found all that put the design in execution, six of these having first laid violent hands upon themselves, the rest were forthwith brought to their tryal . . . [where] twenty seven condemned whereof twenty one were executed, one being a woman with child, her execution by that means suspended, some were burnt others hanged, one broke on the wheele, and one hung a live in chains in the town, so that there has been the most exemplary punishment inflicted. . . . Severall others were apprehended, and again acquitted by the Court, for want of sufficient evidence. . . . I am informed that in the West Indies where their laws against their slaves are most severe, that in case of a conspiracy in which many are engaged a few only are executed for an example. In this case 21 are executed and six having done that Justice on themselves more have suffered than we can find were active in this bloody affair.[85]

Here Hunter's numerical tables devolve into lists of those who were discovered, tried, and condemned. At this juncture Hunter was willing to identify only one of the rebels as female by virtue of a pregnancy that stood in the way of her execution.

Hunter was quite aware that he had to balance the value of enslaved men against the need for a sufficiently punitive response to the revolt by the colonial officials. He subsequently justified the severity of the 1712 Negro Act by saying that it was the will of the public: "After the late barbarous attempt of some of their slaves nothing less could please the people."[86] Yet in the same missive, he clarified that the owners of some of the accused wanted them to be acquitted. His interest in staving off further executions may well have been purely financial; the cost to the colony of the executions and the compensation to those whose slaves were executed was considerable. In 1715 the Board of Trade attempted to settle a number of debts the colony of New York had incurred, totaling 22,749 ounces of silver plate.

---

84 Governor Hunter to the Lords of Trade, June 23, 1712, in O'Callaghan, *Documents*, 5:341.
85 Governor Hunter to the Lords of Trade, June 23, 1712, in O'Callaghan, *Documents*, 5:342.
86 Governor Hunter to the Lords of Trade, March 14, 1713, in O'Callaghan, *Documents*, 5:356–58.

Of nine categories of debt, the one "For Negroes Executed for Rebellion" was by far the largest, at 6,009 ounces.[87]

Hunter's interest in forestalling the executions of some of the accused rebels may well have been entirely pragmatic, but it was also embedded in political conflicts between slave-owning adversaries who used the guilt or innocence of accused slaves to fight their own internecine battles. Still, Hunter mobilized the pregnant woman's child to stake his claim: some of the accused were not guilty but rather "as innocent . . . as the child unborn."[88] His interest in saving the child is fascinating, as it occurs in the context of an urban landscape where women predominated among the enslaved and yet children rarely survived infancy. Those same factors must be considered when we wonder what compelled this unnamed woman to participate in the revolt while she was visibly pregnant. Her commitment to some kind of reconfigured future was clearly powerful. Note that Hunter, who wrote in some detail about the particulars of the revolt and the circumstances of the accused (there were some "Spaniards unjustly kept in slavery here" among them), says nothing to suggest that she was the only woman involved, only that her pregnancy made her stand apart and justified the delay of her execution. Indeed, based on the laws passed in the aftermath of the uprising, the English authorities clearly understood both women and men to be suspect. In late February 1713, the Common Council ordered that a law be prepared to prohibit all "Negro or Indian Slaves from going in the Streets of this City after Night without a Lanthon and a lighted Candle." A week later, the law was introduced but with an important modification: "Any of Her Majesties Subjects who apprehended a slave without a Lantern were Authorized to Carry him her or them" to the court for "his her or their Contempt."[89] Members of the Common Council recognized, to some degree, that, alone in the dark, an enslaved woman posed as much of a danger to Her Majesty's subjects as a man did.

More than a year after the April 1, 1712, uprising and the executions that followed, Governor Hunter wrote to the colonial officers in London asking for additional pardons for enslaved persons who were still in prison. Two of them, Tom and Coffee, were "proper objects of mercey" because of a lack of evidence against them. In addition, there was the woman, still un-

87 Lords of Trade to Lords Justices, June 4, 1719, in O'Callaghan, *Documents*, 5:522–24.
88 Governor Hunter to the Lords of Trade, June 23, 1712, in O'Callaghan, *Documents*, 5:357.
89 Meeting of the Common Council, February 28, 1713, and March 3, 1713, in *Minutes of the Common Council*, 3:28, 30–31.

named. Governor Hunter wrote, "There is likewise a negroe woman who was indeed privy to ye conspiracy but pleading her belley was reprieved. She is since delivered but in a woefull condition ever since, and I think has suffered more than death by her long imprisonment."[90] We do not know the fate of this woman and of the child she had "since delivered," including whether the child had remained with her in jail. The gruesome process of watching those with whom she had been arrested meet their ends, coupled with knowing that six others had taken their own lives rather than meet the executioner, must have been excruciating. Was it made more or less so by the birth of her child? Had her pregnancy compelled her to join the attempted revolt? A hope for something better for the baby she carried? Or did the pregnancy portend nothing more than illness, premature death, and a lifetime of sorrow and thus lead her to align herself with the rebels out of desperation rather than hope? Finally, if Governor Hunter was capable of situating her long imprisonment as worse than death on the wheel, was her suffering compounded by the death of the infant? Or by her owner snatching the child from her in the hope that its small life might be financial compensation in the face of her impending execution? What is crucial for our purposes is that the pregnancy rendered her knowable to us.

Refusals of Demography

The colonial city of New York, then, home to a female majority among the enslaved and the site of two major conspiracies to overthrow slavery, offers up little in the way of archival traces of the women who were there. These peculiar demographics illustrate particularly well the conundrum that those who study resistance in the early modern Atlantic world must contend with. How do we account for the fact that the female majority in the city warranted little or no comment from colonial officials, even in their documentation of the 1712 and 1741 uprisings of the enslaved?[91]

Given the paucity of records that indicate the presence of women in marronage, it comes as no surprise to find a similar vacuum about women's

---

90 Governor Hunter to Mr. Popple, September 10, 1713, CO5/1050, 81, Colonial State Papers, National Archives, Kew, England.
91 It should be noted that of the seventy-six slave ships arriving to the colony of New York recorded in the Trans-Atlantic Slave Trade Database, only the *Gideon* (with a cargo in which women constituted 46.7 percent) includes information on the sex ratio. Voyage 11414, *Gideon*, http://Slavevoyages.org/voyage/database.

involvement in colonial slave revolts. In the seventeenth- and early eighteenth-century English Atlantic world, slave revolt was an endemic problem. From New York to South Carolina and from there into the English West Indies, the members of legislative bodies—almost all of whom were slave owners—waged a constant battle against enslaved men, women, and children who failed to accept the terms of their enslavement.

The mechanisms that propelled some enslaved women to resist the terms of their enslavement in ways that were rendered visible in the colonial archives were the same ones that colluded to render them enslavable. The early modern system of hereditary racial slavery relied on an alchemy of nascent ideas of hierarchy and difference, home and market, and enslavability and sovereignty. Any person in the colonies who refused these newly emergent categories of order and control was situated as unruly or dangerous. For women of African descent, there were very few spaces of interiority that slave owners did not assume they had legitimate access to. Because of this, we should pay particular attention to evidence in the historical record of women who enacted strategies of resistance that could have been motivated by the existence of, or the reclaiming of, elements of domestic life, interior life, or private life. Thus, the evidence of the numbers of women "making generations" in Maroon communities does not contradict evidence that women worked to impede conception or wrench the time and space of their children's lives out of the hands of the plantation economy. Women who ran away with an eye toward a permanent departure shared the same relationship to the geography of containment that those who engaged in truancy or simply assisted the truant did. And, finally, those who fed the rogues, harbored the fugitives, or took up arms and joined the rebellion faced the promise of exceptionally brutal punishment for the temerity of imagining themselves to be harbingers of freedom.

CONCLUSION. Madness

Slavery broke the world in half, it broke it in every way. It broke Europe. It made them into something else, it made them slave masters, it made them crazy. You can't do that for hundreds of years and it not take a toll. They had to dehumanize, not just the slaves but themselves. They have had to reconstruct everything in order to make that system appear true.
—TONI MORRISON, in Gilroy, "Living Memory," 1993

Being very fond of her Child, Carrying her up and downe, wore her to nothing by which means fell into a feavour and dyed.
—CAPTAIN OF THE SLAVE SHIP *JAMES*, 1675

In 1675 the crew had been loading men and women on board the ship *James* for months. As we have seen, death came even before the ship left the African coast. One woman who died within view of the land to which she would never return demands attention. As she suffered through the days after the fetus inside her died and she then succumbed to what the captain described as an illness brought on by the rot of "the child dead within her," all the other women on board must have viscerally felt the link between her pregnancy and her death.[1] Indeed, her death may have compelled the

1 "Voyage of the *James*, 1675–76," in Donnan, Documents Illustrative, 1:207.

behavior of the other woman whose death the captain accounted for: the woman who "being very fond of her Child, Carrying her up and downe, wore her to nothing by which means fell into a feavour and dyed."[2] In the ship's register, we see the transformation of pregnancy by Atlantic slavery with a clarity that certainly escaped the attention of the captain. We see kinship converted to accounting by the disease and rot of the slave ship. We see the desperate effort of a woman to hold onto her kin as she grieves, perhaps, the loss of one of her sistren to a death untethered from the collective grievability it would have produced in her community prior to her capture.[3] We see a reckoning. The reckoning that subtends the history of Atlantic slavery.

At the heart of Atlantic slavery there was an unnervingly simple proposition—that women and men purchased in African and American markets were a predictable investment, one that could reap returns both during and after the life of the enslaved worker, even in a landscape of precarity. Reproduction, that is, childbirth, was rare in American slave societies—notwithstanding the babies on board the *James*. Yet their possibility served to bolster the stability of investments in colonial ventures.

Human property was marked by the captives' capacity to convey enslavability to their progeny, and buyers of such property could rest easy that their investment would return profits and could be passed down to their own progeny—premature death through brutal labor regimes notwithstanding. In this way, slave ownership and the heritability of enslavement produced speculative possibility, boundless estates, and the idea of expanded wealth for generations. This economically rational proposition was built on the unstable wealth embodied in a mother grieving over the market demand for her child. In the words of historian Michelle Murphy, the economic rationality that attached to slave-based economic projections might usefully be considered "*phantasmagram*—quantitative practices that are enriched with affect, propagate imaginaries, lure feeling, and hence have supernatural effects in surplus of their rational precepts."[4] The economy of

2 "Voyage of the *James*, 1675–76," in Donnan, *Documents Illustrative*, 1:206–9.
3 Butler, *Frames of War*, 15.
4 Murphy, *Economization of Life*, 24. Murphy goes on to write that "the concept of phantasmagram draws attention to the affectively charged and extraobjective relations that are part of the force of numbers. Phantasma accompany quantification as another kind of output, as the felt, aspirational, and consequential imaginaries that structure the world in profound ways, as a potent aura in surfeit of facticity."

transatlantic slavery was embedded in a rational phantasmagram on which all manner of things could be built—both real and imaginary, both tangible and amorphous. The wealth was real, as were the financial risks. The phantasms were the notions of slave ownership without entanglement or culpability, of endless returns on investments, of the gentle and Christian slave owner, of the griefless and uncalculating mother.

The reproductive capacity of enslaved women is at the heart of this fantasy. The appropriation of the Black future through the transformation of enslaved women into "generative forms of capital" was the ideological foundation of hereditary racial slavery.[5] I have argued this before, but I would like to expand this point; there is still much to understand about the gendered notion of futurity in the context of an emerging racist regime. As slave societies developed, they did so by legally distinguishing childbearing from kinship. They structured women's bodies at the center of a "bare genealogy" in which, as literary scholar Nancy Bentley has argued, "kinlessness operates to make the facts of the body serve the sociopolitical order of New World slave societies."[6] By providing a context in which the economization of the enslaved made moral and economic sense, kinlessness rendered hereditary enslavement legible to both slave owners and the enslaved. Slavery destroyed, exploited, and remade kinship among the enslaved through a contradictory claim about African women: that they birthed strangers, or property, rather than kin.

Émile Durkheim said of kinship that "it is a social tie, or it is nothing."[7] Kinship may reference procreation, but it is embedded in social life. It is the process by which people create interdependence. Marshall Sahlins concluded, rather poetically, that kinship is "a mutuality of being" and that kinfolk are "persons who belong to one another, who are members of one another."[8] In the foundational study of gender and racial ideology, Hortense Spillers argued that overlapping the concept of kinlessness onto that of property would enlarge our understanding of the condition of slavery.[9] This is the core intervention that I make in this project, an intervention

5 Murphy, *Economization of Life*, 13.
6 Bentley, "Fourth Dimension," 271. I have explored the legal and cultural aspects of kinlessness in J. L. Morgan, "*Partus Sequitur Ventrem*."
7 Émile Durkheim, "Review of *Zur Urgeschichte der Ehe* [The prehistory of marriage]," quoted in Sahlins, "What Kinship Is (Part 1)," 9.
8 Sahlins, "What Kinship Is (Part I)," 11.
9 Spillers, "Mama's Baby, Papa's Maybe," 74.

rooted in my understanding that kinship is antithetically tethered to the processes of commodification and capitalism set in motion in the early modern period.

While my work is fundamentally an expansion of Spillers's intervention, I nod to Durkheim's "nothing" with the word *kinlessness*—meant to indicate not an ontological state but rather a rebuke, the charge from European travelers, slave traders, and slave owners that Africans produced only procreative ties, that they had no capacity to belong to one another.[10] In the face of such attempts at erasure, kinship became key to enslaved persons' efforts to endure enslavement and to identify slavery's core violations. The novelist Nathaniel Mackey says the relationship between Africa and America is defined by the ruptures of maternal estrangement—"wounded kinship."[11] And, indeed, through the pens of the formerly enslaved, kinship became a crucial space from which to launch a relentless critique of racial slavery, whether it was in Harriet Jacobs's seven-year-long domestic exile to a three-foot-tall crawl space in her grandmother's attic, secretly watching over her children, or in Frederick Douglass's lament that his mother had many children but he had no family.[12] Formerly enslaved people very clearly unpacked the meaning of "wounded kinship": the discovery that your family ties were regarded as illusory and the assertion that they were not.[13] When they did so at the very onset of the transatlantic slave trade, they constitute evidence of the proximity between the affective logics of family and the construction of the edifice of racial capitalism. Those ensnared in the hold of hereditary racial slavery at its very beginning have much to tell us.

The evocation of kinship by nineteenth-century abolitionists (like Douglass and Jacobs) cements family as a key index of the immoral horrors of slavery. But the problem of kinship in regard to the *business* of slavery enters the records much earlier. And it is in relationship to the business

---

10 The feminist theorist Judith Butler writes that kinship is a "set of practices . . . which negotiate the reproduction of life and the demands of death . . . that emerge to address fundamental forms of human dependency, which may include birth, child-rearing, relations of emotional dependency and support, generational ties, illness, dying and death (to name a few)." Butler, "Is Kinship Always Already Heterosexual?," 15.

11 Moten, *In the Break*, 6, 258–60. Nathaniel Mackey elaborates these ideas that are so foundational to Moten in "'Song Sung in a Strange Land.'"

12 Jacobs, *Incidents in the Life of a Slave Girl*; and Douglass, *Life and Times of Frederick Douglass*, 27–28.

13 Hartman, "Venus in Two Acts."

of slavery that kinlessness acquires its most pointed analytic potency. For early European travelers and slave traders, kinship and its alleged absence emerged early as they constructed stories of rulers with massive harems, of women who abandoned children rather than impede their tribal wars, of childbirth as neither private nor painful, of incest and the free giving of wives and daughters as tokens of friendship to European adventurers. Their stories of sexual depravity and bodily strangeness testified to the absence of legible family forms. Kinship was weaponized to define Africans as debased and to rationalize their debasement through the language, to again reference Spillers, of absent structures of familial feeling.[14]

This has led me to another set of questions: What can we learn about racial capitalism's relationship to kinship from the woman whose subjugation is rooted in the claim that she produces nothing other than bare life, a claim thrust upon her aboard a slave ship as she descends into madness and death with her child clutched in her arms? The ability to translate or convert biology into affect is what makes us human. To build an economy on the claim that such a capacity was the province of only a few was an astonishing feat of violence. Hereditary racial slavery made "the mark of the mother a death sentence for her child"; it turned the act of birth into an act of death and, in the words of Saidiya Hartman, made the birth canal into a Middle Passage.[15] My sojourn in the archives has been an attempt to not only put flesh and bones on the apparition of the madwoman on board the slave ship—though I confess to an almost irrepressible desire to do so—but also understand the overlap among her death, her child's birth, and the birth of capitalist modernity.

Scholars of slavery have begun to mobilize the concept of racial capitalism to mark our reanimation of the overlapping origins of slavery and capitalism and often begin that project through the work of Cedric Robinson.[16] Robinson introduced the concept of racial capitalism in 1983 in *Black Marxism*. There he argued that the conditions from which early capitalism

---

14 Spillers, "Mama's Baby, Papa's Maybe"; and Perry, *Vexy Thing*. Spillers writes that kinship *loses* meaning when one's family can be wrenched away by the market at any moment. What I am after here is a recognition that kinship retains its meaning in the face of its disavowal.

15 Hartman, "Belly of the World," 169.

16 Much has been said recently about capitalism and slavery, fueled (as the editors at *Boston Review* wrote) by the conclusion that "Marx's history of capital is incorrect—capitalism did not originate in eighteenth-century British factories, but began with the slave trade." Giles, "What Marx got Wrong."

developed required the preexistence of ideas of human hierarchy that would subsequently become captured under the nomenclature of race. Through such a lens, the existence of slavery at the onset of early modern capitalist formations is neither coincidental nor incidental; rather capitalism, which he termed *racial capitalism* to capture this process, depended on slavery, violence, and imperialism.[17] He mounted his evidence about the concurrence of race and capitalism using the reorganization of labor practices predicated on ideas of ethnic or regional particularity in medieval Europe, or on what he called "antagonistic differences" directed at racialized subjects such as the Jews, Irish, Slavs, Roma, and others.[18]

Robinson also notes that women and girls were the majority of those enslaved in Europe before the birth of the transatlantic slave trade. Scholars of the ancient and medieval periods have long concurred that enslaving women was a route toward incorporation, toward growing the wealth and prominence of a slave owner's household or a slave-owning polity's power through the acquisition of captives who would become kin or citizens. There is something deeply contradictory, then, in my insistence that it is through a turn to unassimilable racialized labor at the onset of the early modern period that we need to both find enslaved women and recognize that as they disappear from the archives of slavery, they become key to our ability to understand both Atlantic slavery and the racial hierarchies that defined it. Robinson's provocation situates racial capitalism as part and parcel of the emergence of modernity, as coeval with the origins of Enlightenment Man, and thus demands a reconsideration of the categories that attend it.[19] Here, it has meant asking how, for enslaved women in the seventeenth century, slave traders' presumption that they were kinless gets folded into historians' explanation for why they are so hard to find.

The presence of women among the captives in the inaugural shipments of enslaved Africans to Europe and then to the Americas was obvious. Our inability to see them—this blindness induced by the accounting practices of ship captains and slave owners alike—is saturated with meaning. Meaning linked to concepts of the fungible, the irrational, and the quantifiable. European writers located the African continent through the alchemy of monstrosity, heathenism, and unregulated trade in texts that are replete with women who mark the process of rendering Africa a legitimate source

17 See Kelley, "What Did Cedric Robinson Mean?"
18 Robinson, *Black Marxism*, 10.
19 Gómez, *Experiential Caribbean*, 4.

of European plunder. African women's disordered presence did important work, distinguishing them from the more familiar European female forced laborers and offering up a strategy for marketing a seemingly endless populace of African slaves. Here and in the capacity of African women to convey enslavability to their children and thus, involuntarily, convey them to the market, reproduction and racial capitalism intersect. The notion of enslavability was attached to the reproductive capacity of a woman perceived as fundamentally different from the household for which she labored, even as her sexual vulnerability to the slave owners testified to her sameness. That space of corporeal contradiction, I believe, allowed the Europeans who became slave traders, slave buyers, and slave owners to perceive African women and men as legitimate commodities, as fungible on the basis of a mark of difference that was both indelible and breachable.

Many scholars of race in the early modern period (Cedric Robinson, Hortense Spillers, Sylvia Wynter, Kim Hall, and Herman Bennett, among others) have explored the ways that racialized ideologies of difference in Europe were firmly tethered to the processes by which Africans were slotted into the category of the enslavable. Less attended to is the precise work that the origin of the *race/reproduction bind* performed in moving racial slavery into the heart of early modern capitalism. This is both ideological, as Alys Weinbaum has argued, and material.[20] By this I mean that we need to more capaciously consider the connection between women's reproductive capacities and the ability to both name and imagine race as producing some human beings who were nothing more than enslavable.

In the sixteenth and seventeenth centuries, new regimes of thought emerged that replaced notions of complex communities with singular claims of racial clarity. Such claims served as cover for the contradictory violences that hereditary racial slavery inserted into colonial projects—and without which such projects would have been impossible. Let's return to the women forcibly separated from their children and spouses on the dock in Lagos and to the woman who walked herself to death and madness.[21] Their refusal to relinquish their kinship ties to the anonymizing record books and to the mathematical divisions of the slave traders suggests a foundational counternarrative to commodification among the enslaved. African women from Senegambia, the Gold Coast, and beyond entered the trans-

20 Weinbaum, *Wayward Reproductions*.
21 Zurara, *Chronicle of the Discovery*; "Voyage of the *James*, 1675–76," in Donnan, *Documents Illustrative*, 1:207.

atlantic slave trade with generational familiarity with complex markets, long-distance trade networks that linked salt and gold merchants across the Sahara, and the fear of capture and captivity at the hands of enemies. These were things they understood. For Robinson, the manifestations of Black radicalism are based in the enslaved's commitment to rejecting the terms on which their captivity was founded, to preserving an ontological totality, a sense of wholeness "not predicated upon Africans' experience of plantation life, but on a total rejection of their lot." Robinson writes, "The Black radical tradition cast doubt on the extent to which capitalism penetrated and re-formed social life and on its ability to create entirely new categories of human experience stripped bare of the historical consciousness embedded in culture."[22] This conviction that capitalism's penetration had limits in the lives of the peoples whose labor produced capitalist economies is at the crux of the matter both for Robinson and for me. It poses a still unanswered question: In the face of the captures, transports, sales, and imposed labor regimes that defined life for African women, who could understand that they were becoming the commodity form on which Atlantic economies were founded, where might ontological totality be found, much less preserved?[23]

As I look to the early colonial archives, I find a conceptual space in which we can glimpse the roots of such preservation of self and such dissent, the nascent articulation of what will become a diasporic theory of power, a recognition on the part of the enslaved that the marketing of their bodies was nothing less than a systematic denial of their kinship ties and, as such, had to be refused. I see it in the actions of women like Dorothe Angola and Maria Portogys, who in the 1640s used the courts to try to place their children in indentureships after the Dutch West India Company used those children to hold their parents in a state of half-freedom in colonial New York. I see it in the court case of Elizabeth Keye, the daughter of an African woman and an Englishman who argued in 1655 that she had inherited freedom from her father, even as the Virginia House of Burgesses moved to insist that children such as herself could only inherit enslavement from their mothers. And I see it in the ubiquitous growth of Maroon communities by

22 Robinson, *Black Marxism*, 170.
23 Robinson finds the clearest expression of such totality in marronage, in Africans running away with one another before they had even become acclimated to the new environment, and in Maroon communities found throughout the Americas and the Caribbean. Robinson, *Black Marxism*, 168–69.

self-liberation and by birth across the West Indies and Latin America, in spite of colonial governors' attempts to write Maroon women into the archive only as slaves and victims of men and never as Maroons themselves.

I have suggested in this book that there was a recognition of the enormity of what racial slavery meant, a recognition that was both intellectual and felt in the body, one viscerally accessed by enslaved and free Black women. I make this argument from a range of sources: sources that situate those women at the heart of market economies before their enslavement, that describe women's capture and transport while pregnant, that describe women's use of the courts and the church to protect their children's future, that recognize the internal growth of Maroon villages. These bits of evidence are inadequate, of course, but lead me to consider carefully the extent to which claims of natural dispossession rooted in the bodies of these women would be perceived by these self-same women. This suggestion builds on Robinson's notion of the desire for ontological totality but departs from it in crucial ways. For Robinson, the urge toward the rejection of enslavement is rooted in an African culture, in the maintenance of a sense of self across the Middle Passage that carries with it the urge and capacity to collectively reject enslavement entirely. These are the roots of Black radicalism—a clear rejection of racial capitalism and a reclaiming of community for life outside of and opposed to the plantation and its attendant structures of domination and extraction. But what is this if not a reclamation of kinship? And might kinship offer a less static view of Africa and of what was both passed and past?[24]

In 1683 the English ship *Dorothy* arrived at the Ghana coast and was loaded with "one hundred and thirty five negroes, whereof some were men and some were women."[25] During the time the ship remained at anchor, the captain was unable to stop the captives from using tobacco. He likely thought it was a harmless concession, especially because other ship captains allowed it, but in this instance it proved disastrous: "A negro woman betweene deck of the said ship who had fire with her . . . did fling the same pipe lighted from her which . . . did fall into the hole of the said Shippe where the [gun]powder was and instantly the shippe thereupon was

24 I reference here Toni Morrison's multiplicity of meanings at the end of the novel *Beloved*: "This is not a story to pass on." Morrison, *Beloved*, 324.
25 "Case of the *Dorothy*," in Donnan, *Documents Illustrative*, 1:308–17, 312. The ship is voyage 21556 in https://slavevoyages.org/voyage/database.

blowne up."[26] A handful of Englishmen survived and testified to the care they had always taken to keep the powder safe. Their story was crafted to indict the woman's carelessness and warn the captains of other ships. But a crucial question is all but ignored: was her act one of carelessness or care? Having lived in proximity to English slave trading *and* firepower for decades, might she not have designed to bring an explosive and liberatory end to the people captured on that ship? Having experienced firsthand the violence of capture, might she not have anticipated the violence to come and made a strategic decision to bring it to a dramatic end, even as she braced herself with a final draw of sweet tobacco smoke from her pipe?

Our understanding of Atlantic slavery must start from the assumption that as early as the fifteenth century, African captives, both men and women, came out of cultures suffused with commerce and thus were aware both of their commodification and of how that process situated them in relationship to the state.[27] Hereditary racial slavery placed their reproductive capacity at the core of what rendered them enslavable. It positioned kinship in the marketplace and thereby rendered enslaved women as vectors of quantifiable kinlessness. What racial capitalism does in its starkest terms is to introduce the human body to the marketplace. And thus in its starkest terms it situates African women at the heart of the structural logics of the business of slavery. This isn't a metaphor. Actual women were laboring throughout the Americas, and—equally important—slave owners were conceiving of Black people as produced for markets. If the roots of racial capitalism are entwined in the emergence of the race/reproduction bind and the harnessing of African women's reproductive capacities to the economies of the transatlantic slave trade, so then are the origins of the Black radical tradition. They offer what Imani Perry has suggested we need: alternative grammars for liberation that are rooted in embodied truths.[28] These are grammars of acknowledged grief, of the acuity and calculus out of which that grief arose. These are grammars formed in the corpo-

---

26 "Case of the *Dorothy*," in Donnan, *Documents Illustrative*, 1:312.
27 Here I understand *state* to reference both the polity from which they came and the entity represented—albeit hazily—by the ship captains and the white inhabitants of the colonies in which they landed.
28 In the end I want to ask, in chorus with Imani Perry, "So what if we were to start here and build out on the alternative grammars and reordering that emerge from embodied truths?" Perry, *Vexy Thing*, 221.

real earthiness of birth and death and the Middle Passages that relentlessly took place inside enslaved women's bodies. They are the grammars of sanity in the face of madness, of care in carelessness around a ship's hold full of gunpowder and kinfolk. They are the grammars that structure the refusal to relinquish a child to the market—a refusal felt so powerfully and clearly that it "wore you down to nothing" and left you dead with your claim to family, to kin, clenched forever in your arms.[29]

29 "Voyage of the *James*, 1675–76," in Donnan, *Documents Illustrative*, 1:207.

Abbot, George. *A Briefe Description of the Whole Worlde*. London, 1599.

Alpern, Stanley B. "What Africans Got for Their Slaves: A Master List of European Trade Goods." *History in Africa* 22 (1995): 5–43.

Alvares, Manuel. *Ethiopia Minor und a Geographical Account of the Province of Sierra Leone*. Ca. 1615. Translated and annotated by P. E. H. Hair, based on the transcription made by Avelino Teixeira da Mota. Liverpool: Department of History, University of Liverpool, 1990.

Álvares de Almada, André. *Brief Treatise on the Rivers of Guinea*. 1594. Reprinted in *The Discovery of River Gambra (1623)*, by Richard Jobson, edited by David P. Gamble and P. E. H Hair, 274–84. London: Hakluyt Society, 1999.

Anderson, Benedict. *Imagined Communities: Reflections on the Origin and Spread of Nationalism*. 2nd edition. London: Verso, 1991.

Appleby, Joyce Oldham. *Economic Thought and Ideology in Seventeenth-Century England*. 1978. Los Angeles: Figueroa, 2004.

Aquinas, Thomas. *Summa Theologica*. 1265. Christian Classics Ethereal Library. http://www.ccel.org/ccel/aquinas/summa.

Arendt, Hannah. *The Human Condition*. 2nd edition. Chicago: University of Chicago Press, 1998.

Arendt, Hannah. *The Origins of Totalitarianism*. New York: Harcourt Brace, 1958.

Atkins, John. *A Voyage to Guinea, Brasil, and the West-Indies*. London, 1735.

Bailey, Amanda. *Of Bondage: Debt, Property, and Personhood in Early Modern England*. Philadelphia: University of Pennsylvania Press, 2013.

Bailey, Anne C. *The Weeping Time*. Cambridge: Cambridge University Press, 2017.

Baker, Lee D. *From Savage to Negro: Anthropology and the Construction of Race, 1896–1954*. Berkeley: University of California Press, 1998.

Baptist, Edward. "'Cuffy,' 'Fancy Maids,' and 'One-Eyed Men': Rape, Commodification, and the Domestic Slave Trade in the United States." *American Historical Review* 106, no. 5 (Dec. 2001): 1619–50.

Baptist, Edward. *The Half Has Never Been Told: Slavery and the Making of American Capitalism.* New York: Basic Books, 2014.

Barber, Sarah. "Settlement, Transplantation and Expulsion: A Comparative Study of the Placement of Peoples." In *British Interventions in Early Modern Ireland*, edited by Ciaran Brady and Jane Ohlmeyer, 280–98. Cambridge: Cambridge University Press, 2005.

Barbot, Jean. *Barbot on Guinea: The Writings of Jean Barbot on West Africa, 1678–1712*, 2 vols. Edited by P. E. H. Hair, Adam Jones, and Robin Law. General editor P. E. H. Hair. London: Hakluyt Society, 1992.

Barclay, Jenifer L. "Mothering the 'Useless': Black Motherhood, Disability, and Slavery." *Women, Gender, and Families of Color* 2, no. 2 (2014): 115–40.

Bardaglio, Peter. "'Shamefull Matches': The Regulation of Interracial Sex and Marriage in the South before 1900." In *Sex, Love, Race: Crossing Boundaries in North American History*, edited by Martha Hodes, 112–40. New York: New York University Press, 1999.

Barrett, Lindon. "Mercantilism, U.S. Federalism, and the Market within Reason: The 'People' and the Conceptual Impossibility of Racial Blackness." In *Conditions of the Present: Selected Essays*, by Lindon Barrett, edited by Janet Neary, 320–51. Durham, NC: Duke University Press, 2018.

Barry, Boubacar. *Senegambia and the Atlantic Slave Trade.* Translated by Ayi Kwei Armah. Cambridge: Cambridge University Press, 1998.

Bartels, Emily. "Imperialist Beginnings: Richard Hakluyt and the Construction of Africa." *Criticism* 34, no. 4 (1992): 517–38.

Bashford, Alison, and Joyce E. Chaplin. *The New Worlds of Thomas Robert Malthus: Rereading the Principle of Population.* Princeton, NJ: Princeton University Press, 2016.

Baucom, Ian. *Specters of the Atlantic: Finance Capital, Slavery, and the Philosophy of History.* Durham, NC: Duke University Press, 2005.

Bauer, Raymond A., and Alice H. Bauer. "Day to Day Resistance to Slavery." *Journal of Negro History* 27, no. 4 (1942): 388–419.

Beckert, Sven, and Seth Rothman. Introduction to *Slavery's Capitalism: A New History of American Economic Development*, edited by Sven Beckert and Seth Rothman, 1–28. Philadelphia: University of Pennsylvania Press, 2016.

Beckles, Hilary McD. *Britain's Black Debt: Reparations for Caribbean Slavery and Native Genocide.* Kingston, Jamaica: University of the West Indies Press, 2013.

Beckles, Hilary McD. "Capitalism, Slavery and Caribbean Modernity." *Callaloo* 20, no. 4 (Oct. 1997): 777–89.

Beckles, Hilary McD. *Natural Rebels: A Social History of Enslaved Black Women in Barbados.* New Brunswick, NJ: Rutgers University Press, 1989.

Behrendt, Stephen D., David Eltis, and David Richardson. "The Costs of Coercion: African Agency in the Pre-modern Atlantic World." *Economic History Review* 54, no. 3 (Aug. 2001): 454–76.

Belgrove, William. "A Treatise upon Husbandry or Planting." Boston, 1755. Sabin Americana, Gale, Cengage Learning. http://galenet.galegroup.com/servlet/Sabin?af =RN&ae=CY101268663&srchtp=a&ste=14.

Benjamin, Walter. "Theses on the Philosophy of History." In *Illuminations: Essays and Reflections*, edited by Hannah Arendt, 253–64. New York: Houghton Mifflin Harcourt, 1968.

Bennett, Herman L. *African Kings and Black Slaves: Sovereignty and Dispossession in the Early Modern Atlantic*. Philadelphia: University of Pennsylvania Press, 2018.

Bennett, Herman L. *Africans in Colonial Mexico: Absolutism, Christianity, and Afro-Creole Consciousness, 1570–1640*. Bloomington: Indiana University Press, 2003.

Bennett, Herman L. *Colonial Blackness: A History of Afro-Mexico*. Bloomington: Indiana University Press, 2009.

Bentley, Nancy. "The Fourth Dimension: Kinlessness and African American Narrative." *Critical Inquiry* 35, no. 2 (Winter 2009): 270–92.

Berlin, Ira. "From Creole to African: Atlantic Creoles and the Origins of African-American Society in Mainland North America." *William and Mary Quarterly* 53, no. 2 (Apr. 1996): 251–88.

Berry, Daina Ramey. *The Price for Their Pound of Flesh: The Value of the Enslaved, from Womb to Grave, in the Building of a Nation*. Boston: Beacon, 2017.

Beverly, Robert. *The History and Present State of Virginia*. London, 1705.

Billings, Warren M. "The Cases of Fernando and Elizabeth Key: A Note on the Status of Blacks in Seventeenth-Century Virginia." *William and Mary Quarterly*, 3rd ser., 30, no. 3 (July 1973): 467–74.

Billings, Warren M., ed. *The Old Dominion in the Seventeenth Century: A Documentary History of Virginia, 1606–1689*. Chapel Hill: University of North Carolina Press for the Omohundro Institute for Early American History and Culture, 1975.

Bindman, David. "Black Presence in British Art." In *The Image of the Black in Western Art*. Vol. 3, *From the "Age of Discovery" to the Age of Abolition*. Part I: *Artists of the Renaissance and Baroque*, edited by David Bindman and Henry Louis Gates Jr., 235–70. Cambridge, MA: Harvard University Press, 2010.

Bindman, David, and Henry Louis Gates Jr., eds. *The Image of the Black in Western Art*. Vol. 3, *From the "Age of Discovery" to the Age of Abolition*. Cambridge, MA: Harvard University Press, 2010.

Blackburn, Robin. "Lincoln and Marx." *Jacobin*, August 28, 2012.

Blackburn, Robin. *The Making of New World Slavery: From the Baroque to the Modern, 1492–1800*. London: Verso, 1997.

Blake, John William, ed. *Europeans in West Africa, 1540–1560: Documents to Illustrate the Nature and Scope of Portuguese Enterprise in West Africa, the Abortive Attempt of Castilians to Create an Empire There, and the Early English Voyages to Barbary and Guinea*. London: Hakluyt Society, 1942. Reprint, 2010.

Blake, William. *The History of Slavery and the Slave Trade, Ancient and Modern. . . .* Columbus, OH, 1857.

Block, Sharon. *Colonial Complexions: Race and Bodies in Eighteenth-Century America*. Philadelphia: University of Pennsylvania Press, 2018.

Block, Sharon. *Rape and Sexual Power in Early America*. Chapel Hill: University of North Carolina Press for the Omohundro Institute for Early American History and Culture, 2006.

Blumenthal, Debra. *Enemies and Familiars: Slavery and Mastery in Fifteenth-Century Valencia*. Ithaca, NY: Cornell University Press, 2009.

Bly, Antonio T. "'Pretends He Can Read': Runaways and Literacy in Colonial America, 1730–1776." *Early American Studies: An Interdisciplinary Journal* 6, no. 2 (Fall 2008): 261–94.

Boemus, Johannes. *The Fardle of Facions*. London, 1555.

Borucki, Alex, David Eltis, and David Wheat. "Atlantic History and the Slave Trade to Spanish America." *American Historical Review* 120, no. 2 (Apr. 2015): 433–61.

[Botero, Giovanni]. *The Worlde, or An Historicall Description of the Most Famous Kingdoms and Common-Weales Therein*. Translated and enlarged edition. London, 1601.

Bowser, Frederick. *The African Slave in Colonial Peru*. Stanford, CA: Stanford University Press, 1974.

Boyle, Robert. *General Heads for a Natural History of a Country*. London, 1665.

Braudel, Fernand. *Civilization and Capitalism, 15th–18th Century*. Vol. 1, *The Structure of Everyday Life: The Limits of the Possible*. London: Phoenix, 2002.

Braudel, Fernand. *Civilization and Capitalism, 15th–18th Century*. Vol. 2, *The Wheels of Commerce*. Berkeley: University of California Press, 1992.

Breen, T. H., and Stephen Innes. *"Myne Owne Ground": Race and Freedom on Virginia's Eastern Shore, 1640–1676*. New York: Oxford University Press, 1980.

Brewer, Holly. "Slavery, Sovereignty, and 'Inheritable Blood': Reconsidering John Locke and the Origins of American Slavery." *American Historical Review* 122, no. 4 (Oct. 2017): 1038–79.

Briggs, Peter. "John Graunt, Sir William Petty, and Swift's *Modest Proposal*." *Eighteenth-Century Life* 29, no. 2 (Spring 2005): 3–24.

Brinch, Boyrereau. *The Blind African Slave, or, Memoirs of Boyrereau Brinch, Nick-Named Jeffrey Brace . . . : With an Account of His Captivity, Sufferings, Sales, Travels, Emancipation, Conversion to the Christian Religion, Knowledge of the Scriptures, &c. . . .* St. Alban's, VT: Printed by Harry Whitney, 1810.

Brown, Christopher L., and Phillip Morgan, eds. *Arming Slaves: From Classical Times to the Modern Age*. New Haven, CT: Yale University Press, 2006.

Brown, Kathleen M. *Good Wives, Nasty Wenches, and Anxious Patriarchs: Gender, Race, and Power in Colonial Virginia*. Chapel Hill: University of North Carolina Press for the Omohundro Institute of Early American History and Culture, 1996.

Brown, Vincent. *The Reaper's Garden: Death and Power in the World of Atlantic Slavery*. Cambridge, MA: Harvard University Press, 2008.

Brown, Vincent. "Social Death and Political Life in the Study of Slavery." *American Historical Review* 114, no. 5 (2009): 1231–49.

Buck, Peter. "Seventeenth-Century Political Arithmetic: Civil Strife and Vital Statistics." *Isis* 68, no. 1 (Mar. 1977): 67–84.

Buck-Morss, Susan. "Envisioning Capital: Political Economy on Display." *Critical Inquiry* 21, no. 2 (Winter 1995): 434–67.

Burnard, Trevor. "Evaluating Gender in Early Jamaica, 1674–1784." *History of the Family* 12, no. 2 (Jan. 2007): 81–91.

Burnard, Trevor. *Mastery, Tyranny, and Desire: Thomas Thistlewood and His Slaves in the Anglo-Jamaican World.* Chapel Hill: University of North Carolina Press, 2004.

Burnard, Trevor, and Emma Hart. "Kingston, Jamaica, and Charleston, South Carolina: A New Look at Comparative Urbanization in Plantation Colonial British America." *Journal of Urban History* 39, no. 2 (Mar. 2013): 214–34.

Bush, Barbara. *Slave Women in Caribbean Society, 1650–1838.* Bloomington: Indiana University Press, 1990.

Butler, Judith. *Frames of War: When Is Life Grievable?* London: Verso, 2009.

Butler, Judith. "Is Kinship Always Already Heterosexual?" *Differences: A Journal of Feminist Cultural Studies* 13 (Spring 2002): 14–44.

Byrd, Alexander X. *Captives and Voyagers: Black Migrants across the Eighteenth-Century British Atlantic World.* Baton Rouge: Louisiana State University Press, 2008.

Byrd, Alexander X. "Eboe, Country, Nation, and Gustavus Vassa's 'Interesting Narrative.'" *William and Mary Quarterly* 63, no. 1 (2006): 123–48.

Byrd, William. *The Westover Manuscripts, Containing the History of the Dividing Line betwixt Virginia and North Carolina: A Journey to the Land of Eden, 1736.* Petersburg, VA: E. and J. C. Ruffin, 1841.

Cadamosto, Alvise Da. *The Voyages of Cadamosto and Other Documents on Western Africa in the Second Half of the Fifteenth Century.* 1455. Edited by G. R. Crone. New York: Routledge, 2010.

Calomiris, Charles W., and Jonathan B. Pritchett. "Preserving Slave Families for Profit: Traders' Incentives and Pricing in the New Orleans Slave Market." *Journal of Economic History* 69, no. 4 (Dec. 2009): 986–1011.

Camp, Stephanie M. H. *Closer to Freedom: Enslaved Women and Everyday Resistance in the Plantation South.* 1st ed. Chapel Hill: University of North Carolina Press, 2004.

Campbell, Gwyn, Suzanne Meirs, and Joseph C. Miller, eds. *Women and Slavery.* Vol. 1, *Africa, the Indian Ocean World, and the Medieval North Atlantic.* Columbus: Ohio University Press, 2007.

Campbell, Gwyn, Suzanne Meirs, and Joseph C. Miller, eds. *Women and Slavery.* Vol. 2, *The Modern Atlantic.* Columbus: Ohio University Press, 2007.

Canny, Nicholas, ed. *The Origins of Empire: British Overseas Enterprise to the Close of the Seventeenth Century.* Oxford: Oxford University Press, 1998.

Carney, Judith. *Black Rice: The African Origins of Rice Cultivation in the Americas.* Cambridge, MA: Harvard University Press, 2001.

Carney, Judith, and Richard Nicholas Rosomoff. *In the Shadow of Slavery: Africa's Botanical Legacy in the Atlantic World.* Berkeley: University of California Press, 2009.

Carretta, Vincent. *Equiano the African: Biography of a Self-Made Man.* Athens: University of Georgia Press, 2005.

Carretta, Vincent, ed. *Unchained Voices: An Anthology of Black Authors in the English-Speaking World of the Eighteenth Century.* Lexington: University Press of Kentucky, 1996.

Cassedy, James. *Demography in Early America: Beginnings of the Statistical Mind, 1600–1800.* Cambridge, MA: Harvard University Press, 1969.

Chaplin, Joyce E. "The Problem of Genius in the Age of Slavery." In *Genealogies of Genius*, edited by Joyce E. Chaplin and Darrin M. McMahon, 11–28. Palgrave Studies in Cultural and Intellectual History. New York: Palgrave Macmillan, 2016.

Chaplin, Joyce E. *Subject Matter: Technology, the Body, and Science on the Anglo-American Frontier, 1500–1676*. Cambridge, MA: Harvard University Press, 2001.

Chapman, Mary. "'Happy Shall He Be, That Taketh and Dasheth Thy Little Ones against the Stones': Infanticide in Cooper's *The Last of the Mohicans.*" In *Inventing Maternity: Politics, Science, and Literature, 1650–1865*, edited by Susan C. Greenfield and Carol Barash, 238–51. Lexington: University Press of Kentucky, 2015.

Clifford, James. *Routes: Travel and Translation in the Late Twentieth Century*. Cambridge, MA: Harvard University Press, 1997.

Cohen, Patricia Cline. *A Calculating People: The Spread of Numeracy in Early America*. Chicago: University of Chicago Press, 1982.

Cohn, Bernard. *Colonialism and Its Forms of Knowledge: The British in India*. Princeton, NJ: Princeton University Press, 1996.

Colley, Linda. *Captives: The Story of Britain's Pursuit of Empire and How Its Soldiers and Civilians Were Held Captive by the Dream of Global Supremacy, 1600–1850*. New York: Pantheon Books, 2002.

Columbus, Christopher. *Journal of Christopher Columbus*. London: Hakluyt Society, 1893.

Connolly, Brian. *Domestic Intimacies: Incest and the Liberal Subject in Nineteenth-Century America*. Philadelphia: University of Pennsylvania Press, 2014.

Costa, Emilia Viotti da. "The Portuguese-African Slave Trade: A Lesson in Colonialism." *Latin American Perspectives* 12, no. 1 (Winter 1985): 41–61.

Cugoano, Quobna Ottobah. "Thoughts and Sentiments on the Evil and Wicked Traffic of the Slavery and Commerce of the Human Species (London, 1787)." In *Unchained Voices: An Anthology of Black Authors in the English-Speaking World of the Eighteenth Century*, edited by Vincent Carretta, 145–84. Lexington: University Press of Kentucky, 1996.

Cummings, Ronald. "Jamaican Female Masculinities: Nanny of the Maroons and the Genealogy of the Man-Royal." *Journal of West Indian Literature* 21, no. 1/2 (Nov. 2012): 129–54.

Curtin, Philip D. "Africa and the Wider Monetary World, 1250–1850." In *Precious Metals in the Later Medieval and Early Modern Worlds*, edited by John Richards, 231–68. Durham, NC: Carolina Academic Press, 1983.

Curtin, Philip D. *The Atlantic Slave Trade: A Census*. Madison: University of Wisconsin Press, 1972.

Curtin, Philip D. *Economic Change in Precolonial Africa: Senegambia in the Era of the Slave Trade*. Madison: University of Wisconsin Press, 1975.

Dadzie, Stella. "Searching for the Invisible Woman: Slavery and Resistance in Jamaica." *Race and Class* 32, no. 2 (Oct. 1990): 21–38.

Daunce, Edward. *A Brief Discourse of the Spanish States*. London, 1590.

Davis, Angela. "Reflections on the Black Woman's Role in the Community of Slaves." *Black Scholar* 3, no. 4 (1971): 2–15.

De Barros, Juanita. *Reproducing the British Caribbean: Sex, Gender, and Population Politics after Slavery*. Chapel Hill: University of North Carolina Press, 2014.

Deng, Stephen. *Coinage and State Formation in Early Modern English Literature*. New York: Palgrave Macmillan, 2011.

Deng, Stephen. "'So Pale, So Lame, So Lean, So Ruinous': The Circulation of Foreign Coins in Early Modern England." In *A Companion to the Global Renaissance*, edited by Jyotsna G. Singh, 262–78. Oxford: Wiley-Blackwell, 2009.

Desrochers, Robert E., Jr. "Slave-for-Sale Advertisements and Slavery in Massachusetts, 1704–1781." *William and Mary Quarterly*, 3rd ser., 59, no. 3 (July 2002): 623–64.

De Vries, Jan. "The Economic Crisis of the Seventeenth Century after Fifty Years." *Journal of Interdisciplinary History* 40 (Autumn 2009): 151–94.

Deyle, Steven. *Carry Me Back: The Domestic Slave Trade in American Life*. New York: Oxford University Press, 2005.

Dillon, Elizabeth Maddock. "Zombie Biopolitics." *American Quarterly* 71, no. 3 (Oct. 2019): 625–52.

Diouf, Sylvaine A., ed. *Fighting the Slave Trade: West African Strategies*. Athens: Ohio University Press, 2013.

Donelha, Andre. *An Account of Sierra Leone and the Rivers of Guinea and Cape Verde*. 1625. Portuguese text edited by Alvelino Teixeira da Mota. Notes and English translation by P. E. H. Hair. Lisbon: Junto de Investigaçõs Cientificas do Ultramar, 1977.

Donington, Katie, Ryan Hanley, and Jessica Moody, eds. *Britain's History and Memory of Transatlantic Slavery: Local Nuances of a "National Sin."* Liverpool: Liverpool University Press, 2016.

Donnan, Elizabeth, ed. *Documents Illustrative of the History of the Slave Trade to America*, 4 vols. Washington, DC: Carnegie Institution of Washington, 1930.

Dorsey, Joseph C. "Women without History: Slavery and the International Politics of Partus Sequitur Ventrem in the Spanish Caribbean." *Journal of Caribbean History* 28, no. 2 (1994): 165–207.

Douglas, Mary, and Baron C. Isherwood. *The World of Goods*. New York: Basic Books, 1979.

Douglass, Frederick. *Life and Times of Frederick Douglass*. Boston: De Wolf, 1895.

Draper, Nicholas. *The Price of Emancipation: Slave-Ownership, Compensation and British Society at the End of Slavery*. Cambridge: Cambridge University Press, 2010.

Drax, Henry. *Instructions for the Management of Drax-Hall*. London, 1679. Ann Arbor, MI: Text Creation Partnership, 2011. https://quod.lib.umich.edu/e/evans/N05794 .0001.001/1:3?rgn=div1;view=fulltext.

Du Bois, W. E. B. *The Suppression of the African Slave Trade to the United States of America, 1638–1870*. New York: Oxford University Press, 2007.

Dunn, Richard. *A Tale of Two Plantations: Slave Life and Labor in Jamaica and Virginia*. Cambridge, MA: Harvard University Press, 2014.

Duquette, Nicolas. "Revealing the Relationship between Ship Crowding and Slave Mortality." *Journal of Economic History* 74, no. 2 (June 2014): 535–52.

Durkheim, Émile. "Review of *Zur Urgeschichte der Ehe* [The prehistory of marriage]." *L'Annee Sociologique* 1 (1898): 306–19.

Eburne, Richard. *Plaine Path-Way to Plantations*. London, 1624.

Edwards, Bryan. *The History, Civil and Commercial, of the British Colonies in the West Indies*. London, 1793. Reprint, Philadelphia, 1807.

Egerton, Douglas R. "Slaves to the Marketplace: Economic Liberty and Black Rebelliousness in the Atlantic World." *Journal of the Early Republic* 26, no. 4 (Winter 2006): 617–39.

Eltis, David. *The Rise of African Slavery in the Americas*. Cambridge: Cambridge University Press, 2000.

Eltis, David, and Stanley L. Engerman. "Fluctuations in Sex and Age Ratios in the Transatlantic Slave Trade, 1663–1864." *Economic History Review* 46, no. 2 (May 1993): 308–23.

Eltis, David, and Stanley L. Engerman. "Was the Slave Trade Dominated by Men?" *Journal of Interdisciplinary History* 23, no. 2 (Autumn 1992): 237–57.

Eltis, David, Frank D. Lewis, and David Richardson. "Slave Prices, the African Slave Trade, and Productivity in Eighteenth-Century South Carolina: A Reassessment." *Journal of Economic History* 66, no. 4 (Dec. 2006): 1054–65.

Eltis, David, Frank D. Lewis, and David Richardson. "Slave Prices, the African Slave Trade, and Productivity in the Caribbean, 1674–1807." *Economic History Review* 58, no. 4 (Nov. 2005): 673–700.

Eltis, David, Philip Morgan, and David Richardson. "Agency and Diaspora in Atlantic History: Reassessing the African Contribution to Rice Cultivation in the Americas." *American Historical Review* 112, no. 5 (Dec. 2007): 1329–58.

Endres, A. M. "The Functions of Numerical Data in the Writings of Graunt, Petty, and Davenant." *History of Political Economy* 17, no. 2 (Summer 1985): 245–64.

Equiano, Olaudah. *The Interesting Narrative of the Life of Olaudah Equiano, or Gustavus Vassa, the African*. Edited by Werner Sollors. 1st ed. Norton Critical Edition. New York: Norton, 2001.

Erickson, Peter, and Kim F. Hall. "'A New Scholarly Song': Rereading Early Modern Race." *Shakespeare Quarterly* 67, no. 1 (Aug. 2016): 1–13.

Fage, J. D. "Slaves and Society in Western Africa, c. 1445–c. 1700." *Journal of African History* 21, no. 3 (1980): 289–310.

Falconbridge, Alexander. *An Account of the Slave Trade on the Coast of Africa*. London, 1788.

Fassin, Didier. "A Contribution to the Critique of Moral Reason." *Anthropological Theory* 11, no. 4 (Dec. 2011): 481–91.

Fassin, Didier. "Moral Economy Redux: A Critical Reappraisal." Paper presented at the Institute for Advanced Study. Princeton, NJ, Spring 2005.

Fernandes, Valentine. "O Manucrito." 1508. Translated by David P. Gamble and P. E. H. Hair. In Richard Jobson, *The Discovery of River Gambra (1623)*, edited by David P. Gamble and P. E. H. Hair, 267–71. London: Hakluyt Society, 1999.

Finch, Aisha. "'What Looks Like a Revolution': Enslaved Women and the Gendered Terrain of Slave Insurgencies in Cuba, 1843–1844." *Journal of Women's History* 26, no. 1 (Spring 2014): 112–34.

Finkelman, Paul, ed. *Slavery and the Law*. Lanham, MD: Rowman and Littlefield, 1998.

Finkelstein, Andrea. *Harmony and the Balance: An Intellectual History of Seventeenth-Century English Economic Thought*. Ann Arbor: University of Michigan Press, 2000.

Finley, Cheryl. *Committed to Memory: The Art of the Slave Ship Icon*. Princeton, NJ: Princeton University Press, 2018.

Flynn, Dennis O., and Arturo Giráldez. "Born with a 'Silver Spoon': The Origin of World Trade in 1571." *Journal of World History* 6, no. 2 (Fall 1995): 201–21.

Fogel, Robert W., and Stanley L. Engerman. *Time on the Cross: The Economics of American Negro Slavery*. New York: Little, Brown, 1974.

Foote, Thelma Wills. *Black and White Manhattan: The History of Racial Formation in Colonial New York City*. New York: Oxford University Press, 2004.

Fortin, Jeffrey A. "'Blackened beyond Our Native Hue': Removal, Identity and the Trelawney Maroons on the Margins of the Atlantic World, 1796–1800." *Citizenship Studies* 10, no. 1 (Feb. 2006): 5–34.

Fosse, Eustache de la. *Crónica de uma viagem à Costa da Mina no ano de 1480*. Paris: R. Foulché-Delbosc, 1897.

Foster, Thomas A. *Rethinking Rufus: The Sexual Abuse of Enslaved Men*. Athens: University of Georgia Press, 2019.

Foster, Thomas A. "The Sexual Abuse of Black Men under American Slavery." *Journal of the History of Sexuality* 20, no. 3 (Sept. 2011): 445–64.

Foucault, Michel. *The Birth of Biopolitics: Lectures at the Collège de France, 1978–1979*. Edited by Michel Sellenart. Translated by Graham Burchell. New York: Palgrave Macmillan, 2008.

Foucault, Michel. *The Order of Things: An Archaeology of the Human Sciences*. Reprint, New York: Vintage Books, 1994.

Foucault, Michel. *Security, Territory, Population: Lectures at the Collège de France, 1977–78*. Edited by Michel Sellenart. Translated by Graham Burchell. New York: Palgrave Macmillan, 2009.

Fuente, Alejandro de la. "Slave Law and Claims-Making in Cuba: The Tannenbaum Debate Revisited." *Law and History Review* 22, no. 2 (Summer 2004): 339–69.

Fuentes, Marisa J. *Dispossessed Lives: Enslaved Women, Violence, and the Archive*. Philadelphia: University of Pennsylvania Press, 2016.

Galenson, David W. *Traders, Planters, and Slaves: Market Behavior in Early English America*. Cambridge: Cambridge University Press, 1986.

Gamble, David, and P. E. H. Hair. Introduction to *The Discovery of River Gambra (1623)*, by Richard Jobson, edited by David P. Gamble and P. E. H. Hair, 1–72. London: Hakluyt Society, 1999.

Games, Alison. *The Web of Empire: English Cosmopolitans in an Age of Expansion, 1560–1660*. New York: Oxford University Press, 2008.

Garrard, Timothy F. "Myth and Metrology: The Early Trans-Saharan Gold Trade." *Journal of African History* 23, no. 4 (1982): 443–61.

Gaspar, David Barry. *Bondmen and Rebels: A Study of Master-Slave Relations in Antigua*. Durham, NC: Duke University Press, 1985.

Gaspar, David Barry, and Darlene Clark Hine, eds. *More Than Chattel: Black Women and Slavery in the Americas*. Bloomington: Indiana University Press, 1996.

Gaspar, Joaquim Alves. "Blunders, Errors and Entanglements: Scrutinizing the Cantino Planisphere with a Cartometric Eye." *Imago Mundi* 64, no. 2 (2012): 181–200.

Gates, Henry Louis, Jr. *Figures in Black: Words, Signs, and the "Racial" Self*. New York: Oxford University Press, 1987.

Geggus, David. "Sex Ratio, Age and Ethnicity in the Atlantic Slave Trade: Data from French Shipping and Plantation Records." *Journal of African History* 30, no. 1 (1989): 23–44.

Geggus, David. "Sex Ratio and Ethnicity: A Reply to Paul E. Lovejoy." *Journal of African History* 30, no. 3 (1989): 395–97.

Genovese, Eugene. *From Rebellion to Revolution: Afro-American Slave Revolts in the Making of the Modern World*. Baton Rouge: Louisiana State University Press, 1981.

Giles, Rosie. "What Marx Got Wrong about Capitalism." *Boston Review*, April 21, 2019. http://bostonreview.net/reading-lists/rosie-gillies-boston-review-what-marx-got-wrong-about-capitalism.

Gilroy, Paul. *The Black Atlantic: Modernity and Double Consciousness*. Cambridge, MA: Harvard University Press, 1993.

Gilroy, Paul. "Living Memory: A Meeting with Toni Morrison." In *Small Acts: Thoughts on the Politics of Black Cultures*, 175–82. London: Serpent's Tale, 1993.

Glimp, David. *Increase and Multiply: Governing Cultural Reproduction in Early Modern England*. Minneapolis: University of Minnesota Press, 2003.

Goetz, Rebecca Anne. *The Baptism of Early Virginia: How Christianity Created Race*. Baltimore, MD: Johns Hopkins University Press, 2012.

Gómez, Pablo F. *The Experiential Caribbean: Creating Knowledge and Healing in the Early Modern Atlantic*. Chapel Hill: University of North Carolina Press, 2017.

Gómez-Moriana, Antonio. "Narration and Argumentation in the Chronicles of the New World." In *1492–1992: Re/Discovering Colonial Writing*, edited by Rene Jara and Nicholas Spadaccini, 94–119. Minneapolis: University of Minnesota Press, 1989.

Graunt, John. *Natural and Political Observations Mentioned in a Following Index, and Made upon the Bills of Mortality by Capt. John Graunt. . . . ; with Reference to the Government, Religion, Trade, Growth, Air, Diseases, and the Several Changes of the Said City*. London, 1662.

Green, Toby. *The Rise of the Trans-Atlantic Slave Trade in Western Africa, 1300–1589*. Cambridge: Cambridge University Press, 2012.

Greenblatt, Stephen. *Marvelous Possessions: The Wonder of the New World*. Chicago: University of Chicago Press, 1991.

Greenfield, Susan C., and Carol Barash, eds. *Inventing Maternity: Politics, Science, and Literature, 1650–1865*. Lexington: University Press of Kentucky, 2015.

Gregory, C. A. "Cowries and Conquest: Towards a Subalternate Quality Theory of Money." *Comparative Studies in Society and History* 38, no. 2 (Apr. 1996): 195–217.

Griffin, Eric. "From Ethos to Ethnos: Hispanizing the 'Spaniard' in the Old World and the New." CR: *The New Centennial Review* 2, no. 1 (Spring 2002): 69–116.

Gronniosaw, James Albert Ukawsaw. "A Narrative of the Most Remarkable Particulars in the Life of James Albert Ukawsaw Gronniosaw (London, 1772)." In *Unchained*

Voices: An Anthology of Black Authors in the English-Speaking World of the Eighteenth Century, edited by Vincent Carretta, 32–58. Lexington: University Press of Kentucky, 1996.

Groot, Silvia W. de. "Maroon Women as Ancestors, Priests and Mediums in Surinam." *Slavery and Abolition* 7, no. 2 (Sept. 1986): 160–74.

Guasco, Michael. "Settling with Slavery: Human Bondage in the Atlantic World." In *Envisioning an English Empire: Jamestown and the North Atlantic World*, edited by Robert Applebaum and John Wood Sweet, 236–53. Philadelphia: University of Pennsylvania Press, 2005.

Guyer, Jane I. *Marginal Gains: Monetary Transactions in Atlantic Africa*. Chicago: University of Chicago Press, 2004.

Guyer, Jane. "Wealth in People and Self-Realization in Equatorial Africa." *Man: Journal of the Royal Anthropological Institute* 28, no. 2 (June 1993): 243–65.

Guyer, Jane. "Wealth in People, Wealth in Things—Introduction." *Journal of African History* 36, no. 1 (1995): 83–90.

Habib, Imtiaz H. *Black Lives in the English Archives, 1500–1677: Imprints of the Invisible*. Aldershot, UK: Ashhgate, 2008.

Hacking, Ian. "Making Up People." In *Reconstructing Individualism: Autonomy, Individuality, and the Self in Western Thought*, edited by Thomas C. Heller, Morton Sosna, and David E. Wellbery, 161–71. Stanford, CA: Stanford University Press, 1986.

Hadfield, Andrew. "The Benefits of a Warm Study: The Resistance to Travel before Empire." In *A Companion to the Global Renaissance*, edited by Jyotsna G. Singh, 99–113. Oxford: Wiley-Blackwell, 2009.

Hagthorpe, John. *Englands Exchequer, or A Discourse of the Sea and Navigation*. London, 1625.

Hair, P. E. H. *Africa Encountered: European Contacts and Evidence, 1450–1700*. Milton Park, UK: Routledge, 1997.

Hair, P. E. H. "Attitudes to Africans in English Primary Sources on Guinea up to 1650." *History in Africa* 29 (1999): 43–68.

Hair, P. E. H., and Robin Law. "The English in Western Africa to 1700." In *The Origins of Empire*, edited by Nicholas Canny, 241–63. Oxford: Oxford University Press, 1998.

Hakluyt, Richard. *The Principall Navigations: Voiages, and Discoveries of the English Nation*. London, 1589.

Hall, Catherine. "Whose Memories? Edward Long and the Work of Re-remembering." In *Britain's History and Memory of Transatlantic Slavery: Local Nuances of a "National Sin,"* edited by Katie Donington, Ryan Hanley, and Jessica Moody, 129–49. Liverpool: Liverpool University Press, 2016.

Hall, Douglas. *In Miserable Slavery: Thomas Thistlewood in Jamaica, 1750–86*. Kingston, Jamaica: University of the West Indies Press, 1999.

Hall, Kim F. "Extravagant Viciousness: Slavery and Gluttony in the Works of Thomas Tryon." In *Writing Race across the Atlantic World*, edited by Phillip Beidler and Gary Taylor, 93–112. New York: Palgrave Macmillan, 2005.

Hall, Kim F. *Things of Darkness: Economies of Race and Gender in Early Modern England*. Ithaca, NY: Cornell University Press, 1995.

Hall, Rebecca. "Not Killing Me Softly: African American Women, Slave Revolts, and Historical Constructions of Racialized Gender." PhD diss., University of California, Santa Cruz, 2004.

Hall, Richard, ed. *Acts, Passed in the Island of Barbados, from 1643, to 1762, Inclusive to Which Is Added, an Index; and Abridgement: With Many Useful Notes, References and Observations, Never Before Published: And Also a List of All the Laws . . . Which Are Now Become Obsolete. . . .* London, 1764.

Handler, J. S. "Survivors of the Middle Passage: Life Histories of Enslaved Africans in British America." *Slavery and Abolition* 23, no. 1 (2002): 23–56.

Hariot, Thomas. *Thomas Harriot's Artis Analyticae Praxis: An English Translation with Commentary.* Edited and translated by Muriel Seltman and Robert Goulding. Sources and Studies in the History of Mathematics and Physical Sciences. London: Springer, 2007.

Harrington, James. *The Oceana and Other Works.* 1656. London, 1737.

Harriot [Hariot], Thomas. *A Briefe and True Report of the New Found Land of Virginia.* 1590. Charlottesville: University of Virginia Press, 2007.

Harris, Cheryl. "Whiteness as Property." *Harvard Law Review*, no. 8 (June 1993): 1707–91.

Harris, Leslie M. *In the Shadow of Slavery: African Americans in New York City, 1626–1863.* Chicago: University of Chicago Press, 2003.

Hartman, Saidiya. "The Belly of the World: A Note on Black Women's Labors." *Souls* 18, no. 1 (Mar. 2016): 166–73.

Hartman, Saidiya. *Lose Your Mother: A Journey along the Atlantic Slave Route.* New York: Farrar, Straus, and Giroux, 2007.

Hartman, Saidiya. *Scenes of Subjection: Terror, Slavery, and Self-Making in Nineteenth-Century America.* New York: Oxford University Press, 1997.

Hartman, Saidiya. "Venus in Two Acts." *Small Axe* 12, no. 2 (June 2008): 1–14.

Hawthorne, Walter. *Planting Rice and Harvesting Slaves: Transformations along the Guinea-Bissau Coast, 1400–1900.* Portsmouth, NH: Heinemann, 2003.

Hawthorne, Walter. "Strategies of the Decentralized: Defending Communities from Slave Raiders in Coastal Guinea-Bissau, 1450–1815." In *Fighting the Slave Trade: West African Strategies,* edited by Sylvaine A. Diouf, 152–69. Athens: Ohio University Press, 2013.

Hening, William. *The Statutes at Large: Being a Collection of All the Laws of Virginia from the First Session of the Legislature, in the Year 1619.* Vol. 2. Richmond, VA, 1819.

Henwick, John. "Islamic Financial Institutions: Theoretical Structures and Aspects of Their Application in Sub-Saharan Africa." In *Credit Currencies and Culture: African Financial Institutions in Historical Perspective,* edited by Endre Stiansen and Jane Guyer, 72–97. Stockholm: Nordic Africa Institute, 1999.

Heywood, Linda M. *Njinga of Angola: Africa's Warrior Queen.* Cambridge, MA: Harvard University Press, 2017.

Heywood, Linda M. "Slavery and Its Transformation in the Kingdom of Kongo: 1491–1800." *Journal of African History* 50, no. 1 (2009): 1–22.

Heywood, Linda M., and John K. Thornton. *Central Africans, Atlantic Creoles, and the Foundation of the Americas, 1565–1660.* Cambridge: Cambridge University Press, 2007.

Higginbotham, A. Leon, Jr. *In the Matter of Color: Race and the American Legal Process; The Colonial Period*. New York: Oxford University Press, 1978.

Hine, Darlene Clark. "Female Slave Resistance: The Economics of Sex." *Western Journal of Black Studies* 3, no. 2 (Jan. 1979): 123–27.

Hodes, Martha. *Sex, Love, Race: Crossing Boundaries in North American History*. New York: New York University Press, 1999.

Hodgen, Margaret T. *Early Anthropology in the Sixteenth and Seventeenth Centuries*. Philadelphia: University of Pennsylvania Press, 1964.

Hodges, Graham Russell. *Root and Branch: African Americans in New York and East Hersey, 1613–1863*. Chapel Hill: University of North Carolina Press, 1999.

Hogendorn, Jan, and Marion Johnson. *The Shell Money of the Slave Trade*. Cambridge: Cambridge University Press, 1986.

Hortob, Job. *The Rare Travails of Job Hortop, an Englishman, Who Was Not Heard of in Three and Twentie Yeares Space*. London, 1591.

Hylle, Thomas. *The Arte of Vulgar Arithmaticke*. London, 1600.

Ibn Khaldun. *The Muqaddimah: An Introduction to History*. Edited by N. J. Dawood. Translated by Franz Rosenthal. Princeton, NJ: Princeton University Press, 2015.

Inikori, J. E. *Forced Migration: The Impact of the Export Slave Trade on African Societies*. New York: Africana, 1982.

Inikori, Joseph. "The Struggle against the Transatlantic Slave Trade: The Role of the State." In *Fighting the Slave Trade: West African Strategies*, edited by Sylvaine A. Diouf, 170–98. Athens: Ohio University Press, 2013.

Ipsen, Pernille. *Daughters of the Trade: Atlantic Slavers and Interracial Marriage on the Gold Coast*. Philadelphia: University of Pennsylvania Press, 2015.

Jacobs, Harriet. *Incidents in the Life of a Slave Girl*. 1862. Reprint, New York: Dover Publications, 2001.

James, Joy. "Afrarealism and the Black Matrix: Maroon Philosophy at Democracy's Border." *Black Scholar* 43, no. 4 (Winter 2013): 124–31.

Jerven, Morten. "The Emergence of African Capitalism." In *The Cambridge History of Capitalism*. Vol. 1, *The Rise of Capitalism: From Ancient Origins to 1848*, edited by Larry Neal and Jeffrey G. Williamson, 431–54. Cambridge: Cambridge University Press, 2014.

Jobson, Richard. *The Discovery of River Gambra (1623)*. Edited by David P. Gamble and P. E. H. Hair. London: Hakluyt Society, 1999.

Jobson, Richard. *The Golden Trade: Or, A Discouery of the Riuer Gambra, and the Golden Trade of the Aethiopians. Also, the Commerce with a Great Blacke Merchant, Called Buckor Sano, and His Report of the Houses Couered with Gold, and Other Strange Obseruations for the Good of Our Owne Countrey*. London, 1623.

Johnson, Michael P. "Runaway Slaves and the Slave Communities in South Carolina, 1799 to 1830." *William and Mary Quarterly* 38, no. 3 (July 1981): 418–41.

Johnson, Walter. "Racial Capitalism and Human Rights." In *Race Capitalism Justice*, edited by Walter Johnson and Robin D. G. Kelley, 105–12. Forum 1. Cambridge, MA: Boston Review, 2017.

Johnson, Walter. *River of Dark Dreams: Slavery and Empire in the Cotton Kingdom*. Cambridge, MA: Harvard University Press, 2013.

Johnson, Walter. *Soul by Soul: Life inside the Antebellum Slave Market*. Cambridge, MA: Harvard University Press, 1999.

Johnson, Walter. "To Remake the World: Slavery, Racial Capitalism, and Justice." *Boston Review*, October 19, 2016. https://bostonreview.net/race/walter-johnson-slavery-human-rights-racial-capitalism.

Jordan, Winthrop D. "Modern Tensions and the Origins of American Slavery." *Journal of Southern History* 28, no. 1 (Feb. 1962): 18–30.

Kammen, Michael. *Colonial New York*. New York: Oxford University Press, 1975.

Kaplan, Paul H. D. "Italy, 1490–1700." In *The Image of the Black in Western Art*. Vol. 3, *From the "Age of Discovery" to the Age of Abolition, Part 1: Artists of the Renaissance and Baroque*, edited by David Bindman and Henry Louis Gates Jr., 931–90. Cambridge, MA: Harvard University Press, 2018.

Kars, Marjoleine. "Dodging Rebellion: Politics and Gender in the Berbice Slave Uprising of 1763." *American Historical Review* 121, no. 1 (Feb. 2016): 39–69.

Kearney, Douglas. "Swimchant for Nigger Mer-Folk (an Aqua-Boogie Set in Lapis)." In *The Black Automaton*, 61–62. Albany, NY: Fence Books, 2009.

Kelley, Robin D. G. "What Did Cedric Robinson Mean by Racial Capitalism?" *Boston Review*, January 12, 2017. http://bostonreview.net/race/robin-d-g-kelley-what-did-cedric-robinson-mean-racial-capitalism.

Klein, Herbert. "African Women and the Atlantic Slave Trade." In *Women and Slavery in Africa*, edited by Martin Klein and Claire Robertson, 29–38. Portsmouth, NH: Hein, 1987.

Klein, Herbert S., Stanley L. Engerman, Robin Haines, and Ralph Shlomowitz. "Transoceanic Mortality: The Slave Trade in Comparative Perspective." *William and Mary Quarterly* 58, no. 1 (Jan. 2001): 93–118.

Klein, Martin A., and J. E. Inikori. *The Atlantic Slave Trade: Effects on Economies, Societies, and Peoples in Africa, the Americas, and Europe*. Durham, NC: Duke University Press, 1992.

Kupperman, Karen Ordahl. Introduction to *A True and Exact History of the Island of Barbados (1673)*, by Richard Ligon, edited by Karen Ordahl Kupperman, 1–36. Indianapolis, IN: Hackett, 2011.

Landers, Jane. "Founding Mothers: Female Rebels in Colonial New Granada and Spanish Florida." *Journal of African American History* 98, no. 1 (Jan. 2013): 7–23.

Landers, Jane. "Transforming Bondsmen into Vassals: Arming Slaves in Colonial Spanish America." In *Arming Slaves: From Classical Times to the Modern Age*, edited by Christopher Leslie Brown and Phillip Morgan, 120–45. New Haven, CT: Yale University Press, 2006.

Lane, Kris. "Captivity and Redemption: Aspects of Slave Life in Early Colonial Quito and Popayán." *Americas* 57, no. 2 (Oct. 2000): 225–46.

Lasser, Carol. "Voyeuristic Abolitionism: Sex, Gender, and the Transformation of Antislavery Rhetoric." *Journal of the Early Republic* 28, no. 1 (Spring 2008): 83–114.

Leibsohn, Dana, and Barbara E. Mundy. *Vistas: Visual Culture in Spanish America, 1520–1820*. http://www.fordham.edu/vistas.

Leo Africanus. *A Geographical Historie of Africa, Written in Arabicke and Italian by John Leo a More, Borne in Granada and Brought up in Barbarie*. Translated by John Pory. London, 1600.

Ligon, Richard. *A True and Exact History of the Island of Barbados*. 1673. Edited by Karen Ordahl Kupperman. Indianapolis, IN: Hackett, 2011.

Lindsay, Lisa. "Extraversion, Creolisation, and Dependency in the Atlantic Slave Trade." *Journal of African History* 55 (July 2014): 135–45.

Locke, John. *An Essay Concerning Human Understanding*. 1690. Kitchener, ON: Batoche Books, 2000.

Locke, John. *Two Treatises of Government*. 1690. London: Routledge, 2010.

Long, Edward. *The History of Jamaica: Reflections on Its Situation, Settlements, Inhabitants, Climate, Products, Commerce, Laws, and Government*. Vol. 2. London, 1774.

Lopes, Duarte. *A Report of the Kingdome of Congo, a Region of Africa: And of the Countries That Border Rounde about the Same. 1. Wherein Is Also Shewed, That the Two Zones Torrida and Frigida, Are Not Onely Habitable, but Inhabited, and Very Temperate, Contrary to the Opinion of the Old Philosophers. 2. That the Blacke Colour Which Is in the Skinnes of the Ethiopians and Negroes &c. Proceedeth Not from the Sunne. 3. And That the Riuer Nilus Springeth Not out of the Mountaines of the Moone, as Hath Been Heretofore Beleeued: Together with the True Cause of the Rising and Increasing Thereof. 4. Besides the Description of Diuers Plants, Fishes and Beastes, That Are Found in Those Countries*. Translated by Abraham Hartwell. London: Iohn Wolfe, 1597.

Lovejoy, Paul E. "Daily Life in Western Africa during the Era of the 'Slave Route.'" *Diogenes* 45, no. 179 (Autumn 1997): 1–19.

Lovejoy, Paul E. "The Upper Guinea Coast and the Trans-Atlantic Slave Trade Database." *African Economic History* 38 (2010): 1–27.

Lowe, Lisa. *Intimacies of Four Continents*. Durham, NC: Duke University Press, 2015.

Mackey, Nathaniel. "'The Song Sung in a Strange Land': An Interview with Nathaniel Mackey." By Andrew Mossin. *Iowa Review* 44 (Winter 2014/2015): 172–92.

Mallipeddi, Ramesh. "'A Fixed Melancholy': Migration, Memory, and the Middle Passage." *Eighteenth Century* 55, nos. 2/3 (Summer/Fall 2014): 235–53.

Mancall, Peter C. *Hakluyt's Promise: An Elizabethan's Obsession for an English America*. New Haven, CT: Yale University Press, 2007.

Manjapra, Kris. "Necrospeculation: Postemancipation Finance and Black Redress." *Social Text* 37, no. 2 (June 2019): 29–66.

Martyr, Peter. *The Decades of the Newe Worlde or West India Conteynyng the Nauigations and Conquestes of the Spanyardes, with the Particular Description of the Moste Ryche and Large Landes and Ilandes Lately Founde in the West Ocean Perteynyng to the Inheritaunce of the Kinges of Spayne. . . . Wrytten in the Latine Tounge by Peter Martyr of Angleria, and Translated into Englysshe by Rycharde Eden*. London, 1555.

Marx, Karl. *Capital: Volume I*. New York: Penguin Classics, 1990.

Mather, Cotton. "Magnalia Christi Americana." London, 1702.

McCormick, Ted. "Alchemy in the Political Arithmetic of Sir William Petty (1623–1687)." *Studies in History and Philosophy of Science* 37, no. 2 (June 2006): 290–307.

McDonah, Josephine. "Infanticide and the Boundaries of Culture from Hume to Arnold." In *Inventing Maternity: Politics, Science, and Literature, 1650–1865*, edited by Susan C. Greenfield and Carol Barash, 215–38. Lexington: University Press of Kentucky, 2015.

McInnis, Maurie D. *Slaves Waiting for Sale: Abolitionist Art and the American Slave Trade.* Chicago: University of Chicago Press, 2011.

McKittrick, Katherine. *Demonic Grounds: Black Women and the Cartographies of Struggle.* Minneapolis: University of Minnesota Press, 2006.

McKittrick, Katherine. "Mathematics Black Life." *Black Scholar* 44, no. 2 (Summer 2014): 16–28.

McManus, Edgar J. *Black Bondage in the North.* Syracuse, NY: Syracuse University Press, 1973.

Meaders, Daniel E. "South Carolina Fugitives as Viewed through Local Colonial Newspapers with Emphasis on Runaway Notices, 1732–1801." *Journal of Negro History* 60, no. 2 (Apr. 1975): 288–319.

Meier, August. *Black History and the Historical Profession, 1915–80.* Blacks in the New World. Urbana: University of Illinois Press, 1986.

Meillassoux, Claude. *The Anthropology of Slavery: The Womb of Iron and Gold.* Translated by Alide Dasnois. Chicago: University of Chicago Press, 1991.

Meillassoux, Claude. "Female Slavery." In *Women and Slavery in Africa*, edited by Martin A. Klein and Claire Robertson, 49–66. Portsmouth, NH: Heinemann, 1997.

Mémoire sur l'esclavage des negres. Schomburg Center for Research in Black Culture, Manuscripts, Archives and Rare Books Division, The New York Public Library. New York Public Library Digital Collections. Accessed November 21, 2020. https://digitalcollections.nypl.org/items/cfc7cd9001-1-f9990-0-13442-2-19550-0-0505686a51c.

Menard, Russell R. "How Sugar and Tobacco Planters Built Their Industries and Raised an Empire." *Agricultural History* 81 (Summer 2007): 309–32.

Menard, Russell R. "Reckoning with Williams: 'Capitalism and Slavery' and the Reconstruction of Early American History." *Callaloo* 20, no. 4 (Oct. 1997): 791–99.

Menard, Russell R. *Sweet Negotiations: Sugar, Slavery, and Plantation Agriculture in Early Barbados.* Richmond: University of Virginia Press, 2006.

Merian, Maria Sibylla. *Metamorphosis insectorum Surinamensium.* Amsterdam, 1705.

Mignolo, Walter. "Literacy and Colonization: The New World Experience." In *1492–1992: Re/Discovering Colonial Writing*, edited by Rene Jara and Nicholas Spadaccini, 51–96. Minneapolis: University of Minnesota Press, 1989.

Miller, Joseph Calder. *Way of Death: Merchant Capitalism and the Angolan Slave Trade, 1730–1830.* Madison: University of Wisconsin Press, 1996.

Miller, Joseph Calder. "Women as Slaves and Owners of Slaves: Experiences from Africa, the Indian Ocean World, and the Early Atlantic." In *Women and Slavery: Africa, the Indian Ocean World, and the Medieval North Atlantic*, edited by Gwyn Campbell, Suzanne Miers, and Joseph C. Miller, 1:1–42. Athens: Ohio University Press, 2007.

Mintz, Sidney, and Richard Price. *The Birth of African-American Culture: An Anthropological Perspective.* Boston: Beacon, 1992.

Minutes of the Common Council of the City of New York, 1675–1776, 8 vols. New York: Dodd, Mead, 1905.

Misselden, Edward. *Free Trade, or The Meanes to Make Trade Florish.* London, 1622.

Moitt, Bernard. *Women and Slavery in the French Antilles, 1635–1848.* Bloomington: Indiana University Press, 2001.

Montrose, Louis. "The Work of Gender in the Discourse of Discovery." *Representations* 33 (Winter 1991): 1–41.

Morgan, Gwenda, and Peter Rushton. "Visible Bodies: Power, Subordination and Identity in the Eighteenth-Century Atlantic World." *Journal of Social History* 39, no. 1 (Fall 2005): 39–64.

Morgan, Jennifer L. *Laboring Women: Reproduction and Gender in New World Slavery.* Philadelphia: University of Pennsylvania Press, 2004.

Morgan, Jennifer L. "*Partus Sequitur Ventrem*: Law, Race, and Reproduction in Colonial Slavery." *Small Axe:* 22 (Mar. 2018): 1–17.

Morgan, Jennifer L. "'Some Could Suckle over Their Shoulder': Male Travelers, Female Bodies, and the Gendering of Racial Ideology, 1500–1700." *William and Mary Quarterly* 54 (Jan. 1997): 167–92.

Morris, Thomas D. *Southern Slavery and the Law, 1619–1860.* Chapel Hill: University of North Carolina Press, 1996.

Morris, Thomas D. "'Villeinage . . . as It Existed in England, Reflects but Little Light on Our Subject': The Problem of the 'Sources' of Southern Slave Law." *American Journal of Legal History* 32, no. 2 (Apr. 1988): 95–137.

Morrison, Toni. *A Mercy.* New York: Knopf, 2008.

Morrison, Toni. *Beloved.* New York: Knopf, 1987.

Moten, Fred. *In the Break: The Aesthetics of the Black Radical Tradition.* Minneapolis: University of Minnesota Press, 2003.

Moten, Fred. *The Universal Machine.* Durham, NC: Duke University Press, 2018.

Muldrew, Craig. "'Hard Food for Midas': Cash and Its Social Value in Early Modern England." *Past and Present* 170 (2001): 78–120.

Mun, Thomas. *A Discourse of Trade, from England unto the East Indies.* London, 1621.

Munford, Clarence. *The Black Ordeal of Slavery and Slave Trading in the French West Indies, 1625–1715.* Vol. 2, *The Middle Passage and the Plantation Economy.* Lewiston, NY: E. Mellen Press, 1991.

Murphy, Michelle. *The Economization of Life.* Durham, NC: Duke University Press, 2017.

Mustakeem, Sowande M. *Slavery at Sea: Terror, Sex, and Sickness in the Middle Passage.* Ithaca, NY: Cornell University Press, 2016.

Muzer, Jeronimo. "Relacion del viaje." In *Viajes de extranjeros por España y Portugal,* edited by J. Garcia Mercadal, 1:328–417. Murcia, Spain: Consejería de Educación y Cultura, 1999.

Newton, John. *The Journal of a Slave Trader, 1750–1754.* London: Epworth, 1964.

Newton, Melanie J. "Returns to a Native Land: Indigeneity and Decolonization in the Anglophone Caribbean." *Small Axe* 17, no. 2 (July 2013): 108–22.

Nwokeji, G. Ugo. *The Slave Trade and Culture in the Bight of Biafra: An African Society in the Atlantic World.* New York: Cambridge University Press, 2010.

O'Callaghan, E. B. *Documents Relative to the Colonial History of the State of New York; Procured in Holland, England, and France,* 15 vols. Albany, NY: Weed, Parsons, 1853–1857.

O'Callaghan, E. B. *Laws and Ordinances of New Netherlands, 1638–1674.* Albany, NY: Weed, Parsons, 1868.

O'Malley, Gregory E. *Final Passages: The Intercolonial Slave Trade of British America, 1619–1807*. Chapel Hill: University of North Carolina Press, 2014.

Painter, Nell Irvin. "Soul Murder and Slavery: Towards a Fully Loaded Cost Accounting." In *Southern History across the Color Line*, 15–39. Chapel Hill: University of North Carolina Press, 2002.

Palmié, Stephan, ed. *Slave Cultures and the Cultures of Slavery*. Knoxville: University of Tennessee Press, 1995.

Palmié, Stephan. "A Taste for Human Commodities." In *Slave Cultures and the Cultures of Slavery*, edited by Stephan Palmié, 40–54. Knoxville: University of Tennessee Press, 1995.

Palmié, Stephan. *Wizards and Scientists: Explorations in Afro-Cuban Modernity and Tradition*. Durham, NC: Duke University Press, 2002.

Patterson, Orlando. "Slavery, Alienation, and the Female Discovery of Personal Freedom." *Social Research* 58, no. 1 (Apr. 1991): 159–87.

Patterson, Orlando. *Slavery and Social Death: A Comparative Study*. Cambridge, MA: Harvard University Press, 1982.

Paugh, Katherine. *The Politics of Reproduction: Race, Medicine, and Fertility in the Age of Abolition*. New York: Oxford University Press, 2017.

Paul, Joanne, and Kurosh Meshkat. "Johnson's Relations: Visions of Global Order, 1601–1630." *Journal of Intellectual History and Political Thought* 1 (2003): 108–140.

Perrin, Liese M. "Resisting Reproduction: Reconsidering Slave Contraception in the Old South." *Journal of American Studies* 35, no. 2 (Aug. 2001): 255–74.

Perry, Imani. *Vexy Thing: On Gender and Liberation*. Durham, NC: Duke University Press, 2018.

Petty, Sir William. *The Petty Papers*, 2 vols. Edited by Henry William Edmund Petty-FitzMaurice, Marquess of Lansdowne. New York: Houghton Mifflin, 1927.

Petty, Sir William. *Political Anatomy of Ireland*. London, 1691.

Phillips, William D. *Slavery in Medieval and Early Modern Iberia*. Philadelphia: University of Pennsylvania Press, 2014. http://www.jstor.org/stable/j.ctt5hjm6x.7.

Pierson, Michael D. "'Slavery Cannot Be Covered Up with Broadcloth or a Bandanna': The Evolution of White Abolitionist Attacks on the 'Patriarchal Institution.'" *Journal of the Early Republic* 25, no. 3 (2005): 383–415.

Pietz, William. "The Problem of the Fetish, I." RES: *Anthropology and Aesthetics* 9 (1985): 5–17.

Pietz, William. "The Problem of the Fetish, II: The Origin of the Fetish." RES: *Anthropology and Aesthetics* 13 (1987): 23–45.

Pina, Ruy de. *Chronica del Rey Dom João II*. 1500. Lisbon: Academia de Ciências de Lisboa, 1792.

Piot, Charles. "Atlantic Aporias: Africa and Gilroy's Black Atlantic." *South Atlantic Quarterly* 110, no. 1 (Winter 2001): 155–70.

Piot, Charles. "Of Slaves and the Gift: Kabre Sale of Kin during the Era of the Slave Trade." *Journal of African History* 37, no. 1 (1996): 31–49.

Poovey, Mary. *A History of the Modern Fact: Problems of Knowledge in the Sciences of Wealth and Society*. Chicago: University of Chicago Press, 1998.

Powell, Robert. *Depopulation Arraigned, Convicted and Condemned, by the Lawes of God and Man: A Treatise Necessary in These Times; by R. P. of Wells, One of the Societie of*

New Inne. London: Printed by R[ichard] B[adger] and are to bee sold in S. Dunstans Church-yard neere the Church doore, 1636.

Price, Richard. *Maroon Societies: Rebel Slave Communities in the Americas*. 3rd ed. Baltimore, MD: Johns Hopkins University Press, 1996.

Pudaloff, Ross J. "No Change without Purchase: Olaudah Equiano and the Economies of Self and Market." *Early American Literature* 40, no. 3 (Nov. 2005): 499–527.

Purchas, Samuel. *Purchas His Pilgrimes: or Relations of the World*. London, 1613.

Puttenham, George. *The Arte of Englishe Poesie*. London, 1589.

Pyrard, François. *The Voyage of François Pyrard of Laval, to the East Indies, the Maldives, the Moluccas and Brazil*. 1619. London: The Hakluyt Society, 1887.

Quinn, David Beers. "Sir Thomas Smith (1513–1577) and the Beginnings of English Colonial Theory." *Proceedings of the American Philosophical Society* 89, no. 4 (Dec. 1945): 543–60.

Radburn, Nicholas, and David Eltis. "Visualizing the Middle Passage: The *Brookes* and the Reality of Ship Crowding in the Transatlantic Slave Trade." *Journal of Interdisciplinary History* 4 (2019): 533–65.

Rediker, Marcus. *The Slave Ship: A Human History*. New York: Viking, 2007.

Reinhardt, Mark. *Who Speaks for Margaret Garner?* Minneapolis: University of Minnesota Press, 2010.

Richardson, David. "Cultures of Exchange: Atlantic Africa in the Era of the Slave Trade." *Transactions of the Royal Historical Society* 19 (2009): 151–79.

Richardson, David. "Shipboard Revolts, African Authority, and the Atlantic Slave Trade." *William and Mary Quarterly* 58, no. 1 (Jan. 2001): 69–92.

Richardson, David, and David Eltis. "Prices of African Slaves Newly Arrived in the Americas, 1673–1865: New Evidence on Long-Run Trends and Regional Differentials." In *Slavery in the Development of the Americas*, edited by David Eltis, Frank Lewis, and Kenneth Sokoloff, 181–218. New York: Cambridge University Press, 2004.

Richardson, David, and Filipa Ribeiro da Silva. *Networks and Trans-cultural Exchange: Slave Trading in the South Atlantic, 1590–1867*. Leiden: Brill, 2014.

Roberts, Lewes. *Merchants Map of Commerce: Wherein the Universal Manner and Matter of Trade Is Compendiously Handled*. London, 1677.

Roberts, Neil. *Freedom as Marronage*. Chicago: University of Chicago Press, 2015.

Robertson, Claire. "We Must Overcome: Genealogy and Evolution of Female Slavery in West Africa." *Journal of West African History* 1, no. 1 (Spring 2015): 59–92.

Robertson, Claire, and Martin A. Klein, eds. *Women and Slavery in Africa*. Portsmouth, NH: Heinemann, 1997.

Robertson, Claire, and Martin A. Klein. "Women's Importance in African Slave Systems." In *Women and Slavery in Africa*, edited by Claire Robertson and Martin A. Klein, 3–27. Portsmouth, NH: Heinemann, 1997.

Robinson, Cedric J. *Black Marxism: The Making of the Black Radical Tradition*. 2nd ed. Chapel Hill: University of North Carolina Press, 2000.

Rodney, Walter. *A History of the Upper Guinea Coast, 1545–1800*. Oxford: Clarendon, 1970.

Roediger, David R., and Elizabeth D. Esch. *Production of Difference: Race and the Management of Labor in U.S. History*. Oxford: Oxford University Press, 2012.

Rosenthal, Caitlin. *Accounting for Slavery*. Cambridge, MA: Harvard University Press, 2018.

Rucker, Walter C. *Gold Coast Diasporas: Identity, Culture, and Power*. Bloomington: Indiana University Press, 2015.

Rupert, Linda M. "Marronage, Manumission and Maritime Trade in the Early Modern Caribbean." *Slavery and Abolition* 30, no. 3 (Sept. 2009): 361–82.

Sahlins, Marshall. "What Kinship Is (Part I)." *Journal of the Royal Anthropological Institute* 17, no. 1 (Mar. 2011): 2–19.

Sainsbury, William Noel, and Great Britain Public Record Office. *Calendar of State Papers, Colonial Series, America and West Indies, 1661–1668: Preserved in Her Majesty's Public Record Office*. London: Longman, 1880. Sabin Americana: History of the Americas, 1500–1926. Accessed Sept. 28, 2020. https://link-gale-com.proxy.library .nyu.edu/apps/doc/CY0101500811/SABN?u=new64731&sid=SABN&xid=dcb8e51f.

Sancho, Ignatius. "Letters of the Late Ignatius Sancho, an African, in Two Volumes, to Which Are Prefixed, Memoir of His Life (London, 1782)." In *Unchained Voices: An Anthology of Black Authors in the English-Speaking World of the Eighteenth Century*, edited by Vincent Carretta, 77–109. Lexington: University Press of Kentucky, 1996.

Sandhu, Sukhdev. "Ignatius Sancho: An African Man of Letters." In *Ignatius Sancho: An African Man of Letters*, 45–74. London: National Portrait Gallery, 1997.

Saunders, A. C. de C. M. *A Social History of Black Slaves and Freedmen in Portugal, 1441–1555*. New York: Cambridge University Press, 1982.

Schiebinger, Londa. "Agnotology and Exotic Abortifacients: The Cultural Production of Ignorance in the Eighteenth-Century Atlantic World." *Proceedings of the American Philosophical Society* 149, no. 3 (Sept. 2005): 316–43.

Schiebinger, Londa. "Exotic Abortifacients and Lost Knowledge." *Lancet* 371 (Mar. 2008): 718–19.

Schorsch, Jonathan. "Blacks, Jews and the Racial Imagination in the Writings of Sephardim in the Long Seventeenth Century." *Jewish History* 19, no. 1 (2005): 109–35.

Seed, Patricia. *American Pentimento: The Invention of Indians and the Pursuit of Riches*. Minneapolis: University of Minnesota Press, 2001.

Seed, Patricia. *Ceremonies of Possession in Europe's Conquest of the New World, 1492–1640*. Cambridge: Cambridge University Press, 1995.

Seijas, Tatiana, and Pablo Miguel Sierra Silva. "The Persistence of the Slave Market in Seventeenth-Century Central Mexico." *Slavery and Abolition* 37, no. 2 (June 2016): 307–33.

Seth, Suman. *Difference and Disease: Medicine, Race, and the Eighteenth-Century British Empire*. New York: Cambridge University Press, 2018.

Shammas, Carole. "Black Women's Work and the Evolution of Plantation Society in Virginia." *Labor History* 26 (Winter 1985): 5–30.

Shammas, Carole. *The Pre-industrial Consumer in England and America*. Oxford: Oxford University Press, 1990.

Sharpe, Christina. *In the Wake: On Blackness and Being*. Durham, NC: Duke University Press, 2016.

Shaw, Rosalind. *Memories of the Slave Trade: Ritual and the Historical Imagination in Sierra Leone*. Chicago: University of Chicago Press, 2002.

Sheales, Fiona. "African Gold-Weights in the British Museum." British Museum, 2014. Accessed March 2016. https://www.britishmuseum.org/research/online_research _catalogues/agw/african_gold-weights.aspx.

Shepard, Alexandra. *Accounting for Oneself: Worth, Status, and the Social Order in Early Modern England*. Oxford: Oxford University Press, 2015.

Sheridan, Richard B. "Letters from a Sugar Plantation in Antigua, 1739–1758." *Agricultural History* 31, no. 3 (July 1957): 3–23.

Shockley, Evie. "Going Overboard: African American Poetic Innovation and the Middle Passage." *Contemporary Literature* 52, no. 4 (Winter 2011): 791–817.

Singh, Jyotsna G., ed. *A Companion to the Global Renaissance*. Oxford: Wiley-Blackwell, 2009.

Smallwood, Stephanie E. "Commodified Freedom: Interrogating the Limits of Antislavery Ideology in the Early Republic." In *Whither the Early Republic: A Forum on the Future of the Field*, edited by John Lauritz Larson and Michael Morrison, 289–98. Philadelphia: University of Pennsylvania Press, 2012.

Smallwood, Stephanie E. *Saltwater Slavery: A Middle Passage from Africa to American Diaspora*. Cambridge, MA: Harvard University Press, 2008.

Smith, Adam. *An Inquiry into the Nature and Causes of the Wealth of Nations 1776*. New York: Dutton, 1910.

Smith, Ian. "Barbarian Errors: Performing Race in Early Modern England." *Shakespeare Quarterly* 49, no. 2 (Summer 1998): 168–86.

Smith, S. D. "The Account Book of Richard Poor, Quaker Merchant of Barbados." *William and Mary Quarterly*, 3rd ser., 66, no. 3 (July 2009): 605–28.

Smith, Thomas. "A Letter Sent by I. B. Gentleman vnto His Very Frende Maystet [*sic*] R. C. Esquire vvherin Is Contiened a Large Discourse of the Peopling and Inhabiting the Cuntrie Called the Ardes, and Other Adiacent in the North of Ireland, and Taken in Hand by Sir Thomas Smith One of the Queenes Maiesties Priuie Counsel, and Thomas Smith Esquire, His Sonne." London, 1572. Early English Books Online.

Smith, Venture. "A Narrative of the Life and Adventures of Venture, a Native of Africa (New London, 1798)." In *Unchained Voices: An Anthology of Black Authors in the English-Speaking World of the Eighteenth Century*, edited by Vincent Carretta, 369–87. Lexington: University Press of Kentucky, 1996.

Smithers, Gregory. *Slave Breeding: Sex, Violence, and Memory in African American History*. Gainesville: University Press of Florida, 2012.

Snyder, Terri L. "Suicide, Slavery, and Memory in North America." *Journal of American History* 97, no. 1 (June 2010): 39–62.

Solow, Barbara L. "Introduction: Slavery and the Rise of the Atlantic System." In *Slavery and the Rise of the Atlantic System*, edited by Barbara Solow, 1–20. Cambridge: Cambridge University Press, 1991.

Solow, Barbara L. "The Transatlantic Slave Trade: A New Census." *William and Mary Quarterly*, 3rd. ser., 58, no. 1 (Jan. 2001): 9–16.

Sontag, Susan. *Regarding the Pain of Others*. New York: Picador, 2004.

Spear, Jennifer. "Colonial Intimacies: Legislating Sex in French Louisiana." *William and Mary Quarterly*, 3rd. ser., 60, no. 1 (Jan. 2003): 75–98.

Spear, Jennifer. *Race, Sex, and Social Order in Early New Orleans*. Baltimore, MD: Johns Hopkins University Press, 2008.

Spicer, Joaneath, ed. *Revealing the African Presence in Renaissance Europe*. Baltimore, MD: The Walters Art Museum, 2013.

Spiller, Elizabeth. *Reading and the History of Race in the Renaissance*. Cambridge: Cambridge University Press, 2011.

Spillers, Hortense J. "Mama's Baby, Papa's Maybe: An American Grammar Book." *Diacritics* 17, no. 2 (Summer 1987): 65–81.

Stark, David M. "A New Look at the African Slave Trade in Puerto Rico through the Use of Parish Registers: 1660–1815." *Slavery and Abolition* 30, no. 4 (Dec. 2009): 491–520.

The Statutes at Large: Being a Collection of All the Laws of Virginia, from the First Session of the Legislature, in the Year 1619, 13 vols. Edited by William W. Hening. New York, 1819–1823.

Steckel, Richard. "Women, Work, and Health under Plantation Slavery in the United States." In *More Than Chattel: Black Women and Slavery in the Americas*, edited by David Barry Gaspar and Darlene Clark Hine, 43–60. Bloomington: Indiana University Press, 1996.

Streeck, Wolfgang. "Citizens as Customers: Considerations on the New Politics of Consumption." *New Left Review* 76 (Jan. 2012): 27–47.

Sublette, Ned, and Constance Sublette. *The American Slave Coast: A History of the Slave-Breeding Industry*. Chicago: Chicago Review Press, 2015.

Sussman, Charlotte. "The Colonial Afterlife of Political Arithmetic: Swift, Demography, and Mobile Populations." *Cultural Critique* 56 (Winter 2004): 96–126.

[Sutton], Belinda. "Petition of an African Slave, to the Legislature of Massachusetts." In *Unchained Voices: An Anthology of Black Authors in the English-Speaking World of the Eighteenth Century*, edited by Vincent Carretta, 142–44. Lexington: University Press of Kentucky, 1996.

Sweet, James H. "Defying Social Death: The Multiple Configurations of African Slave Family in the Atlantic World." *William and Mary Quarterly* 70, no. 2 (Apr. 2013): 251–72.

Sweet, James H. *Domingos Álvares, African Healing, and the Intellectual History of the Atlantic World*. Chapel Hill: University of North Carolina Press, 2011.

Sweet, James H. "The Iberian Roots of American Racist Thought." *William and Mary Quarterly* 54, no. 1 (Jan. 1997): 143–66.

Swift, Jonathan. *A Modest Proposal and Other Satires*. 1729. Introduction by George R. Levine. New York: Prometheus Books, 1995.

Tadman, Michael. "The Demographic Cost of Sugar: Debates on Slave Societies and Natural Increase in the Americas." *American Historical Review* 105, no. 5 (Dec. 2000): 1534–75.

Tannenbaum, Frank. *Slave and Citizen: The Classic Comparative Study of Race Relations in the Americas*. Boston: Beacon, 1992.

Taylor, Eric Robert. *If We Must Die: Shipboard Insurrections in the Era of the Atlantic Slave Trade*. Baton Rouge: Louisiana State University Press, 2006.

Teelucksingh, Jerome. "The 'Invisible Child' in British West Indian Slavery." *Slavery and Abolition* 27, no. 2 (Aug. 2006): 237–50.

Thirsk, Joan, and J. P. Cooper. *Seventeenth-Century Economic Documents*. Oxford: Clarendon, 1972.

Thomas, Deborah A. "Caribbean Studies, Archive Building, and the Problem of Violence." *Small Axe* 17, no. 2 (July 2013): 27–42.

Thomas, Keith. "Numeracy in Early Modern England: The Prothero Lecture." *Transactions of the Royal Historical Society* 37 (1987): 103–32.

Thompson, Peter. "Henry Drax's Instructions on the Management of a Seventeenth-Century Barbadian Sugar Plantation." *William and Mary Quarterly*, 3rd ser., 66, no. 3 (July 2009): 565–604.

Thornton, John K. "African Dimensions of the Stono Rebellion." *American Historical Review* 96, no. 4 (Oct. 1991): 1101–13.

Tillet, Salamishah. *Sites of Slavery: Citizenship and Racial Democracy in the Post–Civil Rights Imagination*. Durham, NC: Duke University Press, 2012.

Tomlins, Christopher. *Freedom Bound: Law, Labor, and Civic Identity in Colonizing English America, 1580–1865*. Cambridge: Cambridge University Press, 2010.

Trouillot, Michel-Rolph. *Silencing the Past*. New York: Beacon, 1992.

Tryon, Thomas. *The Good Housewife Made Doctor*. London, 1682.

Turner, Sasha. "Abba: Grief, Sympathy, and the Negotiation of Motherhood in Slavery." Paper presented to the New York University Workshop in the History of the Atlantic World. New York, NY, November 27, 2018.

Turner, Sasha. *Contested Bodies: Pregnancy, Childrearing, and Slavery in Jamaica*. Philadelphia: University of Pennsylvania Press, 2017.

Ungerer, Gustav. *The Mediterranean Apprenticeship of British Slavery*. Madrid: Verbum, 2008.

Ungerer, Gustav. "Printing of Spanish Books in Elizabethan England." *Library* 20 (Sept. 1965): 177–229.

Van den Broecke, Pieter. *Pieter van den Broecke's Journal of Voyages to Cape Verde, Guinea and Angola, 1605–1612*. Edited by J. D. La Fleur. London: Hakluyt Society, 2000.

Vaughan, Alden T. "The Origins Debate: Slavery and Racism in Seventeenth-Century Virginia." *Virginia Magazine of History and Biography* 97, no. 3 (July 1989): 311–54.

Vilches, Elvira. *New World Gold: Cultural Anxiety and Monetary Disorder in Early Modern Spain*. Chicago: University of Chicago Press, 2010.

Voyages aux côtes de Guinée et dans Ameriques faits en 1702 [Voyages to the coast of Guinea and the Americas, 1702]. Amsterdam, 1719.

Waldstreicher, David. "Reading the Runaways: Self-Fashioning, Print Culture, and Confidence in Slavery in the Eighteenth-Century Mid-Atlantic." *The William and Mary Quarterly* 56, no. 2 (Apr. 1999): 243–72.

Walker, Tamara. *Exquisite Slaves: Race, Clothing, and Status in Colonial Lima*. New York: Cambridge University Press, 2017.

Wallerstein, Immanuel. *The Modern World System I: Capitalist Agriculture and the Origins of the European World-Economy in the Sixteenth Century*. Berkeley: University of California Press, 2011.

Watson, Alan. "Seventeenth-Century Jurists, Roman Law, and Slavery." In *Slavery and the Law*, edited by Paul Finkelman, 367–78. New York: Rowman and Littlefield, 1998.

Watson, Alan. *Slave Law in the Americas*. Athens: University of Georgia Press, 1989.

Wax, Donald D. "Preferences for Slaves in Colonial America." *Journal of Negro History* 58, no. 4 (Oct. 1973): 371–401.

Weaver, Karol K. "'She Crushed the Child's Fragile Skull': Disease, Infanticide, and Enslaved Women in Eighteenth-Century Saint-Domingue." *French Colonial History* 5 (2004): 93–109.

Webb, Mary. *Memoir of Mrs. Chloe Spear a Native of Africa, Who Was Enslaved in Child-hood, and Died in Boston, January 3, 1815, Aged 65 Years*. Boston: James Loring, 1832.

Weheliye, Alexander G. *Habeas Viscus: Racializing Assemblages, Biopolitics, and Black Feminist Theories of the Human*. Durham, NC: Duke University Press, 2014.

Weinbaum, Alys Eve. *The Afterlife of Reproductive Slavery: Biocapitalism and Black Feminism's Philosophy of History*. Durham, NC: Duke University Press, 2019.

Weinbaum, Alys Eve. "Gendering the General Strike: W. E. B. Du Bois's Black Reconstruction and Black Feminism's 'Propaganda of History.'" *South Atlantic Quarterly* 112, no. 3 (Summer 2013): 437–63.

Weinbaum, Alys Eve. *Wayward Reproductions: Genealogies of Race and Nation in Transatlantic Modern Thought*. Durham, NC: Duke University Press Books, 2004.

Weissbourd, Emily. "Race, Slavery, and Queen Elizabeth's 'Edicts of Expulsion.'" *Huntington Library Quarterly* 78, no. 1 (Spring 2015): 1–19.

Wennerlind, Carl. *Casualties of Credit: The English Financial Revolution, 1620–1720*. Cambridge, MA: Harvard University Press, 2011.

Wennerlind, Carl. "Credit Money as the Philosopher's Stone: Alchemy and the Coinage Problem in Seventeenth-Century England." *History of Political Economy* 35 (2003): 234–61.

Wheat, David. *Atlantic Africa and the Spanish Caribbean, 1570–1640*. Chapel Hill: University of North Carolina Press for the Omohundro Institute for Early American History and Culture, 2015.

Wheat, David. "The First Great Waves: African Provenance Zones for the Transatlantic Slave Trade to Cartagena de Indias, 1570–1640." *Journal of African History* 55 (Mar. 2011): 1–22.

White, Deborah Gray. *Ar'n't I a Woman?: Female Slaves in the Plantation South*. New York: W. W. Norton, 1985.

White, Deborah Gray. *Telling Histories: Black Women Historians in the Ivory Tower*. Gender and American Culture. Chapel Hill: University of North Carolina Press, 2008.

Wilks, Ivor. "Wangara, Akan and Portuguese in the Fifteenth and Sixteenth Centuries. 1. The Matter of Bitu." *Journal of African History* 23, no. 3 (1982): 333–49.

Wilks, Ivor. "Wangara, Akan and Portuguese in the Fifteenth and Sixteenth Centuries. 2. The Struggle for Trade." *Journal of African History* 23, no. 4 (1982): 463–72.

Williams, Eric. *Capitalism and Slavery*. 1944. Edited by Colin A. Palmer. Chapel Hill: University of North Carolina Press, 1994.

Wingate, Edmund. *Mr. Wingate's Arithmetick: Containing a Perfect Method for the Knowledge and Practice of Common Arithmetick*. Revised by John Kersey. London: Printed for Philemon Stephens at the Gilded Lion in St. Pauls Church-yard, 1658.

Wood, Betty, and T. R. Clayton. "Slave Birth, Death and Disease on Golden Grove Plantation, Jamaica, 1765–1810." *Slavery and Abolition* 6, no. 2 (Sept. 1985): 99–121.

Wood, Marcus. *Blind Memory: Visual Representations of Slavery in England and America, 1780–1865*. New York: Routledge, 2000.

Wood, Marcus. "Celebrating the Middle Passage: Atlantic Slavery, Barbie and the Birth of the Sable Venus." *Atlantic Studies: Literary, Cultural, and Historical Perspectives* 1, no. 2 (Oct. 2004): 123–44.

Wood, Peter H. *Black Majority: Negroes in Colonial South Carolina from 1670 through the Stono Rebellion*. New York: Alfred A. Knopf, 1975.

Wynter, Sylvia. "Beyond the Categories of the Master Conception: The Counterdoctrine of the Jamesian Poiesis." In *C.L.R. James's Caribbean*, edited by Paget Henry and Paul Buhle, 63–91. Durham, NC: Duke University Press, 1992.

Wynter, Sylvia. "1492: A New World View." In *Race, Discourse, and the Origin of the Americas: A New World View*, edited by Vera Lawrence Hyatt and Rex Nettleford, 5–57. Washington, DC: Smithsonian Institution Press, 1995.

Wynter, Sylvia. "Unsettling the Coloniality of Being/Power/Truth/Freedom: Towards the Human, after Man, Its Overrepresentation—an Argument." CR: *The New Centennial Review* 3, no. 3 (2003): 257–337.

Wynter, Sylvia, and Katherine McKittrick. "Unparalleled Catastrophe for Our Species?" In *Sylvia Wynter: On Being Human as Praxis*, edited by Katherine McKittrick, 9–89. Durham, NC: Duke University Press, 2014.

Yang, Chi-Ming. "Silver, Blackness, and Fugitive Value: 'From China to Peru.'" *Eighteenth Century* 59 (2018): 141–66.

Zahedieh, Nuala. "Making Mercantilism Work: London Merchants and Atlantic Trade in the Seventeenth Century." *Transactions of the Royal Historical Society* 9 (1999): 143–58.

Zahedieh, Nuala. "Overseas Expansion and Trade in the Seventeenth Century." In *The Origins of Empire: British Overseas Enterprise to the Close of the Seventeenth Century*, edited by Nicholas Canny, 398–422. Oxford: Oxford University Press, 1998.

Zakim, Michael. "The Political Geometry of Statistical Tables." *Journal of the Early Republic* 38 (2018): 445–74.

Zurara, Gomes Eannes de. *The Chronicle of the Discovery and Conquest of Guinea*. Edited by Charles Raymond Beazley and Edgar Prestage. London: Hakluyt Society, 1896.

African women (continued)
  division of labor in West Africa, 125, 138–40;
  fears of capture, 157; as illegible, 5; numbers
  of in slavery, 29; offspring of as products,
  106–8; perceptions of, 53–54. *See also* enslaved women; erasure of African/enslaved
  women; sex ratios, 1500–1700
Agamben, Giorgio, 42
agnotology, 217
Agrin (Arguin, Mauritania), 122
alchemy of race and commerce, 14, 20, 24, 30,
  37, 39, 244, 250–51; gold and, 67–68, 77;
  transmutation, 98
Alexander (slave-trading ship), 193
alienation, 25, 156, 158, 172; of reproductive
  labor, 6, 209, 223
alphabetic writing, 62–64, 84
Alvares, Manuel, 70, 129
Álvares de Almada, Andre, 69–70, 80
America. *See* English Americas
Anderson, Benedict, 200
Anglo-Dutch War of 1665–1667, 215–16
Angola, 49–50, 120
Angola, Dorothe (enslaved woman), 238, 252
Antigua, 215–16
apes, racist linking of Africans with, 134
Appleby, Joyce, 76–77, 89
apprenticeships, 238
appropriation, x, 16n31, 24, 209: English confidence in, 57–58; of kinship, 237–43
appropriation of labor, 35, 68, 76, 99–100; African understanding of, 160; sexual division of
  labor, 125, 138–40
archive: African experience missing from, 5–9,
  20, 209; critical strategy for, 169; production
  of data demographics in, 40–44; distorted
  evidence and erasures in, 21–22, 29, 36–37,
  42, 214; newspapers, 197–206, *198*; erasure of
  women and Middle Passage, 25; resistance
  erased in, 214; unsettling of, 54; violence
  transferred to documents, 8; visual, 151–55.
  See also logbooks, slave traders'
Arendt, Hannah, 42, 233n59
Arte of English Poesie (Puttenham), 63
Artis Analyticae Praxis (Hariot), 91
Atlantic history, 29, 109; English Atlantic in
  longer history of, 3; new ways of thinking, 14
Atlantic Slave Trade: A Census, The (Curtin), 30
auction block, 51, 164, 173–75

Aunt Hester (enslaved woman), 220–21
autobiographical accounts, 158–61, 165, 168–69,
  204–5
Azanaghis, 123

Bailey, Amanda, 68
Barbados, 34–36, 51, 184–86, 202–3
Barbados Ledger, 184–86
barbarianism/savagery, imputed to Africans,
  62–64, 69, 82, 104n147
Barbot, Jean, 180–82, *183*, 185
bare life (Agamben), 42
Barreda, Ignacio Maria, *105*
Barrett, Lindon, 90
Barry, Boubacar, 139, 140n90
bastardy laws, 178
Baucom, Ian, 50–51
Beckles, Hilary, 56
Belgrove, William, 190
belonging, politics of, 5, 200, 204
Benin, 144
Benjamin, Walter, 42
Bennett, Herman, 61, 71, 80, 118n16, 251
Bentley, Nancy, 247
Berlin, Ira, 2
birth rates, 246; in Maroon communities, 230;
  New York City, 240; in West Indies, 182, 186,
  194–95, 223–24
Black Marxism (Robinson), 10, 15–16, 160, 234,
  249–52
Blackness: as enslavability, 1, 10, 108, 138; logbooks and origin of, 23, 54
Black radical tradition, 10, 16–17, 208; accounting practice rooted in, 17; Maroons and, 234;
  origins of, 145, 160, 232–33, 249–52
bodies: appropriation of women's, x, 16n31,
  102–4, 209; as commodities, 141–42; as corporeal metaphor for national sovereignty,
  17–18; in ledger books, 115–16; as praxis for
  understanding resistance, 208–9; as site
  of pleasure and resistance, 217–20; "three
  bodies" of enslaved people, 219, 224; value
  ascribed to Black, 8, 18. *See also* pregnancy;
  reproduction
body politic, metaphor of, 17–18, 106–7
Boemus, Johann, 119, 125–26
Bolas, Juan de (Maroon leader), 234
Bologna, Italy, painting, x

Borucki, Alex, 33
Boston News-Letter, 200
Botero, Giovanni, 83–84, 89
Braudel, Fernand, 55, 56
Briefe and True Report of the New Found Land of Virginia (Harriot [Hariot]), 92
Briefe Description of the Whole Worlde, A (Abbot), 82–83, 129–30
Briggs, Peter, 104–5n149
British Lords of Trade, 241
Brookes (slave-trading ship), 20, 153–55, *154*
Brown, Vincent, 5–6, 228
Buck-Morss, Susan, 18
Budomel (Jalof lord), 123–24
Burnard, Trevor, 203n82
Butler, Judith, 48, 166, 246
Byrd, William, 102–3

Cabo Blanco, 65
Cadamosto, Alvise da, 117–19, 117n12, 122–24, 133
Calomiris, Charles, 194
Camp, Stephanie, 217–18, 224
Campbell, John (slave owner), 200
Canary Islands, 117
cannibalism, 124; cannibal shop, 85–87, *86*; in satire, 104–6
Cantino planisphere of 1502, 145–47, *147*
Cape of Good Hope, 75, 83
capitalism: erasure of African women as central to, 37; insurance claims, 50–51; print, 200–201; slavery's unacknowledged role in, 56, 236–37, 249–50. *See also* commodification; racial capitalism
Capitalism and Slavery (Williams), 11, 16, 56
Caribbean, slave ship voyages to, 45, 51, 51n64
Carney, Judith, 138
Carolina House of Assembly, 213–14
Carolinas, slave ship voyages to, 45
casta (mixed-race) paintings (Spain), 104, *105*
Catherine of Aragon, 62
Chapin, Joyce, 92, 94n110
chattel property laws, 99, 178
children: birth rates, 182, 186, 194–95, 223–24; as commodities, 182; as cost to slave owner, 114, 192–95; currency linked with, 134; enslavability follows condition of mother, 3–6, 102, 106, 178, 178n17, 194; erasure of, 37; Europeans' inability to recognize, 157; internal slave trade and, 227; labor of, 190, 192; Middle Passage

and, 38, 39, 42, 45; numbers of in slave trade, 32; as "plunder," 217, 229–30; property rights to in English Americas, 192; on slave ships, 25, 46, 166–67, 192–93; used as lures, 127, 141, 156, 165; women tasked with protecting, 25, 46, 166–67
citizenship, 18, 49, 57n6, 93, 97
civility, 64, 84n82, 92–93, 132–34, 150, 207; infanticide used to discuss, 225–26
Civil War, 56n2
coin. *See* specie
collective identity, 90, 93, 234
colonialism, 90–91; English imperial expansion, 100–101; Iberian contact with West Africa, 26, 59–67, 108, 112; illiteracy as justification for, 62–64; native mortality as justification for, 64; numeracy linked with, 91–93; peopling nations as rationale for, 93–100; population linked with, 91–100; settler, 4, 14, 15, 17; sex ratios in English colonies, 103–4; Spanish, Dutch, English, and French economies, 17; "tyranny of the alphabet," 62–63. *See also* English Americas
Columbus, Christopher, 62, 64, 65, 110, 132–33
commerce: affective relationships and, 3, 20–21, 60–61; demographics reduce people to monetary value, 55; denial of kinship facilitates, 37; language of, 61, 64, 66, 70–73; rupture of parental bond by, 61; slavery as instrument of, 26, 30; spatial aspects, 57, 60–61. *See also* exchange; market
commodification, 68n35; affective relationships as bulwark against, 3; as antithesis of humanity, 205; counternarratives of, 25, 60, 252; European, 13–14; generational, 220; human, linked to rise of market economies, 11–12; of humans, 4, 11–12, 52, 58; illiteracy as justification for, 64; of kin, 156–57; naturalization of female, 128; racialized maternity as synchronous with, 20; reiterative articulation of, 66, 174; resistance to, 17, 26; stages of, 66; systemic, 52–53; understanding of by African and enslaved people, 7–8, 25–26, 53–54, 108, 140, 149, 156–61, 170, 176, 252, 255; West African concepts of, 25. *See also* capitalism
commodities: Africans as, 18, 80–89, 106–7; African women's bodies as, 141–42; biotic, captives as, 66; children as, 182; early forms of exchange, 122–23; ideas as, 43; kinship as,

commodities (continued)
24; phantasmagorical powers of, 33, 109; racial hierarchy used to separate forced labor from, 101–2; slaves, in lists of, 69, 71, 99, 129;
Common Council (New York), 242
common law, 177, 178
commons, 90
Company of Royal Adventures, 184
condition, as term, 5–6
Congo, 85–89
consumption, 57n6, 75, 97
containment, geographies of, 217–18, 244
Council of New Netherland, 237
counternarratives, 160, 233; of commodification, 25, 60, 252
court cases and petitions, 1–5, 178–79, 203, 237–38, 252
credit, 68, 81, 108–9
Creoles, 2, 199
critical fabulation, 169
Cromwell, Oliver, 116
Cudgoe's War (First Maroon War), 236, 241
Cugoano, Quobna Ottobah, 157, 161
cultural logics, 16–17, 19, 56–57, 77
currency, 75–77; children linked with, 134; coinage crisis, 59n8, 75, 77; English guinea coins, 72; enslaved people as, 19, 34, 66, 68, 74–80, 136; goods as, 77; ideological, 215; Luandan, 87; Lumache (cowrie shells), 87–88, 123, 136–38; as new concept, 24–25. See also specie
Curtin, Phillip, 30, 67n34

Daunce, Edward, 116n10
Davis, Angela, 7, 217
death sentence, slavery as pardon in face of, 69
debt, 68, 242
de la Fosse, Eustache, 144
Delight (slave-trading ship), 166
demographics, 12–14, 32, 55–109; in archives, 40–44; clarity needed, 29–30; normalizing work of, 43, 55; racing economies, 58–61; refusals of, 243–44. See also colonialism; numeracy; population; sex ratios, 1500–1700
Deng, Stephen, 77n66
De Novo Orbe (Martyr), 85
Description of a Slave Ship, 153–55, 154
Descrittione dell'Africa (Description of Africa) (Africanus), 83, 90, 130
Diagram of the Decks of a Slave Ship, 154

diasporic theory, 11, 60–61, 113–14
difference, 19; antagonistic, 8, 59, 61, 250; early modern notions of, 11–12, 25, 59, 67; extra ecclesium, 61; as heritable, 39; Iberian views of, 59, 61; numeracy and production of, 110–40; racialized, 11–12, 165; socioreligious, 55–56; white slavery and, 72–73
Dillon, Elizabeth, 6
Donelha, Andre, 134
Dorothy (slave-trading ship), 253–54
Douglas, Mary, 57n6
Douglass, Frederick, 161, 220–21, 248
Drax, Henry, 190–91
Du Bois, W. E. B., 40
Duke of Argyle (slave-trading ship), 166–67
Durkheim, Émile, 247, 248
Dutch slave traders, 49–50, 69
Dutch West India Company, 179, 182–83, 234–36, 252

Eannes, Gil, 65
Eburne, Richard, 94, 95
economic institution, slavery as, 30
economics, 15, 17, 57–59; as site of rationality, 8, 83–85, 200, 207
economic suffering, 160–61
economies: African, 135–40; amoral, 115–35; moral economies of slave trade, 41, 127, 174, 203, 210, 210n7, 215; racing, 58–61; of reproduction, 73, 134, 190; rooted in slavery, 14–17, 100–101, 202–3
economy, the, 76, 81
Eden, Richard, 90
Edward IV (England), 67
Edwards, Bryan, 236
Egyptian social order, 125
Elizabeth I, 74, 90
Elmina (fort, in Ghana), 82
Eltis, David, 30, 31–32, 33, 36
empires, 14, 17, 59, 72, 74, 113
Engerman, Stanley, 31–32, 36, 187–88, 187–88n43
England: abolitionist movement, 37; Africa, ideas of, 15, 25, 36–37; African slavery and, 1–2, 57–58; alleged insularity of, 11; American colonies, 93–94; confidence in use of enslaved people, 57–58, 62; data of slave-ship captains used in, 46–47, 52; economic crises, 14, 75–77, 100, 108; Elizabethan era,

femininity, European imaginary of, 147–48, 213
feminist theory, 10, 16n31, 65n25
Fernandes, Valentine, 129
fetish: credit fetishism, 108–9; language of, 85
feudal labor, 98–99
Finch, Aisha, 209–10
Finley, Cheryl, 153
flos pavonis (peacock flower; *Caesalpinia pulcherrima*), 224
Fogel, Robert, 187–88, 187–88n43
Foster, Thomas, 189
Foucault, Michel, 13, 18n37, 89–90, 90n97
freedom: alternative grammars for, 254; court cases and petitions, 1–5, 178–79, 203, 237–39, 252–53; exchange relations and, 204–5; freedom-as-movement, 233; "half-freedom," 237–39, 252
French, Anglo-Dutch War of 1665–1667 and, 215–16
Fuentes, Marisa, 8, 171
fungibility, 58, 61, 211; gold and captives equated, 65–68, 78
futurity, gendered notions of, 149, 153, 167, 188, 224, 247

Gamble, David, 81–82n75
Games, Alison, 72
Gante, Pedro de, 62–63
Garner, Margaret, 161
Gaspar, David Barry, 186
Gates, Henry Louis, Jr., 133–34
gender, politics of, 161, 164
geographies of containment, 217–18, 244
geography, 63, 80, 92, 112–13; maps, 121, 131, 145–47, 147
Gideon (Dutch slave-trading ship), 52, 243n91
Gilroy, Paul, 42
Glorious Revolution (1688), 107
gold: captives equated with, 65–68; centuries-old trading routes, 85; in East, 64, 65; New World, 58, 64; salt trade and, 117–18, 123; trans-Saharan trade, 82. *See also* currency
Golden Trade: Or, a Discouery of the Riuer Gambra, and the Golden Trade of the Aethiopians, The (Jobson), 73–74
Gómez, Antonio Enrique, 146
Gonçalves, Antam, 65, 124, 127
governance, 14, 89, 101
government, population and, 96–98

grammar, race as, 165, 165–66n63
Graunt, John, 96–98, 100, 104, 106–7
great chain of being, 134
Green, Toby, 144
Grenville, Richard, 91
grief, 5, 38, 59–60, 160, 205, 240, 246–47; as knowledge production, 254; necessary for life, 48, 166, 246
Gronniosaw, James, 159
Guasco, Michael, 57
Guinea, 130
Guyer, Jane, 18

Hacking, Ian, 100
Hagthorpe, John, 94
Hair, P. E. H., 81–82n75, 122
Haitian Revolution, 199n72
Hakluyt, Richard, 63–64, 70–73, 77, 81, 117n12
half-freedom, 237–39, 252
Hall, Catherine, 37
Hall, Kim, 11–12, 57, 77, 251
Hall, Rebecca, 232n56
Hariot, Thomas, 91–93
Harrington, James, 95
Hart, Emma, 203n82
Hartman, Saidiya, 13n28, 44n49, 54, 169, 249
hauntings, 10, 30, 50–51
Hawkins, John, 68–69, 70–73, 81, 81–82n75, 122
headright proposals, 189
heathenism, 70, 81, 250
Hegel, Georg Wilhelm Friedrich, 22
Henry, Prince, 65, 124
hereditary racial slavery, 1, 5, 67 reproduction of white population and, 103, 106; African women as central to, 18–19, 26, 37–38, 108, 222; change in European concepts of, 39–40, 67; kinlessness as rationale for, 37–38, 126, 155, 247–49; kinship as basis of, 10, 26, 38; New Amsterdam, 238; racialist logics of, 56, 67, 109; recognition of, 220–21, 227–28, 253; refusal/inability to bear children, 220; refusal to acknowledge kinship, 60–61, 83; role in modern economic systems, 15, 32, 59; slavery as distinct from, 72–73; subjection produced through, 150. *See also* racial capitalism; slavery
Heywood, Linda, 139
Higginbotham, A. Leon, 238
Hine, Darlene Clark, 222–23
Hispaniola, 64, 65–66, 148

history, philosophy of, 204

History of Jamaica, The (Long), 36–37

Holland, 97, 98

humanity, commodification as antithesis of, 205

Hume, David, 89

Hunter, Robert, 236, 240–43

Hussick, Shill (slave owner), 184–85

Hylle, Thomas, 55

Iberian contact with West Africa, 26, 59–67, 108, 112; difference, views of, 59, 61; *extra ecclesium*, 61; prior to English contact, 61–62; sex ratios in slave trade, 143–45. *See also* Portugal; Spain

Ibn Khaldun, 132, 133

ideology: 11–14; demographic data and, 42–43; refusal to record age and sex ratios of captives, 49–50, 52; religious, 57. *See also* racial ideology

imagination, public, 108

"imagistic memorial site," 151–52

increase, laws of, 178

indentured servitude, 2–3, 18, 19, 103, 179, 192, 217, 252

Indies, 62, 67, 72

infanticide, 223, 225–28

infant mortality rates, 182, 194, 223, 225–28, 240; New York City, 240

inferiority, "natural," 64

infrastructure of slave trade, 171–72

Inquiry into the Nature and Causes of the Wealth of Nations, An (Smith), 17–18

Instructions (Drax), 190–91

interdisciplinarity, 10–11, 23

interiority, violations of, 204, 223, 225, 235, 244

intimacy, 203–4

investing public, 108

Ipsen, Pernille, 103n145

Ireland, 90, 98–99, 107

Isabella, Queen, 68, 89

Isherwood, Baron, 57n6

Jacobs, Harriet, 205, 248

Jamaica, 36–37, 116, 224–25, 227–28; Cudgoe's War (First Maroon War), 235, 240; Spanish Negroes, 234

James (slave-trading ship), 166, 245–46

James, Joy, 233

Jerven, Morten, 139

Jobson, Richard, 73–74, 81, 81–82n75, 116, 125, 128–29

Johnson, Walter, 171, 205

Jordan, Winthrop, 11

Josephus, Flavius, 91n102; Josephus problem, 91, 91n102

Kars, Marjoleine, 209–10

Keye, Elizabeth (enslaved woman), 1–3, 5, 108, 203, 252–53; as economic thinker, 3, 7–8, 19

Keye, Thomas, 1

Khan and Cathay, 64

kinlessness: African women's reproduction of, 4, 10, 15, 16n31, 126; emergence of new forms of, 57; material consequences of, 179–80; as means of promoting capitalism, 35; parental disregard alleged, 126–29; presence of children gives lie to, 46, 59–60; property overlapped with, 247–48; as rationale for hereditary racial slavery, 37–38, 126, 155, 247–49; as resistance, 220; simultaneity of with kinship and racialized thinking, 179–80

kinship, 1–5, 249n14; affective relationships, commodification of, 3–4, 60, 71, 165, 181; African women's understanding of, 3–4, 19, 25, 108, 207–8; appropriation of, 237–43; as basis of hereditary racial slavery, 10, 26, 38; Black, 173; capitalism linked with, 32; as commodity, 24; erasure of, 35, 37–38, 49, 60–61, 83; family vs., 150; fictive, 114, 149–50, 149–50n28; foundational generations in New World, 44; incorporation into existing networks, 172–73; Irish and English intermarriage, recognition of, 98; kin-based "democracies," 139; machine metaphor and, 149–50; market dependence on, 4, 6–7, 59–61, 254; networks, 156, 172, 250; possibility of only among enslaved Africans, 38–39; property inextricable from 5, 172–73; reclamation of, 253; recognition of, 4, 38, 98, 141, 156–57, 183, 252; recurring rupture of parental bond, 61; refusal to relinquish, 251–52; reproduction delinked from, 4, 10, 15, 16n31, 19, 247; resistance and, 204, 213–14; sale of children within networks of, 156–57; in slave narratives, 159–60; white, 108, 206; women's protection of children during Middle Passage, 25, 46, 166–67; wounded, 248. *See also* affective relationships; family

placelessness and, 80–81, 113–14; politics of belonging in, 5, 204; revolts during, 46n54, 162–64, 168–69; secondary shipments after, 44–45n50; sexual violence during, 25, 50, 52–54, 161–62; visual records of, 151–55, 163; women's protection of children during, 25, 46, 166–67. See also transatlantic slave trade

Mignolo, Walter, 63

Mina (Portuguese fort), 82, 138–39

mining, 148

Mintz, Sidney, 9–10n20, 32, 149, 172

Misselden, Edward, 75, 76

modern world: African women's centrality to, 18–19; racial capitalism and slavery as central to, 18–19, 41–42, 155, 205–6; refusal to record sex and age ratios in logic of, 49; universalism and, 18

Modest Proposal, A (Swift), 104–6

monstrosity, 13, 81, 121, 124, 150, 250; cannibal shop, 85–87, 86

moral considerations, 13–14, 22, 24, 41–42, 57–58, 203

moral economies of slave trade/slavery, 41, 127, 174, 203, 210, 210n7, 214–15

Morgan, Gwenda, 201

Morris, Thomas, 177

Morrison, Toni, 245

mortality rates, 20, 182, 190; during Middle Passage, 46n54, 142–43, 159, 164, 166

motherhood, 219–22; children used to lure onto ships, 127, 141, 156, 165; child's status follows condition of mother, 3–6, 102, 106, 178, 178n17, 194; dysselection of, 221–22, 222n32; slave owners' view of women as antimothers, 221–22

Mun, Thomas, 71, 75, 76, 77

Murphy, Michelle, 33, 43, 246, 246–47n4

Mustakeem, Sowande, 162

naming, 172, 172n3, 238

Nanny (female Maroon leader), 218, 234, 236

natality, 233n59

national identity, 62, 63, 74, 77n66, 92

national sovereignty, corporeal metaphor for, 17–18

nations, peopling, 93–100, 134

Native Americans, 65–66, 68; justifications for colonialism and enslavement of, 64, 89, 134; population and colonialism linked, 92–93;

reproduction of Englishness and, 95–96, 102–3, 104n147

Natural and Political Observations Mentioned in a Following Index, and Made upon the Bills of Mortality (Graunt), 96–98, 100, 104, 105–7

Negro Act of 1712, 242

neutrality, 9, 24–25, 33, 53, 101–2

Nevis harbor, 192–93

New Amsterdam, 179, 182–83, 237–39; half-freedom in, 238–39

New Netherland, 237–38

newspapers, 197–206, 198

New World: gold, 58, 64, 74; in seventeenth-century economic writings, 58–59; Spanish America, 32–33, 83, 143; Spanish claims to, 64. See also English Americas; Latin America

New York City, 51–52, 240–43

Niño, Pedro Alonso, 68

Nocco, Moncky (enslaved driver), 190

North African refugees, 22

North America, 223–27; New York City, 240–43

numeracy, 5–6, 237; African, recognition of, 122–23, 131–32, 135, 137–38; African cultural formation and, 114; Africans said to lack, 25, 63–65, 84–85, 87–88, 110, 116, 120, 123, 124, 132–34; algebraic symbolism, 91; colonialism linked with, 91–93; counting women in Middle Passage, 44–52; dehumanization and, 9–10n20, 13, 82, 104–5, 153; demographics, 13–14; disciplinary power of, 55; figurative language and, 8–9n18; increase in, 8, 12; innumeracy used to justify slave trade, 133; lists of commodities, and normalization of slavery, 69, 71, 99, 129; mathematics, early modern, 43, 91; phantasmagrams, 33; production of difference and, 110–40; quantification in Enlightenment thought, 55, 93–94, 103; racial thinking and, 91–92, 106–7; and, 214; role in production of slavery, 26, 110–11; violence and, 55, 91, 106; visual archive linked with, 153. See also accounting; demographics; political arithmetic

O'Malley, Gregory E., 44–45n50

origin stories, 111, 248; first person captured (1441), 141, 143, 148

"other," European notions of, 59

Oursel, Pretaxat, 163

palimpsest, 26

Palmié, Stephan, 7, 88

pamphlet literature, 71

partus sequitur ventrem, 3–6, 102, 106, 178, 178n17, 252

paternalism, 190

paternity, 2, 5, 95, 98, 208, 232

Patterson, Orlando, 5–6

Paugh, Katherine, 194

Perrin, Liese, 222

Perry, Imani, 65n25, 173, 254

personhood, 204, 218, 220; legal, 173–74, 178

Peru, 33, 66, 148

Petty, William, 96–100, 104, 107

phantasmagrams, 33, 109, 246–47, 246–47n4

Phillip II, 62

Pietz, William, 67, 81, 85, 133

pieza, 171, 196, 214

Piot, Charles, 156

placelessness, 80–81, 113–14

plantations: records of women on, 49; sex ratios on, 34–38; sugar, 101, 106, 148–49, 187–88, 230–31

political arithmetic, 3, 8, 13n28, 37, 44n49, 96–100, 104–7; enumeration as invasive, 107; in Hariot's writings, 91–93; refusal to see history of slavery and slave trade, 42–43; rise of, 12–14, 96. *See also* numeracy

political economy, 17–18, 41, 53, 90, 160, 226; capitalist, 56; population and, 71, 102; of women in slavery, 22

Poovey, Mary, 8–9n18, 43–44, 98, 100n134

population, 13–14, 89–93; abstraction of, 37, 43, 100n34, 101, 105–6, 108, 111; biotic commodities as outside, 66; colonialism linked with, 91–93, 91–100; depopulation fears, 89–90; enumeration and, 107; government and, 96–98; incentive and punishment for, 95–96; as "natural," 90n97; peopling nations, 93–100, 134; political economy and, 71, 102; racing, 100–109; "unfit subjects of Trade," 97. *See also* demographics

Portogys, Maria (enslaved woman), 238, 252

Portrait of an African Woman Holding a Clock (Carracci), x

Portugal, 59, 65, 69; forts in West Africa, 82, 129–30, 138–39, 145; transatlantic slave trade, 141–43

Powell, Robert, 90

predicament, slavery as, 5–6

pregnancy, 1, 47, 49, 155–56, 165–67, 180; abortion and infanticide, 223, 225–28; execution suspended due to, 242–43; infant mortality rates, 182, 194, 222, 225–28, 240

Prester John (legendary Christian ruler), 83, 112, 121

Price, Richard, 9–10n20, 32, 149, 172

Princess Henrietta of Lorraine, Attended by a Page (van Dyck), 77, 79, 80

Principall Navigations, Voiages and Discoveries of the English Nation (Hakluyt), 63–64, 70–73, 117n12

Prinses (slave-trading ship), 49–50

print capitalism, 200–201

prisoners of war, as slaves, 40n37, 50, 128

Pritchett, Jonathan, 194

property law and rights, 4–5, 177–79, 192

public-private divide, 49, 150, 210–11

Pudaloff, Ross, 204

Puerto Rico, 142, 148

Puttenham, George, 63

Pyrard de Laval, François, 88

race making/race thinking, 14, 17, 59, 110, 165, 208

race/reproduction bind, 251, 254

racial capitalism, 6, 15–17, 25–26, 41, 180, 248–50; reproductive, 140, 145. *See also* capitalism; hereditary racial slavery

racial categories, hardening of, 2–4, 6, 213

racial hierarchy, 2, 9–10, 14, 16, 213; enumeration and, 107; erasure required for, 25, 37; gold, language of, 56, 75; infanticide discussions, 225–26; population linked to, 93, 100; two types of slavery, 72; Spanish tradition of, 104; used to separate forced labor from commodities, 101–2

racial ideology, 11, 14, 17, 24–25, 31, 99–102, 201, 213, 215, 219; African women as central to development of, 29; development of, 41, 56n2; historicization of, 59; Irish and, 99; in mathematics, 91, 91n102; nineteenth-century racial science, 58; numeracy and, 91–92, 106–7; simplistic notions of prejudice, 177; tools of dominance, 181

racialist logics, 3, 13–20, 49, 55–56, 81, 109, 131, 161, 218; applied to economies, 58–61; ideology, 58

rape, 5, 47, 50, 65, 162–63, 167, 189n49

rationality, 6–8; "correct" relationship to possessions, 75–76; dehumanizing violence of, 104–5; economics as site of, 8, 83–85, 200, 207; monetary value and human subjects linked, 64–65; moral judgment couched in, 91–92; moral standing, 76; quantification and scholarship, 42; religion in service of, 70–71, 82; used against African and New World peoples, 75–77, 85–87, 86, 102, 110–11. *See also* Enlightenment thought

rationalization, 12–14, 20, 59; political arithmetic's role in, 42–43; of transatlantic slave trade, 17, 36–37, 42–43, 49, 108–9, 150

recognition, 9–10n20, 35, 37n30, 50, 73, 82; agony of, 157, 160–61; of hereditary racial slavery, 60, 220–21, 227–28, 253; of kinship, 4, 38, 49, 98, 141, 156–57, 183, 252; language of irrationality and, 82; moment of sale and, 173, 176, 185; of money and value, 64, 123, 131; of moral challenges, 70, 73; nonrecognition, 164–65, 173–74c, 190; performance of nonrecognition, 173–74; of trade complexity, 132, 140n89; transatlantic slave trade and, 43–44, 48

Rediker, Marcus, 149

refusal: to acknowledge kinship, 60–61, 83; to relinquish kinship, 251–52; rooted in an African culture, 253. *See also* recognition; resistance

Relatione Univerali (*The Worlde*) [Botero], 83–84, 89

religion: English coin and, 75; manumission in exchange for conversion, 234; Protestant, 116, 235; slavery justified by, 55–59, 70–71, 75–76, 82, 111

Renaissance scholarship, 12

Report of the Kingdome of Congo (Lopes), 85–89, 86

reproduction, 6–8, 16; alienation of reproductive labor, 6, 209, 223; alleged to be pain-free, 120, 213, 247; attempts to pair enslaved people, 185; birth rates, 182, 186, 194, 195, 223, 246; breeding of enslaved people, 95n116, 187–88n43, 187–92, 194–95, 222–23; economy of, 73, 134, 190; "encouragement" of, 189; enslaved women as reproducers, 19, 33–35, 53, 104, 124, 138, 222, 227–28, 254; fertility and fertility control by women, 220, 222–28; infanticide, 223, 225–28; of kinlessness/delinked from kinship, 4, 10, 15, 16n31,

19, 247; in Spanish America, 33; pronatalist policies in 1800s, 194; speculative finance and, 188–90; visual imagery of slave ship, 153–55, 154; white as hereditary, 6

resistance, 10, 41, 207–44; Anglo-Dutch War of 1665–1667, 215–16; body as site of, 217–20; categories of, 203–4, 207–8; clothing materials, rejection of, 219; to commodification, 17, 26; day-to-day, 209–10, 221, 225; diasporic theory of, 60–61; enslaved women's bodies as praxis for understanding, 208–20; execution for, 241–42; extreme responses to, 211–12; as "form of strike," 222; infanticide as, 223, 225–28; kinship and, 204, 213–14; as male-only, 213–14; Maroons and, 215–16, 228–34; military experience of African men and, 40n37; New York conspiracy, 241–43; numeracy and, 214; as personal response and collective/political critique, 222; physical forms of, 203–4, 219–20; pleasure as oppositional, 217–19; plunder, rhetoric of, 215–28, 229–30, 231; recognition and, 60, 220–21, 227–28, 252; refusal to be rendered as "thing," 66; reproductive control by women, 220, 222–28; runaway slaves, 175–76n11, 197–206, 198; slave revolts, 26, 46n52, 162–64, 166–68, 232n56, 240–44; specter of white women's rape used to inflame war, 215–16; surveillance, breaking, 201–2; women's, absent from archive, 209–12; women's leadership of, 162–64. *See also* Maroons; refusal

Richardson, David, 149

Robert (slave-trading ship), 163

Roberts, Lewes, 132

Roberts, Neil, 218

Robertson, Claire, 138

Robinson, Cedric, 10, 15–16, 160, 234, 249–52

Rodrigues, Jan, 239n78

Royal Academy, 133

Royal Africa Company, 166, 192–93

Royall, Isaac, 157–58

runaway slaves, 175–76n11, 197–206, 198; slaves as self-stealing, 25, 199, 201; Virginia advertisements, 201–2

Rushton, Peter, 201

Sahlins, Marshall, 247

Saint Christopher (Caribbean island), 215

Saint-Domingue, 194

sales of enslaved people, 53, 170–206; acts of sale and theft, 197–206, *198*; auction block as symbolic image, 173–74; children, 192–95; divide between enslaved and enslaver clarified by, 207; education into understanding of, 170–72, 175n13, 179–80, 196–200; gendered market pricing, 183–84; incomplete knowing required, 176–77; internal and external markets, 156n37, 196–97, 227; by kinship networks, 156–57; legalizing, 177–80; legal personhood and, 173–74, 178; locations of, 174; marketing families, 180–97; moment of, 25, 172–74, 197; performances of nonrecognition, 173–74; "prime male equivalents," 196; public market, 171, 205–6; runaway ads vs. sales ads, 199; "scrambles," 175; sexual exploitation implicit in, 183–86; women said to be purchased for enslaved men, 184–85, 212–14; women's higher price, 146

salt trade, 117–18

Sancho, Ignatius, 165

Santiago (slave-trading ship), 142–44, 148–49, 151

Sapes lineage, 142

Schiebinger, Londa, 217

scholarship, 40, 41–42n40, 41n39, 113–14, 251; assumptions about women's productivity, 144–45; Black feminist theory, 10, 222–23; customs, ethnological description of, 119; cultural approaches, 11, 53; feminist theory, 10, 16n31, 65n25; formal histories, 23; historiography, 10, 17, 40, 46, 214n13, 217; marginalization of slavery in, 15, 42, 55–57; on Maroons, 231–33, 232n56; relatedness, methodology of, 10; visual imagery and, 152–55

"scrambles," 175

Seijas, Tatiana, 33

Senegambia, 68, 81, 83, 117; first enslaved person taken from (1441), 141, 143, 148; Portuguese forts at, 129–30

servitude, as juridical category, 8

Seven Years' War, 194

sex ratios, 1500–1700, 29–54, *48*, 243n91; among English settlers, 38–39; among Maroons, 231; counting women, 44–52; eighteenth-century figures, 51n64; in English colonies, 103–4; erasure of women, and violence, 52–53; Iberian slave trade, 143–45; in New Netherland,

239–40; on plantations, 34–38, 51; refusal to record, 49; *Santiago*, 142–44, 148–49; from slave sales account books, 51; women and children as percentage of captives, 47

sexual economy of slavery, 73, 73n52, 185; as amoral, 115–35; West African, 123–24, 128–29

sexual violence, 15, 162, 189, 189n49, 208, 211–12

Shakespeare, William, 68

Shammas, Carol, 103

ship, as metaphor, 113

Shockley, Evie, 23

Sierra Leone, 70, 142

Sierra Silva, Pablo Miguel, 33

silver, 64, 66, 67, 74–75

slave, as term, 35, 214n13

slavery: afterlife of, 13n28, 29, 44; cannibalism linked with "taste" for, 88–89; capitalism linked to, 56, 239, 248–50; captives vs. slaves, 72–73; as condition, 5–6, 14; as constitutive of commerce, value, money, and capitalism, 15–17, 89; hereditary racial slavery vs., 72–73; gendered male, 34–35, 231; hardening of racial categories, 2–4, 6; Mane incursions, 142; marginalization of in scholarship, 15, 42, 55–57; political economy of women in early modern era, 22; as predicament, 5–6; racialized, transition to, 12; social relations as antithesis of kinship, 4; as human trafficking, 52; white, 72–73. *See also* enslaved people; enslaved women; hereditary racial slavery; transatlantic slave trade

"slave ship icon," 153

slave societies, 222

slave trade. *See* transatlantic slave trade

"Slave Trade and the Numbers Game, The" (Curtin), 30

Slave Voyages database, 30–31, 44–45

Smallwood, Stephanie, 43, 52, 66, 68n35, 113, 151n30

Smith, Adam, 17–18

Smith, Thomas, 90

Smith, Venture, 159

social death, 5–6, 204

social history, x, 10, 19, 29, 41, 113

social spheres, 49, 57

socioreligious difference, 55–56

Solow, Barbara, 31

Sontag, Susan, 20

South Carolina, 40n37, 175, 189

South Sea Company, 108–9

space, 57, 80

Spain, 61n13, 62–66, 74, 116n10; *casta* (mixed-race) paintings, 104, 105

Spanish America, 32–33, 83, 143

specie, 66, 68, 74–80, 136; Africans as, 77; English, 74–77, 77n66. *See also* currency

Speed, John, 121, 130

Spiller, Elizabeth, 62

Spillers, Hortense, 4, 6, 10, 113, 164, 247–49, 251; enslaved women's bodies and American violence, 208–9

state, as term, 254n27

statute law, 178

"stealing oneself," 25, 199, 201

St. Jacob (slave-trading ship), 183

Stuyvesant, Peter, 183

subjectivity, 17–18, 64–65;

sugar plantations, 101, 106, 148–49, 187–88, 230–31

suicide, 161, 164, 165, 168, 169n73; conspiracy plot and, 241, 242

surnames, 235–36

surveillance, breaking, 201–2

Sutton, Belinda (enslaved woman), 157–58

Sweet, James, 204

Swift, Jonathan, 104–5n149, 104–6

Teelucksingh, Jerome, 193

"thingness," 66, 176–77, 205

Thistlewood, Thomas, 189, 189n49

Thomas, Keith, 8, 91n102

Thompson, Peter, 190

Timbuktu, 65

Time on the Cross (Fogel and Engerman), 187–88, 187–88n43

Tomba, Captain (enslaved African), 163

trade: conventional narrative structure, 122–23; transformations in, 75–77; women's roles in West Africa, 138–39. *See also* transatlantic slave trade

transatlantic slave trade, 3; 1444 as date of onset, 29, 59, 127; 1807 ban on, 194, 227; all-male workforce presumed, 34–36; children on slave ships, 25, 46, 166–67, 192–93; as cultural phenomenon, 15, 17; demographics of, 40–44; English ability to ignore, 101, 108–9; ideological developments in, 13–14; kinship networks built on board slave ships, 172–73; knowledge regimes of, 6; large-scale impact

of, 40; materiality of, 24, 57, 67, 113–14, 138, 215; overcrowded ships, 143, 152, 153–55, 154; political arithmetic's concurrent development with, 12–13; Portuguese, 141–43; as quantitative problem, 30; rationalization of, 17, 36–37, 42–43, 49, 108–9, 150; sex ratios, 1500–1700, 29–54; to Spanish America, 32–33; tax on, 227; traders as reluctant observers, 164–65; values/valuelessness set in motion by, 6; wrath and, 20–21. *See also* Middle Passage; sex ratios, 1500–1700; slavery

Trans-Atlantic Slave Trade Database project, 30–31, 44

transmutation, 97–98, 106–7

transportation, as population solution, 98

Transport des négres dans les colonies (Oursel), 163

travel accounts, 62, 75–76, 81–82, 111–12; amoral economies in, 115–35; as guides to trade, 88; inverted norms alleged in, 119, 125–26

treaty and trade negotiations, 70–71; with Maroons, 229, 234

tribute, people as, 69

trinkets, exchange of used to justify irrationality, 62–64, 81–82, 87–88, 121, 123, 133

Trouillot, Michel-Rolph, 199n72

True and Exact History of the Island of Barbados (Ligon), 34–35

Tullideph, Walter, 186

Turks, 75; Josephus problem, 91, 91n102

Turner, Sasha, 194

"tyranny of the alphabet," 62–64, 84

understanding by African and enslaved people: affective relationships and women, 3–4, 19, 108, 160, 207–8; of commodification, 7–8, 25–26, 53 54, 108, 140, 149, 156–61, 160, 170, 176, 252, 255; of kinship, 3–4, 19, 25, 108, 207–8; of market value, 199–200; of racial capitalism, 25; sales of enslaved people as education into, 170–72, 175n13, 179–80, 196–200

"unfit subjects of Trade," 97

Ungerer, Gustav, 122n29

United States: American South, 194; Massachusetts, 157–58. *See also* Virginia

universalism, 18, 21, 65n25, 83, 111, 111n2, 116, 219; natural rights claims, 64–65

universalization of value, 64–65

unthinkable, 18n37, 106, 188–89, 192, 199n72. *See also* erasure of African/enslaved women value, 4–5; ascribed to Black bodies, 6, 8, 18; "correct" relationship to possessions, 74–76, 81, 83–84; degraded systems of, 6, 55–56, 59, 61, 67; local concepts, West African, 156; merchants' systems of, 59; misidentified, 67–74; mystery of, 81; neutrality imputed to, 33; sale of human beings and, 24–25, 58; specie and, 67, 74–80; status and, 107; universalization of, 64–65; West African views of, 8, 18, 111, 204

values, social and cultural, 74–80

Van den Broecke, Pieter, 120, 125–26, 128

van Dyck, Anthony, 77, 79, 80

Varmahaly Negroes, 229–30

Vaughan, Alden, 11

Vilches, Elvira, 64, 78

violence, 4; Black paternity and, 208; comprehension of, 7, 40, 50, 102, 115, 135, 158–59, 161, 165, 209; economic suffering, 160–61; erasure of women and, 50, 52–53; incomplete knowing required, 176–77; modernity rooted in, 16; New York conspiracy and, 241–43; normalization of, 6, 55, 71, 135; numeracy and, 55, 91, 106; property law and, 178; rape, 5, 47, 50, 65, 162–63, 167; rationalization of, 8–9, 9–10n20, 109, 150; sexual, during Middle Passage, 25, 50, 52–54, 161–62; speculative planning, 106; wrath, 20–21

Virginia, 77, 91–93, 92, 96, 102–3, 178–79, 201–2; Black women as taxable wealth, 189; children follow condition of mother, 3–6, 106, 178, 178n17, 194; runaway slave advertisements, 201–2; legislature's request for Carolina slaves, 213–14; *partus sequitur ventrum* code (1662), 1–5, 178, 178n17, 253

Virginia Gazette, 202

Virginia House of Burgesses, 1, 102, 178, 252

visual records of Middle Passage, 151–55, *163*

Walker, Tamara, 33

war, 227; Anglo-Dutch War of 1665–1667, 215–16; Civil War, 56n2; Cudgoe's War (First Maroon War), 235, 240; Maroons and, 229, 230, 232–33, 235; prisoners of war as slaves, 40n37, 50, 128; Seven Years' War, 194

Weaver, Karol, 194

Weinbaum, Alys, 204, 251

Wennerlind, Carl, 108–9

West Africa, 12, 14, 23; agricultural system, 138–40; alleged killing/selling by kin and rulers, 69, 83, 126, 130, 131, 156; commodification, concepts of, 25; domestic economies, 139; Gambia River area, 69, 73, 80; Iberian contact with, 26, 59–67, 108, 112; kinship structures in, 38; political diplomacy and trade, women's sexual role in, 19, 69, 73n52, 103n145, 104n147, 115, 118, 140; sexual division of labor, 125, 138–40; trading complexity and expertise, 122, 131–32, 135, 137–38, 139–40n90; worldviews, 19, 66. *See also* Africa; Middle Passage; transatlantic slave trade

Western Design (Cromwell), 116

West Indies, 40n37, 175, 193–95, 223, 244; birth rates; 182, 186, 194–95, 223–24, enslaved people transported from, 240

Wheat, David, 33

Wheels of Commerce, The (Braudel), 56

White, Deborah Gray, 214n13

whiteness, construction of, 6, 77, 95, 150, 176n13, 208n1; femininity, European imaginary of, 147–48, 213

white slavery, 72–73

white women, 5, 19, 104, 215–17

Williams, Eric, 11, 16

Williams, Goodwife, 206

Wingate, Edmund, 91

women: appropriation of bodies of, ix–x, 16n31, 102–4, 209; as carriers of sexual disorder, 134–35. *See also* African women; enslaved women; pregnancy; reproduction

Wood, Peter, 201

wrath, neutralization of, 20–21

Wynter, Sylvia, 110n1, 171, 222n32, 51

Yang, Chi-Ming, 78

Zakim, Michael, 96

zombie biopolitics, 6

Zong (slave-trading ship) massacre (1783), 50–51

Zurara, Gomes Eannes de, 59–60, 65, 68, 70, 71, 124, 126–28, 165, 171, 173